26-5-46

D1071141

ESSAYS
IN HONOR OF
JOHN DEWEY

John Dewey

Reproduced from the bust by Jacob Epstein

ESSAYS
IN HONOR OF
JOHN DEWEY

ON THE OCCASION OF HIS
SEVENTIETH BIRTHDAY
OCTOBER 20, 1929

THE
CARNEGIE LIBRARY
OF OTTAWA

NEW YORK
HENRY HOLT AND COMPANY

COPYRIGHT, 1929,
BY
HENRY HOLT AND COMPANY, INC.

B
29
.E8
1929

THE
CARNEGIE LIBRARY
OF OTTAWA

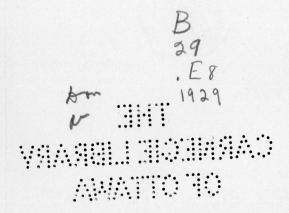

PRINTED IN THE
UNITED STATES OF AMERICA

THIS VOLUME IS PRESENTED TO
JOHN DEWEY
BY HIS STUDENTS AND ASSOCIATES
ON THE OCCASION OF HIS
SEVENTIETH BIRTHDAY

139187

PREFACE

THESE essays are written by former or present colleagues of John Dewey and are presented to him on the occasion of his seventieth birthday. Though the contributors are now widely scattered, they were all at some time associated with Professor Dewey either at the University of Chicago or at Columbia University; they are a symbol of that larger group, scattered still more widely, of students, friends, and admirers of a great philosophical teacher. It is manifestly impossible to include in this volume contributions from all those who could and would join in such a tribute. Among those whose names might appear here, but do not, mention must be made at least of Professor A. W. Moore, who was among the first to suggest this volume, but who was prevented by illness from contributing to it.

Though there is no unity of subject-matter nor organization in the arrangement of the essays, they all reflect a single source of inspiration. They have a common stimulus in the leading ideas of a fertile mind, but they are not intended to represent a " school " of thought, nor to suggest a consistent body of doctrine.

October 20, 1929.

TABLE OF CONTENTS

ix

TABLE OF CONTENTS

ESSAYS
IN HONOR OF
JOHN DEWEY

PERSONALITY: HOW TO DEVELOP IT IN THE FAMILY, THE SCHOOL, AND SOCIETY [1]

Felix Adler

I shall consult in this paper the utmost brevity consistent with clearness, since the ground to be covered is extensive, too extensive indeed, and the space allotted necessarily limited.

The subject announced asks of us such light as we have on the means of developing personality. But what is personality? If we are to develop a thing we ought surely to know what the thing is which we undertake to develop. I urge, therefore, that we consider at the outset what meaning we are to attach to the word " personality."

> Without the way there is no going.
> Without the truth there is no knowing.

says Thomas à Kempis. Without a true notion of the object in view, true at least to oneself, we shall certainly go far astray.

In common parlance, personality is used as an honorific term. When we say of a man that he is a personality we imply that at any rate he is not to be overlooked, that he is not negligible, is not just one of a crowd, stands out salient in one way or another. He is supposed to be impressive, too, that is, to leave an impression of himself on others. In brief, the word as currently employed implies two things, distinctiveness and distinction. A personality is marked off in some way from others, is different, is distinguishable, but also somehow distinguished. But the two notions which, if analyzed, may prove useful, when left in the vague, as they generally are, can certainly not serve to guide the educator, and we must go beyond common parlance for help.

If we turn to the philosophers for explicit definition, we find a perplexing variety. I happen to recall at the moment the following: *Substantia per se subsistens, per se operans;* and again, *persona est substantia intelligens, individua, incommunicabilis, non sustentata ab alio, nec in alio.*

[1] Printed in the Report of the Fourth International Moral Education Congress, Rome, 1926.

But with no disposition to rule metaphysics out of court it is difficult to see how a substance such as defined in the formulae just quoted, or in others like them, can be capable of being developed. Perhaps personality cannot be developed, perhaps it is something which, the right conditions being given, appears, manifests itself, and our task as educators would then be to supply the right conditions. But at any rate the metaphysical interpretation of personality at this stage of our inquiry will not greatly serve, and we had better try a different line of approach.

To clarify thought, I shall set down the following questions:

Why is no animal beneath the rank of man called a person? The human family is subdivided into the white-skinned (Caucasian), the yellow (Mongolian), the black-skinned, etc. Why does the fact that a man belongs to the Caucasian division not entitle him to be regarded as a personality? The Caucasians are sufficiently distinguishable from the Mongolians, and conversely. And yet mere membership in any one of the large subdivisions of mankind does not suffice to constitute personality. Distinctiveness alone without distinction does not, and the distinction must itself be a genuine distinction. But what is genuine distinction?

Neither does the circumstance that I am an American, and you are Italians, or Frenchmen, etc., establish my title to the honor implied in the attribution of personality, for the same reason as the one just given.

Again, there are the "Characters" of Theophrastus, masterpieces of psychological discrimination, with outlines sharply edged, and hence exceedingly distinguishable, but certainly without distinction (that is measured by some standard which we have not yet found), undeserving of the eulogistic term with which we are concerned.

But perhaps the most important point to elucidate is the difference between personality and individuality. A person is an individual; an individual is not therefore a person. (We must keep on reminding ourselves that person is an honorific term. In England the clergyman is called the parson, that is *the* person.) Personality includes individuality, but is something superadded to it. We shall therefore come to close quarters with our subject by grasping first the meaning of individuality.

The word "individual," derived from the Latin, is equivalent to "atom," derived from the Greek. Etymologically it just means indivisible, irreducible, a last term, an ultimate unit of which a multitude is composed. Taken in this way the word is colorless, and connotes a

meaning the very opposite to that of which we are in search.   For taken
in this way the very mark of the individual would be its replaceableness.
If the individual is regarded merely as one of a multitude or class, any
other will do as well.   But our interest in the individuality of human
beings (let the physicist deal with atoms as he will) is clearly in some
sort of irreplaceableness.   If a man is just like any other, if anyone else
will serve as well, he is not in any case a personality, and does not possess
even what we really mean by individuality.

There are a number of synonyms of "individual" which come nearer
the notion here forecast, such as private *versus* public, particular as against
universal, peculiar, which seems to express intimate qualitative difference.
Idiosyncrasy also pointedly stresses the apartness, the unlikeness denoted
by individuality.

Let me fasten on the last word, "unlikeness," and see how far it will
carry us.   The unlike human being may be regarded as the center of a
series of concentric circles.   The outermost circle would be mankind.
Proceeding inward the next circle would be the Caucasian or some other
grand division of the human race.   The next is the nation of which he is
a member — the French, the American, the Italian, or some other.   Next
would be the vocational group, industrial, commercial, professional, etc.,
of which he is a member.   Within this is enveloped the closest group, the
family.   The unlikeness which we are seeking to vindicate for the man
is not unlikeness *in vacuo*.   It is a dissimilarity which stands out against
many similarities which he shares with others, whereby he is physically
and psychologically determined.   He is a man, and shares the general
traits that characterize his species.   He is a Caucasian, he is a Frenchman,
if you will, he is a merchant, lawyer, etc.   In virtue of heredity he reproduces the traits of his family connection.   His unlikeness, his intimate,
private self must then consist in what he does not share, in what remains
after all those determining factors have been discounted.   But what is it
that he does not share?   What makes him peculiar (we may use this
word in a good sense)?   Is individuality a modified feature on the face
of humanity — a smile in one instance, a grimace in another?   Is it a
flourish embroidered on a general pattern?   Is it the variant of a type,
the type as a whole being preserved intact, he representing only an aspect
of it?   None of these metaphors exactly fits.   Take the last, and select
from the series of concentric circles that of nationality — the French, for

example. Does François Ier represent the French type? Does Pascal? Does Voltaire? Does Robespierre? Each of these individuals represents, not the French character, the French type as a whole, but some deflection of it, some over-accentuation of one of its traits. And the man would not have been what he actually was had he not suppressed in himself certain other traits which go to make up the type, had he not been a kind of excrescence of the type instead of its representative. The elements are never so happily mixed in any individual that "nature can rise up and say — This is a man," or this is a Frenchman, or for that matter this is a scientist, the typical scientist, or the typical artist. There are among artists romanticists and classicists. There are scientists who lean toward generalization, and others who lean toward particularization. There are mechanists and vitalists. And if there be any man who creates the impression that he is all-of-a-piece, a towering, superhuman individual, whose actions are dominated by a single master-impulse, like Napoleon, the fact in his case is all the more apparent that he has achieved this compactness, this unity, at the frightful cost, for himself and for mankind, of abolishing or suppressing in himself tendencies and faculties without which real humanity is unbelievable. He has attained distinctiveness at the sacrifice of genuine distinction. Individuality as an empirical phenomenon is attained only by suppression.

While we have thus traced in a large way the meaning of differentiation, and the series of determining factors by which it is reached, the second indispensable requisite, that of distinction, has not been justified anywhere in the process. Distinction implies evaluation. Distinctiveness describes a man as he is. Distinction involves that in some degree he is up to the standard of what a man ought to be. Distinction is an ethical term, whereas distinctiveness is a naturalistic term.

But the moment we raise the question of values, we enter on debatable ground. From time immemorial controversies have raged as to what is the right standard of value, as to what are its grounds. Here the various schools of philosophy and the various religions clash. Here Theists and Pantheists, Hedonists and Rigorists, Finalists and Pragmatists, are forever at strife, and unanimity is less in sight today than it ever was.

It would seem then that we have arrived at an *impasse*. We are asked to develop personality, and we discover among ourselves, as well as in the world at large, the widest divergence of opinion as to what the thing is that we are to develop. And out of this predicament, if we are completely honest, if we are not disposed surreptitiously to impose our own philosophy upon others, there seems to be no escape. The way out, it seems to me, is to remember that a philosophy, as well as a religion, may be judged by its fruits. Whatever our philosophy, it should lead to certain practical educational procedures. These practical results can be tried out and tested, and even adopted by those to whom the philosophy as such would not appeal. (For instance, one may be a good deal of a Stoic in practice without in the least accepting the Stoic metaphysic.) One can drink from the stream without going back to the source.

Nevertheless, in addressing fellow-educators, and not a public of laymen, it seems proper for me to state, at least in a few paragraphs, my own philosophical conception of personality, not for purposes of propaganda, but in order that the practical proposals to which I have been led may become the more transparent. These practical proposals can then be judged on their own merit or demerit, as I have said above.

Here, then, is a brief philosophical confession. I am not a Kantian, but go with Kant in affirming that every human being is an end *per se*. To say that he has value is not enough. He has value on his own account. Mere value is relative. Water has value to the thirsty, food to the hungry. Some things have a higher value, some have a lower value, but all such values are relative to the use that is made of them. But man as an end *per se* is intractable to being merely used. He declares a *noli me tangere,* he claims an intimate core of selfhood which resists appropriation. The law of the jungle is that life feeds on life. The law of an ethical community is that life shall at the least respect other cognate life, forbear to infringe upon it.

In the world, the law of the jungle still prevails. The exploitation of labor goes on, barely mitigated by the legislation in the more civilized countries. The social evil spreads its black plague-spots over the globe. The stronger nations crush the weaker. Trade, confused with civilization, takes toll of millions of lives in Africa, in the Far East. Group ambitions and antipathies are barely beginning to be held in leash by the new device of the League of Nations. And the wisest counselors insist that only a change of heart, a change of mental and moral attitude, can avail to establish the foundations of peace. Accordingly, if we as educators are to train a generation capable of promoting this new turn in human affairs, a new respect for man as such, for the human being as an end *per se,* seems to be the *sine qua non.* Personality, as I see it, is one aspect of it at least, may be defined as that quality in every man which makes him worth while, aside from the uses to which he may be put by his fellows.

But this is only one aspect of it. And here precisely we hit upon the fundamental ethical problem, the ethical paradox.

The paradox is that beings whose claim to independence is recognized must at the same time live in a state of mutual dependence. How can a self which repels from its inviolable precincts invasion *ab extra* be drawn out of its solitude into the service of others? Society is as necessary to us as the air we breathe. Even creatures lower than man, like bees and ants, are socially orientated, and man much more so than they. Society exists inevitably where creatures have wants for the satisfaction of which they depend on fellow-creatures. If, then, in regard to a human being we urge his dependence on others, we declare the natural fact of his situation, but seem to contradict the ethical dictum of his independence, his sovereign selfhood. If, on the other hand, we emphasize his independence, we seem to deny the mutual dependence. We do not deny that he may make others dependent on himself, may subjugate them. Society, ideally conceived, is a system of reciprocal give and take. It has never been really so; the strong, the unscrupulous, the cunning, have always taken more than they have given. But the urgent impulse of mankind today is towards rectification of such unfairnesses, the creation of a social order in which the give and take shall be more justly reciprocal. And yet the tantalizing paradox remains: how can such a social order even theoretically be conceivable? How can independence and dependence be reconciled? How can selfhood and service be compatible? How can a man be at once an end *per se,* and a means to the ends of others? Kant declares that a man is an end *per se,* and should never be treated *merely* as a means to others' ends. But the word " merely " disguises the difficulty, without removing it. The question is: how is it ethically possible that a man should be treated as a means at all? And where can the line be drawn between the respect I owe to my fellow as an end in his own right and the extent and the manner in which I may use him as a means? Kant nowhere indicates the solution. He cannot, because the two terms which he couples in his formula are from the point of view of his system irreconcilable.

And there is no solution, not even an ideal solution, so long as the equality that is predicated of all men on moral grounds is interpreted as similarity. (In that case the sole relation that ought to subsist between these sovereign beings would be that of respect and aloofness.) The solution lies in another direction, namely, in construing equality as equivalence, in regarding the associated selves as representing each some one differentiated mode of being, and their relation to one another as that of eliciting unlike differentiated modes of being in each other. Intrinsic selfhood would thus not be sacrificed, but accentuated, the play of interaction being the means of accentuating it.

In the beginning I stated that individuality is comprised in personality; here I can add that individuality and personality both are ideal goals which can be worked towards, but never fully attained. Individuality stands for distinctiveness, personality for distinction. Ideally, individuality is the same as uniqueness. It is the exquisite, intimate, entire exfoliation of a single mode of being, as such induplicable, and therefore indispensable in the world of being. Ideal personality is this same individuality so directed in its effects on other cognate individualities as to produce in them their intrinsic unlikeness.

Ownness and alienness are the two poles between which spiritual being moves. The impact of alienness ideally is such as to force the self from foreign ground, from ground which does not belong to it, to force it on its own ground, and thus to produce genuine ownness. When I say alienness I am speaking relatively, for there is an underlying ground of unity of which the differences are the effulgence.

To use a homely illustration, men may be said to resemble not the bricks of which a house is built, but the pieces of a picture puzzle, each differing in shape, but matching the rest, and thus bringing out the picture. Or they may be likened to a color scheme in which each of the colors has the effect of modifying its neighboring colors and being in turn by them modified. Or, better still, they may be compared to the actors in a noble play in which no star actors are permitted to concentrate attention upon themselves, but each performs his rôle in such a way as to enable his fellow-actors to do the fullest justice to their rôles, with a view to the adequate rendering of the meaning of the play. A certain unity of the spiritual nature among men, as I have said, is presupposed. This unity blossoms out into differences. The interaction between them is their perpetual reconciliation.

And now as to the application of this conception to the educator's business of developing human beings, in the family, the school, the state, the international society.

Let us keep the simile of the actors and the play in mind. Every social group — the family group, the school group, the vocational group — is a functional group. It has a certain meaning for life to be produced in its members. These meanings are successive, those of the smaller groups broadening out into the larger.

In each case the meaning or object for which the group exists is twofold — the concrete object imposed by nature, and the ideal or spiritual object. (I use the word "spiritual" in the following sense. The law of the jungle is: Live at the expense of other life. The law to be derived from Hedonism is: Live and let live. The spiritual law is: Live in promoting life.) Thus the natural object of the family is to replace the generation now existing by a new generation. Mountains, rocks, and seas remain for thousands of years; human beings after a short duration wither and pass away. The family recruits the ranks in order that the species may not die off.

Again, the natural object of the school, considered as a social group, is to serve as an organ for the transmission of the knowledges, skills, and insights of the past, through the present generation to future generations. The ideal or spiritual object in each case is to produce in the members of the group the functional attitude which I have just described: the will to do one's part in such a manner as to enable one's associates in the group to do their part with the greatest possible excellence. It is this relation that counts most in the development toward personality. Personality, so far as it is attainable, consists in this attitude of mind, nay, of one's whole being, towards the being of others. To put it succinctly: the natural purpose for which the group exists is the occasion (I had almost said the pretext) for the envisagement of the ideal purpose. The natural object is commonly considered the product, the personal relations the by-product; from the spiritual point of view the reverse is true — the personal relations are the true product, the natural object is the by-product. The formula which I have used in expressing my ethical thought is: Seek to elicit the best in others, and you will thereby challenge and bring to light the hidden best in yourself. That best in others I may now explicitly define as the best performance of function. And in order to elicit that in others every one will discover that it is necessary to transform himself, to reconsider perpetually the manner in which he performs his part, and to improve on it.

In this way, I may add, the conflicting claims of egoism and altruism are transcended. Egoism leads to the over-emphasis of the self and its separateness; altruism leads to the under-estimation of the self in its relation to others. A distinguished scientist quoted the other day the phrase: *Aliis serviens, ipse consumor.* This expression has a noble sound, but taken too literally is really unsound, for genuine self-love is as indispensable as its antithesis. The two, in fact, are inseparable. Genuine service implies spiritual growth.

In applying the functional conception to the family, the following points may be enumerated. The part of the husband towards the wife is to evocate in her the most widely horizoned womanhood of which she is capable; that of the wife is to evocate in the man the most integrally related energy of which he is capable. The function of the pair towards their children is, by the interaction that takes place between them, by the spiritual life which they produce in themselves, to evocate the latent potentialities of their offspring.

The part of the father in his influence on the children is differentiated from that of the mother.

The rôle of the children towards their parents is reverence based on the experience of superior wisdom, and on the touch of something higher than wisdom which they can feel without analyzing it, and gratitude for benefits received. Among these benefits there is one that should be specially signalized. It has to do with the idea that the child, like every human being, is an end *per se.* To be an end *per se,* as has been shown, is to be regarded as possessing worth, that is, an intrinsic possibility of merit independent of any actual evidence of it, nay, to be affirmed despite contrary evidence. The love of the parent for the child is the natural basis for this affirmation: since the love which the normal parent feels instinctively — the mother more directly, the father more indirectly — for the young beings that were once a part of their own being, is irrespective of any performance, or of any show of deserving on the part of the child. And the child which is the object of this love has thereby received the foundation of moral self-respect for its entire future. This is one reason why the plan of state education proposed by the communists, to replace the bringing up of children in the family, is a desperate error. The instincts of parents will vigorously rebel against such a plan, and the spiritual interests of mankind protest. The most ignorant parent is capable of giving his offspring what the most enlightened kindergartners and teachers, whose affection is necessarily dispersed over the many, cannot supply — the concentrated interest, the home feeling in the heart of the parent, which is the condition of the future man's home feeling in an alien world.

The function of brothers and sisters towards one another is likewise of fundamental importance. Fraternity is often construed as meaning the sympathy of like for like. But brothers and sisters are often different in character and disposition, and when these differences are discovered and become accentuated in the course of time, the consequence is a sundering of the tie, a break, each going his own way in hatred or indifference. The ethical significance of fraternity, on the other hand, is precisely that of learning to understand and to adjust each other's differences, the bond of consanguinity and the common life aiding those concerned to do so.

Coming next to the school, with which educators have more directly to do, the writer asks leave to refer to the Ethical Culture School, which he established nearly fifty years ago, and which, as its name indicates, has personal development for its maximum aim. There are other major aims, but this is the maximum. The principles and methods of this school may be reported as follows:

The school is not a mechanism, but an imperfect organism, which is ever to be in process of more vitally organizing itself.

The different members of the school society have different offices to perform. The rôle of the teacher is sublime. No one can ever flatter himself that he is adequate to it. The office of the teacher is for one thing to carry on the tradition of mankind; next, to carry it forward. The mental and moral capital of the human race, like the physical capital, is forever in danger of perishing, and must forever be renewed. The office of the teacher, as was said above, is to transmit the knowledges, skills, and insights from the past to the present generation; but in transmitting, he must also purify, separate the grain from the chaff, that which is viable from that which is decayed.

Above all, however, the teacher must be himself forward-striving. He does not even begin to be worthy of the name unless he constantly seeks to augment his mastery of the subject which he teaches, and, in whatever minor capacity, to increase the treasure of which he is the custodian.

If I may introduce a personal reminiscence — I had the good fortune, in my student days, to be in touch with certain great teachers. I became a disciple of no one of them, being led by experience and reflection to follow a different way. But all the same, what I gained from them was invaluable; it was the contagion of forward striving — and this every teacher can, in a degree, communicate to his pupils. In the Ethical Culture School this is attempted by friendship and close contact between the subject teachers and those students who show a particular talent for the subject. The teacher initiates them into his own studies, his own strivings, and acquaints them with the problems that await solution in his particular branch.

The teachers of the different subjects included in the school curriculum, as of science, mathematics, languages, fine arts, mechanical arts, are expected to give in each case at least an elementary survey of the history of the subject, of the evolution of it, laying special stress on the great outstanding figures, treating the history biographically, showing that it was through the labor and the mental toil of human beings that every advance in knowledge and method was made.

The teaching force of the school are a body, and must act as a whole. Their relations to one another are crucial. Single teachers often exert a deep and salutary influence, and special devotion to one or the other master is not discouraged. But there must be no star actor in the play that goes on in the school — or, let me rather say, in the interplay. The mutual support of each teacher by his colleagues, the evident desire (evident to the pupils as well) to promote the most fruitful activity in each branch of the school work, is the common concern of all. As the attitude of the parents towards one another, the support each gives to the other, creates the right atmosphere in the home, so the like attitude on the part of each teacher towards the rest creates the right atmosphere in the school.

For the ethical development of the young, the formation of certain habits is of prime importance. Aristotle rightly insists on habits (*hexeis*) as the foundation of principles. In the habits are implicit the principles which may afterwards be explicated. The conditions in the Ethical

Culture School are intended to generate certain habits. For instance, it is not a class school, or a sectarian school. All the social strata are represented — children of the wealthy, of the fairly well-to-do, and of the utterly poor, are among the pupils. Among the nine hundred, three hundred are so-called "free scholarship" pupils. All pupils meet on the level of perfect comradeship. Often the poorest are elected to class honors, such as class presidencies. The habit of looking on every human being as an end *per se,* irrespective of externals, irrespective also of religious and denominational distinctions, is thus fostered.

As in every modern school, the teachers endeavor to discover and to cherish the individual bent of each pupil, and for this purpose a great amount of freedom is encouraged. But in many of our progressive schools, freedom is carried to extremes, when it leads to anarchy. Discipline is no less necessary. The idea of individuality supplies the principle of freedom; the idea of personality, of mutual influence, supplies the principle of discipline.

The variety of opportunities for the display of individual aptitude afforded in the science, art, manual training, etc., departments, furthermore, contributes to the appreciation by the pupils of types of excellence differing from their own. A pupil may be behind in the literary work of his class, but then on the other hand he may excel in the art work, or in the shop work, or in the science. The habit of respect for differences is thus inculcated.

The more advanced students act as volunteer pupil-teachers of the less advanced in any branch after school hours. The habit of promoting the development of others with a view to self-development is thereby encouraged.

What is called community service has been established; that is to say, in the shop-work in the school, in the art department, in connection with the athletics and the music, the more competent students, say of the age of sixteen and seventeen, undertake to give instruction and training to poorer youths and girls of the neighborhood, not members of the school, who do not enjoy the same opportunities. *Docendo discimus* is recognized with respect to the adult teacher — the adult teacher gains by giving, gains a surer grasp of what he knows by so simplifying his knowledge as to put it within the range of the less mature. The adolescent who is put in the way of *docendi* gains a similar advantage, and besides is initiated into that habit of which I am here speaking, that of developing others, and thereby achieving self-development.

In discussing the habits I have already passed over into describing the function or rôle of the pupils in the school organism. Their most important function perhaps is to be seen in the system of self-government. The object of this self-government is to produce the concept of law. To learn by doing is the general rule in education; to learn the true understanding of what law means by law-making is an application of this rule. Ideally law embraces the totality of those conditions which are indispensable to the development of human beings towards personality, and which are capable of being enforced. Positive law is a transcript of the ideal in so far as the community at any time is intellectually and morally capable of willing such conditions. In the school these conditions include partly such externals as order, punctuality, courtesy between the sexes (the school is co-educational), fair play in the games, etc., partly they cover certain deeper factors, such as the concept of authority and the administration of justice — under the concept of authority is comprised what may be called the civil law of the school, under the concept of justice the criminal law, if that term may be used. Authority must be freely accepted by the pupils. It must be made to rest on the greater experience, the greater ripeness of the governing body, in particular on that forward-striving attitude of the teachers, which has been already characterized as the leaven and life of the school. Their authority is that of leaders on the path which the students themselves are to follow. Democracies especially are wont to shy at authority, to resent or at best to regard it as a necessary evil, a contrivance to prevent sheer anarchy. It is all the more desirable that the intrinsic grounds on which authority depends should be apprehended by the rising generation.

The administration of justice in the school also should be understood and managed by the students under the guidance of their teachers. Even in the most advantageously situated schools there will be infractions of moral obligation, falsehood, deception, even theft. It matters greatly, especially for the progress of penology, that the students should at an early period be assisted to comprehend the true purpose of punishment, and to this end that they should be themselves judges of the backsliders amongst them. The object of punishment is to abolish the evil and to reclaim the evildoer. But it has also another aspect, which is to teach humility to those who have not slipped or fallen into wrongdoing. The judge, be he an adult on the bench, or an adolescent in the council room of the student government, is the mouthpiece of the social conscience. The judgment he pronounces attains its due effect only in its repercussion on himself.

It has been said that in ancient times the individual existed for the sake of the state, and that democracy is a government in which the state exists for the benefit of the individuals. Neither of the two limbs of this statement is exact, and both are unsatisfactory, especially the latter. If the state exists only for the advantage of the individuals, then the law is shorn of its majesty, and turned into a mere convenience. And this meager conception of law is actually entertained in not a few schools where self-government has been introduced. There are unwritten laws which man has not made, and of which the positive laws are but a provisional translation. To make the actual law a more adequate rendering of that high pattern laid up in the heaven of the ideal is the work of progressive society, and for this business the members of a self-governing student body should be trained. (The term " self-government " is not precise; co-operative government, that is co-operation in government between students and faculty would be the better designation.)

In the school about which I am reporting there has also been from the first what had been called moral instruction in all the classes. The direct teaching of moral ideas has been criticized on the ground that it is supposedly addressed merely to the intellect, and is therefore abstract, and also for the reason that moral guidance given as occasion arises is apt to be more to the point, and more lasting in its effect. But the one does not exclude the other, and the occasions for casual moral direction are not sufficiently numerous or varied. Nor is the kind of teaching actually given abstract. The appeal is made vividly to the imagination and the feelings. Picturesque stories from the Old and New Testaments are used to illustrate the family relations — the devotion of sons to fathers, and of fathers to sons, delicate charity, the finding of the pearl of great price in the heart of sinners and publicans. The Greek epic is used; the heroisms of secular biography are used. The story of the slave-trade is told to arouse indignation against the habit of using other men as mere tools. Literature is drawn upon to present the noblest ideals of manhood and womanhood as they were conceived by the poets, Homer, Dante, and the others. Above all, the purpose of the specific moral teaching, or, to designate it as what it really is, the presentation and discussion of the vital problems of life so far as the young are competent to understand them, consists in explicating what is implicit in the habits and in the experience of the young themselves, and in thus forming clear concepts, capable of application to situations in which they will find themselves later on.

In addition it is possible to give adolescents, in the later period of adolescence, a certain ideal prevision of relationships of which as yet they have no experience, by treating of the ethics of marriage, of citizenship, etc.

The third subject mentioned in the title of this paper is the development of personality in society. Now society is not an aggregate of atomic individuals, a heap of pebbles, as it were; it consists of vocational groups, such as the commercial and industrial group, the agricultural group, the various professional groups, etc. I stated in the beginning that in each of the groups to which a human being successively belongs, the family, the school, the vocation, the nation, etc., there is ever a twofold object to be attained — an obvious concrete object and an ideal object. In the case of the vocational groups the concrete object is the rendering of a social service — in the commercial and industrial group, for instance, it is the production and exchange of commodities — while the ideal object is the internal, functional organization of the group in such a way that the work done by each shall react on the workers, the result of his work being the birth in them of personality, or at least the envisagement of the sublime ideal of it. Now a glance at the actual state of the different vocational groups shows how far we are, not only from the practical realizations, but even from the bare conception of so exalted an object. Complaint is made today that even the professions of medicine, law, etc., are being commercialized. That the vocation of the merchant and manufacturer should be "commercialized" seems to be taken as a matter of course. But is the business of producing and exchanging commodities itself mean? Is there any reason why the individual who does this kind of work for society should have less dignity in his own eyes as a business man than the lawyer or the doctor? Where does the fault lie?

There are two evils that must be clearly exposed before there is any chance of even gradually remedying them — the one is individual egotism, the other vocational egotism, as I shall presently explain. By individual egotism I mean, not self-love, but selfishness of the base sort, which consists in rendering a service to society in order to make money. To make money it is true one must render some kind of service; but if I am individually selfish I regard the service as secondary, and the pecuniary gain as primary. This is what is really meant by " commercialism." The bare recognition, however, of the fact that the men engaged in business do constitute a vocational group who are required to do a certain work for society, would of itself tend to invert the wrong attitude which is at present taken. The service would then loom big in the forefront of men's imaginations, and not the riches, the pleasures, the prestige to be gained for the pushing business man by incidentally rendering a certain service to society.

But the deeper transformation of industry, for example, is not possible unless the functional principle is applied to bring about a new internal organization of industry. The manager, the executive, the workers of every rank, the scientists in the laboratories connected with the industry, the artists who co-operate, for instance, in the textile industry — all these should be regarded as having their distinctive rôles to play. They would, of course, be salaried as such, the salary being regarded, not as remuneration for the work done, but the means of enabling the man or the woman to do it in the best possible way.

Of course, what I am describing is an ideal to give direction to the reformation of society, and not a result to be actualized out of hand. The internal organization of industry, as every one knows who has the slightest acquaintance with the existing situation, is especially difficult, because of the ever more general utilization of the machine to replace hand labor, and because of the drudgery. The aim, however, should be to reduce hours of monotonous labor, and increasingly to release time, not for leisure, but for genuine work, work such as will net development to the worker. On this subject I have expressed myself in somewhat greater detail in my Hibbert Lectures on " The Reconstruction of the Spiritual Ideal."

The capitalistic system has for its object the accumulation of wealth, the increase of the product by the stimulation of initiative. The various social reform movements now afoot have for their main object a more equitable distribution of the product. The functional or ethical system here indicated has for its main object the effect of production on the producers themselves. Under the head of producers are included the highest as well as the humblest of the workers.

But there is a second evil which I have called vocational egotism. I have just applied the ethical principle, conceived as functional, to the internal organization of industry, but what is supremely needed has as yet hardly been envisaged, namely, the organization, on the same principle, of the relations of the different vocational groups to one another. There are certain major interests of mankind with which the different vocational groups are intrusted. Until now, and still at the present time, each of the major interests is pursued, so to speak, in single-track fashion. This is what I mean by vocational egotism. Science aims at the advancement of science, reckless of the effect which its discoveries and methods may have on human life and the other lines of human activity which are no less to be valued in the interest of progress. Thus chemistry has employed elaborate methods to produce the poison-gas which was used during the last war. Science and invention combined have created instruments of destruction from which even primitive savages might have shrunk in horror. Similarly, at the time of the Renaissance, art was pursued in single-track fashion with the result of corrupting Italian society, and at least contributing to leave the Italian states at the mercy of foreigners. And so at present the trade interest, in itself legitimate, is set up in isolated fashion, is indeed vaunted as if trade and civilization were identical, and is followed to the ends of the earth, breeding unappeasable rivalries, destroying the native industries of India, sacrificing millions of lives in Africa, and threatening to shatter without regard to what is worth preserving the age-long structure of Chinese culture.

But while we declaim against these excesses of commercialism, we are not at liberty to forget that the radical fault, the root of the evil, is to be found in each of the vocational groups, in the vocational egotism which seeks to promote its own ends heedless of the effect thereby produced on other interests no less important. Thus, to point to one more example, religion at the time when it was paramount in the world suppressed science and halted the advance of knowledge; today, when science is paramount, it tends to paralyze religion, and to chill and discourage the spiritual aspiration of the race.

In the Ethical Culture institution a system of prevocational schools is now being planned, the object of which is to promote an attitude of mind in the student favorable to the internal organization of each vocation, and to the organization of the vocations in respect to one another — in other words, to overcome vocational egotism. Since the institution is situated in the City of New York, a great commercial center, the first prevocational school contemplated is a school of commerce and industry. Other prevocational schools are included in the project. The plan of the Prevocational School of Commerce and Industry is the following. Whatever subjects and methods are employed in the best commercial schools in order to create efficiency are adopted. The future business man is to be efficient as well as progressive. He is to have his feet on the ground whatever star in the high heavens he may follow. But the main intention is ethical. To this end history especially is utilized — not commercial history as it is commonly taught, but rather the history of commerce and industry as exemplifying the beneficent and the evil effects which the pursuit of business in single-track fashion has had on other major interests. There have been beneficent influences. Greek science arose in the seaport-town of Miletus; Galilei flourished at Florence. Venice, England, Holland illustrate the influence of the commercial class on the development of political institutions. In Venice, for instance, we have a state all-of-a-piece, a monolith, so to speak, commercial in motive and method from foundation to apex. In England we witness the abolition of the absolutist monarchy by the pressure of the commercial class; in Holland the successful struggle against the despotism of Spain; in the French Revolution too the uprising chiefly of the middle class is instrumental in the destruction of feudalism. Again we note the influence of commerce and industry on art and manners. The account taken of these happy influences is designed to give to the student an initial sense of pride in business, enabling him to see it, not as black as it is painted by its extremist critics, but rather as a vocation which might acquire a nobility not now possessed by it, and to think of himself as working in it with a sense of dignity not inferior to that of the most disinterested followers of the higher professions.

Per contrast, commercial history has its dark side, and this also must not be concealed from the student, but rather fully exposed to him — the middle class getting the purchase to rise by pressing downward on the class beneath it, the recrudescence of the slave trade in the eighteenth century (in which England, the most liberal country in Europe, was the principal offender), the unbridled exploitation of labor, the horrible opium traffic, the white-slave traffic, etc.

The chief mischief in the above group, as in the others, I repeat, has been the single-track pursuit of its object. Good and evil results have ensued. But neither the good nor the ill, save now and then exceptionally, were deliberately intended. Commerce in particular has gone on its way like one of those fast trains that we sometimes see rushing through our Western prairies, scattering sparks to the right and left, and spreading far-extending conflagrations, while it carries its passengers and its freight to their destination. In the students of these prevocational schools a frame of mind is to be promoted which will lead them deliberately to consider the effects of the social service they render on the other major interests of the world, and to measure their success by the degree to which their pursuit redounds to the advantage of science, of the arts, of government, and of the spiritual life of human beings. Modern industry, for instance, has by its demands powerfully contributed to the advance of electricity, chemistry, etc. It is beginning to perceive that for its own sake it must permit the scientist to work without insisting prematurely on practical utilization, that it must give as well as take, that in giving it will gain. Functional representation, when developed in any industry, will have a potent effect on the more adequate organization of political democracy. Art and industry will profit by the more intimate connection between them, and the spiritual life of the world will be reanimated in the degree in which idealism actually enters into the work-a-day life.

Of all the imperfect organizations that remain to be organized, the society of nations is the most imperfect. It is hardly as yet even a society — rather a chaos of conflicting factors and forces. Hitherto the rule has been for the strong nations to live at the expense of the weak. Now in the Covenant of the League the rule proposed is, live and let live, let the strong and the weak live side by side, each pursuing its own path of happiness and prosperity.

Life at the expense of other life; live and let live; is it possible to advance to a higher rule of each nation flourishing in the process of promoting the best that is in the life of sister-nations?

I have space only for a single illustration of the rule of gaining by giving as applied to the intercourse of peoples. Every one of the chief peoples of the earth has produced a certain type of civilization. Each of these types has its own peculiar excellences and also its profound defects. The intercourse of the peoples, according to the spiritual rule, should be such that each people, regarding the excellence of its neighbor as a treasure and desirous of enhancing it, would endeavor so to modify the faults of its own type of culture as to be able through its influence to correct the faults in these other types. Thus at the present day the Orient needs the effect upon itself of the active, energizing Occident in order to prevent its contemplativeness, its serenity, from deteriorating into stagnation; it needs the stir of movement that comes from the West in order to make its distinctive virtues more virtuous, while the Occident needs to temper its incessant energizing by meditation and repose. Each by undergoing the modifying influence of the excellences of the other types thus fits itself to expunge their faults. The same might be said of the mutual influence of the Latin, the Anglo-Saxon, and the Teutonic types. And the gradual organization of mankind would then result in a *corpus spirituale* in which, on the largest scale, the essentially human law, the law of living in promoting life, would be honored.

RELIGIOUS VALUES AND PHILOSOPHICAL CRITICISM

EDWARD SCRIBNER AMES

In his work, *Experience and Nature,* Professor Dewey marks the point at which philosophy " departs from the arts of literary discourse. They have a freer office to perform — to perpetuate, enhance, and vivify in imagination the natural goods; all things are forgiven to him who succeeds. But philosophic criticism has a stricter task, with a greater measure of responsibility to what lies outside its own products. It has to appraise values by taking cognizance of their causes and consequences; only by this straight and narrow path may it contribute to expansion and emancipation of values. For this reason the conclusions of science about matter-of-fact efficiencies of nature are its indispensable instruments. If its eventual concern is to render goods more coherent, more secure, and more significant in appreciation, its road is the subject-matter of natural existence as science discovers and depicts it."

The values which religion has cherished are inner peace and security, spiritual fellowship and communion, blessedness and joy. Peace and security have meant a guarantee of triumph over disaster and death. The saints have been able to endure outward affliction and defeat through the sense of possessing an inner and final superiority. Their vindication might not be realized in this life but they have held to the conviction that ultimately, if only in a future life, their faith would be justified. They could support the burdens of a present evil existence in view of an immortality in which their righteousness would avail. In all the trials of earthly striving they could find comfort in association with others who shared their beliefs and hopes, and could rest their souls upon the invisible presence of the divine Companion. In a future life this comradeship would be made perfect and enduring. In the light of this deep security and satisfying fellowship the heart was filled with immeasurable joy running on into unending life beyond this vale of tears.

The ground of these values was the eternal, unfailing character and infinitely good will of God. In his rulership and dominion of the world, justice and love could not be defeated. The Lord of heaven and of earth would care for his own and reward those who trusted in him.

The means of attaining and making certain of these spiritual values was through such a conduct of life as was divinely prescribed. By keeping the divine commandments, observing the law of the heavenly way, and maintaining union with the Divine through prayer, the soul could ward off the shafts of evil, gaining forgiveness and recovery from all sin. On every hand were the lighted altars and the living Word of the temples of faith to shelter the weary, to revitalize their trust and hope in the realities of the spiritual life. By obedience to the authority of revelation, and by implicit devotion to the Church man surely could find and hold fast the security, the fellowship, and the happiness he craved.

These values and the frame of divine ordinance within which they were set belonged to a static and unexplored world. That world has been transformed by scientific knowledge into distances of light years and durations of geological ages; the whole has been found to be vibrant with the ceaseless motion of electrons and solar systems, the changing forms of a vast evolutionary process. What is still more astounding is the discovery that the records which were taken to be the revelation of the divine will were inscribed by the hands of many fallible men, through successive stages of imperfect cultures. Upon the great figures of the heroes and divinities of the old legends has fallen the disillusioning light of historical knowledge. The standards and the commandments which were taken as the unquestioned guides to the attainment of religious values have proved to be the formulated customs and taboos of ancient folk ways and tribal mores. Where, then, is man now to find satisfactory guides to those values which the religious souls have cherished? Do those values still remain the supreme objects of the religious quest? Does there, indeed, exist such a divine Being setting the goals and furnishing the guarantees of achieving them in this life or the next? These are some of the searching problems propounded to the present age. In the confusion which these questions beget, some cling blindly to the old order; others discard it completely; and still others seek to discover in the new world the values that belong to it, with the means of making them accessible and appealing. Of those who find abundant and satisfying values there are many who do not regard them as religious, or as the material of religious experience, preferring to drop the name with the world-view in which it arose.

At last the greatest difference between the old and the new worlds lies in the fact that the old was the creation of the uncritical judgments of naïve men, through immediate sense impression and unconsciously formed customs and fancies, while the new world has been examined, measured, and tested by more reflective thought. At least we know that the earth is not the center of our solar system, and that it has existed through millions of years, and that man himself has lived through millenniums, amidst widely diverse and slowly shifting cultures. Still more important is the knowledge gained about human nature itself, about language, habits, customs, imaginative legends, poetry, dreams, and thought processes. One of the greatest changes has come with the conception of evolution and the lengthening future of man on the earth which awakens an expectant, inquiring attitude, and suggests the possibility of discoveries, experiments and achievements as remarkable as any yet experienced. The present machine age, so suddenly developed as compared with the slow cultural changes of the past, has stirred the imaginations of men to further hopes for the mastery of nature and the release of human energy into new channels. The impatience of mankind with poverty, disease, and passive acceptance of fate, with the arousing of a spirit of hopeful inquiry to eliminate these and other sources of suffering and evil, marks a new attitude towards existence in striking contrast to the old dutiful sense of resignation and acceptance of natural events. With this discovery of the power of intelligence rightly applied to the concrete problems of living has come a different appraisal of the value of human nature and a disposition to stand erect in the face of the universe and to look about with intelligent caution and chastened assurance.

It is obvious that for this new spirit there are new values, such as adventure in the discovery of further secrets of nature, and of vast experiments in material, in social, and in moral ways of life. These are not mere imaginary projects but are adventures actually in process. The beneficial results attained through doubt of traditional systems, and through rejection of old pieties, has made doubt itself a value, and has enhanced the cultivation of originality and novelty. It has suggested the ideal of progressive achievement, opening to human imagination the vistas of indefinite growth and enrichment of life in this present world. Even the conception of a life hereafter has been recast in terms of the attractiveness of continued work and growth. The old values of security and blessedness have been made over to include adventurous risk in creative labor.

It is not strange that these changes have raised questions concerning the nature of value itself. Does value belong to the realm of existence as known and experienced, or does it pertain to a transcendental realm? Are there two orders of value, that which belongs to natural experience and that which is above and outside the scene of change and time? Or are the values that man undergoes merely subjective and unrelated to the real world of existence? Or are the experienced values of human life as real as man's physical and mental life, and accessible to some comprehension with reference to their conditions and consequences? It has been the contention of the idealistic philosophies most closely allied with historic Christianity that the religious values belong to the realm of pure reason, independent of the changing world of concrete existence, yet setting the standards of moral worth and endeavor in the life of man. Religion has therefore seemed to involve a peculiar set of values, non-empirical, authoritative, and final. Never has the question been so urgent as to whether religion is possible on the basis of values which belong to nature and to human life, as these are found in common experience. It is a common remark that there is no sharp demarcation between the sacred and the secular, that life is unitary and unbroken by such divisions. But it is uncertain whether this comment represents a reasoned conviction or is only the expression of the wish to affirm that all interests are subject to the dominion of religious standards and authority.

Höffding, in his great work on *The Philosophy of Religion,* holds that religion has to do with values arising in immediate experience, in man's struggle for existence. Man's faith in their significance and preservation springs directly from his feeling, from his needs. These values are represented in vivid forms of the imagination, in myths, legends, drama. Such ideas as arise in connection with them are emotionally conditioned, and have the nature of motivated rationalizations. They lie within the interests which generate them and are the embodiment of custom, tradition, and authority. Höffding says: " For every religious standpoint, and especially for the great popular religions, knowledge is certainly not without importance. During its classical ages, religion is everything to man, satisfying also his thirst for knowledge. But the thirst for knowledge is here subordinate to the impulse of self-preservation, to the need to develop and maintain life. . . . Only by remembering this can we understand how it is that certain ideas are developed in defiance of the intellectual interest in clear and consistent thinking. . . . If the religious ideas are to have any significance at all, therefore, it can only be in serving as symbolical expressions for the feeling, the aspirations, and the wishes of men in their struggle for existence; thus they are secondary not primary both in significance and origin."

The great transition from natural to ethical religion sets the problem of values in a new light. The ethical values pertain to personality and to the relations between men in their associated life. It is impossible, Höffding thinks, to determine that the highest values originating here are preserved permanently in the universe, but this does not destroy their value. They arise in experience and belong to reality and are good while they last. Even if there is no future life for man, a question impossible of scientific solution, still there is ground for cherishing the good that appears. It would be childish to renounce what is experienced as the higher values because we are unable to determine by the measure of scientific thought that they are not preserved forever, or that human personality in which they arise does not possess immortality. We have no means of comprehending the universe in its totality and cannot demonstrate the permanence or the final relation of our human values to the whole of reality. But we do have within our experience needs and wishes whose fulfilment brings satisfaction. These are subject to change with growth and enlarging experience and some are felt to be more rewarding than others in their pursuit and realization. "The problem is how the self-development of the individual can assist the self-development of other men. All spiritual and material culture, all individual and social striving, finds its place in the ideal here indicated. In its work at the shaping and applying of this idea, ethics itself becomes religion, for it is here working for the all-holiest, and everything which men call and have called holy must finally be estimated by means of the criterion which this idea supplies."

Such a view of religion brings it into unity with life; its values are the values of actual experience; its norms are verifiable. It does not leave religious values to the decrees of arbitrary will, or of blind custom, or of external authority. They become subject to observation regarding the conditions under which they arise and the consequences to which they lead. In this way they become accessible to rational estimates and subject to processes of stabilization and enlargement. The possibility thus arises of distinguishing between the secondary accretions which have gathered around historic religions and the vital elements that carry satisfying conviction to enlightened and cultivated minds. Plenty of mystery remains in religion as in all other types of experience: there are always possibilities of new events with their attendant goods and evils. The recognition of the fact that values arise, increase, and decay, turns attention to the circumstances under which such changes occur, and may lead to the discovery of the controlling conditions. In this way intelligence may become the instrument of maintaining religious values and of freeing them in human life. The quality of adventurous, experimental living in the direction of richer and fuller relations is involved in the finding of values in the natural course of events.

A further characteristic of this doctrine of value is that it makes possible appreciable and intelligible criteria for comparing and estimating values with reference to their function in experience. If it is true that there can be no argument about differences of values in their immediate occurrence — since whatever is found to be good is good to the subject experiencing it — still it is obvious that the approval of some things as good may lead to disastrous consequences. There can be no question but that the drug addict finds indulgence a value, but it is also clear that such indulgence tends to habits that are devastating to the efficiency of the individual and indirectly to other persons. Intelligent observation may show good reasons why the cherishing of some values is beneficial, and of others bad. In general those values that lead to fuller values, to harmony, fruitfulness, and growth proclaim themselves as supremely desirable; while such as have the opposite consequences are to be discarded. The " highest values," accordingly, are those which in the long run bear the best fruits in the life process. These are judged highest, not in terms of any fixed and final standard outside of experience, but within describable and verifiable ways of concrete living. They are always the highest from the standpoint of the growing life itself and because they point forward to other values that may supersede them.

It follows that the religious values are not special kinds set off from others such as health, economic goods, and social interests, but rather the religious values are just these common values in so far as they are fitted into a well-proportioned, working system where each makes its proper contribution to the whole. The religious values are always also at the same time other kinds of values. Religion is the integration of various concrete values in the way which ministers to the fullest and most harmonious and expansive living. Because life goes on under changing and precarious conditions, emphasis from time to time falls upon different aspects. At one time it is important to give special consideration to health, at another to income, at another to recreation, at another to public affairs, and all of the time to maintain a watchful regard for the support and cultivation of all of them in relation to one another and in due proportion. Any good thing, good in its due relations and as a participating value in a complex existence, may be emphasized and developed until it becomes an unbalancing and disturbing factor and thereby takes on a negative and sinister character. Religion, conceived in the narrow sense of special virtues of humility or self-sacrifice, may become irreligious from the larger and more organic conception of the good life. It is through the ceaseless application of intelligent criticism and appraisal that such extremes and one-sidedness are avoided. For this reason, it is dangerous to attempt to pattern an individual life after that of another person, especially one in another culture or social milieu. The values of the individual move within the general culture of his time and circumstance, and are therefore intimately related to his period and station. Just because the highest values are always highest within the field of concrete duties and opportunities it is impossible to isolate and fix particular attitudes and forms of behavior once and for all. Religion moves with the general life and is to be estimated in every age by the success with which it contributes to the projection and fulfilment of the noblest ideals possible to that age.

It is extremely difficult for those of one culture adequately to assess the spiritual life of another, because each is conditioned by its own outlook and evaluations. But the more effectively one is able to reconstruct the living interests of other times and peoples, the more evidence is afforded of the meaning and the force of the ideals found there. It has been all but impossible for the adherents of positive or revealed religions to appreciate the values of the religions they call natural or pagan. The claims of direct, supernatural inspiration have assumed a source of knowledge quite outside the scope of man's natural reflection and insight. In this conception there is a barrier between peoples and religions in addition to that common sense of superiority which every culture tends to generate with reference to its own customs and ideals. But recognition of the fact that all human experience gives rise to values, furnishes a principle for a more constructive interpretation and appreciation of it. Even the birth of critical, self-conscious reflective thought that has set a wide gap between the epoch which understands it and all others, becomes also the surest guide to the values of those civilizations that did not possess it to so great a degree. In the light of modern studies of preliterate, remote cultures it is now possible to reconstruct more clearly the values which they cherished and to sense the common human characteristics which appear in all of them. The most fantastic ceremonials of the Aruntas and the Kaffirs reveal the working of those selective and evaluating attitudes which operated in the discerning Greeks, though with quite different results. Through the unconscious influences of environment and accidental causes, the savage societies had their hearts set upon some things as better than others, and upon some experiences that constituted for them the supreme goods of existence. All had their convictions as to their highest good and the qualities of bravery, endurance, and shrewdness by which those goods were sustained. Their values were for them as real and as commanding as those of any higher societies can be for them. That which sets the great distances between cultures is not the intensity of devotion to their ends, but the discovery of critical, conscious means of investigating the conditions and the consequences of selecting and freeing any values whatsoever. Values which rest upon custom and magic, upon force and prestige, are just as absorbing and mandatory in their immediacy as those that flow from discriminating judgments and free insights, but they are not as capable of extension and of reconstruction. It is true that there is no argument about tastes in the direct experience of them, but there is opportunity for enlightened judgment as to their conditions and results. Religions may not be compared in terms of the fervors and raptures which their devotees feel in the observance of their ceremonials, but it is abundantly evident that some religions rest more upon external authority and blind faith, and that there are great differences between them as to their moral, spiritual freedom and power of social fruitage.

Religion, in the past, like other forms of social organization, has been largely controlled by conservative attitudes, but in an age which prizes invention and discovery, religion itself begins to be "adventurous." When authority, wealth, and heredity ruled in the state, they also were embodied in religious appraisals, but with the emergence of democracy and appreciation of creative personality, religion champions the equality of men and the development of the individual. There is not lacking evidence that religion is also far on the way to include within itself the free spirit of scientific inquiry. What else is the meaning of the great labors of historical criticism as applied to its sacred scriptures by religious leaders themselves; of the acceptance of scientific accounts of the creation of the world and of man, with the candid dismissal of old myths and superstitions; of the founding of institutions of learning with the fullest freedom of inquiry; of the current searching studies of religious experience in human nature; and of the fearless, critical investigations of the ideas of the soul, of immortality, and of God? Even churches have become experimental, too often no doubt with the hope of saving themselves, but also in larger measure than is generally recognized, in order to discover new and better forms and organizations for the liberation of the minds and habits of men. The "faith" cultivated by religion tends more and more to be faith in the power and disposition of human nature to experiment responsibly and fruitfully with life, to welcome from experience those discoveries that enrich and further life itself. No true estimate of the nature and possibilities of religion can be made which does not take into account the profound changes that are taking place within religious institutions themselves. Many persons, reared in strict, traditional forms, who participate in modern scientific and social enterprises, remain curiously unaware of the spirit which informs the more recent religious literature and religious practices. Frequently they have failed to generalize their own scientific method to include the larger social and cultural interests, and do not take the trouble to inquire whether it may be possible also to restate religion in terms of the inherent, urgent values of modern life.

The theory of value upon which this paper rests, recognizes that scientific truth is itself one kind of value, and that there are also other real and legitimate values in human experience. There are values of friendship, of aesthetic appreciation, of imaginative creation which do not wait upon scientific knowledge. Living is a much more rich and varied experience than the process of scientific knowledge, no matter how important the latter may be. Only a few individuals, relatively, ever become scientific with reference to the values they cherish. They find the values of love, of labor, of art, and of religion in the full stream of practical life. They go directly to the theater or to their vocation and *live* there. While they do not elaborate theories of criticism, they nevertheless constantly employ critical judgments concerning the events and experiences encountered. It is by building up standards and principles of taste through concrete participation in life that they clarify and deepen their moral and aesthetic values. Through such interests the expert judgments of the connoisseurs reach people and contribute to the illumination and diversification of their experience.

The same practical appropriation of informed and intelligently guided religious experience occurs. Religion is itself a kind of poetic translation and interpretation of the supreme values of life, but it should be a poetry based on reality. It employs for its purpose the arts of architecture, literature, and music. Processions, costumes, and symbolic devices are used. The congregation is a kind of dramatic expression of religious experience, and is more or less recognized as such. It is the great chorus of the drama. Such a setting invites to further symbolism and this appears in the discourse made up, at its best, of parables, pictures, dramatic incidents, and poetic prose. In religion, as in other forms of art, what is sought is the presentation, in appealing symbols, of the struggle and the meaning of human life. It demands a living enactment of life itself in such ways as will bring home to the will and the emotions the ideal meanings present in human experience. In the religious interest the imaginative representation of the web of life and its various values is the most effective, and therefore religion in its great, fresh, energizing periods has employed legend, parable, and dramatic story. Only in the secondary epochs, at the hands of systematizers and administrators, has it fallen into the mistake of trying to make these literary and artistic forms into formal, logical, and epistemological determinants of absolute Truth and Reality. So long as such formulas are regarded for what they really are, namely, speculative reflections, they serve useful purposes. They are then significant, orderly summaries of the world-view in which they arise, and they furnish frameworks through which individuals may behold in intellectual perspectives the relative place and importance of various interests. But so long as they are held to be the tentative and sketchy outlines which they are, they invite further study and continuous critical restatement. When dogmas are taken for what they are, they perform valuable functions, not the least of which is that they invite thoughtful improvement, as well as furnishing provisional guidance for action. Then the creeds are worthy of respect as the embodiment of serious philosophies of life, and are shorn of their deadening effect as rules for slavish acceptance and obedience. It is quite essential that there shall always be creeds of this kind, but the recognition of this is the dismissal of all creeds of whatever age or recency as statements of absolute and final wisdom.

The need for critical religious philosophies of life in the present age is one of the great characteristics of the time. The profound revolutions in scientific thought and in practical life demand summations and interpretations to make clear the values which are inherent in it and to clarify the conditions and the consequences which may be involved concerning them. Perhaps no age has so suddenly been confronted with such radical questioning of old values and the forms in which they have been cast. Science and the machine have vastly enlarged man's outlook upon nature and upon human life and have transformed the conditions of human existence. Whether this means a deadening mechanical and materialistic conception, or a richer humanistic and spiritual evaluation, is the crucial moral and religious problem demanding consideration. It is evident that there is no easy and ready-made solution such as the return to other " ages of faith " with their dependence upon authority, special revelation, and emotional ecstasy. The values of common life stand in their own right, subject to the tests of living experience, and open to discovery of ways and means by which they may be stabilized and made fruitful for further development and enhancement. These values can no longer be regarded as merely means to ends which lie outside themselves, but are at once both means and ends. The instruments of material production and mobility cannot be relegated to the realm of mere machinery and technique if they are the carriers of greater power and freedom for the human spirit. They become " spiritualized " by the satisfactions which their use involves and by the contributions they make to greater security and progress. We live in the present, and unless the work of the day brings its own rewards of achievement and joy, it cannot create them for some detached future. At the same time the natural, future results of present endeavor become qualities of immediate experience so far as they are imaginatively grasped in the implications of the task in hand.

A religious philosophy of life, conceived in consistency with scientific knowledge, recognizes the limited nature of man's knowledge and achievement, but finds in this very fact certain profoundly significant values. One is the thrill of adventure into the unknown. The zest of experiment and adventure is present in the humblest scientific experiment and in the most modest social enterprise. If it were a closed world of absolute, fixed values, and known to be such, man would either revolve in the circle of dead familiarity, or grope in a maze of blind faith. But everyday experience disproves such a view, for all common, practical living is infused with the sense of some degree of continuity between the plans and endeavors we put forth and the expectation of fulfilment. This expectation is justified by the results, though they seldom come easily or in the exact form and degree anticipated. Life intrigues us constantly by its partial successes and partial failures, but just on this account it is interesting and alluring. There is ever the reward of increasing accumulation of these experimental undertakings, broadening knowledge, multiplication of tools, enriching records, and enlarging sympathy for those who strive, whether they win or lose. Ours is not a sheltered, guaranteed existence on this planet, yet it is not wholly without its boons and findings. The very conditions of emotional excitation lie in the character of the world as we know it, and give significance to the moral qualities of courage, patience, co-operation, and sympathy.

This contingent character of the world also induces a befitting humility. The vast powers of nature surge around us, they extend far beyond our little niche in space and time. The clearest fields of science have their lacunae, and are bounded with fathomless immensities. This fact has tempted many devout souls to conceive these unknown areas as the proper sphere of religion, and for these they often surrender the realities which lie upon our shoal and bank of time. But to stand upon the solid realities of experience, recognizing the fact of its limits, is a very different thing from plunging off into the abyss where nothing is seen or tested.

The contemplation of the unknown from the footing of the known has decided advantages over discarding what is in hand for the emptiness and darkness around it. Our knowledge about things provides handles by which we take hold of them, though each thing has filaments or atmospheres which we cannot grasp. Surely what is felt and handled belongs to the universe as much as any other conceivable entities, though the realization that all we know is set in the indeterminate, gives an air of mystery and marvel to all that we behold. This fact may well beget the realization that man's life is beset throughout by necessary resignations. Values appear and disappear, sometimes tragically and irremediably. Storms, accidents, social upheavals, occur with fatal power, and men are often helpless in the face of them. Not all the powers of life and death are in their control. They must live cautiously and prudently, as well as adventurously and dangerously. Religion therefore justifiably enjoins reverence, humility, and the fear of the Lord, as well as a stout heart and quiet trust. To ignore either side of experience is to lose all one's practical bearings in the depths of mysticism or despair, or to live in a false security with the illusions of vain, blind conceit. The wisdom of the wise is to cling to the values which prove themselves in the shifting scenes of life, and to labor for the conditions that give them greater accessibility, continuing growth, and new progeny in the colorful and thrilling life of man lived at its highest levels and fullest capacities.

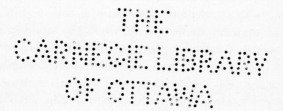
THE CARNEGIE LIBRARY OF OTTAWA

EVOLUTION AND TIME

Albert G. A. Balz

I

METAPHYSICAL speculation may occasionally anticipate changes in the human scene. But more often, perhaps, it is the bird of wisdom that takes flight, as Hegel said, with the twilight. In the nineteenth century the human scene made historical process and development, growth and evolution, the central idea in the reflective mind. Absolute Idealism, viewing all things as process, effected an anticipatory use of the idea. Naturalistic metaphysics performed the odd feat of translating the process of Absolute Idealism into an evolutionism, with great renown accruing to the philosophies of evolution. With all of this came new metaphysical reflections of changes in the human scene. Reality evolves — is it then creative? Things are historical or else they are nothing — what, then, of time?

Metaphysicians of more than one school have agreed with Alexander's retort to Russell:[1] with the former they would change the latter's dictum to the effect that to take time seriously is a sign of metaphysical incapacity into the mere admission that particular times cannot be taken seriously by the philosopher. And again in agreement with Alexander many metaphysicians would urge that the recognition of the fundamental place of time is the first condition of progress in philosophical reconstruction. Bergson, with the definition of reality as both evolution and creation, reflected admirably the new sensitivity. The world in which men live and which they operate upon appears to be replete with uncertainties, with unanticipatable futures, with novelties and beginnings, with spirals rather than cycles. To reduce these suggestions to traits of a merely phenomenal world seemed perilous, and the definition of reality by means of a systematic neglect of them seemed arbitrary. The thought of reality as an evolution and as creative, moreover, brought a renewed interest in the problem of time. Bergson, sharply distinguishing real from clock

[1] *Space, Time, and Deity*, Vol. I, 1920, p. 36.

time, defines the reality that is creative and evolving as duration. The doctrine of emergence and Whitehead's "creative advance of nature" seem to be expressions of the same reorientation in metaphysics.

What is the motivation of this renewed interest in time and of this tendency to view reality as creative? And what is the relation of the concept of evolution to these tendencies? Negatively, of course, these movements express a reaction against a metaphysics that defines reality as static and complete. In the background lies the non-temporal, or supra-temporal, Absolute, with time reduced to a dimension of the phenomenal world. Moreover, the human adventure, to the modern mind, seems inextricably bound up with time: the concept of evolution has made even the man on the street think in this way. Nature, life, and society possess a temporal character or they are nothing at all. From the standpoint of those who would take the human adventure, and in accord with this would take time, seriously, the supra-temporal Absolute appears singularly remote.

This feeling for the temporal aspect of the human adventure must have been both cause and effect with respect to the redirection of mind signalized in the triumph of evolution. Genesis, growth, historical process, development, evolution — these have become the dominant conceptions of mind. They came to prevail, doubtless, because experience and the needs of inquiry demanded them. But the mind's sensitivity to the need must have depended, in part, upon an internal change of attitude. The change did not occur without strain. The genetic and evolutionary point of view cut across many ingrained habits of mind. As the peculiar character of modern civilization became more and more clearly defined, this mental readjustment followed as effect, and metaphysics was in so far a laggard. But the readjustment brought an intensification of the movement. The dynamic thrust of things, the dazzling picture of the reconstruction of nature and society, daring and even ill-judged aspirations and anticipations precipitated into the Idea of Progress — all these were causes and effects. Within a civilization such as this, where mind learns to think of human destiny as lying within the natural world, time is a vital factor in human calculation. To view things genetically, to find the meanings of things in their history, to think in terms of development and evolution, are extensions of the calculation dictated by need. Things unquestionably have a history. Genesis, development, and evolution are discoverable in things if it once occur to us to look for them. Yet the modern mind did not find them until the discovery was demanded by the urgencies of experience.

In this situation is born the renewal of the metaphysical interest concerning the reality of time. Even moral interests gave reinforcement to this reorientation, as was picturesquely expressed when James found the Absolute to be of value mainly as an excuse for a moral holiday. Out of this situation, again, and with the co-operation of moral interests, came a predilection for the view that reality is not merely a flux, but a creative thrust. It seems a safe conjecture — and if safe, of the first importance — to urge that the *élan vital* brought about the intensification of interest in the metaphysics of time rather than that the latter gave rise to evolutionism. We perceive that things have a history. And then, when things become virtually identified with their history and with their evolution, the problem of time becomes acute. Bergson, advancing from duration to memory and from memory to the *élan vital,* does not recapitulate, but systematically reverses, the order of discovery.

Beneath this movement of mind, however, lies a crisis in the history of modern thought. To take time seriously; to regard it as constitutive of the nature of things; to define reality as creative and as displaying its character in an evolution: these are not obviously coimplicative. But as defining a nascent point of view they are in conflict with another point of view. Mind won its greatest triumphs, especially in reconstructing the stage of the human adventure, by interpreting the flux as a series of mechanical redistributions while confusing, as Bergson would urge, clock time with real time and making of time merely a factor in an equation. With the fruits of this interpretation, however, came a reaction. In success were found inadequacies. The flux, having been explored as redistribution, is felt to be something other than, or something in addition to, redistribution. Genesis, history and historical process, development and evolution, express the reaction. The situation is repeated. A new success, that of the evolutionary schema, is attained. But with the new success comes a conflict of categories and a crisis. This crisis defines the problem of much recent metaphysics.

II

"No more fundamental question can be raised than the range and force of the applicability to nature, life, and society of the whole-and-part conception." The context of this statement of Dewey's [2] is defined by a discussion of analytical realism. The importance of the question, however, is not limited by the context. This is true also of the sentence immediately preceding it: "A theory which commits us to the conception of a world of Eleatic fixities as primary and which regards alteration and organization as secondary has such profound consequences for thought and conduct that a detection of its motivating fallacy makes a substantial difference." These remarks are quoted both for their suggestiveness and because they bring to mind a parallel. "No more fundamental question can be raised than the range and force of the applicability to nature, life, and society of the conception of evolution." The latter question is as important as that formulated by Dewey. If this does not appear to be the case, it is largely because confidence in the adequacy of the whole-and-part conception has been undermined precisely by the extraordinary success achieved by the historical and evolutionary scheme of interpretation.

If the whole-and-part conception (with "parts" taken as Eleatic fixities) had not been uncritically extended in its application, Dewey's question would lack point. For there can be little doubt that the whole-and-part schema has range and force of applicability, and this can be maintained of the evolutionary schema. It would not be difficult to furnish illustrations both of the excessive application of the whole-and-part schema and of its valid uses. Daily life, with its manipulation of things, indicates sufficiently that valuable results accrue when things in nature, life, and society are considered as whole, and these wholes as analyzable into parts not further analyzable. The study of the world as a whole of fixed parts, adopted by modern science and reflected into modern epistemology and metaphysics, called forth the reaction embodied in the evolutionary point of view.

Greek thought, of course, worked out the plan of interpreting the flux as consisting of changes of combination and dissolution of combinations with the entities involved defined as fixed. In this manner there was secured a point of view from which qualitative differences could be placed

[2] *Essays in Experimental Logic,* pp. 45–6.

in correlation with quantitative differences. The qualitative differences, from this point of view, were necessarily regarded as having only a preliminary methodological importance. After the mediaeval episode [3] and for reasons which must be omitted, scientific inquiry found in quantity the common denominator of things, and replaced the qualitative diversity of things by the inexhaustible possibilities of combination of fixed units. The preliminary methodological rôle of qualities became confused with questions of their ontological status, especially as a result of the impact of the Cartesian dualism of substances. The mediaeval particular becomes a combination of parts and for the multitude of genera and species are substituted a few kinds of Eleatic portions. "For thinkers of the seventeenth century," as the matter has been excellently summarized, "to whom all ideas of development were entirely foreign, the place which is now filled by the conception of evolution was occupied by the idea of composition, with the implied distinction between the simple and the complex. A complex whole being regarded as the mere sum of its constituent parts, these latter were not thought to undergo any modification as the result of their combination; similarly, the whole was supposed to be directly resolvable into its parts without remainder. The whole temporal process containing nothing but different combinations of the same

[3] Aristotelian concreteness, defining a thing as the unity of matter and form, impeded the incipient process of reducing and simplifying the world by placing thought in a dilemma: On the one hand the thing as the unity of matter and form, or as determined by the four causes, reassigns to the particular its individual specificity. So conceived, an account of the world could be given only by describing each particular within it. On the other hand, if methodological simplification were sought by the use of common denominators, the latter could be nothing other than the species, the essentially qualitative formal component as providing a basis for the classification of things. A systematic account of the world, accordingly, must necessarily have the shape of an elaborate classification in terms of genus and species. This procedure, however, is not amenable to control. The genus and species reflect the qualitative richness of perception, which is always of the particular; moreover, from the standpoint of qualitative characteristics, a vast number of classifications, each relevant to things, is possible. In terms of unanalyzed perception, the genus and species must retain the qualitative variety of the perceived thing, in which case classification is literally impossible; or else classification must take the form of an abstraction from perceived resemblances, and the class is only an hypostatization of qualitatives. In the movement towards the genus and species, thought cannot on this basis readily distinguish between essential and non-essential resemblances. In fact, one similarity is in principle as good as another. Differentia may well become fanciful, or, if it seek to avoid this, it may become essentially verbal. From this dilemma followed the sterility of what is called, none too happily, mediaeval science. In reaction, modern thought sought to reinstate the quantitative point of view. Descartes, asserting that the infinitude of figures suffices to express the diversity of things, states the fundamental principle of the readopted point of view.

simples, out of which nothing genuinely new could emerge, the historical point of view from which we trace development in time, and seek to comprehend the new determinations which arise in its course, was without significance. To comprehend a complex whole, all that was required was a process of direct analysis by which the simples contained in it were distinguished. Then, starting with the simples, thought could retrace with perfect adequacy the process by which the whole had originally been constituted." [4]

The whole-and-part schema had immediately two quite diverse applications, within nature and within mind.[5] A second set of simples appears: these are mental simples, the idea, the states or contents of consciousness. Experience becomes, in Dewey's phrase, not a method but a subject-matter. The contents of consciousness, however, receive definition by the extrusion of qualitative diversity from the external world that science envisaged. The part of the common-sense thing assigned to mind is just that part unassimilable by science — its variable qualitative features. If, then, the schema of simples and compounds be applied to mental existence, these Eleatic portions are qualitative irreducibles.

With this came both triumph and failure. Science had provided control over nature; technological achievement, presumably, indicated a grasp of the nature and meaning of things. But scientific success was epistemo-

[4] Gibson, J., *Locke's Theory of Knowledge and its Historical Relations,* Cambridge, 1917, pp. 47-8.

[5] The objects, i.e., the objectives, of science were nature, as diluted as possible with respect to qualities, and patterned in terms of wholes and fixed parts, susceptible of quantitative determination. Scientific method instituted a contrast between its objectives and common sense things of perception. The mind's acquaintance with things, and even with the objectives of science, was first of all dependent upon these things of immediate perception. Thus an apportioning is suggested: a part of what seems to be nature is really nature; another part is really mind. This is effected through many influences: moral and religious and theological interests recoil from the apparent implications of science. The epistemological tangle arises: perception itself is a mechanical process; the organs of perception, the human body as a whole, are common sense perceptual things; accordingly, the apportioning that applies to other things applies to the perceiving organism. Mind, proposing a science of the living body, stands in a relation to it that is precisely the same as that obtaining with respect to any existential subject-matter. The apportioning suggested by method, desirable from the standpoint of moral and theological interests, is seemingly required by epistemology. The situation points to a dualistic ontology; and the dualistic ontology that lies to hand gives point to the situation. It is important to note that the apportionment *does not furnish two sets of things both known to common sense,* but two sets of things *neither of which is known to common sense.* The common sense world is replaced: in part by a Nature known only in and to science; in part by a Mind known only in and to epistemology and metaphysics.

logically unintelligible save, possibly, at a serious metaphysical price. Hume and Kant may be appealed to in witness of the statement.[6]

The situation, however, was not merely a dialectical puzzle. Mind had reached the whole-and-fixed-part schema because nature and experience had forced it upon attention. There could scarcely be a question as to whether the schema had range and force of applicability, but only a question as to its limits. The schema became a problem because of difficulties residing in that frame of thought itself. Moreover, if fruitfulness of use gave assurance that nature is not suggesting the whole-and-part plan in mockery, it is nature that suggests the danger of absurdity in its application. In revulsion from the world of Eleatic fixities, mind perceived that things are historical, and turns to the genetico-evolutionary scheme of interpretation. Finally, with this comes the problem of the relationship of the two schemes of thought.

Eleatic fixity and vital movement, whole-and-part and organic integration of differentiations stand in opposition. Are all things, and each thing, to be thought of both as whole-and-fixed-part and as a unity in or of evolving process? Do the two schemes obtain as correctives of each other, each defining the limitations of the other? Or are things divisible into two classes, the one class sufficiently characterizable in terms of the one, the other class characterizable in terms of the other conception? Or finally do the two sets of conceptions represent two interpretative strata,

---

[6] The problem was triple: the combinatory in nature must be made intelligible; the compounding of simples in mental nature needs explanation; and the relationship between the two sets of simples forms a problem. Occasionalism sought to correlate the two fields through the agency of God, and was forced to the same device within nature itself. Moreover, it was apparent that the knower is not, so to speak, exhausted when the mental simples and their compoundings are indicated. The common-sense distinction between the perceiver and the things perceived is duplicated in the distinction between the knower and his ideas. Hume represents the reduction of the triple to a single problem. There is but one set of simples and their ordering is inexplicable. Montague's admirable article, " A Neglected Point in the Philosophy of Hume," seems to me not quite complete. The net result of Hume is not that the Humean impressions and ideas are non-mental things of common sense, and not mental at all, but rather that they are neither things nor ideas, neither physical nor mental. By Hume's application of the Berkeleian argument against matter-substance to soul-substance, all substance disappears. Therefore the contexts within which an idea can be defined as mental and not physical, or as physical and not mental, are destroyed. Hume's use of the terms " impression " and " idea " may be justifiable within the context of his psychological analyses, but not without that context. Epistemologically, the Humean impression and idea is an entity of Eleatic fixity, and cognitive relations are unintelligible; and ontologically it is neither a thing nor a mental state, for concerning its ontological status nothing can be said. Science is impossible on a double count.

the genetico-evolutionary plan giving the more profound insight into the nature of things?

This is the historical moment of Leibnitz. The monad preserves the radical isolation of the Eleatic unit. Its fixity, however, is defined only by its insulated self-containedness. Internally, the monad is an unfolding, a continuous self-explication. Inasmuch as it cannot be influenced by other monads, it is fixed: in so far as it is an internal development, the monad is a vital irreversible process. Presumably the monads are not things, but the units of composition of things, while things are aggregates.[7] The integrity of the monad is unaffected by composition and decomposition, for these can refer only to changes in which the monads are unaffected internally by virtue of the changes. Whole-and-part relations are purely external and non-constitutive. It may be assumed that the whole-and-part view of things — in general, the field of matter and mechanism — is phenomenal rather than real. Change is accordingly twofold: there is change within (and of) the monad — change, in this case, being an unfolding, a development, a microcosmic evolution; on the other hand, there is change in the sense in which things arise by aggregation and disappear in disaggregation. The atomic constituents of the world must be thought of in genetico-developmental terms; but the world at large must be understood in terms of the whole-and-part schema. The radical disparity of change and process could scarcely be made more emphatic.

The disparity, moreover, is macrocosmic as well as microcosmic. The pre-established harmony is the metaphysical expression of the strife between two sets of conceptions. In so far as the pre-establishment is emphasized, the implication is that the harmony is imposed from without and is not in itself evolutionary. Reality as a whole (or in theological terms, creation) is an aggregate, not a unity that can be called " organic."

7 This statement may require reservation. Leibnitz, especially where living things are concerned, hesitates between the definition of the living organism as itself one monad, and the view of the organism as an aggregate of monads. His treatment of body and soul is peculiarly instructive. Three tendencies may be discriminated: First, the organism is a monad, and the soul is the active aspect of this monad, the body its passivity. Second, the human being is a collection of monads, soul being the harmony of the active aspects of this plurality of entities: i.e., the pre-established harmony of the microcosm. Finally, there is the soul as a monad, a central (and highly evolved?) monad, with the body an assemblage of monads. Views then current concerning the development of the individual organism naturally inclined Leibnitz toward the first view, and by extension, to the view that every particular is a monad, thus giving an Aristotelian matter-and-form concreteness. But the tradition of body-soul dualism, and scientific conceptions of matter, effectually checked this tendency.

In so far as the emphasis is placed upon this, that the monads are so made by the Divine Architect that harmony results, giving an appearance of interadjustment where there is really no interrelation at all, this apparent harmony is presumably an evolution. Leibnitz' metaphor of the orchestra must be carried beyond the point to which Leibnitz himself carried it if the metaphor is to represent effectively his meaning. We have to imagine that the monadic musicians not merely cannot hear one another, but that they possess no score: each musician's playing is wholly improvisation, the expression of his own soul in its radical individuality.[8] That these improvisations should constitute a symphony — or supply the illusion of symphonic system for the imaginary listener — expresses one of two possibilities: it is a miracle or it is mechanism. A miracle if the symphonic unity be the result of an unpredictable harmony of improvisations; but mechanism if God so made the musicians that, in expressing their inmost souls by their improvisations, harmony necessarily results. In the latter case, indeed, the musicians are not monads but Robots. The orchestra is an aggregate, and there is no improvisation. The score has been pre-established, and the parts have been written out. The orchestra has no conductor precisely because it is composed not of musicians but of machines. With this the category of whole-and-part is perceived to be not phenomenal but real.

The outcome is instructive. Leibnitz seeks to save the reality of the individual, but does this only by the adoption of the whole-and-part schema. This schema, however, involves the paradox of explaining change by aggregation and disaggregation of units in themselves subject to no change. There arises from the paradox the adoption of the developmental and evolutionary conception. Neither plan, it seems, admits of real beginnings, of genuine novelty, of creativeness in reality in a sense comfortable to the aspects of experience suggesting the concept of evolution. In terms of one set of conceptions, only a particular aggregation, as an aggregate, can possess any novelty whatever. In the other case, when evolution is pluralized by the whole-and-part conception, every unit is a creative process, an historical career. Each of these processes, however, is an unfolding through inner necessity. There radical individuality implies that each process is itself an independent develop-

---

[8] This extension of the metaphor was brought to my attention by the late Professor Lefevre.

ment, a microcosmic evolution. Since there are no interactions between
the monads, there is no creative novelty, for the one monadic development
is as ultimate as any other. Each monad, leaving to one side the theological *deus ex machina,* is an eternal reality in itself, thinkable only in
terms of its own unending and internal history. Thus again intelligible
beginnings are possible only as aggregations. The unification of the
plurality of histories into one — which is the meaning of the pre-established harmony — is either a mystery for which the fact that the world
is the best possible is an explanation denying the independence of the
monads, or else it is a unity of aggregation.

Thus each schema acts as a curb upon the other. If categories, however, are to be judged by their fruits, nature validates both interpretative
schemes by the intellectual fruits that accrue. Nature suggests that a
consolidation of the two conceptions should be valid and bring economy
for mind. But the history of philosophy seems to disclose that the competition between the conceptions is not to be ended by assigning to each
its peculiar subject-matter. Moreover, the Leibnitzian dilemma points
to the fact that nothing can be gained by making the one schema metaphysically more primary than the other. It seems idle to regard the one
conception as applying to the " phenomenal " world while the other
applies to the noumenal world. If it be experience and nature, the
" phenomenal " world, that forces mind to take cognizance of discontinuity and to think in terms of a redistribution of fixed elements, it is
equally the case that from the same source come the suggestions for a
developmental and evolutionary interpretation.

III

The immense success of the genetico-evolutionary schema and the
historical method obscured the Leibnitzian dilemma. Many evolutions
having been discerned, evolution became Cosmic Process, and reality is a
History.[9] As the whole-and-part conception swept from one field to
another and all things became parts of one Whole, so the mind passed
from evolutions to Evolution. If the former extension legitimately
prompts Dewey's question as quoted above, so the latter extension prompts

[9] I must acknowledge here my indebtedness — and indebtedness incurred throughout
this paper — to Woodbridge's *The Purpose of History,* Columbia Univ. Press, 1916, and
especially to his chapter on " The Pluralism of History."

a parallel to Dewey's question. The problem of the range and force of applicability of the conception of evolution is as pressing for the advance of science and metaphysics as the problem indicated by Dewey. The Leibnitzian dilemma was anticipatory. It reappeared in many shapes after Leibnitz. Most strikingly it appears in the paradoxical fact that an evolutionary interpretation is imposed upon a subject-matter already organized in terms of the whole-and-part pattern, while the latter pattern is continually employed to give exactitude in interpreting developments and evolutions.

Is the Leibnitzian dilemma resolvable? Is it perhaps overbold to offer more than the suggestion that the dilemma itself points the direction in which philosophical criticism promises to be fruitful. The celebrated definition of evolution offered by Herbert Spencer correctly describes the manner in which evolution was taken when the conception was regarded as a master-key opening many, if not all, scientific and metaphysical locks. It is not inapplicable to the Leibnitzian monad. It is, moreover, inevitably the definition of evolution that reduces all monads to one Monad, or otherwise reintroduces Dewey's question in acute form. Evolution means an unfolding; a change whereby that which was implicit becomes explicit; it is a self-disclosure, a continuous and progressive manifestation of an inner nature, a " realization " of " potentialities." Negatively the meaning of evolution according to the definition is indicated by this, that any and every influence arising from a source external to the evolving thing can have no positive contribution to make to the career of that thing. Such influences from without are occasioning causes, releasing agencies; they are detonators that set free a train of changes quite incommensurable with the detonating agency. The external factor may somehow counteract a constrictive and oppressive element, thus permitting the series of changes whose determinate character is given in the thing itself. Development and evolution come to have primarily the same meaning, the restriction of one term to an individual and the application of the other to a process involving a plurality of individuals becoming unessential.

Mind, however, over-reaches itself in the definition. The schema of evolution with which we seek to take account of vital and dynamic aspects of experience turns into a new and rigid determinism. Suggested by the appearance of " creative advance," evolution comes to deny advance by a systematic interlocking of all advances. If things in their severalty are just so many evolutions, and if growth, development, be exhaustively an inner unfolding, then these several things cannot even be detonators with respect to one another. On the other hand, if the unfolding from within of one thing seems to bear a determinate relation to other things, then the plurality of things becomes illusory. That is to say, if evolution be what it is usually taken to mean, then there is one evolution and not many. We may then say of reality that it evolves. But for this we must pay a double price: on the one hand it cannot be said of anything less than the whole of Reality that it evolves, save by way of an equivocal use of terms; on the other hand, if we affirm that reality evolves, there is no creative advance in things. The detonators, the releasing agencies, lie within the one Monad. They are of its substance, which is to say that they do not exist and that there are no detonators. The one evolution must contain within itself that character whereby the implicit becomes explicit with inexorable necessity.

With this, it may be conjectured, we come upon the vital defect of the traditional definition of evolution. For time cannot be taken seriously if reality be one vast evolution. The unfolding of the implicit into the explicit may not be thinkable in terms of a redistribution of fixed parts. But the one comprehensive unfolding in its predetermined and determinate majesty reduces particular times to " moments " of unfolding, the Annals of the Absolute, and of Time as a whole a *totum simul*. We cannot, in short, begin with a plurality of growths, histories, developments, and evolutions and reduce them to one evolution without sacrificing time. It is time that points to evolutions, and not evolutions to time. If seeds sprout, not in midwinter, but in spring-time, it would seem that the seed must wait for spring and a detonator. But there can be neither mid-winter nor spring-time in a reality that is one Evolution. Nothing can check this evolution; and there is nothing to serve as a releasing cause. The unfolding of the implicit is either timeless or nothing. Indeed, it must be both timeless and nothing if it be a timeless evolution, and we are to avoid the equivocation of using the term with respect to reality in a sense hopelessly unrelated to those facts of nature and life and society which forced upon us the employment of the conception. The evolution of the stellar system and the growth of the flower from the daffodil bulb may be informative concerning reality. But if this be granted, it is not because reality is an evolution but because time is fundamental in the nature of things.

To take time seriously; to report experience faithfully; to acknowledge in nature, life, and society creative advances — to do all this requires a report of correlations of histories, careers, of processes and evolutions. When this is done, however, evolution becomes the name of a type of metaphysical problem rather than the solution of problems. The extent to which sequences in time are unfoldings of the implicit to explicitness is everywhere problematic. The problems are specific reflections of variable characters in different subject-matters, and the subject-matters alone can throw light upon the range and force of applicability of the schema of evolution. For metaphysics the problem is that of discovering in the temporal character of reality the basis of the radical pluralisms of histories, processes, developments, and evolutions.

ART, ACTION, AND AFFECTIVE STATES

Harold Chapman Brown

The argument of this paper may well start from Professor Dewey's criticism of the isolationist theories of art. "It is sometimes said," he writes, "that art is the expression of the emotions; with the implication that, because of this fact, subject-matter is of no significance except as material through, which emotion is expressed. Hence art becomes unique. . . . In such a statement emotion either has no significance at all, and it is mere accident that this particular combination of letters is employed; or else, if by emotion is meant the same sort of thing that is called emotion in daily life, the statement is demonstrably false. For emotion in its ordinary sense is something called out *by* objects, physical and personal; it is response *to* an objective situation." (*Experience and Nature*, p. 390.) The consequences to be drawn here, however, are slightly different from those emphasized by Professor Dewey; if aesthetic emotion is not different in kind from emotion as it occurs incidentally to living, it should be important to reflect upon the relations of emotion to thought and action and the consequent significance for living of aesthetic expression and appreciation. It is this theme with which the present paper is concerned.

Contemporary aestheticians exhibit a rather remarkable agreement that, whatever else art may be, it is at least a language of the emotions, but they differ as to whether language is an instrument of expression or of communication. The separation of these two functions, however, is quite impossible as applied to language, for communication can only exist if something is expressed, and a form of expression that can communicate nothing is neither language nor art. At least the intent to communicate seems to be what differentiates vocalization, gesture, or action, as language, from such expressive but non-communicatively intended activities as scratching our heads from nervousness and swearing when we "madly cram a right hand foot into a left hand shoe," — performances which have no communicational intent, hence are not generally classified as language or art.

The tendency to deny to a work of art the capacity to communicate an emotion as something essential to its being art rests upon a confusion. It is true that a work of art is a work of art before it is exhibited, if it is never exhibited, or if it is cast as pearls before swine. Nevertheless, if art, it has the potentiality of communicating emotion to a properly educated and receptive audience. The artist may not intend to exhibit his work; he may merely record feeling states lest he forget, or seek to attain clarity as to his feelings for himself alone as we note down ideas for our private eye or to clarify our thought, but such records, whether of emotion or thinking, are instruments of potential communication between our present selves and our selves at some later time. In brief, if art is a language of the emotions it must be both a medium of expression and of communication. Either without the other is not language.

Unfortunately we have no adequate and generally accepted physiological theory of affective states. It is, however, generally believed that they are closely related to visceral and glandular processes, and to the operations of the autonomic system. (Cf. Lloyd Morgan: *Life, Mind, and Spirit,* pp. 174–180.) Why physiological psychologists should stop at this point is not at all clear. These processes are merely incidental to adjustments of metabolic correlations in the organism necessary to maintain a balance between its complicated structures amidst the varied and complicated activities an ever-changing environment induces. If emotion is to retain any sort of sensory character, as James maintained, that sensory character is surely better interpreted as related to these metabolisms than to the processes by which they are brought about. It is hard to understand the emission of hormones as contributing a sensory component to mind, but it is compartively easy to see how a metabolic change might; at least metabolic processes are of the same order of physiological fact as the peripheral changes that give rise to other sensory qualities.

Lloyd Morgan distinguishes two stories that can be told of the organism: one, the life-story, is told in terms of physiological processes; the other, the mind-story, is told in terms of psychological states. If we adopt this mode of description, in terms of the life-story there is at any normal moment a certain prevalent and more or less persistent type of metabolic correlation; for example, the relaxed muscles, light breathing, and diffused nerve action of a man lying under the shade of a tree on a sunny day, thinking of nothing in particular. In terms of the mind-story there is a mood of lazy contentment. A wandering ant may suddenly nip the nape of his neck. Both life- and mind-story undergo a spectacular change. He slaps wildly at the injured spot, may even leap to his feet. His breathing rate, pulse, and muscular innervations are suddenly transformed. New metabolic correlations for intense activity are set up. This is the changed life-story. On the side of the mind-story, he would report anger with, perhaps, a touch of fear or disgust.

This sudden transformation, however, is no longer described as mood but as emotion. In general it may be noted that emotion always goes with a life-story of more or less violent readjustment of metabolic correlations to meet the demands of a rather abruptly induced new type of activity. In the above case, when the offending ant has been removed or slaughtered, the former mood may be recovered or a new mood replace it. Perhaps day-dreaming under the tree is succeeded by leisurely strolling. In the life-story this means the establishment of new autonomic correlations and a consequent change in the type of metabolic balance. Moods seem to be characters of persistent states in the mind-story, while emotions represent metabolic conditions during readjustments to new conditions. Emotions only lapse into moods when the emergency that gives rise to them has been met. Perhaps some forms of emotional expression that Darwinians have vainly tried to interpret as survivals of actions once useful may turn out to be essential phases of such readjustment processes, and of no further objective significance.

Our actual behavior involves at least the co-operation of two types of nervous processes, the one, sensory-motor, by which events in the environmental world cause the innervation of action patterns built up in the course of the experiences of living; the other, autonomic, serving to control the distribution of energy flow within the organism in such fashion that some sort of metabolic balance can be recovered and maintained no matter what the organism is called upon to do. (Cf. Kempf: *Autonomic Functions of the Personality*.) We may be justified in going even further than this. In the course of living we build up, not one action pattern to a stimulus-situation, but a repertoire of action patterns. A book seen on the table may be picked up and read, thrown at the cat, dropped in the waste basket, or ignored. If it is legitimate to read back from the mind-story to the life-story, and if we neglect the case when seeing the book is incidental to some activity already commenced, such as house cleaning, the selection from among our repertoire of action patterns is determined by mood. In terms of the life-story, this seems to mean that those actions are most easily innervated which the musculatory system is best energized to perform. That is, the selection is not made by the nervous system, although it may be limited by acquired patterns, but is made by the prevailing type of autonomic balance, present in the mind-story as mood.

There is one restriction that must be put upon this thesis. Some stimuli win for themselves such ready discharge into action patterns that, regardless of mood, they pass over into action. Autonomic adjustments that prevent the action from being harmful follow along after. This is the condition in emotional situations. One may be crossing the street in a reflective mood, but the sharp honk of a near-by auto-horn leads to precipitate, although often confused, action in spite of mood, and the affective state is one of fear, anger, or both. It is the function of the sympathetic nervous system to bring about the correlations that are to result in the new energy distribution, but as this is not brought about smoothly and at once, many action patterns within our repertoire get brief play, hence hesitance and confusion in conduct. Whatever instincts may be and however they arise, whether as a result of heredity or of unconscious learning, perhaps prenatal, their close association with emotion arises from the fact that they represent the sort of close connection between sensory stimulus and action pattern that tends to make the stimulus affective, although against mood, and hence compel those metabolic readjustments of which the mind-story is emotion.

Apart from such critical situations where instinct or habit dominates the stage, the effective character of mood is manifested both by a selective influence in determining which of the many sensory stimuli that beset us at any instant shall attain the dominance constituting attention, and which of the action patterns this stimulus might innervate shall become actually innervated. When stimuli leading to conflicting lines of action are permitted by mood to gain attentive dominance, we are in the situation initiative of thought. This, as Professor Dewey has pointed out in *How We Think*, leads to a series of relevant memories and imaginative images, each initiative of an action pattern repertoire. Mood exercises a selective influence, until a congenial *Gestalt* is found or formed, or until a persistent action pattern brings about a shift of mood suited to the action involved. Thought always prepares possible action, but such action is only actualized when contributing to the restoration or preservation of some state of metabolic balance within the organism.

One might be tempted to speculate that if Professor Watson is correct, and if the three fundamental emotions of the child are fear, anger, and love, called out respectively by sudden noises or removal of support from the body, restriction of movement, and stroking or gentle rocking, we have in them examples of the three types of metabolic readjustment that it is possible to produce. In fear, the stimulus innervates action patterns that demand a redistribution of energy-bearing materials to replace katabolic exhaustion. While this adjustment is being made, the demanded action is carrying the energy level of certain muscle groups below its normal state of balance — hence the general unpleasant character of fear. In the case of anger, accumulated energy is ready for movement and an over-supply accumulates, since the natural action is prevented, hence an overflow in spasmatic action results. Lastly, in the case of love, an unfortunate name, gentle stimuli merely provoke the responses that are normally adequate to restrain the energy level that would otherwise rise to that over-accumulation which is, in terms of mind-story, the irritability of inaction. Bergson has pointed out that the animal organism, as a storehouse of assimilated energy, must constantly release energy in movement, but he does not emphasize the fact that over-accumulation without release by action is as harmful as action that drains energy below its normal level. Kempf has, I believe correctly, found in this need the basis of spontaneous movements.

In brief, the theory on which I wish to base what follows is that mood is the most influential factor in selecting what we perceive from the range of possible perceptions of the moment, barring, of course, the cases where fundamental instinctive or habit processes are the primary control; secondly, that mood sets limits to the range of relevant memories and images that can be evoked; thirdly, that mood exercises a restrictive influence on the kinds of anticipatory solutions of problems that thought imagery can present; and lastly, that mood confers that final sanction on some imaged solution which is identical with its acceptance as a final preparation for action. Emotion is merely a state of transition from one mood to another. Its significance lies largely in the conditions which provoke it and in the mood in which it results. It has been an intellectualistic mistake on the part of philosophers to try to eliminate emotion, for that is physiologically impossible, but it is possible to learn to direct its course and to bring it to desirable mood culminations.

The claim that aesthetic emotion, as such, is in some way distinct from the emotions of everyday life is due, I think, to its place in the behavior cycle rather than to its character as an emotion. In the aesthetic situation the stimulus is either a direct play on metabolic adjustments with the aid of the autonomic system, as in the case of pure music, or the stimulating condition is an emotion evoking representation that enhances the effects of the direct factors. The consequent action is postponed or diverted because we are always quite aware that we are stimulated by a *representation*. No one would try to eat painted fruit, because he sees that it is painted fruit, or to rescue Desdemona from Othello, because he knows that the actress will soon appear for a curtain call. If we are deceived, as in the case of wax works, we no longer consider the effect aesthetic. If it is an actual scene in nature that provokes the aesthetic response, we are always detached from it so that immediate participation is not instigated. This situation may arise either because of the character of the object, a forest or a distant mountain range, or from some peculiar state into which we have been brought, as when hopelessness in the face of some cataclysm throws us into a state of detachment in which we watch destruction and terror about us as if events of another world than ours.

In this detachment lies the explanation of the fact that so many affective states are pleasant when aesthetically presented that are rarely pleasant when they occur in connection with the activities of living. If pleasure, as is usually admitted, is a part of the mind-story relative to organic conditions that are on the whole beneficial, while unpleasantness arises in the mind-story of the immediately harmful, any successful readjustment of the metabolic balance must result in pleasure. Immediate harm can only follow when the energy drain of prematurely forced action overtaxes the local metabolic provision. This, of course, does not occur when there is no demand for action. Particular aesthetically induced moods may be uncongenial and unpleasant when a persistent mood-set resists reorganization and so refuses to further the impelled empathic movements (I am using *empathic* in Langfeld's sense) that the reorganization would entail.

Of the two ways of producing aesthetic effects, the direct and the representational, music alone seems to be capable of succeeding by exclusive use of the direct method. This is because of the great power of heard rhythms and tonal changes to modify our empathic states. No combinations of line, form, and color can grip us with the vigor of a march rhythm, and although some combinations of color may almost nauseate, they cannot make us shiver as a squeaky slate-pencil does. But even music usually invokes indirect aids such as imitative sounds, suggestive titles, or even a complete program. Painting and the plastic arts are always representative, barring some futuristic experiments of doubtful worth, and architecture, a seeming exception, really exhibits manifestations of use that have the emotional value of representations.

It follows that in so far as direct stimuli can be used, art is relatively independent of a special form of culture, but not necessarily of prior experience of the art form. More complex reactions cannot be attained without the prior acquisition of simpler ones that can be integrated into them. This is generally true of all learned activities. We cannot learn to write until we have attained the control of movements necessary to holding an object and directing its movements in a rather subtle fashion. Similarly we cannot make a complex empathic response until we have acquired a repertoire of simple ones from which it can be integrated.

On the other hand, the emotional effect of a represented object is always dependent upon personal and cultural experience. The direct empathic response to a representation of two crossed sticks of wood might be the same for all men, but as a representation of the Cross they have a peculiar significance within Christian culture, differing somewhat for the Catholic and the Protestant, for the unbeliever and for the devout. A cultivated man can yield himself to cultural beliefs that he understands but does not share, but he is helpless before what he does not understand. But even in such cases there may be direct elements in the representation, as in the arts of primitive peoples, that give a true aesthetic effect, although not all the effect that could be obtained by those immersed in the represented culture. Tolstoi's demand that all art should be of universal appeal, if met, would narrow the field of art far more than he imagined — or it would presuppose a common culture spread throughout the whole world.

Aesthetic states may be distinguished as reminiscent or expansive. Of the first type are those utilized in popular art, mere revivals of feeling states with which we are already familiar that have the congeniality of old friends. Such art is easily appealing, but it soon grows tiresome with repetition. On the other hand more subtle art, by its combinations of empathic and associative instrumentalities, succeeds in building up in us new feeling states or in adding to the profundity and completeness of states before but superficially developed. It expands our capacity for emotionality. To get such new experiences takes time and repetition. The first contact will give us much less than the art is capable of giving, so we do not readily tire of it, but go back again and again, each time finding, as we say, something new in it, a deeper meaning.

Of these two sorts of aesthetic effects, the reminiscent is usually produced by suggestive representations and the expansive by direct empathic instigation, but it is impossible to make this distinction rigid since a new combination of representations can result in an integration of their emotional concomitants into an affective state that is genuinely expansive, and the trite rhythms and harmonic progressions of popular music may easily be of merely reminiscent value. One has only, however, to compare the emotional significance of a child's death as presented in the old melodramas with the subtle working of the same theme in Andromache's great speech at parting with her son, or in Ibsen's use of it in the last act of *Brand,* to recognize the emotional varieties combinations of imagery may work. It is difficult to denote these, for our vocabulary in dealing with emotions, as in naming colors, is poor beside the wealth of experiences met. Indeed the effect of much untitled music is so delicate that the resultant affective states, being unnamable, are often unrecognized as such, hence the illusion that the result is a pure intellectual pleasure. The art may then be thought of erroneously in terms of mere formal composition. (Cf. Dewey: *Experience and Nature,* pp. 391–2.)

All profound or habitual aesthetic experiences leave traces that are not eliminated from our nervous dispositions. Since more complex capacities have to be acquired, the process of acquiring them is open to the control of education. This sort of instruction in art is not to be gotten from the study of technique, but by repeated opportunities for appreciative experience, beginning with the less complicated and difficult forms and rising by degrees to the more difficult, always remembering that the first materials from which we must build are from our daily experiences in living. The situation is quite parallel to that of learning denotative language where we first learn to talk about what we can see, hear, or touch and then come to understand combinations of words that take us beyond our personal experiences.

Our educational system, unfortunately, seems to have directed itself to destroying the capacity for the appreciation of art. In literature the selected readings are sufficient to guarantee this. No healthy high-school boy will have had the psychological experience that would enable him to appreciate *Hamlet*. His teacher may recognize this, but at any rate her training has been to assume the futility of the task of teaching appreciation, so she makes him repeat the story, memorize quotations associated with characters, and all in all drives what nails she can into the coffin of his aesthetic potentialities. She teaches him that literature is a bore and only to be approached in the spirit of routine labor.

This would not be serious, perhaps, if it were not for the fact pointed out above that affective states limit the possible sphere of thought and action. The child whose potential emotional development has been thus thwarted is henceforth less of an individual than he should have been. When emotion is aesthetically developed, the emotional capacity attained is as truly material on which we may draw in the situations involved in living as if it had been attained through them. The detachment of art may free us from the need of immediate precipitation into action, but nevertheless the affective preparation due to training in appreciation will be drawn upon in actual experience just as truly as the engineer will draw upon his learning to make a dam safe, or the pianist upon the agility acquired in five-finger exercises to interpret the work of a master. It might be, for example, that we would have fewer divorces if the liberation of the mind from the intellectual prejudices that held the unfit together were accompanied by a development of a capacity for sympathetic appreciation that might result in more fitting unions. At any rate it is a tragic commentary on our educational system that so many are allowed to arrive at adult years with the emotional equipment of a child of six. Emotional defectives, whether the defect is due to birth or education, are quite as useless and probably more dangerous than intellectual defectives.

Most works of art, moreover, have a double purpose. They not only develop an emotional reaction, but also attach it to an interpretation of some situation that is met in living. Thus we learn to feel about such situations as our art has taught us and come to think and act accordingly.

This point is touched upon but inadequately covered by Professor Dewey's conception of art as "education in forms of perception." The contact with a work of art is really a very complex experience, and there are at least five different aspects of that experience that can give rise to significant judgments often confused under the title "aesthetic judgment," but really expressive of independent attitudes of interest.

In the first place there is the question of whether the artist really gets over the effect he intends, or any effect. This is analagous to the question whether a writer has anything to say and succeeds in making his idea clear to others. If a work of art fails in this respect it may still be a pretty, formally correct, combination of lines, tones, or colors, as the work of a writer can be a model of grammar but barren of ideas. If the subject-matter has little significance in itself, as in the case of still life, the feeling excitation due to technical versatility may be enough to satisfy us, but if the subject-matter is such that we expect some significant revelation from it, we experience a sense of disappointment at mere technical display. The interplay of light, form, and color may be adequate for an interpretation of still life, but we feel a distinct antagonism to the representation of a human being as having no greater significance. Formal technique, like correctness of diction, is a favorable condition for aesthetic presentation, but it is not in itself sufficient to make a true work of art.

There is also the judgment of personal taste, elevated by some schools of criticism to be all important. It is really, however, an evidence of the aesthetic maturity of the observer, or of his momentary mood. Appeal to personal taste gives rise to the dogma *de artibus non est disputandum*. But one may fail to like a work of art that effectively conveys a mood merely because that mood is one that the individual's past experiences or present prejudices render insufferable; or one may fail to care for it because he is incapable of getting the potential effect from lack of training in the art in question. There are many who fail to appreciate Dante from lack of the culture that would enable them to respond to the affective stimuli through which his effects are produced. But capacity to appreciate does not guarantee liking. Mr. Arliss is reported to have said that the Jews will not attend his performance of the *Merchant of Venice* because of the uncongenial emotional atmosphere in which their race is there presented. Such judgments of personal taste are interesting and may have a social value, but they should not be confused with judgments pertaining to other characteristics of art.

Another sort of judgment arises when the artist attempts to attach a feeling-value to a represented situation. It is directed toward the truthfulness of his presentation of fact. Thus when Strindberg, from analogies to insect life, reports that woman looks to man only for the needs of herself and her children, and that when these are satisfied rids herself of him by way of death or the madhouse, it can well be doubted whether this is a truthful representation of fact, although we may recognize that Strindberg has accomplished the aesthetic part of his task well and, in cynical moods, we may find his representation congenial.

Again we may pass judgment as to whether the mood conveyed by a truthful representation, however pleasing to us, is really appropriate to the situation involved. We may, for example, feel that there is something dignified or encouraging about the very crudities of Main Street that make it unfitting to treat it as is done by Sinclair Lewis. This is not to say that the situation has been falsified, but that real aspects have been blended and worked together to produce an aesthetic effect that is inappropriate to the subject-matter. Where Nietzsche rejoices in Wagner's beautiful presentation of the love of Siegmund and Sieglinde, especially in the convention-flaunting phrase " sister and wife of thy brother," some feel that triumph by incest is inappropriately clothed in such exalted mood, however deeply they may enter into that mood for the time being. This sort of judgment stands somewhere between the judgment of personal taste and the moral judgment of evaluation. It is not a question of culture inadequate for the appreciation of a present mood, or of a doubt as to fact, as in the former sort of judgment, but of a clash with more deeply rooted and intellectually accepted attitudes toward life. It is apart from the moral judgment in that it does not necessarily imply the belief that harmful results from the aesthetic experience are likely to manifest themselves.

The moral judgment of art has aroused violent protests from artists. I think this is partly due to a preoccupation on their part with the effectiveness of techniques and also to anger at the stupidities of censors. That no moral judgment of art is possible could only be maintained by demonstrating that the work of art produced no effect on the observer that would ever in any way influence his conduct. If we come to love mountains, forests, sea, to be inspired by the creative drive behind the master works of man, or fear the mechanization of industry, because artists have aroused in us such feelings toward these things, we carry these attitudes over into daily life and become better or worse men because of them. This is of ethical significance. Stupid censorship confuses the presentation of immoral situations with immorality of the art, failing to recognize that the morality or immorality does not lie in what is exhibited to us, but in the attitudes we carry over from the presentation to situations we may meet. It would be hard to find a man made worse by witnessing the censored *Damaged Goods* of Brieux, but easy to find those who are less desirable citizens from being intrigued by movie interpretations of the allurement of vice, pleasurable and profitable, with consequences easily escaped by trivial acts of penance.

What has been said above about the physiological-psychological bases of affective states should leave no doubt that aesthetic experiences have significant consequences in our lives. The argument is reinforced by everyday experience. It is the justification of Wilde's aphorism that it is not art that imitates nature, but nature that imitates art. Also it is manifest in our use of the arts for the ends of advertising and propaganda.

The final goal of advertising is, of course, to increase the sale of the articles advertised. This involves bringing to the reader's attention the name and use of the article, fixing this in his memory, together with suggestions as to where it can be obtained and possibly the price. Plain print, striking headlines, catchy captions, etc., could accomplish this end, but that is not sufficient. There must also be created a desire for possession, and here the aid of the artist is invoked. Pictures serving to make the article itself look desirable or to associate it with things that the prospective purchasers may be assumed to desire, envelop it in an effective setting such that the act of purchase may become more probable. The advertising illustrations may have an independent value as art, but they are nevertheless used with the justified belief that their aesthetic effects will influence conduct.

Propaganda also utilizes art to influence conduct. It differs from advertising chiefly in that the latter aims only at instigating a specific act with respect to specific articles while propaganda is usually aimed at developing an attitude toward a general situation from which a diversity of acts may flow. Most of us recall the war propaganda aimed at increasing hatred of the enemy, promoting willingness to conserve food, and the like. The danger of both propaganda and advertising is their success in heightening emotionality to the point of discharging into action without the intervention of thought, hence both can easily take advantage of misrepresentations of fact and lead to undesirable conduct. In the service of good ends both are usually held to be desirable and socially necessary. This may be true, but if the Kantian dictum that human beings should always be treated as persons and never as things is practicable, both are to be, in the long run, condemned.

It is difficult to draw the line between propaganda and much of our best art. The distinction perhaps lies in the fact that true art has sufficient restraint to remain thought-provocative rather than to precipitate action. Shaw and Ibsen both seek a reconstruction of our social life, the one by showing the ridiculousness of many of our social conventions, the other by exhibiting the tragedies that may result from them. Shaw is more close to the propagandist, for he prefaces his plays with discussions indicative of what he believes is the remedy, while Ibsen is more content to let his audience think out its own means of relief. The Belgian sculptor Meunier is also remote from propaganda in that he merely awakens our horror and sympathy by exhibiting the dehumanizing effect of long hours of repetitious labor in the bowels of the earth. He has been called the sculptor of socialism. Perhaps he believes that socialism can furnish a panacea. His work as a sculptor does not show that; yet no one could view it without a heightened impulse to think and act for better conditions. Such thought-provocative use of art, if the facts represented are true, cannot be held objectionable by even the strictest adherent of the Kantian code.

Everywhere the disinterestedness of art is open to question. Hirn points out that " some of the world's finest love lyrics were originally composed, not in aesthetic freedom, which is independent of all by-purposes, but with the expressed end of gaining the ear of some beloved woman . . . The further the biographer pushes his indiscreet researches into the private life of individual artists, the more often he will find that some form of interest — personal, political, ethical, religious — enters into the so-called aesthetic activity." (*Origins of Art,* p. 9.) This is not the place to discuss the motives that lead to aesthetic creativeness, however, but it is to be noticed that even in these cases the appreciative observer is led to enter into the feelings that the artist has expressed. In the case of the love lyric, for example, he may learn to search out and appreciate all sorts of hitherto unnoticed traits in the beloved of his choice. Both his selection of the object and his technique of courtship may markedly alter. Again nature imitates art, and we are led to introduce new perspectives into our world by the emotional values the artist has attached to it.

The " peculiarly instrumental character of art " to which Dewey refers is its capacity to clothe our world with appropriate feelings that lead us to fruitful thought and action. " Emotions come to be organized around those objects that we regard as the good things of life; and without these emotions we should not pursue them; but remain indifferent and apathetic to their appeal," (Shand: *Foundations of Character,* p. 4) writes Shand, but I should modify this to read that what we regard as the good things of life are those about which certain emotions have become organized and that art is the chief means, other than accident, by which this organization can be consciously controlled. In a sense the place of art with respect to the emotions is exactly parallel to the place of science with respect to thinking. As by science we rid ourselves of harmful superstition and the misleading interpretations of a too exuberant imagination so that we can act with a real foreknowledge of consequences, so by art we can rid ourselves of accidental emotional associations and intelligently invest objects with the emotional glow that makes them joyously sought.

Educators and moralists have been very slow to recognize the potentialities of this function of art for the development of civilization. At least they have made little or no use of it. To be sure, in a well-known passage, Poincaré attributes the triumph of Greek culture over Europe, and even our scientific advance, to the influence on the mind of Greek art (*Foundations of Science,* p. 368), but this utterance of his has never been treated with the seriousness it deserves. Even Plato, with all his earnestness to master the secret of moral education, did not quite grasp this point. He was convinced that virtue is akin to intelligence and hence should be something that can be taught, and at the same time, from the failure of virtuous men to have their sons taught it, he doubts that it can be. Yet in the discussion of the arts in the last book of the *Republic* he makes a radical selection of arts that shall be permissible in the ideal state on the grounds that the others do not make for the good life. Why did he not see that virtue, to be inculcated, must be presented as lovely. In the fourth book of the *Republic* he issues the warning that " any musical innovation is full of danger for the whole State and ought to be prohibited. . . . When modes of music change, the fundamental laws of the State always change with them." He seems to understand this to mean merely that the new modes reflect a growing restlessness, but I recall hearing a distinguished scholar of Russian history maintain that the whole political development of Russia could be anticipated in the history of Russian music. His explanation was that the changes in music represented the appearance of new sensitivities leading to new or increased irritation with certain evils. There followed efforts at thinking and impulses for reconstruction, but in directions the aesthetic character of the music rendered congenial. If this is true, the capacity of art to socialize emotions, as stressed by Guyau, becomes of prime importance as the key to developing virtue both in individuals and in the state.

The greatest defect of our contemporary educational system, perhaps of our present-day civilization, is its preoccupation with the means of doing and its almost exclusive dependence on the mirage of economic reward to supply motive for doing. But even as thoroughgoing an economic thinker as Taussig, when he gets away from the technique of his subject (Money Making and Invention), has to admit that the deepest motivations of action do not lie in the economic returns, but in the emotional coloring in which actions are steeped. Philosophy may concern itself with the evaluation of ends, but to do is not the same as to know what it is good to do, so we can still complain, with the Emperor Julian, that although the philosopher may " expound to you the inward essence and outward signs of all the virtues," there is something else needed ere they blossom forth in life itself.

There exist scarcely any studies of the use of the arts in education for social progress, and such attempts as have been made vacillate between a half-hearted development of aesthetic appreciation, a thing good so far as it goes, and a sort of propaganda use of art, as in history, where truth is sacrificed for the sake of patriotic emotions in such fashion that either disillusionment must follow, or a flaunting vaingloriousness almost more inimical to healthy national development than the cynicism of the disillusioned. Yet the building up of emotional capacity, *appropriately associated* with experience, should be the very foundation of any educational system, and the materials are at hand.

Literature, of all the arts, is the most available for such purposes; pictures, music, sculpture, or architecture are not everywhere at hand. Hence the appreciation of literature and the understanding of it should be fostered at all costs. We should be taught to look to it not merely for recreation in the idle hour or as a refuge for the tired business man, but as a part of all vocational training, as a means of extending our understanding of life itself. We can learn from it how men have felt and do feel about the world around them, its institutions, and their fellows, and we can learn to understand wherein these attitudes have brought them happiness or the reverse, and develop ourselves accordingly.

Nature does imitate art. Who can doubt that the anticipations of modern unrest as to the relations of the sexes, or our growing disillusionment as to the finality of a merely economically prosperous civilization has been fostered in the literature of the last century? Contemporary plays and stories are full of impatience with the old virtues, but unfortunately they are so training us that no healthy boy wants to be called *good*, and many men and women feel this epithet an insult. Just as our realtors have taken away from us the glow of the word " home " to substitute the triviality of the thing " house," so we are being robbed of the beauty of virtue for the colorlessness of indiscriminate toleration. Surely there is no more stupid way to face life than with a universal tolerance of all things. Dull intolerance, like dull moral criticism of art, has led to a present-day stressing of its opposite, but one cannot translate into serious living the attitude of the nonsense verse:

> " Willie put poison in Grandmother's tea;
> Grandmother died in agony.
> Willie's mother was very much vexed;
> And Willie's father said, ' Well, what next? ' "

Intolerance is quite as important as tolerance, but it requires discrimination to make either attitude virtuous.

The significant artist then must be something more than a mere artist, and great artists have been. He must be a sensitive individual but one whose character or thought leads him to formulate attitudes that are of healthy significance to the society in which he lives. He can make real virtue lovely and real vice abhorred. He is not a propagandist for sentimentalities, but promotes deeper appreciation and understanding of the complex world about us. If I might paraphrase Plato I should write: Now then do I meet that which I liken to the greatest of the waves; yet shall the word be spoken, even though the wave break and drown me in laughter and dishonor; and do you mark my words. Until the discriminative appreciation of art is taught to men or until the teachers of this world have the spirit and power of art, and virtue and loveliness meet in one, and those common natures who pursue either to the exclusion of the other are compelled to stand aside, cities will never have rest from their evils — no, nor the human race, as I believe — and then only will true civilization have a possibility of life and behold the light of day.

TWO BASIC ISSUES IN THE PROBLEM OF MEANING AND OF TRUTH

Edwin Burtt

Let us examine and clarify if we can two questions which must be answered clearly in any tenable theory of the nature of meaning, with particular reference to the meaning of the very important concept " truth," but which contemporary discussions all too often deal with vaguely. Does it not often happen in the progress of philosophical enquiry that decided differences of opinion, even marking the gulf between one school and another, appear on a question which has not yet been stated in the happiest form for fruitful discussion? In such a situation the attempt to formulate precisely the real bone of contention is a service. The reader may judge whether it is correct to hold that the first issue to be mentioned in the following pages is the clue to the essential epistemological difference between realism and pragmatism, while the second marks the vital difference between the Jamesian and Deweyan types of pragmatism. If this be the case, the endeavor to drag them to the front is surely pertinent.

We may begin with the very general preliminary query: How is the meaning of a concept to be determined? This will, of course, lead to various types of answer according as the query is construed, and so I hasten to delimit it. By the word " how," I have in mind such questions as these: In what direction do we look? To what kind of thing do we appeal when we try to fix a meaning about which doubt has arisen? This will make the matter sufficiently precise to open discussion.

Now does not the history of philosophy disclose that the most basic difference of conviction between philosophers on this question is the difference between the view on the one hand that our appeal is to an external structure involving no reference to the mind or organism interested in determining the meaning, and the view, on the other hand, that the meaning cannot be determined without such reference? We may expand this query slightly by suggesting that the issue is whether the meaning is to be construed in terms of the properties or structure of the object whose meaning is in question, or whether it should be expressed in terms of what is done about the object by the observer who is interested in discovering the meaning. The traditional position in philosophy is the former, and it has taken two prominent forms. In the Aristotelian logic, with its characteristic theory of definition, the meaning of any substance was to be stated in the form of a hierarchical structure of genera and species, the determining differentia being found in those properties of the substance which marked it off from other members of the genus. This structure, which was after all but an extension of our common-sense way of analyzing the relations of objects, was supplanted in the early modern period by the notion of mathematical order; to give the meaning of anything was conceived by this mathematical rationalism as involving its location and motion in the geometrical field in terms of which God had created the world. The realistic school today in general adheres to the same essential assumption, though with a broader and more critically developed notion of mathematical or logical order, and with but sparse references to divine creation. From its point of view to state the meaning of anything is to analyze it into its logical simples, whose relations are determined in terms of logical presupposition. If a presupposes d, while d does not presuppose a, then d is a more ultimate and elementary concept than a. By pursuing the analysis in the direction of logical simplicity we sooner or later reach elements whose concepts resist further analysis, and the structure revealed by these elements furnishes the ultimate meaning of the concept analyzed. The realists follow the main trend of modern science in characterizing this ultimate structure as a mathematico-logical order. All other things presuppose mathematical simples, while the latter presuppose nothing beyond themselves. In all this there is no appeal to the interests or actions of the person engaged in carrying out the analysis, these being supposed quite irrelevant to the structure in terms of which the meaning is to be found.

The main forces which support this type of doctrine are apparently two. First, there are the habits which are a part of our common-sense outlook upon the world. We begin mental life by turning our attention outward, not inward, and at every stage of our development practical daily needs foster concentration upon what is happening in the objects which we need to master, and require us to minimize preoccupation with what is happening in us while we study them. It is clear that unless habits of this sort had been early formed the human race would have been easily overwhelmed by the ruthless power of an ill-understood environment. Their survival value is thus indubitable, and they naturally tend to persist even when they are not so strongly needed.

Second, it is precisely this achievement of common sense that science has made its foundation and has considerably extended, so far as concerns all its branches except introspective psychology. (I assume that the latter will be taken by most readers as the exception that proves the rule.) It was dimly seen by the champions of early modern science that the mediaeval contentment with teleological explanations both rested on an unfortunate preoccupation with human destiny and also issued in a mischievous blindness to many promising facts of nature and readiness to distort others. Accordingly, a definite effort to turn attention away from ulterior human interests and fasten it upon external events became a central and decisive aspect of the method of science. If we add the circumstance that by the application of this method science has actually attained approximate success in uncovering systems of occurrences that can be exactly formulated without appeal to any subjective factor, we may easily understand why realistic philosophers distrust the introduction of references to anything smacking of subjectivism, feeling that it is decidedly an unscientific retrogression and likely to offer a cover to a novel, but just as harmful, reading of the universe in terms congenial to human interest. The important thing from the realist standpoint is to extend this scientific hatred of final causes to philosophic discussions and leave no standing room at any point for the unfortunate human tendency to keep a side glance upon its own desires while looking at the facts of nature.

The contrary position was first affirmed in influential form in Protagoras' saying that "Man is the measure of all things," and was expanded at the inception of modern philosophy in Bacon's treatment of the idols of the mind with the accompanying assertion that though the effect of these tendencies could be minimized there was no way of banning it from human thinking entirely. The subjective type of idealism has ever made capital of it, and today it is finding vigorous championship in the pragmatic school, following the lead of C. S. Peirce in the essay which has now become the classic of pragmatic discussion.

The pragmatist is one with the realist in eagerness to follow the sig-

nificant achievements of modern science and avoid distortion of his reflections by preoccupation with matters of personal destiny. But he parts
company at the next step. For he is not willing to assume that this
eagerness can be satisfied without more ado, as the realist is. In his haste
to ban teleology the realist takes for granted at this point, unwittingly,
a very tempting teleological belief that the pragmatist deeply distrusts.
Just why does he distrust it? I take it that the main influence is represented in the following considerations. Let us revert to the realist's
procedure of determining the meaning of a concept by analyzing it into
simple constituents fixed by the relation of presupposition. What right
have we to assume, asks the pragmatist, that such notions as this procedure
involves are as unambiguous and self-justifying as the method of logical
atomism assumes? Do the facts of the history of philosophy show that
we can really transcend our variable biases at will and lay hold on an
external structure of meaning that is common to all of us? The answer
candor compels him to make is "No." Even scientific analyses are by no
means universally accepted. Defeat met in the attempt to maintain such
transcendence forces the pragmatist willy nilly to appeal in his quest for
a concept's meaning to something located in himself and not external.
He surrenders the teleological faith of the realist, for he sees that what
presupposes what, depends on one's point of view and in particular on
what he takes the process of explanation to be, while any object is simple
if one can offer in terms of it the kind of explanation that one wants.
God was a simple being for mediaeval and early modern rationalism,
whereas for contemporary realists the concept of such an entity presents
itself as highly complex, far indeed from an ultimate product of analysis.
Indeed, many members of the school would be inclined to question
whether such an inclusive notion is a legitimate concept at all. If we
conceive the nature of explanation in the terms expressed by the scholastic
dictum that the cause must be equal to the effect " *aut formaliter aut
eminenter,*" then the relation of presupposition will lead in exactly the
opposite direction to that assumed by the present-day realist — it will mean
that every other concept presupposes that of God, while the latter presupposes nothing further. This conception seemed so natural to Descartes that after reaching the most thoroughgoing state of scepticism
possible he made use of it without critical question as directly known " by
the natural light "; it is an essential principle in Spinoza's theory of ex-

planation if we interpret " *eminenter* " in terms of the idea of perfection; and it presents itself as thoroughly cogent to the common man today who has any vivid religious or aesthetic interest. But it is rejected by all who feel it necessary to follow without reservation the trend of modern science in rejecting final causality as a tool of explanation. The method of realism, we must remember, is not analysis simply, but analysis accompanied by such rejection.

Do not such prominent historical differences indicate clearly that however much we should like to do so we cannot really leave out in our notion of the meaning of a thing reference to the observer and the way he is reacting to it? How else can the difference be objectively accounted for? They cannot be stated in terms of the external structure of the object, for it is precisely differences in that external structure that they affirm. They must point to differences in the organism dealing with the object, and if we are willing to grant this we must say that the meaning of the object itself involves in part the behavior of the organism whose attention is focused upon it. For in that case a statement of meaning in terms of external structure alone will not be complete; by recognizing that it means what it is taken to mean because of some characteristic of the observer we accept the obligation to call attention to that characteristic of the observer in order to render the statement objective. Otherwise we are leaving it a matter of personal idiosyncrasy, partially camouflaged by dogmatic claims to universality.

The same points, of course, might be urged to justify the metaphysical use of the term " *experience* " as equivalent to *reality* in the manner common with idealists and pragmatists. The truth of an idea becomes identical with its versification in the experience of those for whom the idea had been problematic. The clinching consideration is that while there may be some structure of reality entirely external to our individual thinking and while it is important for us to fasten upon that structure as closely as we can, yet we dare never assume that we have attained it. For any structure that we find ourselves at any time actually conceiving is necessarily infected by the limitations of our personal thinking. Our notion of a world transcending our own perspective is still a notion rooted to that perspective and no other. To suppose otherwise is to suppose that we can jump out of our skins and entirely swallow up the experience of others by a magic and omnivorous gulp.

If we incline to the conclusion that the pragmatist is essentially right in this position, we are committed to a definite approach to further metaphysical problems, and our answers will be quite different from those which rationalism in all its forms has offered to them. But we shall need to face a further issue which has cleft pragmatism into two wings on the problem of meaning and of truth. If what we are doing in relation to an object is a part of its meaning, shall we say that any and every reaction thus occurring is to be taken as revealing its meaning, or that certain reactions only are to be regarded as fulfilling this function? In the latter case we shall need to determine what limitations are to be made and how they are to be justified.

We may open the attack on this issue by considering certain positions which attempt to rule out all limitations of the sort just suggested. In the *Logic of Modern Physics* Professor Bridgman outlines what he defends as the *operational* method of determining the meaning of a concept. After criticizing the early modern physicists for assuming that the meaning of terms can be stated by referring to their intrinsic properties he explains his own position in the following words:

"We may illustrate by considering the concept of length. What do we mean by the length of an object? We evidently know what we mean by length if we can tell what the length of any and every object is, and for the physicist nothing more is required. To find the length of an object, we have to perform certain physical operations. The concept of length is therefore fixed when the operations by which length is measured are fixed: that is, the concept of length involves as much as, and nothing more than, the set of operations by which length is determined. In general, we mean by any concept nothing more than a set of operations; *the concept is synonymous with the corresponding set of operations.* If the concept is physical, as of length, the operations are actual physical operations, namely, those by which length is measured; or if the concept is mental, as of mathematical continuity, the operations are mental operations, namely, those by which we determine whether a given aggregate of magnitudes is continuous. It is not intended to imply that there is a hard and fast division between physical and mental concepts, or that one kind of concept does not always contain an element of the other; this classification of concept is not important for our future considerations.

"We must demand that the set of operations equivalent to any concept be a unique set, for otherwise there are possibilities of ambiguity in practical applications which we cannot admit."

There are two things to be particularly noted in this statement. In the first place Professor Bridgman wishes to impose on the notion of operation only those limitations which define the actual procedures of science. Since the interest of the scientist in dealing with any concept is to use it as a tool in the quantitative determination of certain data, the operations he has in mind are limited by that purpose. But the conception is not intended to be limited in any other way. To be sure, the author is tempted occasionally to commit the typical scientist's fallacy in assuming that this is the only purpose that can properly function in relation to these concepts; because there was no way of measuring absolute time he assumes that the concept is meaningless, forgetting that although it may be sterile for scientific purposes it may have had extra-scientific meaning to the minds of Newton and others. In the second place he mentions specifically the possibility that the operations determining the meaning of a concept may not be overt physical performances, but may be mental, as in the case of the concept of mathematical continuity. But it is evident from his discussion that he does not notice in the case of mental operations a difficulty not present in the case of physical operations, namely, that the latter are open to the observation on the same terms of more than one person, while the former are not. In the case of the concept of mathematical continuity this does not lead to serious ambiguity in interpreting the meaning of the concept, possibly because such mental operations as are here involved can be symbolized in conventionally accepted physical marks whose meaning is fixed. Can mental operations that do not enjoy this privilege yield any standardized meaning? It is impossible to point them out to another in the same definite way as physical operations and thus identify and fix them. This suggests that there may in fact be an important limitation to the operations that determine the meaning of a concept that Professor Bridgman's discussion has not uncovered, or at least a limitation that *ought* to be recognized if meaning is to fulfil a social function and become more than a matter of personal taste in dealing with the thing whose meaning is in question.

In William James's theory of truth we apparently have an attempt to validate in general philosophical terms the thesis now applied to scientific concepts by Professor Bridgman, though he does not explicitly develop a general theory of meaning by its aid. The truth of an idea is determined by the satisfactoriness of the consequences that ensue when the idea is acted upon. Of what sort must these consequences be, and what kind of action is legitimate as revealing a meaning or establishing a truth? As in the scientist's case, James is reluctant to impose any limitations. In the most generous statements of his position it appears that any consequence satisfactory to anybody which follows as a result of any action on an idea, makes that idea true " in so far forth," the latter phrase meaning that it makes it true to that person till some later experience throws doubt upon it. " At each and every concrete moment, truth for each man is what that man ' troweth ' at that moment with the maximum of satisfaction to himself." While under the stress of criticism James showed a disposition elsewhere to restrict the scope of this theory, his religious essays clearly indicate that he would certainly not wish to eliminate, any more than Professor Bridgman, inner mental consequences, as legitimate for purposes of verification. It was in large part James's interest in justifying by pragmatic means experiences of emotional comfort secured by the adoption of religious faith that made pragmatism a vividly appealing theory.

It will be worth our while to consider briefly the central thesis of James's *Will To Believe* in order to note the precise difficulty that arises when occurrences of an inner emotional sort are given legitimacy for revealing a meaning or verifying a truth, on the same basis as overt physical behavior. The doctrine is that when anyone faces a live, forced, and momentous option between two hypotheses that cannot be decided on intellectual grounds (by which James means, cannot be decided by appeal to overt physical data) he is justified in believing the hypothesis that is most satisfying to his emotions. Now the question of the existence or non-existence of God being such an option, the above principle applies to it; if I want to believe in God it is legitimate for me to do so. On exactly the same ground, though James was not interested in pursuing this implication, if I dislike the notion of God it is legitimate for me to refuse to believe in his existence. And if satisfying consequences continue in each case, both beliefs are pragmatically verified. This, of course, equates truth with personal taste in ideas, at least ideas on such subjects, and makes it quite possible for mutually contradictory hypotheses to be true at the same time. To return a moment to Professor Bridgman's position with reference to scientific thinking, we see in the light of James's doctrine that there is really no guarantee that such an inconsistent situation might not appear in dealing with scientific concepts also, unless it so happen that all mental operations used in science can be symbolized by conventionally accepted physical marks whose meaning is fixed for all users. If operations may vary as between individuals, then the meanings of terms determined by them may vary, and the truth of statements expressing or developing such meanings may vary.

This brings our analysis to a focal point. For I think it will be admitted without the need of explicit defense that such a situation would not be tolerated in science. For scientific thinking a meaning is something that can be determined in the same definite way for all minds, and a scientific truth is something that can be verified as such by any competent observer who wishes to do so. If we grant this assertion then it becomes evident that scientific method does involve in fact a limitation of the operations or consequences that may be admitted as revealing the meaning of a concept or verifying a hypothesized truth about the thing it denotes. Just what is this limitation and what can be said by way of furnishing a justification for it? Does it apply to thinking in general or merely to the field of scientific enquiry?

To take these questions in order, is it not clear that at this point we introduce what is frankly an ethical consideration into scientific method, and that unless we recognize that the foundations of our logic (and perhaps our metaphysics too) are affected by this ethical consideration it will not be possible to understand the nature and ground of this limitation. We hint at this fact by our use of the term "normative" in discussing the nature of logic.

Taken as a matter of plain empirical fact, without introducing any ethical postulate, is it not fair to say that on a general pragmatic basis the meaning of any concept is just what it happens to be at any given time to any individual who is using it, and that any statement is true (as James's broadest statement of the pragmatic principle indicates) to anyone who finds himself disposed to believe it. Taken in this factual way, there are inconsistent elements in the meaning of the same term, and contradictory assertions are accepted as true. Some people believe in God as existent, and others are atheists. But if we erect a theory of meaning or of truth which simply justifies this individualism, as James appears to do, we can make no social progress in our thinking. We sit down, content each to believe what we happen to feel like believing, and not worrying about the fact that other people will believe something else. This attitude is the complete negation of the scientific spirit. If we ask why, the answer must be given in ethical terms. We feel that meaning and truth carry the implication of universality, that a certain social responsibility is bound up with them, that the reflective progress we desire is precisely in the direction of such responsibility, that, in short, concepts *ought* to mean the same thing to all minds, and that if any statement is to be called true it *ought* to be possible for any interested person to verify it as such. A concept may, at present, in point of fact, mean something different to you from what it does to me, but if so, we *ought* to find some way of interpreting the meaning so that it may become a common possession. You may, at present, take some assertion to be true that I take to be false, but if so, we *ought* to devise a technique of verification that will determine as between these conflicting claims and definitely refute one or the other of them. It is perhaps the very essence of the scientific attitude to make this ethical postulate.

Once this view gains plausibility, we see on the one hand that the operations that may be accepted as establishing meaning or truth will be definitely restricted in nature by this ethical consideration. They must be operations such as will make possible the attainment of social agreement on the meanings in question, and any operations not of this character cannot be regarded as having any relation to meaning or truth. We see on the other hand why it is that certain prominent characteristics of scientific method have become such. Why is science empirical? Because only externally observable data that can be pointed out to the senses of other people on the same terms as to our own can furnish an adequately common basis of scientific truth. Other foundations of knowledge prove in the end too esoteric. Why are hypotheses and theories to be tentatively held? Because no matter how much they may appeal to their inventor, he must not assert them as true till he has discovered some way of establishing them as such to the satisfaction of other inquirers. Why is mathematics the preferred tool of deductive analysis in science? Because mathematical thinking is the one sort of mental operation on which we seem able (for whatever may be the reason) to mean the same thing at each step of the game as our neighbor does. Why is verifying experiment an external physical performance with the aid of physical tools? Because thus alone may the process be a co-operative affair, and the achievement of each stage of the verification be subject to social check. It appears to be the business of science to give meaning and truth social universality. Why, finally, to take a further illustration from the field of recent psychology, does behaviorism restrict itself to the phenomena that it does? It is surely a very plausible answer to say that the reason is found precisely in our ethical postulate: by restricting its data to the things that individuals overtly do, it is giving socially objective meaning to its terms in a way that could never be done when the attention of psychologists was focused mainly on private states of consciousness that could never be co-operatively studied and measured.

If this be so, then the question becomes pressing: is it the responsibility of science only to restrict its investigations in this manner, or does this ethical insistence apply to all our thinking, on general philosophical questions as elsewhere? We may gain a clue to the answer which appeals to the Deweyan branch of pragmatism if we return to the concept of God already discussed in connection with James's theory of truth. In the case of any religion that has outgrown sectarian and nationalistic limitations (and no student of philosophy is likely to be satisfied with a religion that has not) the concept of God is consciously thought of as having universal validity — he is not my or your private God, but the God of the whole world, rightfully claiming the reverence and worship of all men. If we cannot think of him as such he does not function as God even to us, for we can have the appropriate religious feeling before him only when we conceive him as universal. Can James's method of argument justify belief in a deity of this character? I think a candid examination shows that it cannot, and precisely for the reason that this way of establishing meanings and verifying truths is inconsistent with the ethical postulate stated above. For if I continue to believe in God while my neighbor does not, I must nevertheless have a grounded conviction that the concept is really valid for him as well as for me, and that under appropriate conditions its validity would become revealed to him; if not, the conception loses the universality essential to it and cannot function even for me. But when I consider James's argument I see that it proves atheism as easily for those who wish a godless world as theism for those whose predilection is for divinity. This means that even for those who want a God this way of reasoning cannot prove a God of universal quality; it can only prove a truncated deity whose realm does not reach beyond those who wish the comforts of religious faith, that is, a God who cannot function as such even for them, as soon as they recognize what it is that they have been seduced to worship under the guise of a universal God. The concept, in brief, is inconsistent with this way of proving its validity. Unless we are willing to worship as God a being who is less than the deity of the whole world and may be nothing but an idealization congenial to the emotions of those whose tastes are similar to ours, we must make the ethical postulate above discussed central in our theological as well as in our scientific thinking. This means that we must hold the concept of God invalid for ourselves, except in so far as we can devise ways of giving it validity for others, with particular reference to those whose experience to date makes them least disposed to see any meaning in such a notion.

I take it that it is in the light of these factors that we should interpret Professor Dewey's doctrine that scientific method is the method of all right thinking and that philosophies claiming either private or super-scientific access to truth are misusing the latter term and leading their adherents into an exceedingly tempting snare but mischievous delusion. The following quotation from the first chapter of *Experience and Nature* is relevant to this assertion:

" The empirical method points out when and where and how things of a designated description have been arrived at. It places before others a map of the road that has been travelled; they may accordingly, if they will, retravel the road to inspect the landscape for themselves. Thus the findings of one may be rectified and extended by the findings of others, with as much assurance as is humanly possible of confirmation, extension, and rectification. The adoption of empirical, or denotative method would thus procure for philosophic reflection something of that co-operative tendency toward consensus which marks enquiry in the natural sciences. The scientific investigator convinces others not by the plausibility of his definitions and the cogency of his dialectic, but by placing before them the specified course of experiences of searchings, doings and findings in consequence of which certain things have been found. His appeal is for others to traverse a similar course, so as to see how what they find corresponds with his report. . . .

" Truth or falsity depends upon what others find when they warily perform the experiment of observing reflective events. An empirical finding is refuted not by denial that one finds things to be thus and so, but by giving directions for a course of experience that results in finding its opposite to be the case. To convince of error as well as to lead to truth is to assist another to see and find something which he hitherto has failed to find and recognize."

The term which Professor Dewey uses to describe his position with respect to fundamental assumptions on scientific method is the traditional term "empiricism." The question may well be raised whether the real novelty and importance of the assumptions are not inevitably greatly obscured and rendered almost certain of serious misinterpretation by this description through a familiar philosophical concept. Professor Dewey is an empiricist, but he is not merely what that word means in the histories of modern philosophy and science. He is an empiricist because, and in so far as, the empirical method is instrumental to the realization of co-operative ends in the work of science and philosophy. He is a rationalist too in so far as the procedures congenial to rationalism are indispensable aids in the same reflective process as socially used. But this is to affirm that the essence of method as this branch of pragmatism conceives it is neither empiricism nor rationalism, nor any other traditional *ism* — it is the functioning consciously within method of co-operative ends. If we are to bring into the forefront this central assumption it should be given a central place in our terminology. Clarity would suggest that those who accept this approach to logic no longer call themselves operationists, or behaviorists, or empiricists, but, if they do not mind what appears at first sight a rather barbarous term, *co-operationists*. The use of such a term would not, of course, indicate that the one who stresses it claims any higher quality of social purpose than is to be found in fellow-philosophers or scientists, but that he sees such a purpose as filling the essential and decisive function in giving right method the character which it must have to be right instead of wrong.

It is nothing new to say that man is the measure of all things as they are experienced, nor to note that all thinking is inevitably affected by selective interests which vary between individuals and groups. It is a novel and important thing, so far as my reading of the history of philosophy goes, to affirm that this effect is sufficiently central to demand recognition in our interpretation of the very foundation processes of logic, to hold that thus objective universality of meaning and truth becomes an ideal of logical value to be approximated rather than a factual structure to be claimed, and to interpret the ultimate meaning of all methodological tools in the light of the ethical principle which thus determines the difference between sound and unsound logic.

KANT, AQUINAS, AND THE PROBLEM OF REALITY

CORNELIUS CLIFFORD

THE quest for Reality, like the quest for the Golden Fleece, has left a various and not always coherent literature in its wake. Though not strictly conterminous with the story of what men have instinctively agreed to call Philosophy, that literature is associated with a very few significant names. Plato and his great pupil, Aristotle, Porphyry, Plotinus, Abelard, Thomas Aquinas, Duns Scotus, Cajetan, who almost created a new Aquinas by the insight and the wisdom of his Commentaries, the Jesuit Suarez, Spinoza, Descartes, Kant — what a list it is, and what memories in the history of thought it evokes! If it reads like an uncanny baker's dozen, let it be noted that it can scarcely be added to, and might, profitably, be made less; for each of these Masters has a metaphysic, or is in search of one; and it is the metaphysician that ultimately counts in this controversy. There are thinkers whose outlook on the mysteries of matter and life and mind is as balanced and penetrating as any of those whom we have ventured to instance; Origen is, conceivably, such a man, and so, without challenge, is Augustine of Hippo; but they are men of the pulpit or the closet; and the majority of those whom we have cited above, some ten in all, were teachers. They were the accredited expounders of a *tradition* in the truest and most literal sense of that term; their home was in the Academy, or the Porch, or the University; their primary business was with systems; their profession was to see the concept steadily; to handle it objectively; to see it whole. If such preoccupation with system-making has its perils — and the long sad history of European thought surely has its warnings in this connection — the pit-falls of occasional or piecemeal thinking are, not unfrequently, more portentous still: but when we have contended for so much it must be conceded, also, that pure metaphysics will not carry us to our journey's end. Any account of the hidden structure of things must involve a theory of mind and its processes. Do these processes lead anywhere? Are they so relative and illusory as to be without value? Is it irrational to expect, we will not say, finality, but a sure and well-mapped field of investigation in this problem?

Leaving aside, for the purposes of this paper, the tentative and partial solutions offered by Greek thinkers on this many-sided mystery, we hazard the suggestion that there have been two and only two supreme protagonists, each appearing at a crisis in the history of European thought, whose contributions to the subject deserve a serious man's notice. The first of these is one of the most modern of men, though, paradoxically enough, he belongs to the thirteenth century. We are speaking, of course, of Thomas Aquinas the influence of whose teaching and the charm of whose personality would seem, for the third time in the six and a half centuries that have elapsed since his death, to be entering upon a new and deserved primacy in the Schools. The other supreme protagonist is Immanuel Kant; and because his influence is more recent, more intimate, more akin to the *ethos* of the modern university type of mind, so to say, we propose to deal with him first.

Obviously it is in the *Critique of Pure Reason* that we must expect to find the real mind of the man. His temperament, in so far, at least, as temperament can be said to reveal itself in writings so sustainedly abstruse and impersonal as his less ambitious lucubrations, is another matter. It is the intentional reach of a man's mind that is most important when we are in search of theories of knowledge; it is the depth and breadth, too, we may add, of that same mind that most concerns us when he tells us that he has thought a good deal about the business in hand and finally assures us — too truthful Hellenes as most of us are in these venturesome matters — that Jason will never come back with the Golden Fleece. Doubtless; but is it not just as possible that the hero will return with something more substantial, if less faery-like and romantic, as an alternative; and that in the bales of the good ship *Argo* may be found some more remarkable commodity, some merchant's stuff that may spell gold, yellow and shining and more real, in the end?

Summaries of Kant's *Critique of Pure Reason,* even in the final and more authentic form in which he left it to us, are easy enough to make. Pointed or pointless, true or only half true, they abound in the philosophic literature of England, France, Italy, and his native Prussia, of the past century; while mere text-book presentations of the same are as unnumbered as the stars for multitude. The greatest and most trivial of minds have burdened us with their fundamental positions and their ultimate significance. It would be invidious — it might be unjust — to single out any one of them. What we should much prefer to do is to attempt with the aid of Kant himself to point out the actual problem which he set before his extraordinary intellect for solution. It has been said that he was no metaphysician; that he was a psychologist groping tentatively after a theory of knowledge; and this in spite of the palpable fact that he gives us an enormous and appalling metaphysic of the mind which is as difficult to master in its several details, its primary *dicta,* its laws, its instincts, its " forms," as the dusty, cut-and-dried, labeled, and pigeon-holed categories of Aristotle himself. The present writer can recall a lecture delivered more than five and forty years ago by a very acute Jesuit professor (the late Father Salvator Brandi) in which Kant was described as a very great and original thinker whose unfortunate rôle it was to be one of the nineteen distinct fashioners of a theory of the origin of ideas and who failed nobly, but egregiously, because he had begun at the wrong end of the stick. He began with the mind and never succeeded in getting outside it. Again, it has been objected that the monotonous recriminations of the Neo-Scholastics for the past three quarters of a century are based upon a fundamental misapprehension of what Kant's purpose in the *Critique of Pure Reason* really was.

His aim was not to establish Reality; it was to explain, possibly even to justify, the mind's processes in reaching out for objectivity. It is not easy to say which is the most crucial in Kant's final analysis — its elaborate epistemology or its cautious and discouraging metaphysic. He himself set greater store by the metaphysical element in his treatise than he did by the epistemological; and when he reissued the *Critique* in a revised form in 1786 he observed — was it a boast? — that he had said the last word on a long-debated matter. Here was a way, an authentically human, yet ontologically justifiable and true way to scientific cognition at last. It led, not to an actual and inward knowledge of the thing in itself (*noumenon*), but to a knowledge of *phenomena.* The distinction, which he took over with curious naïveté from Hume whom he affected to correct, was big with controversies that the next century was to label — not always with discriminating accuracy, be it observed — as the ever recurring battle between the Realist and the Idealist. The book had an enormous *succès d'estime.* Kant's place in the history of Western European philosophy was henceforth assured. Königsberg became a place of pilgrimage. The prestige of its hero was fated to lie like a shadow — *magni nominis umbra* — across the pathway of every serious thinker for many a year to come.

It was in keeping with the simplicity of Kant's character that he should admit how much he owed to Hume; not Wolff, nor Leibnitz, be it remembered; nor even Descartes, who seems, in spite of his " clear and distinct ideas," his " intuitions," his mathematician's concept of corporeity, and the rest, to have made little or no impression on the development of his thought; but Hume who " first roused him from his dogmatic slumbers." He would double on Hume's assumptions and inferences to show that there was another, and less sinister, way out of the plausible *impasse*. It was a precarious, if chivalrous, acknowledgment, at its utmost; but could the Scotch sceptic have lived to discover how great a creditor he had unwittingly become since his death, he might have felt that he had been flippant in his day to some purpose after all. For behind the " Synthetic *a priori* Judgments " of the *Critique of Pure Reason* there lurked, not only the more far-reaching problem of the nature of all our human assents, practical or speculative, but the profounder question of the relation of sense-knowledge in general to the *dicta* of the understanding; the relation, that is, of our percepts and apperceptions — if we must use the inept words — which are a joint derivative of the manifold activities of the outer and ultimately subsistent world, and the equally manifold energies, not yet fully mapped by experimental psychology, of the inner and, in a sense, more perfectly subsistent world of mind on its lower or sense levels. Mind and body in this connection are not two entities but one; and that a vital entity. We may separate them for purposes of intelligent analysis. In that sense they are other and other, if you will, but always with an incomplete otherness. To forget that basic truth is to commit one of the deadliest sins against a sound metaphysic.

The key to Kant's logic has been sought for in many directions by supporters and adversaries alike. Wherever else it may be found it is, assuredly, not in the " Categories," which are largely gratuitous in the first place, and in the second place altogether too numerous for the purpose in hand. That purpose is to furnish a sure, if very much delimited, ground for science and to give objective validity to those general statements without which neither science nor philosophy can move forward each in its way to its ever receding goal. Kant himself was by temperament and

education profoundly interested in the scientific achievements and speculations of his time; and the devotees of science since his day have repaid
him, not perhaps in kind — for who would say they have cared for metaphysics? — but in something of larger consequence to the world of
university-trained men. These latter have quietly adopted his untroubled
disbelief in the " Principle of Causality "; and they have taken over, bag
and baggage, the fardel of his " Synthetic *a priori* Judgments " as well.
The transference seems to have been costlier than the majority of them
are at present aware; but if the rapid shift towards the Neo-Realistic
School of late years may be taken as a sign, a goodly company is rousing
itself from a deeper " dogmatic slumber " than even Hume disturbed in
the ruminating brain of the recluse of Königsberg.

In the course of elaborating his theory Kant was acute enough to see
that the Categories, as aboriginal, or innate, laws of the understanding,
achieved a universality of so wide a sweep as to require a kind of intermediary determination which would make them capable of being applied
to the perceptions of sense. And so, with that meticulous and patient
thoroughness which is characteristic of nearly all his thinking he introduces a transcendental device, or piece of mental machinery, to which he
gives the name of *schemata*. A *schema* would seem to be a mediating
representation, without empirical content, which somehow is both sensile
and intellectual. " On the one side it is homogeneous with the Category
and on the other side with the phenomenon." * * * * * " In itself it is
always a mere product of the imagination." By the imagination we are
to understand " the faculty of representing an object even without its
presence in intuition." If we keep in view that the philosopher is here
speaking of the *productive* imagination, and not of the *reproductive*
faculty, we get as near to his meaning as seems possible in this labyrinthine
journey in his company through those dark corridors that lead — too
deviously, it might be objected — from sense perception to ultimate mind.
Reduced to its lowest terms it is an attempt to describe the problem that
has baffled every epistemologist from the beginning of philosophic time;
and students of Aristotle and St. Thomas can hardly avoid comparing
this inverted bit of psychic bridge-building with the processes that take
place (according to their own system) when the " phantasms " of the
image-making faculty are brought under the denuding energy of that
wonderful and ceaselessly transforming thing, still described by School-

men of every shade of thought, even in our own day, as the *intellectus agens*. Perhaps we are all mystagogues when we find ourselves halting at such a parting of the ways. " It is quite clear," says Kant, as he offers us this ingenious clue to the direction we must take! We think the generations that came after him judged the matter with less bias. It was not thus that Hume's scepticism could really be met. The " conceit of imaginary knowledge " still went whistling, boylike, down its perilous way. The objectivity thus attained was arrived at too circuitously not to raise grave misgivings. The wise inquirer today feels that he has been treated too much like a country man come to town. He trusts himself over guilelessly to an alert and plausible cab-driver, who gives him a good run for his money; but disillusionment awaits him when he discovers that he has paid to be set down in a street provokingly near the corner from which he started.

In a compact, but very illuminating, footnote to the introductory pages of one of the most remarkable books published during the past year, Dr. S. Z. Hasan, a Moslem, but English-university-trained scholar, now Professor of Philosophy in the well-known Anglo-Oriental foundation at Aligarh, attempts to show that Kant's commentators, even when sincerely and intelligently sympathetic, have for the most part misunderstood him. The real purpose of the philosopher was an ideological one; and, in that sense, he prevailed. In the body of the text of the same introductory essay, however, while developing along abstract lines the Realist doctrine that " the external world exists and is directly apprehended in perception " (Preface), Dr. Hasan contends for some interesting, but challengeable, positions of his own which a modern Thomist can scarcely help noting. " Knowledge," he tells us, " like existence is an ultimate fact not further analyzable. *Es ist einmal da.* Nothing further can strictly be said of it. But because ultimate, when realized, it appears like existence, most wonderful. We stand aghast before it. We do not understand it. To understand is to reduce to ulterior elements, to go behind the thing. But because we do not understand it, we try to understand it — we try to describe it in terms of facts with which we are more familiar. Existence seems to be more familiar. We therefore describe knowledge in terms of existence." (*Realism:* Introduction p. 14.)

In a footnote, intended to clarify this series of statements, he warns the reader that " the concrete corresponding to knowledge is subject, and that corresponding to existence is substance. The empirical reality corresponding to the former is mind, and that corresponding to the latter is matter."

Whatever an Aristotelian may say on this particular point, we venture to suggest that a Thomist would put it differently. The concrete corresponding to knowledge we may allow to pass. Whether it be mind, or that something more than mind that we call an *ego,* Peter, James, or John, compact of soul and intellect, of brain and nervous system and organized body, is of no immediate importance here; but the concrete corresponding to existence is not substance any more than it is accident; it is essence — this particular, concrete essence of which we affirm that it exists. Essence and existence in Aquinas's courageous and far-reaching metaphysic are by no means identical. They too are other and other. It is thus, on the very threshold of finite being, that we are brought face to face with a fundamental dichotomy that gives a uniqueness and a consistent lucidity to all of St. Thomas's subsequent treatment of *potency and act.* The key to his Theory of Knowledge — for he, too, has a theory that is never permitted to go beyond the facts, external or internal, of human experience — is to be found in that primary, if provokingly unimaginable, distinction. We call it unimaginable in the sense only that we cannot form a picture of it; but it is real for all that; more real, we should say, than any of the findings of the new physics that are so disturbing to the plain man in these mathematico-revolutionary days.

And this brings us, without undue affectation of insight, we trust, to the second half, which is really the crucial half, of this essay. It is quite conceivable, of course, that the problem which St. Thomas and his predecessors in their far-off day, Kant in his own day, and the Neo-Realists only the other day, set themselves to solve, is in truth too fundamental for solution. One must begin somewhere and with somewhat in philosophy. The " somewhere " and the " somewhat," however, need not necessarily be assumptions, pure and simple. They may involve a fact, or a principle of dialectic, or a palpable condition of things, to ignore which is to expose oneself to shipwreck in harbor. However hard-headed and unromantic the disillusionments of time have made us, we are all Argonauts — if we may go back to the parable with which we started — when the thirst for such primary knowledge comes upon us; and, young men and old, we dream dreams of the Golden Fleece. The sense of mystery is often a

stimulus in such junctures, especially when we are clearing the ground
for religion. That is as it ought to be; for religion, revealed or only
natural, is an unappeasable need of all men; whereas philosophy, in its
more considered aspects, at least, is for the few. And the few who venture
into its intricate domain must move there with candid and open eyes.
Even St. Thomas, whose mysticism was beyond that of most men, insisted on walking by sight, and not at the command of authority, in the
" ontological world " which he built up so bravely in defense of the
Catholic faith.

It will be worth while, even at this late day, we suggest, to turn to him.
Has he anything to say? Much, indeed; and, what is almost more germane to the matter, he says it with a curious note of modernity in the not
unmusical flow of his clear and impersonal simplicity of statement that
may prove disconcerting to the many who are accustomed to dismiss him
without ever having read so much as a page of his closely packed prose.

He offers a solution of the question in terms, of course, of the long
controversy about the nature of the universal concepts which played so
large a part in the university life of the century and a half that preceded
his own. To expect to find the problems stated in any other way, would
be to court the imputation of the most childlike anachronism. St.
Thomas knew nothing of ganglia, or grey matter, or brain-centers, or
hormones, or ductless glands; neither he nor his kind were directly interested in morbid psychology; their physical concepts were of the crudest
sort; if they knew anything about atoms, it was as Lucretius had imagined
them; though they were willing to allow that when corporeal matter
underwent chemical change it was probably through its minutest portions
— *per particulas, seu per partes minutissimas* — that the alteration was
effected. Their general and considered outlook upon the universe was
entirely different from our own; but not necessarily their insight into
those aspects of its being which Aquinas taught them to regard from the
angle of the revised texts furnished by the industry of Adam of Morbeke.
Even in the purely physical order they were not wholly without data.
If they were too easily satisfied with the minor premises of their inter-
minable syllogisms, their major propositions were seldom, if at any time,
in hopeless case. Aristotle was not an inept guide; and they wrote
commentaries on the metaphysics of substance, of quantity, of intrinsic
and extrinsic extension with a penetration that went closer to our latter-

day notions on these elusive points than Newton's had ever done. Nor should this greater insight of theirs surprise us. The world was for them a reality as well as a cosmos; a naïve, and mathematically unmanageable cosmos, as even Aquinas himself was beginning to suspect — witness his cautious note about its astronomy — but a real cosmos, none the less, and it could be understood analogously, at least, by mind, since absolute Mind had originally conceived it. It was the old doctrine of the wayside omens stripped of its superstitions and brought back to school again. If only man, the pilgrim, could be taught to construe its primary lessons!

The evidence for St. Thomas's teaching on these fundamental positions will be found scattered throughout his works. They would make a bulky but interesting volume if they were gathered together into one book. The idea has been attempted from divers points of view and at various times during the past three quarters of a century; but the result has seldom been satisfactory, chiefly because the compilers, even when they had scholarship, were not uniformly agreed among themselves on the actual scope of their editing. The modern student, however, is more fortunate in his opportunities because he lives in a day when special lexicons and books of reference abound; though it may well be doubted whether the index-maker of these latter times has either the intelligence or the wide sweep of technical and ordered knowledge which were so conspicuous a note in his predecessors of the sixteenth and seventeenth centuries. The *Summa Theologica,* the *Contra Gentiles,* the group of questions discussed in the *De Veritate,* and a fairly large number of other treatises, to be found in the *Quaestiones Disputatae* and the *Quodlibetales,* represent, perhaps, too vast a field for a beginner to try his mettle on; but the two *Summae* and the discussions grouped under the *De Veritate,* will furnish him with mines in which to dig. St. Thomas, of course, approaches the epistemological problem from the point of view of a Realist; but he is not an out and out Realist; neither do his findings place him, as has even been suggested, among the *Naïve,* and much less, the student may be certain, among the *Neo-Realists,* who have been making more noise of late than their arguments seem entirely to justify. The outside world is for him an existent, that is, a real world. It no more depends for that existence, or that reality, or, even for its wonderful and all but inexhaustible knowableness, upon his feeling, or his thoughts about it, than his own individual understanding depends for its *esse* upon the brute forces of that world, or even upon the world taken in all its bewildering height and might and depth together.

And his reasons for this attitude are many and fundamental; though not all of them are direct. We must ever remember, not only that Aquinas is a Christian and an Aristotelian, but that the great Stagirite himself is at once two distinct, but not radically opposed, personalities. He also is a " Christian " in the Tertullian sense; or, as we should put it perhaps, with a less aggressive front of paradox, he is the " plain man " with his spontaneous assents as well as the philosopher, who, in Newman's finely tolerant phrase, " has thought out our great thoughts for us ages before we were born." As a wise man the Saint is aware of many problems; but, as a philosopher, he knows that not all of them are *true* problems. The problem of the essentially modal otherness between *phenomena* and the *Ding-an-sich* is not a *true* problem, because it assumes something worse than an unworkable hypothesis. It is really based upon a false *suppositum*. It is a pseudo-problem, in a word, without even the poor merit, the cunningly contrived speciousness, of a child's conundrum. It is built on a bottomless misunderstanding that has become far too common since the days of Locke — the misunderstanding, namely, of the old Aristotelian distinction between Substance and Accident and the un-differentiated significance attaching to the words " real " and " reality " in mediaeval and modern minds. For Aquinas the *real* is not necessarily the actually existent. Every *possible,* that is, every conceivable entity, the sum of whose contemplated properties does not involve an ἄλογον is also a *real;* it is a " thinkable," and may, with many a hazard, no doubt, be handled by the speculative intellect. With these elementary distinctions kept well in view, the *true* problem in this matter for Aquinas, as it must be for all who find healthy satisfaction in his school, is primarily twofold; and the two aspects of it are reciprocal. To see the significance of that last clausular statement is of capital importance. It is not a chaotic mass without form or void, a mere aggregate of disparate and unconnected entities, in which we " live and move and have our being." Reality is as hierarchic as human nature. It might almost be said, in a sense, to be as hierarchic as the Church of Christ. There are grades and planes and scales of being. *Tout est en tout;* though it need knowledge, as well as the insight that wisdom brings, to see the all-pervasive golden thread of this authentic relationship.

The first element, then, of this two-sided problem which Aquinas is concerned to discuss, whenever it breaks through the surface of his everyday Scholastic teaching in philosophy or divinity, is the question of the outer world. What is that external thing which both sense and intellect combine spontaneously within one, each in its measure, to call real and existent? Surely it is a *real* thing; and it is there. (*Id quod concipitur — universale a parte rei.*) The second element, corresponding to this first, is the more abiding question of the medium and process by which the outward thing has entered into a vital and immanential union with oneself. It is the question of the *modus quo;* and it introduces us into that ghostly realm within the borders of which the understanding seems to be endowed with the characteristics of omnipotence. *Mens quodamodo fit omnia,* says the Saint. *The mind in a certain sense becomes everything.* It is one of those brave statements which he owes originally to Aristotle; but which rises to an almost mystical directness in his use of it in after days, when he comes to the higher reaches of theology. So long as he is content to play the philosopher, however, he will deal with these issues, for the most part, under the aspect of *esse intentionale.* It is a pity that the term — not peculiar to himself, or even to his school, in mediaeval days — has ever been allowed to pass into desuetude.

It is clear that no thinker could undertake to answer two such fundamental questions, much less formulate them, without having thought out his argument in the light of a well-considered theory of truth to give point and meaning to his solutions. Such a theory Aquinas has; though it might be misleading to the modern enquirer to be told to look for it in the twenty-nine *Quaestiones Disputatae* which the Saint himself, or his earliest editors, grouped together under the sub-caption of *De Veritate.* The *Summa Theologica* furnishes undoubtedly his riper and more considered statements; yet ten of the earlier group of discussions will reveal a good deal of his most suggestive thinking on points which not a few of the Masters of our own time have strangely confused. He holds quite simply that truth lies formally in an equation; perhaps we ought to call it, if the English language will permit us to do so, an *adequation;* it is a relationship, actual or possible, between reality and mind. *Est adequatio rei et intellectus:* and the phrase runs like a burden or refrain through all his pronouncements on cognition. He distinguishes between the truth of things (*veritas ontologica*) which, though predicated primarily and essentially of their relation to the divine Intellect, is also predicated secondarily and accidentally of their possible relationship to ourselves. Therein lies the penultimate secret of their knowableness for us. We do not create truth by our thinking. We discover it, easily or with difficulty, early or late. Nothing in reality is, or is existible even, unless Absolute Mind has first conceived it. Truth so understood has obviously a transcendental aspect and is interchangeable with being; but it has a predicamental aspect too. In this latter sense it is found formally and explicitly only in judgments. Concepts are neither true nor false in themselves, save inchoatively and by way of occasion. They constitute a beginning, so to say, of truth or of its opposite which is error; it is only by being synthesized in the complex act of judgment (*componendo vel dividendo*) that they take on this quality. There would seem to be no finality about ideas in themselves in the Saint's view of them. It is only when they move forward to a mental juxtaposition, so to say, with other ideas that the mind, becoming more alert and quickened to a greater output of energy, approves or disapproves, affirms or denies, the character of their oneness. The perception of this relationship according to Aquinas is the essential note of the *copula*. In Scotus and Durandus and in not a few of the Spanish scholastics of the sixteenth century it needs an act of the will to complete the process. Was this an anticipation of the *Voluntarism* of certain Neo-Kantian thinkers of our own day? Whatever may be urged on that point there is no doubt about the main contentions of Aquinas's position.

Even that inner and seemingly artificial world of logical being (*ens rationis — ens logicum*) by which we group our direct concepts, review our spontaneous judgments, venture upon inferences even, with the aid of codified systems of reflex universals, genera, species, syllogisms, and the rest, derives its validity in the last resort from that aboriginal and potentially mystical adequation between the divine Thought and all finite being. The substance of what we have endeavored to explain in the preceding paragraphs will be found embodied in a singularly concise and lucid statement in the *Summa* (I, Q. XVI, a. 1) where the Saint makes use of the familiar illustration of the idea in the mind of an architect and the idea externalized in the house which he has built and which is described as indeed a *true* house, because it corresponds to his plans as definitely conceived. The point of the illustration evidently lies in the fact that this house depends *per se,* that is, essentially, on the mind of the architect in question; whereas it would have a merely accidental dependence upon the mind of everyone else. In this sense art is a kind of parable of reality when we try to understand the ontologic truth of things.

That is why before summing up the body of the "article," he observes by way of conclusion, *truth is primarily a matter of mind and only secondarily a matter of things in so far as these are compared with mind* as with their source. All of which accounts, he adds, for the various explanations of truth given by Augustine, Hilary, Anselm, and Avicenna.

If we have insisted on this underlying theory of truth at more length than the actual problem of Aquinas seems to call for, it is because it will throw a good deal of light on the first half of his argument. He is a Realist, as we have pointed out, but in a partially restricted sense. Our concepts are objective, direct, and universal. They are objective, because what we *understand* is there, outside of, and distinct from, ourselves; and he makes this assertion, not arbitrarily and only half awakened from an age-long "dogmatic slumber," naïvely characteristic of his School, but because he cannot help adverting reflexly, if you will, to the fact that that same thing which he knows or understands directly as something other than himself, has a potential universality about it. If he sees another like it a moment or an hour after, or even long years after, he *re-cognizes* it; he has a second or third or tenth thought about it, each one of which is a kind of "second first," in a sense not meditated perhaps by the poet who originally hit upon that happy phrase. This *re-cognition* is as *direct* and *objective* as the primary cognition; otherwise he would not know anything at all; and so he formulates a primarily *metaphysical,* not a *psychological,* principle (though it may turn out to have that aspect also) to the effect that the *proportionate object* of the human understanding is a something in the material world outside of ourselves which we have got hold of in an immaterial way. That something he describes as an *essence* or *quiddity* of a corporeal thing.

We said just now that that thing, external to ourselves, (*id quod concipitur*) which we seem to have got hold of mentally is not an actual, but a potential, universal. Even that statement, however, needs further modification if we are to interpret the Saint's meaning with precision. To describe the potential character of this universality he uses the word "*fundamentaliter*"; that is to say, there is ground for calling it a universal.

What is this ground or *fundamentum in re?* Perhaps the acutest and most satisfying answer to that question will be found in the *Opusculum de Ente et Essentia.* It is a tentative piece of work belonging to St. Thomas's earlier years, when he was contending in his persistent but unruffled way for a new and more intimate consideration of Aristotle's teaching on the major problems then agitating the Christian Schools. It is a treatise of most engaging compass; but it manages to sum up in its seven short chapters the cardinal issues which even a modern enquirer would have to meet in establishing a theory of ideas. "*Aureum et perinsigne opusculum,*" says Cajetan in the opening paragraph of his own penetrating and luminous commentary, "a very remarkable essay, but worth its weight in gold." It is indeed all that and something more. In its sure directness of statement it anticipates the great *Summa* and does it in such wise that the student will find it difficult to believe that this Master is a pioneer in the new peripateticism of the thirteenth century. Genius seldom shows traces of the "prentice hand." It may look like a piece of trivial advice, the youthful lecturer hints, to stop and clear up our minds on primary meanings; but, after all, is it not a case of the *parvus error in principio,* which becomes *magnus in fine?* A mere misstep in the beginning and what tragic pitfalls in the end! That Aristotelian warning has never had more ironic significance than in this perpetually recurring matter. "What, then, do we mean by the terms 'essence' and 'being'?" How are their formalities found, out there, in the infinite variety of the concrete world? How are they related to the inner and abstract world of our logical concepts? These are the capital points of his enquiry; and that is why we have insisted that obviously the first question is a metaphysical one for Aquinas. The second has to do more specifically, but not exclusively, with epistemology. The true opposition is not between appearance and reality; it is between *esse reale* and mind. That initial blunder is the small, because unwitting, sin of the post-mediaeval world; but what insanities of misbelief it has bred in the "plain-man" of today who is too busy, too superficially educated — may we say it? — to look back! *Esse reale* may not be so easy to track down; but nothing can shake the Saint's conviction that the quarry is there.

The human mind by its very nature has an "intentional" — a modern might say, an apprehensional — note about its activities. It is a mirror which is all life. It is forever reaching out to its primary, proper, and proportionate object; that which is real and most significant — for him, here and now — in material things. These entities he calls quiddities. They begin for him the intricate and complex process, partly sensible, no doubt, of knowing, which ends in a simple, vital, and characteristically spiritual act of understanding; but that is not the limit of the mind's scope.

It has an *adequate* object as well. It can reach anything under the aspect of *ens* — being. The actual relation of these aspects or objective formalities to the existent and individual thing known confusedly to be out there, a particular something with its rich concretion of being, furnishes a good deal of the matter for the seven chapters of *De Ente et Essentia*. Merely to enumerate them without analyzing the arguments involved will show what is commonly meant by calling Aquinas, not a Realist pure and simple, but a Realist with a reciprocal regard for mind — a Moderate Realist, that is, with his feet firmly planted in that outer world of ponderable, or at least mensurable, matter, which plays so variously, so illusively sometimes, upon sense when observation flags; but which he ultimately understands *sub-specie-aeternitatis*. The eternity, let it be remembered, is a purely negative one, and is not to be identified, except, perhaps, as an arguable, and possibly parabolic, beginning of that other and more real eternity which Boethius defined and of which the Silurist sang:

> I saw Eternity the other night,
> Like a great ring of pure and endless light.

The same must be said of the immutability, the hypothetical " necessity," which puzzles and scandalizes so many sincere, but alien, amateurs when they approach this problem of Scholastic " essences " with the determination to be fair to it and not to condemn its defenders unread.

An insidious and prolific source of misunderstanding in the discussion of this problem from St. Thomas's day — indeed, we might say from Abelard's day — down to our own is undoubtedly to be traced to a certain chameleon-like character in the concepts which inevitably come into play. They belong to two orders of being, the real and the intentional; each requiring the very fullest measure of abstraction of which the human mind seems capable. The result is that the enquirer often unconsciously passes back and forth from one to the other, but the drift of this unwitting movement is predominantly in the direction of *esse intentionale*. We are meticulously prone to stop at each stage of our findings and give the provisional result a name. Now there is an incalculable amount of psychological mistiness, to say nothing of the deeper ontological mystery, involved in the bestowal of a name, especially when the name has to be really significant and worth while, in these tenuous matters. If concrete reality is deeper and fuller than our thought about it, we may be sure that it is deeper and fuller than the labels we attach to it in the stately museums of the mind. No one felt this human inadequacy of the word and the concept more keenly than St. Thomas; but his consciousness of the disability never turned him into a sceptic. He was too wise, too patient, for that. Again and again he harks back to the truism that, because there are grades and grades of knowledge, we must expect to find *grades and grades of real being*. Of the seven chapters of *De Ente et Essentia* the last three are devoted to making that point clear; he achieves this sure result with an amazing economy of statement, because his words, like his concepts, have been disfurnished of all the disturbing emotionalisms of sense. The light of his understanding is a dry light — *siccum intelligentiae lumen*. And this brings us to the second or epistemological side of the problem as he sees it.

Except when he deals with the much subtler questions connected with the assents of religious faith, St. Thomas is satisfied for the most part to be an Aristotelian *sans peur et sans apologie*. It will not be necessary, therefore, to attempt to outline his theory at great length; but it will be more to the purpose, we imagine, if we call attention to certain points which are too often overlooked by the modern student.

(1) In the application of his favorite metaphysical principle of potency and act to the question he insists — appealing always to the fact of inward experience — that the human intellect, as an immaterial and passive faculty, *needs to be determined by its object,* that is, it needs to be determined by the intelligible. This is obviously a metaphysical statement; and it is characteristic of St. Thomas, who is, beyond all else, a metaphysician in these matters even before he is an epistemologist.

(2) Sense knowledge is true knowledge as far as it goes; and it plays an indispensable part in the formation of our ideas; so indispensable, in fact, that the Saint is of the opinion that real thinking cannot go on in this life without the aid of what he calls the *phantasmata*.

(I, Q. LXXXIV, a. 7; item; Q. CXI, a. 3.) A *phantasm* (in this technical and scholastic use of the term) is an inward and vital product of the data of sense. The mind, on the other hand, before acquiring its first concepts, may be likened to a *tabula rasa*. It is a sort of schoolboy's slate, radiant, undenotive, receptive, clean, awaiting in naïve passivity the characters or notions that childish fingers will commit to it. He describes it as a faculty, indeed, because it is an instrument whereby the soul can act; but it is a *passive faculty and needs to be determined by its object, the intelligible*. How is this determination effected? It is here that the phantasm serves a material purpose. There is an active side to this essentially passive mind of ours; and it is on this active side that it gets close to the images of the outer world. It invariably turns to them before the process of real understanding begins. So characteristically human, but instinctive, is the mind's recourse to these images in the formation of its ideas, that Aquinas does not hesitate to link it with the propensity which impels us to turn to illustrations and examples when we wish to help another to understand what we have first understood ourselves. The mind, then, depends in some way upon the phantasm; but how is that dependence to be described? It is an exclusively objective dependence; if there is no image to turn to, the mind will have nothing on which to begin.

(3) Intellectual knowledge is truer than sense knowledge, because it goes farther and helps us to understand. It goes farther because it began by throwing away practically all its *impedimenta*. It reaches greater depths and heights; it has a wider sweep. *Singularium nulla est scientia.* The singular, as singular, takes one nowhere; it is only when its singularity is universalized that *understanding* comes in. In English *to know* is not the same as *to understand*. A like profound distinction runs through the general Scholastic use of *cognoscere and intelligere;* but it is in St. Thomas that the significance of this distinction is most clearly brought out. The intellect works upon the *phantasm* by de-individualizing it. The process is a real, vital, and transforming one, though it is commonly described, with essential accuracy, as one of illumination and abstractive representation. The first net result of this vital act is the *species intelligibilis impressa;* it is the work of the active intellect (*intellectus agens*) and its function is to bring the passive element of mind (*intellectus passivus*) from potency into act; it conceives an idea and

brings it to the birth; it utters the mental word (*verbum mentale —
species intelligibilis expressa*); it has achieved a simple apprehension of
reality. Whatever we are to think of the theory as a whole its crucial
element lies here. How does the *intellectus agens* which Aquinas undoubtedly regards as an immaterial and inorganic faculty of the soul,
get hold of the phantasm which is, *ex hypothesi,* an organic and material
product of the sense-life? St. Thomas, to his credit, seems ever to be
aware of the possibility of such a challenge; and he never shirks a plain
answer. The answer, moreover, is always the answer of a metaphysician.

(4) The answer to this fundamental difficulty will be found in two
noteworthy passages from the Saint's writings which we venture to summarize by way of closing this appeal for a fresh consideration of his
theory on the origin of our ideas.

The first, which we take from the *Summa* (I, Q. LXXXV, a. 1, ad
3), contrasts the individually representative character of the phantasm
as found in the organism with the more abstract, but still essentially
representative, character of the species *intelligibilis impressa* which determines the passive intellect to act. Phantasm and intelligible species are,
alike, representative; the former of the concrete and individual thing;
the latter of this same thing viewed as an abstract nature without its in-
dividuating notes — *solum quantum ad naturam speciei*. We are also
warned not to regard this exercise of its abstractive energy on the part
of the active intellect as a crude process of lifting, as though something
had to pass spatially from the phantasm to the passive and spiritual mind.
The phantasm is a vital, if material, image which the active intellect uses
instrumentally to produce something immaterially, but still veraciously,
representative of the thing we are said to *understand*. There is nothing
arbitrary or blindly *a priori;* nothing " dogmatic " (in Kant's contemptuous sense of the word) about all this. It is just a consistent application
of Aristotelian metaphysics to the data of sense and to the primary processes of mind.

The second passage which we take from the *De Veritate* (Q. X de
mente a. vi, ad 7) is more noteworthy still; because it boldly attacks in
Aristotelian terms the question of the nature of the efficient causality
invoked to explain this interaction of sense and mind. The phantasm is
a true, but secondary and instrumental, cause. The active intellect is the
principal and primary agent in the immanent process from first to last.

What wonder, then, that the ultimate, vital result should bear the mark, so to say, of both instrument and agent (not of agent alone, or of instrument alone) whose opposition fundamentally disappears in the essence of the soul itself. Aquinas is no believer in a pluralism of forms. For him the soul is the one, exclusive, living principle of the body, which it vitalizes, gives unity and sense to, and stamps authentically as the body, not of a mere brute, but of a rationalizing and thinking man. Read in the light of this doctrine of *forms,* and of the ever-recurrent reminder that the human soul, as he puts it, is not a form totally immersed (*totaliter immersa*) in the matter to which it gives meaning as well as dignity, the difficulties commonly urged against the theory will be found to be based largely on misunderstanding.

A PRAGMATIC APPROACH TO BEING

William Forbes Cooley

But is there any such thing? Can there be if pragmatic enquiry is self-limited to what makes a difference in experience? I think there can; [1] for the idea of Being is now affecting questions of existential relations in the domain of science — witness the present issue in physics between " field " theories — hypotheses of basic continuity — and the various forms of *quasi*-atomism, or basic discreteness.[2]

The starting point of such an approach must manifestly be empirical. I find it in the *fragmentariness of knowledge* — that persistent aspect of *incompleteness* which characterizes our acquaintance with the world, together with the many empirical indications of connection with elements or situations unknown. In scientific inquiry solutions lead to new queries. Every discovery — as, indeed, all experience — is " fringed "; residual phenomena point intriguingly to undiscovered things *beyond* themselves — a mysterious *more*. Were there need, it would not be hard to give factual evidence of this fragmentariness in every field of science; but there is abundant expert authority in support of it. When St. Paul wrote, " For we know *in part,* and we speak new insights [prophesy] *in part,*" he might have cited many concurrent testimonies in Greek philosophy from Heraclitus — with his " Nature loves to hide " — down. In our own times a recent utterance of Sir J. H. Jeans is representative: " Our physics and our chemistry are only the fringes of far-reaching sciences; beyond the seashore we have explored in our laboratories lies the ocean, the existence of which we are only beginning to suspect." [3]

The emotional effects of this situation, where mysteries peep over the shoulders of mysteries like snow peaks in the Himalayas, is no doubt

[1] Should the experts of pragmatism decide, however, that the title is a linking of incompatibles, the word " empirical " may be substituted, my pragmatism being of quite a Fabian type, and with dubious claims to orthodoxy.

[2] No doubt this is a structural question on one side (the scientific), but that question turns upon the further metaphysical one of intrinsic nature.

[3] *New York Times,* December 9, 1928.

wholesome — religious in a large way — at least so long as reason remains enthroned. My concern, however, is with its intellectual aspects, its *implications*. As Jeans says, " Interpretation has become more important than discovery. . . . Man is no longer content to stare through a telescope as at a raree-show; the dumb attitude of astonished wonder has passed, and he is beginning to ask insistently what it all means. . . . What, in particular, is the relation of our puny planet and our ephemeral existence to the terrifying grandeur of the universe outside? " [4]

(1) One implication of the fragmentariness of knowledge is, naturally enough, that in greater or less degree the " beyond " is a *continuation* of the here and now, and homogeneous with it. This is implied, or reasonably to be inferred, because without such existential continuity nature's processes would be magical and scientific prediction impossible; that is, it is a corollary of the uniformity of nature. The " beyond " is, therefore, to be conceived as consisting in no small measure of further examples of the natural order with which we are already acquainted.[5] In this sense fragmentariness is evidently mere quantitative incompleteness, and is unavoidable until all that exists in a particular field has been fully explored.

(2) Continuity is by no means, however, the whole story. Sooner or later the progress of research makes us aware that there is another kind of " beyond," not homogeneous with the content of our present knowledge, but different in *quality,* and strikingly different. At every stage of the advance an all-important factor, which is elusive and not to be brought to view, is nevertheless evidently present. We must believe in it, since without it our best results are meaningless. That factor is *the functioning agency*. Its place is best seen in connection with those mechanical situations which, with movements as their functions, constitute the favorite interpretive device of natural science — quite properly, too, for many purposes.

Do empirical substances, supposedly elementary, act in surprising ways? Forthwith the physicist conceives them as masses of imperceptible, organized units whose associated activities are held to account for the behavior of the whole. If we wonder why these posited constituents act

---

[4] *Id.,* January 6, 1929.

[5] Speaking of the possibilities of stellar observation, Jeans remarks: " The universe appears to be uniform, and the traveler in far-off regions does not encounter new species of objects, but merely further examples of the species which abound nearer home." — *New York Times,* January 6, 1929.

out the rôles assigned to them, we are instructed to resolve them severally into still minuter units, and these if need be into others even more elementary. Thus, a grain of table salt is said to consist of a multitude of *molecules,* each of which is an extremely minute physical unit never beheld by the eye of man. None the less it is organized, and, at least in part, its structure is known. It consists of an atom of sodium joined to an atom of chlorin in some definite stereometrical pattern so as to constitute an organized existential whole, the activities of the molecule, although quite different from those of either of its constituents, being persistently maintained even in the face of agencies strongly adverse. Now, even at this stage it is to be suspected that there is a "beyond" not included in the mechanical account; for why do the sodium and chlorin atoms alter their own native behavior and join in maintaining that of the salt molecule? [6]

Nevertheless, the explanation might yield a certain satisfaction if we knew what these constituent atoms are in themselves; but again mechanical analysis omits the functioning agency, and passes the problem of intrinsic nature on to a more elementary stage. The atom, on inquiry, proves to be another theoretical structure constituted of imagined units — an even more complicated mechanism made up of a *quasi*-swarm of "electrons" with a "proton" as queen of the hive. The electrons are, of course, unobservable *a fortiori,*[7] but are held to be units of electricity, whatever that may be. What, then, is the *intrinsic nature* of the atom? Has it any? Is this much-used unit more than a mathematical *symbol,* a postulated plexus of relations? There is evidently no limit to the process of theoretical analysis and sub-analysis, so long as it proves useful; but, like all

---

[6] The zealous mechanist answers: Because the molecule's activities are mere mechanical resultants of the activities of the constituent atoms; but the word "mere" in this claim seems quite doctrinaire.

[7] Eddington has recently pronounced them "dummies." It seems to be common among physicists to regard this electronic theory as a final and satisfactory simplification of the physical world, since the electrons can be conceived as *qualitatively* identical and the various properties of perceptual objects reduced to differences in the numbers and positions of the electrons. Perhaps this hope of the ardent simplifier will survive the shocks of accumulating facts; but it is rather early to acclaim it as realized. On many a previous occasion new fields of research, *in which consequently knowledge was scanty,* have been covered by speculative thought with a screening mist of simplicity that vanished with the increase of real knowledge. In this case a pretty radical distinction has already been found necessary between electrons and protons, and between the activities of the nuclear and the satellite electrons.

utilities, it should somewhere lead to that highest use or value, immediate satisfaction — in this case, *understanding*. If mechanical explanation in its bold descent of the hierarchy of mechanisms which it invokes is not to be a mere infinite regress, it is manifestly needful that sooner or later it should lead us to stable qualitative existence — things with a nature of their own.

Men of science feel this need, at least at times; but the difficulty for them is that their conceptual units lie far beyond the range of observation, without which, directly or indirectly, qualitative acquaintance is impossible. Atoms, supposing them to exist, can at best have only the properties which are imputed to them *through analogy,* and analogy is all too often a broken road in this search. In the physical world we are acquainted only with *masses,* and why should they disclose the intrinsic character of their constituents? The latter are unitary organizations, individuals; the former in the main are not. And what is such inferring but the old fallacy of division, which thought has had to abandon? All empirical objects in nature are imperfectly elastic; but science has found it needful to think of molecules as destitute of friction and perfectly elastic. Evidently atoms, at their still greater remove from observation, and electrons, *a fortiori,* are likely enough to be quite different intrinsically from any conception of them we can form on the basis of sense perception. What, then, is the intrinsic character, or essence, of the functioning agent in these various theoretical systems of physics? That is a problem which, not being one of structure, cannot be solved by mechanical constructions alone. To resolve theoretical units into systems of lesser theoretical units is to say not a word as to the essential nature of any of them. In this judgment so rigorous a natural philosopher as Mr. Bertrand Russell fully concurs. "Physics in itself," he tells us, "is exceedingly abstract, and reveals only certain mathematical characteristics of the material with which it deals. It does not tell us anything as to the intrinsic character of this material." [8] Since it is "concerned only with structure," physics cannot "*per se* warrant inferences as to any but the structural properties of events." "We know the laws of the physical world, in so far as these are mathematical, pretty well; but we know nothing else about it." [9]

[8] *Analysis of Matter,* p. 10. This seems to be going Descartes one better.

[9] *Id.,* pp. 390, 264, 227. Cf. Prof. Eddington's remark in his *Nature of the External World* that, "the frank realization that physical science is concerned with a world of shadows is one of the most significant of recent advances."

Now, for calculation and control acquaintance with structure may suffice, but not for the ends of *understanding*. For that at least a likeness to *qualitative* cognitions (experience) must be established. Process without any acquaintance with what it is that proceeds can never satisfy the mind. " In describing a structure," Russell remarks, " the terms are as important as the relations, and we cannot rest content with terms which we believe to be fictitious." [10]

The question of the intrinsic in nature is, of course, an old one. It is persistent, however, and seems to me as genuine a query as in the time of Thales. Am I told that this very persistence is proof of its lack of profit, for evidently it is unanswerable and is not worth following up? I cannot agree; for it has not altogether failed of answer. The slow but wide advance of science, as distinctly as did the intuition of the first Greek philosophers, favors at least its essential *singleness*. No doubt there is still much diversity of opinion as to its character, and even more perhaps as to its names. Some like to call it the *Absolute*, but they are wont to load that august word with cherished assumptions that more or less beg the question. Much the same is to be said of Mr. Spencer's *Unknowable*. Kant's term, *the thing in itself*, is encumbered with epistemological doctrines; while the ordinary word " *Substance*," of Spinoza and the Scholastics, needs to be accompanied by a definition. At the dawn of philosophy it was called the *arche*, a term rooted in the hypothesis of hylozoism. Plato's name for it was *Being*, a term which, when freed from later connotations and construed in accord with the knowledge of today, I am disposed to think is still the most fitting one; for what we seek is still an existence standing in antithesis to Becoming, something which *is* in the deepest and most persistent way, existence continuing with virtual stability through and somehow behind, or beneath, all the panoramas of the natural process.[11]

---

[10] *Op. cit.*, p. 277.

[11] Heraclitus and some of his followers have tried to exclude any such stable factor, but without avail. Determinateness and order — the existential bases of natural law — are abundantly in evidence in nature, and we cannot at all account for them, and for the reign of law, without positing something that abides, something relatively permanent. Otherwise even change becomes meaningless, there being no means of determining it. It is open, of course, to the critic to urge that merely *relative* permanence and " *virtual* stability " are only change at a slower pace; but the point, however valid logically, is mostly verbal. It does not touch the question proper — the need of a continuing background to account for the reign of order in a phenomenal, changeful world.

What Plato meant by Being has been much clouded by the common disposition to confuse his antithesis of Being and non-Being — especially the latter in its ceaseless rôle of Becoming — with the wider one of reality and unreality. But non-Being was not unreal for Plato, much as he disparaged it at times. It was, as for Descartes, a real physical existence — substantial space. Nor was Becoming unreal. His criticisms of it are based upon two of its aspects which were distasteful to him — the transiency and the phenomenality of its features. It was hopelessly inconstant, and even while it lasted it was not what it seemed! Over against this phantasmagoric reality of Becoming Plato posited an enduring and far superior reality, namely, Being. Now, on the purely metaphysical side, that antithesis is present still. Kobold-like the X of intrinsic nature still attends all those myriad natural functionings which constitute the subject-matter of science; but Being seems a more distinctive term for it than X.

It is evident in advance that Being is not likely to be discovered by simple observation of nature, however intent and patient; for by general critical consent all sensory objects are *phenomena,* Becoming, not Being, mere effects upon the psyche of causes undisclosed. In these perceptions Being must, indeed, be in touch with us, but we are aware only of the *touch,* as from beyond a screen, not of any touching agency. Nor, as we have seen, will the far-reaching inferential machinery of the natural sciences reveal that agency — except in one elementary respect — for, when we ask for Being, physics offers us structure — *relations* not intrinsic properties.

The one exception referred to is the familiar, *quasi*-borderland attribute of *extension.* This is apparently a genuine implicate of structure when it is meant literally and seriously. Despite idealistic criticisms physicists remain matter-of-fact realists, believing in a literally extended world: and I have no disposition to quarrel with them on that issue.[12] Extension is no longer a word of power, however. We wonder today how Plato and Descartes could have construed the physical universe in terms of it, so meager is its content.

Extension excepted, there remains, then, apparently only one line of

---

[12] The sweeping claim that no inference from phenomena can apply to what is beyond phenomena seems to me an unwarranted limitation of constructive thought. No doubt a superstructure cannot be firmer than its support; but it can be much stronger than the *uncombined materials* of that support, as every concrete foundation illustrates.

approach to Being — that through *the inner life.* A demurrer is to be expected at this point, a claim that the psychic is an illegitimate bypath, a turning aside from fact to fancy. What, it is asked, have the phantasmagoria of consciousness to do with the substantial, coercive realities of the world? The reply is that for thinkers with naturalistic leanings this objection is out of date. Can one hold that the mental is a branch of the biological and mind a product of nature, and still deny the evidential legitimacy of mentality as regards the natural order of which it is a manifestation? That would be much as though the needle movements in the mariner's compass were denied relevance in a study of magnetism! Assuredly if we seek any adequate account of our world, we shall not be able to avoid looking within, especially for sources.

Yet we shall, of course, have to discriminate, and with care. Our manifold *percepts per se,* our *feelings* of pleasure and pain, our *emotions,* our *desires* and *purposes,* so far as these are simply features of consciousness — all have notable claims to reflective attention. Genetically they are primary — the very constituents of consciousness, the empirical elements of all other knowledge and belief, and the objects of which in the last analysis we are surest. Yet they are quite certainly " Becoming," and so not the object of our search. We cannot believe that things proverbially so transient and changeful are themselves modes of Being. Rather do they bear the earmarks of *functions* — forms of activity of something other than themselves. So far as they are concerned, the " beyond " which we seek is still beyond. It is otherwise, however, with those personal *powers* which seem to be the *sources* of the objects just considered, and which, as organized into a persisting unity capable of consciousness, we think of as our personality, or ego. These wear at least an aspect of stability, full many of them being manifestly generic and so fundamental.

It is a secondary, but not unprofitable, query whether these stable underlying factors are cognitively simply needful inferences or are themselves objects of consciousness. Some seem to think that, if they have standing inferentially, they cannot be also objects. In that case our personal powers, which are, of course, actually vouched for inferentially, lose the status of data; and one upshot of our inquiry appears to be before us, namely, that Being, if knowable at all, is *purely inferential,* never experiential. Mr. Santayana puts the case neatly in his sweeping conclusion that "nothing given exists," [13] or, conversely, no existents (modes of Being) are objects of consciousness. I venture to think, however, that this denial is quite insufficiently based, and that there is likely to enter into it a subjective bias due to the common predilection for a conveniently divided and classified subject-matter. Assuredly in experience it is not at all uncommon to support (or disparage) obscure perceptions by resort to inference, and this without impairing their actuality as objects. Furthermore, there is reason to think that in the very act of cognition, especially of objectives, the ego, or "psyche," is immediately and functionally aware of itself, both as recipient, or subject, and as initiating agency. No doubt introspection is far from unanimous on this point. What was self-evident to Berkeley was undiscoverable to Hume. But the shift in psychology from intellectualism to voluntarism, man's spontaneous feelings of agency and responsibility, together with his inveterate use of the pronoun "I" despite all philosophical criticisms — these seem to me to favor the theory of *self* consciousness in the literal immediate sense.[14] On the other hand, the idea that an integrated unit of force *cannot* be aware of itself seems to have only the meager justification that, owing to the exigencies of action, we are accustomed in cognition to stress the objective side.

A more probable view to my mind is that psychic activity starts in as impulse, which, when intensively rich enough and sufficiently complicated by conflicting conditions, rises above the threshold and the new feature of awareness occurs, somewhat as heated iron assumes the new function of light on passing 1000 F. In this higher phase conation is still dominant at first, and awareness is flooded with it, so that the cognitive contents are objectives rather than distinct objects — crudely but vividly visioned *ends*. At this stage the self is immediately and strongly, albeit inchoately, present *in* consciousness. But with the multiplication and competition of objectives and the increase of specialization, the impulsive and self-feeling factors tend to drop toward, or below, the threshold, and leave chiefly *objects* in the field of awareness. On this theory subjective and objective situations are primarily *stages* in psychic impulse rather than distinct forms of activity, or even attitudes fundamentally diverse. Any

---

[13] *Scepticism and Animal Faith,* p. 42 ff.

[14] Cf. Whitehead's reference to the "awful ultimate fact, which is the human being, consciously alone with itself, for its own sake." — *Religion in the Making,* p. 16.

mental functioning of the individual will then include a self feeling if it is interesting enough to arouse a lively conative reaction, while cognition of objects of doubtful concern to the percipient may seem to be quite free from self awareness — completely objective. Man's generic personal powers then become, at least potentially, immediate data of consciousness, data which, owing to their stability, must be recognized as legitimate candidates for the status of Being, say, modes of it recurrently present in consciousness. This question is not integral to our inquiry, however. It has to do rather with the vividness and felt actuality of Being than with its character.

Our main concern is as to possible clues to that character discoverable in human nature, however known, regarded as a developed form of cosmic existence — human nature in its essential, generic endowment, of course, apart from all particular acquired traits of individuals or groups. Moreover, clues, to serve our purpose, must be traceable also in the great domains external to human nature. To discover seemingly basic human factors will avail little unless they are in such continuity with reality elsewhere as to be capable of use therein for interpretation and guidance. So restricted, I think there are at least four fundamental properties of our human nature which may reasonably claim to rank as cosmic attributes. They are: *impulsiveness, typicality, modifiability,* and *appreciativeness.*[15]

(1) *Impulsiveness* — We have seen that we search in vain throughout the structural explanations of science for any disclosure of the essential nature of the functioning agents. Nor can we see how mechanical explanations carried down to any imaginable level can possibly improve the logical situation. At every stage the same question as to intrinsic character faces us, and the procedure in itself is necessarily an infinite regress. Mechanism, being purely a matter of relations, does not deal with the inner nature of the things related. We are not to suppose, however, that the man of science actually excludes the intrinsic from his thought. On the contrary, it is probably more or less present with him continually, not as a discovered existence, but as a basic posit, the content of which he hopes will be clearer

---

[15] It may be remarked that this list omits the basic property of extension, already conceded, and that the principle of continuity requires that extension should be attributed to the ego. This may be true; but extension is not as yet a *known* attribute of the ego, and so is not suited to serve as a connecting link between inner and outer. Then, too, in this case the inferential movement is *opposite in direction* from the one I am pursuing; it is from the outer to the inner.

in future. The atom, for example, is for him more than a mathematical, symbolical system of relations; he conceives of it as, also, a truly unitary, highly organized, *actual existence* with intense self-activities, tensions, and potencies. That is, he endows it with an *impulsive* character which is itself not a part of the mechanism proper but its *ground* — something assumed in all mechanical explanations of nature. *All* his organized units are *self*-active; and self-activity is for him part of the intrinsic nature of things, that is, of Being.

For ages this was not the case; the postulate of inertness, based upon impenetrable extension, dominated physics. Natural philosophers were devoted to the task of preserving the integrity and eternity of Parmenidean Being by making all activities *external* to it. Nor is this strange, for the idea of impulsiveness, or inherent force, was not derived from the field of physics itself; and still is not logically derivable therefrom, as Hume made clear enough. Spontaneous activity is not a phenomenon of perceptual physics. It is not observable externally. When an aspect of it appears, it can always be explained away and reduced to external agencies (push and pull) — a feat which hitherto physicists, not to mention materialistic philosophers, have delighted to perform. Now, intrinsic character is *qualitative,* and in the nature of the case can be known only through qualitative experience, never by intellectual processes alone. Hence, self-activity, as an intrinsic characteristic, must have an experiential source; and since that source is not in the *external* field, it must be in the *internal,* that is, in the domain of human life, where in an inchoate way it has been a familiar datum [16] from time immemorial.

There is, of course, no question as to the present dominance of the idea in natural science, despite the fact that its new sovereignty in the inorganic realm has been a kind of Norman Conquest — the rule of a master conception coming from across a wide channel of difference. Within the present century impulsiveness has become a manifest common denominator of the internal and external worlds. Now that physics has discarded materialism, the discoverable residue of the traditional matter-mind distinction is merely that in the mental realm the functioning agent

---

[16] We have only two ways of knowing causes — critical *inference* from events and *immediate awareness of ourselves* as efficient agents. In the last analysis these virtually reduce to one, for apart from the second causality shrinks to mere regular sequence — an agnostic outcome which may suffice for the descriptions of pure science but is incredible to the engineer.

is more or less conscious of its objectives and courses while in the realm of physics it apparently is not. Whatever else matter and mind may be — two or one, for instance — both are evidently modes or functions of something impulsive — self-active existence. This common denominator is, of course, one of the major links in contemporary naturalism, a link by which existential continuity from the physical to the mental is strongly indicated — a single basic existence being regarded as functioning in more or less similar, but successively higher, ways as the evolutionary movement passes from the physical to the self-directive stage. In view of current advances in biology and psychology this doctrine seems very reasonable.[17]

(2) *Typicality* — It is a familiar fact, of course, that our most lively interest as spectators is aroused by *living* forms and other objects that act as though they were alive. This is obvious as regards children, but it is perhaps quite as real as regards most adults. Witness the perennial power of the drama and of fiction. Indeed, primitive man carried this interest into the inorganic field and regarded all things that moved, especially in a way to affect himself, as also concrete living forms; that is, he personified them. Of course, he made some distinctions, the first perhaps being that between friend and foe. Out of this propensity, in part at least, seems to have arisen that deep-rooted trait of human nature, and indeed of sub-human nature, which Professor Giddings has called the " consciousness of kind," and which he holds to be the tap-root of human and brute sociality. From earliest experience we perceive that other men, and especially some kinds of men, are our fellows — a recognition which is not primarily an inference. We feel it before we reflect upon it, in fact before we are capable of reflecting. It is a basic form of consciousness. Later there arises gradually an equally strong conviction of our personal distinctness, becoming at length a feeling of self. In each of these antithetic forms of experience the presence of a distinctive kind of organization, or type [18] — one generic, the other individual — is recognized, and felt to be elemental. A like, but more advanced and theoretical, interest in definite characteristic forms is evidently present in the preference of constructive thought for the discrete, the individual in the organized sense, notwith-

---

[17] Cf. Russell's theory of " Neutral Monism."

[18] This term is used at times with a generic, and at times with an individual stress. Properly it stands for persistent, characteristic form, whether single or plural. A unique object may, therefore, be typical as well as a member of a class.

standing the fact that most physical objects — soils, clays, rocks, waters, gases — are empirically *continuous* quantities. Quite as instinctively apparently in science as in early naïve speculation, thought in seeking to explain now resorts to discrete, and sooner or later to organized, forms — not to widely extended *continua,* but to molecules, atoms, electrons, dynamic systems, etc.

This characteristic interest and method of the mind can no doubt be traced back in part to man's primitive concern about those features of the environment which seemed to carry threat or promise to his welfare; but that environmental fashioning of thought applied rather to the *particular* discrete objects feared or coveted than to his interest in individual objects in general. As a matter of fact, continuous things — minds, waters, sunshine, etc. — did affect his well-being most vitally, but commonly he gave them little heed. When they forced him to take them into account, he *personified* them. Man's concern about discrete things, however modified by environment, is more deeply rooted than any acquisitions of experience as such. Fundamentally it may well be a product of human nature's basic principle of habit, or tendency, to assume or fall into fixed forms of functioning. From a naturalistic point of view it is reasonable to regard all types as forms of functioning acquired (by Being) through the agency of habit. If the hypothesis holds good, man's regard for them or trust in them may well, from the voluntarist point of view, be a freer kind of effort toward established, *quasi*-determinate functioning. The same sort of analytico-synthetic reasoning which has reduced *ideas* to highly specialized ends, or values, may be expected to reduce preferences for types to refined and specialized forms of the type-forming propensity.

In the outer world of nature in general the presence, and indeed reign, of typical forms is manifest enough. Plato seems to have been quite right as to the cosmic supremacy of his " Ideas." Unitary organized types constitute the great existential discoveries and characterize the great theories of science. It may, of course, be denied that these are truly Platonic. Certainly they are not static — highly dynamic rather — and they do not appear to be external. Yet they are *stable forms of reality with characteristic ways of functioning.*

In the field of life their primacy has been recognized from the very dawn of reflection. There the subject-matter is *all* discrete; all the units are organisms — collectively *typical,* not miscellaneous, organisms.

The discovery of a like situation — the reign of unitary *systems* — in that " inorganic " world which perceptually is the domain of continuity, is a notable achievement of the new physics. Men and brutes, insects and plants, are no more truly typical structures, self-active and self-maintaining, than are solar systems on the one hand and molecules and atoms on the other. The full importance of this far-reaching truth is not appreciated until we realize that these distinctive systems are true *individuals* — indivisible unities. They cannot be divided without destroyng the type.[19] And they are uniquely, or distinctively, active. No other type will function in quite the same way. So far as we know, they are *the only seats of efficiency,* as evidently they are also *the only seats of values.* It seems indubitable, therefore, that typicality, actual or potential, and more or less akin to that which is immanent in human nature, is to be recognized as universal, and as therefore properly attributable to Being. It would seem, then, that fundamental existence reveals itself as (1) susceptible of a wide variety of forms, or modes, and (2) as conservative of those modes which somehow *fit*. The facts supporting the " quantum theory " may prove to be but new and surprising manifestations of the second of these characteristics. As to the first mentioned, the question of the origin of the typical forms remains open. If they could be shown to be *acquired* in the course of cosmic development, we should have opened to us a vista of self-active Being as also self-differencing and progressively attaining — an advancing *" causa sui,"* or adventurous evolution realized.[20]

(3) *Modifiability* — The biologist, in developing the doctrine of natural selection, has found it needful to endow protoplasm with the property of *accommodation*. Organisms, he tells us, have sufficient play, or range, of function to adjust themselves to considerable changes of environment. On a larger scale a like power is present also in the species as a phylogenetic factor, called *adaptation,* by virtue of which the organic type, through gradual changes of structure, is able to increase the extent of its environmental adjustments. Such adaptation through structural

[19] For example, a piece of iron is evidently divisible indefinitely, but not so the iron atom. When that is broken up, the parts are no longer iron. They will not do the hundred, or more, things of which the iron atom is capable.

[20] One may, no doubt, reject my adjective " adventurous " in favor of the Platonic claim that natural types are eternal; but to do so in the face of natural selection's ascendancy requires that one should follow Mr. Santayana in relegating experience and science to the realm of " animal faith " and confining the " realm of essence " to abstract, or logical, *possibilities*. The pragmatic service of so doing is not very evident.

change is characteristic of all forms of life; but in its higher forms it is not confined to the phylogeny.

Nowhere has it been more wonderfully effective than in the inner life of man. Indeed, civilization itself in its many stages, from arboreal to industrial and scientific man, is a kind of dramatic presentation of its achievements, achievements which must be attributed largely to structural modifications in the psyche. In the conative domain the new adaptations are manifest, especially in the way of the expansion and complication, the elevation and intensification, of interests and aims. Moral and aesthetic progress is due to them. Nor are they less remarkable in the intellectual domain. When one considers analytically how knowledge is built up generation after generation — the gropings and naïve experimentations, the incessant putting together in experience of a medley of obscure and disconnected percepts and later the pushing of inferences farther and farther from the data of the senses, until a boundless but orderly universe is brought into the field of belief and action — he must be impressed, and deeply impressed I think, with the remarkable powers of insight and construction of the human psyche, *all of which involve reconstructive modifications within itself.*[21] This achievement, this psychic construction of our universe, is repeated, each for himself, in greater or less degree by each new individual, the measure of his success depending on many conditions, among which cortical plasticity and a suitable environment are chief. He has not only a certain power of apperceiving and assimilating perceptions and of articulating and construing them, but in the experience process itself *he grows in ability to do these things.* Even such elementary psychic functions as apperception and memory call for structural changes.

It is plain, then, that in man as well as in the lower organisms modifiability is a fundamental and ever-present characteristic. *Protoplasm is essentially plastic,* albeit also relatively persistent in type. The problem is as to the *existential range* of plasticity. Does it obtain in the physical world, also, and so through its universality have claim to be an attribute of Being. Certainly modifiability is not patent in the inorganic field. On the contrary, this is ordinarily regarded as the hereditary domain of

[21] Cf. the *New York Times* (Nov. 2, 1928) editorial comment following Prof. Shapley's location of the center of the universe, to the effect that the prospective 200-inch telescope "will also give new evidence of the potency of man's mind. The most encouraging phenomenon is that which is at the human end of the telescope. . . . It is after all the human mind that is the centre of the universe."

determinism. Fixity of structure, often glorified as the "reign of law," is the prevailing aspect of the physical world, at least on the perceptual plane. Molecular physics, however, which has to do with physical individuals, does find certain indications of structural modification in accommodation to environment, such as the increased tensile strength developed in metals by intermittent subjection of them to strains gradually increased.

The metaphysical reasons for affirming modifiability in this field, however, are more serious than the empirical. One is the mind's demand for some unity, or continuity, of the organic and the inorganic which shall effect a unification of science. How is the universality of modifiability in the realm of life to be accounted for on an inorganic foundation of absolute fixity? Is it suggested that the elements — if not the Daltonean atoms, then the (more speculative) electrons — may be conceived as absolutely determined and yet their compounds regarded as modifiable owing to their mechanical articulation? Such a view has in its favor our familiarity with changes of structure imposed upon mechanisms in the interest of human ends, but on the other hand it suffers from the lack of the superintending intelligence to which the forms of man-made mechanisms are due. It seems a possible view on one condition, namely, that the structural modifications involved can be regarded as *due wholly to external mechanical agencies*. To me such a situation is scarcely conceivable, certainly not likely. It requires us to transfer the onus of organic modification from the intensive, or highly organized, individual to the much less intensive environment, from the side of the response to that of the stimulus, *the latter then becoming a mechanical cause*. In default of an adequate shaping environmental matrix and in view of the fact that all the existential factors in organisms are physical elements, there seems to be left no explanatory resource short of endowing those elements with at least some of that power of accommodation displayed by the organic structures which they so largely constitute.

Another reason for thinking of Being as modifiable is the great principle of evolution, as generally understood by men of science. More than ever today is this the master-key to the world. If Being is not modifiable, evolution has no serious significance in the cosmos. We can, of course, conceive of incessant shiftings of position by unchanging units throughout the ages, with corresponding changes of cosmic pattern; but that is mere kaleidoscopic play, and not at all a structural *progress,* in fact as likely to be destructive as constructive. It is conceivable enough when we think only of the inorganic world, but it quite fails to tally with, still less account for, the ascent of life. There is in it no *attainment,* no *new* character. To reduce evolution to such a process is no doubt an easy way out — a suspicious circumstance — but it is a way that yields the minimum of intellectual value — no cause for the orderliness of nature and its unitary articulations, nor even any genetic simplification, since it requires us to think of the universe as *eternally just as diverse and heterogeneous in nature as it is now.*

(4) *Appreciativeness* — Feelings of value, which play so large and varied a part in our inner life, we have been wont to deny to the physical world, a denial which — apart from the difference in perceptual awareness — appears to be the principal remaining distinction between the animate and the inanimate. No longer can we distinguish these domains by the presence of organization, for both are organized. Nor will the mark of spontaneity suffice, for self-activity is present in both. It is still held, however — and plausibly enough — that in the field of life activity has reference to *ends,* while in that of physics it has not. For ordinary purposes this is evidently a sound distinction; metaphysically, however, there is reason to think that it is relative, not absolute.

So long as we think only of *our conscious* appreciations, nature seems to be indifferent enough — heedless of our eager desires; but, then, would cosmic appreciativeness, if actual, necessarily take these into account? These empirical ends of ours are rarely *direct* objectives of our fundamental cravings, still less of any one of these acting alone. They are *personal* ends, that is, objectives *as* conditioned — perhaps turned aside or biased or perverted — by varying internal combinations and by particular and often conventional circumstances. Interests which are genetically and functionally so complicated it is, of course, not reasonable to look for in the elementary situations of the physical world, and the lack of them is not proof of a complete absence of values in that world.

That appreciation in the wide sense is the tap-root of *human* activity probably no longer needs to be argued. The new psychology has established it. Nor, with all their real services in psychology, are mechanical explanations at all likely to banish it. Values and movements are no more akin today than in the days of the ancient atomists, although it is true now as then that indirectly they may be causally related. On the other hand, through the new material of anthropology, psycho-analysis, and animal psychology, not to mention the obsolescence of dualism, man now seems more closely linked than formerly to his biological sources, his "low-vaulted past." There are phases of his conative life, largely obscure and subliminal and strangely interrelated, which offer striking glimpses of the *process* of human development *under the urge of desire* — its confused and groping movement, its many deviations and reversions, and yet withal its gradual progress from the primitive and loosely connected to the organized and unitary, from the elementary to the developed and richly intensive.[22] To the psycho-analyst what is finest in man, and what was once cited as proofs of his essential spirituality, is now taking shape as a kind of bloom of the roots and stalks of his inherited biological cravings. Thus more than ever is it manifest that appreciation in one form or another is a cardinal dynamic, a kobold-like basic factor, in human nature — a true *property,* not an accident, an *essential,* not an acquired, socially induced, characteristic. It is strong in the brute inheritance itself and in the brutish kin of primordial man. Consequently to evolutionary thought it is a reasonable hypothesis that its roots extend to the lowest protoplasmic depths — to plant life in a rudimentary way and even, at least in potency, to the *organized units* of the physical realm.

Already in the latter, teleological situations and processes begin to outline themselves through the curtain of mystery — as in the broad fact of *selection,* so widely in evidence. Chemical "affinities" and organized types, in the last analysis, seem inexplicable when all appreciation is excluded. So far as the activity itself is mechanical we can conceive of the selection as due to mechanical causes, but not below that stage; and, as we have seen, *the roots of activity are always below it.* Underlying non-mechanical existence is the condition precedent of any mechanism whatever; so that at that level, the level of Being and original sources, mechanical explanations lose not only adequacy but pertinence. When in our mental constructions we devise stereometrical configurations which we think might account for the selections, a closer scrutiny reveals that we have thereby merely pushed the problem a stage further down, not solved it. Moreover, on the evolutionary principle the organized type,

---

[22] With Plato's *Symposium* before us we cannot pronounce this process an altogether new discovery, but it is now vouched for by a body of facts of which Plato, of course, knew nothing.

whether high or low, is a *spontaneous* construction of and from some less organized basic material; and it remains inscrutable why, say, the electrons adopt that particular configuration and maintain it. Since the types are so persistent, so characteristic, and commonly so widely distributed, it is not possible to view them as products of accident. It seems much more reasonable to regard them as essentially teleological structures of a basic existence with a certain rudimentary appreciativeness. Certainly in the new physics such self-constructed, self-maintaining, variously and distinctively active systems play almost as important parts as in biology, and appear severally to involve an end as truly, and in much the same sense — the maintenance of the type and its functions — as a living organism.

The postulate of basic appreciativeness is supported, also, by sound analogy. In the domain of life organized types prove on development to be *seats of values,* that is, sentient individuals. On principles of taxonomic continuity it is a reasonable view that in the domain of physical nature, also, they are in some measure seats of values. Such a teleological continuity is evidently a part of that quasi-unity of the animate and the inanimate worlds, with only a difference in *degree* of organization between them, which, as we have seen, is a demand of our minds, and which, as constituting a sufficient "unification of science" and as furnishing a new clue for inquiry and interpretation, is a recognized scientific desideratum.[23]

As a matter of fact all the subject-matter of zoölogy is in a quasi-ferment through its manifold appreciations. The fortunes of all organisms are controlled by them. If one denies that they are in any way rooted in Being itself, it seems to be incumbent upon him to show in what other way they could have come to be. If it is asked, how can we possibly imagine appreciative functioning in the simple, purely mechanical situations offered us by physics, my answer must be that I do not know. The most likely hypothesis — and I regard it as very likely, indeed — is that those situations (when actual) are *abstract,* presenting at best only aspects of reality and by no means its fulness. Hamlet's remark to Horatio may well be the true answer. Nor do I see why such a conclusion should be distasteful to any but the devoted partisans of simplicity and eternity. We have had to carry impulsiveness and typicality down, or on, into the heart of Being, and we have found serious reasons for doing the like as

[23] Cf. J. Hjort, *The Unity of Science.*

to plasticity: the hypothesis is reasonable enough that appreciation may be seated there also.

If Being has, indeed, these four attributes; if the ever-present basic cosmic Existence whose marvelous kinematic play environs us throughout all our days and whose modes we ourselves are — if it is thus self-active, individuated, persistently attaining from level to level, and increasingly appreciative in higher and higher ways, then, albeit the outlines are few and vast areas remain to be explored, we have at least adumbrated for us a stupendous stage and drama in which a vast and age-long adventurous development seems to be proceeding, the end of which, just because it is adventurous, the human mind cannot even surmise, but the nearer reaches of which may well reward exploration.

CONSOLATION AND CONTROL

A Note on the Interpretation of Philosophy

John J. Coss

THE writings which have gained enduring regard from men interested in the significance of physical and spiritual relationships may be read in various ways. Sometimes they are consulted as final arbiters in the court of truth, sometimes they are sought as solace or inspiration, sometimes they are studied as human documents which reveal even while they hide the loves and hates of those who wrote them.

Doubtless each way of reading has its justification and reward. Philosophers have inquired with what seems very great objectivity into the meaning of God, of matter, and of man; they have recorded insights into the perplexities of life; and they have shown in the objects of their interest, in their opinions, and in their praise and censure the limits of that which they found real and the hopes and fears which shook their souls.

To deny to any of the readers the existence within philosophy of some part at least of that which he finds there would be folly. To assert that any one of the readers is exclusively correct would not be more wise. But to consider the views of the reader who sees within philosophy one phase of the human drama, and for the time to neglect the other discoveries, may be enlightening and at least tolerable to those who see some truth even in partial truth.

Philosophers as other men have looked out over the past and into the future and found something which to them was worth more than anything else. This value or good they have come on with an immediacy and intensity so compelling as to seem, for them, to need no argument. Argument, or rather, the statement of the grounds of belief might, to be sure, satisfy their own delight in completeness, certainty, and order, but its value would be in large measure its utility for others who had affirmed that same good thing as they themselves had found compelling, or for others still who had rejected it, or yet for others who had no opinion.

The values which men find past denying, the things which they hold to be good, past all doubt and, for themselves at least, past all need of proof, these are the ultimates on which philosophies rest, and from which philosophical structures, built with consummate art and subtle argument, rise above their origin as spires and arches tower above a holy spot where some inquiring spirit saw within the veil or found peace after years of restless struggle and desire.

Two types of value appear most frequently in philosophical writings. They are predominantly present in philosophers because they are constantly recurring in life. For generic distinction these values may be thought of as a contrasting pair. They are satisfactions for those who are seeking consolation or are absorbed in some method of control. Escape and conquest signify these recurring motifs in the life of man; and philosophies have projected in ideas the elemental rhythms of the human spirit between quiescence and activity.

Consolation and control represent two types of desires; and their presence in men, as indicated by the beliefs in ideas which are beyond true and false, gives significant evidence of life histories, of individual and group difficulties, prospects, and successes. Consolation and control taken as interpretive keys to philosophies bring these structures of the imagination into the most direct connection with the affairs of men, and slight perhaps the view of philosophy which would make of it a steady progress from ignorance to the single and ultimate truth. If philosophies are elaborations of ineradicable trends toward escape and conquest, philosophers come into the market place and leave the gods to dwell alone within the intersteller spaces. If consolation and control are dominating emotional acceptances of values, philosophies, at least beneath their arguments, put off the immortality of finality, and join the passing and all too human record of man in a world which alternately oppresses and inspires him. The view of philosophies as the encrusted revelation of desire gives not only zest in the interpretation of individual philosophies, but carries with it an estimate of philosophy itself.

The ritual and vestments of philosophy have become so rich, and the interest in them so absorbing that they seem sometimes to obscure the objects of devotion. Logic as a handmaiden is worthy of her place and station but, become the goddess, she often turns her worshipers into slaves and transforms the noble science in which she one time played her part into a thin and empty formalism. There can be no question but that many figures in philosophic history have been willing and happy slaves. They have elaborated most splendid liturgies that have withstood the ravages of time and through their perfection have made converts to their faith who have carried on the ancient tradition with scarcely less brilliant accomplishments than crowned the efforts of the founders. All this is true; and yet each new philosophy in which some great conviction flamed called down the goddess from her throne and changed her back into a handmaiden.

As one calls to mind the great figures in the philosophical tradition and tries to order them into those who look for consolation and for control one becomes aware that these two terms have various fringes of meaning even while their mass remains the same. Plato and Aristotle did not seek consolation, but their interest in control was scarcely that of Francis Bacon. They sought control of human life in a mundane society. Man's political existence for them appeared potentially a thing of ordered beauty and they described its forms and its discipline. They also looked into reality and saw in the nature of being basic support for their contentions about man. And, if perchance they grew tired of the limitations of the practice of virtue in the approximations of a temporal order, they still kept fast hold of man's ability to find in speculation enduring satisfaction as he exercised his mortal glory and found himself anticipating divinity. Plato seems to justify Platonism by transcending humanity in his description of the utmost which man may experience, but Aristotle extends rather than transcends the human. Dominant as is the theme of societal control in both Plato and Aristotle it is interesting and illuminating to find them seeking a supplement to the normal order — a kind of consolation, yet a thoroughly different one from the joys of the senses, the equilibrium of the passions, or the glories of salvation in the company of the saints and martyrs.

These consolations were the chief preoccupations of those who followed Aristotle and lived in the decline of the ancient world and the early centuries of the barbarian chaos and its gradual ordering. The Epicureans, the Stoics, the Neoplatonists, and the Christian philosophers had also an interest in control, but in a control which was purely subordinate. They sought a control that would assure them the enjoyment of the consolation which alone seemed to them the compensation for existence.

With the dawn of a reviving appreciation of nature and the natural man, a change came over the character of philosophy. Two currents are still visible: consolation does not cease to be an interest, but for many it is subordinated or even lost in the absorption of philosophers in the search for a method which would give man control over his own thinking and assure him of certainty or else, or in addition, give him control over nature and his own destiny.

The early physical philosophers, Descartes and Francis Bacon, the French philosophers of the eighteenth century, Hume, the Utilitarians of the nineteenth century, and the Instrumentalists of the twentieth scarcely seem to warrant a double classification. They are in search of methods of control. It is control of nature, of wealth, of inequality, of poverty, and of ignorance. It is not such control as Plato and Aristotle sought. It is rather control in a society seeking stability and determined on the limitation of human ills. As Bacon would have put it, they are bent upon " the enlarging of the bounds of human empire to the effecting of all things possible."

The consolations of " God, freedom, and immortality " were not without their devotees. Spinoza, when control was becoming a chief interest, had sought consolation and found it in the acceptance of the limits of man and the inclusiveness of God. Kant sought both consolation and control, but in Fichte, Hegel and the right-wing Hegelians and Neohegelians, in Schopenhauer, in Nietzsche, and pretty generally throughout the Romantic movement, the main current has flowed toward some sort of consolation, passive or active, as the ocean to which it made its way.

One wonders if the two interests are destined to continue as two separate themes in philosophy. There seems no reason to doubt it. Man seeks to rule and fails forever of omnipotence. The more keenly men feel this contrast the more likely they are to find themselves turning away into such an interpretation of reality as will bring unity and serenity at last by adding to the immediate scene some vision which is beyond the eye of the body. Perhaps when men temper their longings to the confines of mortality they will find in the endeavor to control that which is within their powers such recompense as will satisfy them. Who knows? Perhaps even God in surveying his handiwork seeks consolation in the thought of a new universe. Who knows?

A PHILOSOPHY OF EXPERIENCE AS A PHILOSOPHY OF ART

Irwin Edman

THEORIES of art and theories of experience have, generally speaking, been remote from each other. A theory of experience has been a theory of knowledge and a theory of art has been a nominally aesthetic footnote to a metaphysical system. This paper is predicated on the assumption that a theory of experience that is actually an account of experience must terminate in and as a theory of art. One may indeed go further. A theory of experience is a theory of art.

For to conceive experience in any pregnant sense is ultimately to conceive a world in which time is genuine, in which present objects or events have meaning, bearing, or significance with reference to a future, in which that future may be controlled and directed by an intelligence which the uncertainties and stabilities of experience both provoke and make possible. A theory of art that is more than a dandified concern with certain aesthetic objects or essences abstracted from the whole context of experience must necessarily be concerned with the technique by which meanings are clarified and organized, with that method by which experience is given order and form. Experience is the name for life in so far as it is meaningful. Art is the name for that intelligence by which meanings are suggested, realized, and embodied. Art and intelligence become identical; they are synonyms for that process by which life becomes articulate and deliberately directed. The recognition that art and intelligence are two names for the same process throws considerable light on what experience is and what is the function of art in the more conventional sense of that term.

There are obviously, as William James and John Dewey have both repeatedly pointed out, various levels of experience. It may be blurred and confused and precarious. It may be clear and stable and precise. It may be merely the brute impingement of meaningless physical data upon a casually and purely physically reacting organism. It may, from a point of view separable by analysis as " subjective," be the unconsidered response of an unrealizing object upon an unmeaning event. A large part even of human experience, all that is merely impulsive and habitual in our behavior, has this character. Taken objectively, with respect to the things, objects, structures, which experience involves, there may be confusion and complexity, an intermingling of processes as yet undeciphered and uncontrolled by intelligence. On this level, consciousness is a blur and existence is a chaos. The function of intelligence is to turn this blur into a clarity, these meaningless sensations into ordered meanings. It is its function, in the complexity and heterogeneity and confounding involvements of the processes of nature, to decipher and distinguish the various natural tendencies at foot and at work. It is its function by selective arrangement and deliberate foresight and direction to marshal them to some fulfillment, to turn them toward some consummation. Intelligence as an art of direction consists in the progressive transformation of a present in the light of some envisaged good which it suggests and supports. This is intelligence in its instrumental and operative aspects or, differently stated, experience as art. Thus art establishes and elicits consummations, fulfilments, forms, and orders which may be enjoyed and appreciated. These enjoyments and appreciations constitute intelligence in its consummatory aspects, experience as appreciative or aesthetic.

Achieved orders, forms, stabilities, may in turn be the instruments of further transformations of experience, as in the case of moral standards, judgments in logic, methods of government, or decisions in law. Or in the case of those forms and consummations which we single out in fine art as consummations, these arresting and consummatory pauses in experience may turn out to be instruments also in widening, deepening, and clarifying further perceptions and enjoyments.

Thus considered, art has a far wider signification than is, in the hands of aestheticians, commonly assigned to it. It has not to do exclusively with the composition of symphonies, the painting of pictures, the chiseling of statues. It is the name for that process of intelligent direction by which the natural tendencies of events, the implicit and unrealized meanings of objects, are furthered and secured. It is that conscious technique by which, out of some uncertainty and crisis, desired goods, first foreseen as ideal possibilities, the self-suggesting hopes of an imperfect present, are achieved and stabilized. It is the technique by which what is problematic, harassing, and confused becomes clear, satisfying, and sustained. Art is the name for that deliberate process by which experience, out of its own fertilities and potentialities, renders itself more perspicuous, more ordered, and more certain.

So much for the changed status of art on the side of creation. On the side of appreciation, art ceases to be simply a passive absorption in a static rapture before certain rarefied objects that are conventionally labeled works of art. It comes to be recognized as implicit in any response to experience that is more than a merely sensuous or merely habitual response, any response that is significant awareness, or awareness of significance. Those consummatory moments of complete, organized, and satisfied awareness can come in love or friendship or more conventionally intellectual contemplations as well as in the presence of those selected objects commonly labeled works of art. Art includes on its active side more than the activities of musicians and painters and poets. On the side of appreciation it includes more than the rapt swoonings of aesthetes, and, indeed, complete appreciation turns out itself to be an active process of intelligence, operative wherever there is significant appreciation of some good that intelligence itself has contrived.

Art thus loses its conventionally aesthetic character. It ceases to be the esoteric byplay of a few gifted or trivial professionals playing with materials, emotions, and subject-matter abstracted from all else in experience. It ceases to be regarded as a virtuoso technique absolutely distinct from and different in kind and in essence from all other types of intelligent activity. What is usually labeled fine art comes to be recognized simply as a subtilized and refined instance of such human activity as is neither the random response of impulse, nor the routine of habit, nor the compulsion of some imposed necessity or authority.

Once all the eulogistically-termed creative arts are seen in the context of the operation of all intelligence, any act of intelligence, even of the most simple and obvious character, is seen to share a claim to the title of creation. All thinking is art. It is the artifice by which present possibilities are discovered, developed, elaborated, and tested in some practical verification. Those elaborate instances of thinking that go by the name of science are merely complicated and involved specimens of that same process of diagnosis, suggestion, deducting, and testing that occur in the simplest cases of human uncertainty, reflection, and decision.

All of industry that is deliberate and controlled practice, all of government that is more than routine or special interest, all of social practices that are more than merely mechanic or the inheritance of habit, are seen to be artistic processes. They are methods for transforming a given present from an unsatisfying confusion and uncertainty to a satisfying and enjoyable stability. They involve creation in precisely the same way that art involves creation. They imply the turning to an examination of available materials, the direction of action in the light of some vision that material suggests, the organization of materials so that they become integrated into some unity, some comprehensive organization, some consummating whole. The statesman, the scientist, and the man of affairs are in their procedure and in their accomplishment no less artists than the creators of conventionally denominated works of art. In so far as their activity is intelligent and not determined by routine or caprice or compulsion they are practicing an art. In so far, on the other hand, as a poet, a painter, or a musician, is a routineer, an academician, or a romantic, explosive and possessed, he is not an artist. The arts of life may degenerate into routines or explosions or regimentations. So may the arts of the poet and the painter and the musician. Government, industry, and law may become crushing stabilities and fixities, cramping rather than releasing life and apprehension and understanding. So may much of what passes for literature and art. Dogmatism in religion, absolutism in government or morals, standardized fixity in industry, have their parallels in formalism and academicism in the fine arts. The failures and successes in both are failures and successes of that disciplined spontaneity and inventiveness which is intelligent procedure.

There are, however, reasons at once plausible and questionable why the fine arts are generally put in a class by themselves. These reasons are questionable morally and socially as well as intellectually, and plausible in all three dimensions as well. In the fine arts the procedure of intelligence, both in its procedure and in the apprehension of what it achieves, is most clear and least impeded. The artist must, like any other deliberate being, use materials and instruments. But within the terms and confines of his own art he is less subject to external compulsions, there are not as many incidental obduracies, as there are in government and industry, to defeat or qualify his intent. The musician can deploy the possibilities of sound, the painter those of line and color, with more complete control, more assuredness of achieving his limited end, than is possible in the grand and complex projects of the statesman or the man of affairs. In the arts intelligence is responsible only to itself. Its discipline is that imposed by the materials and the technique germane to the artist's conception. The end or the achievement is not, as is so often sadly the case in the practical arts of life, divorced from the means. The fine arts are relatively pure areas for the operation of free intelligence. So felicitous indeed may be the operations of intelligence in the fine arts that one is inclined to forget that intelligence is operative there at all and to set down what is due to intelligence operating under auspicious conditions, to some divine possession or inspiration. What is " inspired " in a work of art is exactly what is " inspired " in any other work of intelligence, the unpredictable uprush of suggestions, the spontaneous origination of possibilities which education may liberate and encourage, but which no device or training can insure.

The fine arts again are distinguished from other deliberate and directed activities by the fact that their product, their result, and termination is apparently so completely consummatory, so final and so self-justifying in character. The poem, the painting, the symphony, the statue are there to be immediately perceived and gratuitously enjoyed, apart from the labor that went into their production. Nor need the immediate sensuous apprehension of and absorption in a work of art involve or refer to the intelligence that contrived the organization which is the soul, the pattern which is the essence of a work of art. That form or pattern is intelligence embodied. But it is incarnate as an immediate object of perception. It is perceptually so arresting and so satisfying that its essence is identified with what is immediately perceived and what is there to be perceived is regarded as an end-in-itself. The end of the process of artistic creation is abstracted from the process by which it was created and from any significance or meaning or consequence it may have. It is abstracted into a kind of aesthetic heaven, a still paradise filled with essences, essences whose definition is in terms of what is sensuously perceived, immediately appreciated, and unquestioningly enjoyed. The whole Platonizing tradition that treats works of art as eternal essences is simply the conversion of a thing whose organization is the product of intelligence, into an essence which is simply that organization abstracted from the materials of which it is the organization and from the process of which that organization is the culmination. Art becomes a paradise of perfect forms that were not created by inventive artists in time, but discovered by them inhabiting eternity. It is the metaphysical tribute that romantic critics have paid to the suasion of objects of art and the enjoyments they confer upon the sensitive observer.

In the sphere of the practical arts it is not so easy to discriminate in analysis (though the separation is sadly true in fact) means from ends. An artistic standard discerned and developed becomes an instrument for further practice. A moral standard becomes something to be used, to be tested, and to be applied. A law is something to operate with, a legal decision constitutes a precedent, something to be followed or modified. What is achieved may be enjoyed, but that which is enjoyed clearly constitutes a means to further enjoyment, which, as will be pointed out in the sequel, is true in the fine arts (though it is not superficially apparent). The end product of intelligence in the fine arts becomes an immediate object of enjoyment, as a unified complex of sensations, a harmonious and organized perceptual thrill. The painting is a consummation of an intelligent assemblage of paints and canvas, line, color, brushwork, in the light of some organizing pattern implicit, but only implicit, in the artist's original conception. But that consummation is an immediately felt value, a good become immediately visible and, seemingly, at once immediate and final. The painting is, as it is put in the vernacular, easy to look at. That act of vision is a satisfaction. It is moreover, as romantic aestheticians like to put it, a form that constitutes a peace and an order that constitutes an escape from the uncertainty and the confusion of the diurnal world. But moments of aesthetic contemplation are interruptions of felicity, pauses of salvation.

Now art enjoyed simply as a perceptual thrill, for all the eulogy that is lavished upon aesthetic contemplation, is not so much intelligent appreciation as it is simply a refined form of animal sensation. Music, it has been said, is for many listeners simply a drowsy reverie interrupted by nervous thrills. To the trained listener, however, music is something more than an excitement. Intelligence follows the moving pattern, the vital structure of music. To the lover of painting a picture is more than a vague impressive splotch of color or a random emotional response to what is suggested by the subject-matter. Appreciation is the intelligent apprehension of what is significant and meaningful in a picture or a poem in pictorial and poetical terms, what emotions are relevant to that aesthetic impression, what light or meaning it throws over other experiences including those not popularly regarded as aesthetic. The form or stability which creative intelligence has produced in a painting or a poem or a musical composition becomes in turn an instrument for further apprehension. One may learn from a picture of a tree by Cézanne to look on all trees hereafter with a renewed and clarified vision; just as a poet or a novelist may teach us to look out upon the colors of the world or the people about us with a fresh and emancipated intelligence. Indeed the refreshing quality of art lies not so much in that it offers a realm of abstracted forms to the sterile contemplation of which one may retreat from the confusions and complexities of experience. It is rather that from the lucidity of works of art, and from their intensity and order, one comes back able to decipher with a more clear and affectionate apprehension the world of confusions in which we continue to live. Generations of men turn to the classics, not because they are escapes from life, but because they are eternally renewing verifications and clarifications of it.

While it may seem reasonable and plausible to identify the process of artistic creation with that of intelligence, it may seem, at first blush, more difficult to identify the latter with appreciation. Much of what passes for appreciation is, as has already been pointed out, merely sensuous awareness whose objects are particularly lucid and intense. Much of what passes for more sophisticated appreciation is likewise merely habitual reaction, custom or fashion or pretense. Where appreciation is both rich and genuine, it is a process of understanding what is presented, its formal unity, its emotional bearing, its intellectual significance. It is to traverse a work of art as one does any other complex object, with an intelligent analysis and *redintegration* of what it means in its own terms, plastic, poetic, or pictorial, and in its context. To the trained observer naturally the process of aesthetic contemplation is so telescoped as to seem, indeed sometimes to be, almost instantaneous. There remains, moreover, even in the most expert contemplation of a work of art, always the perceptual thrill of the sensuous medium, and the excitements of those emotional associations half suggested or half embodied. But neither of those facts is sufficient to constitute a valid denial that appreciation, like artistic production, is a process of intelligence. That peace which Schopenhauer long ago insisted came from the fine arts, is indeed a peace. But it is a peace that comes with understanding. For that Essence, that Platonic Idea which Schopenhauer insisted a work of art incarnates, is nothing but the name for that patterned unity which artistic intelligence has established out of its originally inchoate materials. It is that patterned unity which requires a parallel aesthetic intelligence to comprehend and fully to enjoy. The processes of creation and enjoyment in the fine arts may be assimilated to the processes of intelligence in any other activity. By the same token the distinction between merely instrumental and fine or final art, that is, that concerned with final values, must be abolished. The distinction is indeed a social rather than a genuinely logical or even genuinely aesthetic one.

There are, especially in industrial societies, procedures marked by routine or performed solely under the stress of economic compulsion, which are neither intelligent as procedures nor enjoyable in their products. A mechanical routine may be necessary to produce many goods cheaply, and those goods may be standard objects that are necessary to maintain existence, but neither to celebrate nor enhance it. What are called useful arts are often so called because they are not arts at all, but mechanized human activities whose results serve some bare physical necessity. Those who engage in them are slaves to a routine, not masters of an art. What they practise is a march in a treadmill, not a process which has a cumulative significance. In so far as our civilization compels thousands of human beings to spend much of their lives in activities that are void of significance in their doing, void of appreciable beauty in their product, we have achieved only the regimental shadow of a civilized life.

In a civilization where art and industry are divorced, the result is not simply that millions are doomed to a life without either intelligent major activities or the possibilities of appreciable objects or even the capacities for appreciation. The result, furthermore, is that both the creation of art by a few and the appreciation of art by still fewer become thin, exotic, and irrelevant. Our serious activities become sordid and routine, our escapes into art and our appreciations become pallid aestheticisms or romantic flights. It is characteristic that the word " art " has for modern ears a museum flavor. It suggests objects totally divorced from the suggestive experience which initiated them, or the uses to which they were originally put. It connotes trifles made by exquisites rather than the transformation of experience by the subtle contrivings of an intelligence nourished by the experience in which it was bred. On the side of appreciation, connoisseurship connotes the over-exquisite concern of aesthetic dandies fleeing to forms as to a puzzle and to technique as to a game, to an esoteric excitement assumed to be somehow socially refined and morally elevated.

In a society where intelligence was genuinely pervasive, creation and appreciation would be wider in their context and the distinction between fine and useful arts, between instrumental and fixed values, would be broken down. There are, doubtless, granted the permanence of industry and the machine, any number of tasks that are purely mechanical in character, any number of objects produced that are without beauty or significance. There are, doubtless, purely play activities in the fine arts that will always persist, the " play of the virtuoso," the expert diverting himself with his materials. But the measure of a civilization may be said to lie in the degree to which the tasks shared in by the members of that society exhibit the character of intelligence, that is, meaningful procedure, and the extent to which what is produced is meaningful and enjoyable and, in turn, instrumental to further enjoyment.

The arts of life, in so far as they are arts, are both instrumental and final. Their practice at any stage is a good in so far as it liberates the imagination and charges doing with meaning. Their products are works of art in so far as their enjoyment renders experience more free, more various and more interesting, and turns enjoyment from a physical excitement to a meaningful absorption. The fine arts, in turn, are not limited either to play with technique or to materials or to a formalized, prettified, or abstracted subject-matter. What we have come to call " classic " art, the tragedies of Sophocles, the sculpture of Phidias, the poetry of Dante, is classic, not simply in point of felicity of form, but because it is transformed into immediately arresting and appreciable symbols of whole wide areas of experience. It is not only a value as form, but a value as meaning. It is not only a felt good, but the expression of a good. It expresses the whole bearing and texture of characteristic crises and achievements and possibilities in experience. It is life become aware of itself in symbols whose surface is arresting and whose bearing is significant. The difference between a merely salon or decadent art and an art that has vitality and importance lies in the range of meanings which are expressed in those sensuously and imaginatively moving symbols we call works of art. The difference between an art that is merely the delight of the exquisite and one that can engage the attention and interest of an adult intelligence lies in the light or transformation that a work of art throws upon or confers upon further experience. A painter playing with a *pastiche,* a dilettante musing upon significant form, are the symptoms of an art that has lost its vital sources and an appreciation that has lost its way. We do not idly say that Greek art expresses Greek life. It did. Its drama was the long, slow, subtle transformation of ritual. Its sculpture was the long, slow fruit of the study of that human form whose tutored discipline was so much a part of Greek civilization. We do not idly say that Renaissance painting and sculpture and architecture were an expression of the life of the age, or that Chartres or the Church of St. Ouen at Rouen were embodiments of the living experience out of which they grew. They were. The French do well to call their treasured national objects of art *" monuments historiques."* That is what they were. Our own age in its skyscrapers, in its novels following the perplexed consciousness of the modern are all beginning to find their living sources in the life about them. The experimental method, the method of intelligence, has begun transparently to affect our science and our practice. In art we are still copying the formulas of experiences that are not ours, and finding suggestions from a world that is not our own. We build Gothic churches in the midst of an urban and mechanical life; our branch banks pretend to be Greek temples on Broadway. So far as our industry becomes humane and our art authentic, the one will become, in so far as may be, the free expression of intelligence, the other will be the incarnation of what is really moving and suggestive in our lives.

Nor will our fine arts be simply objects to be enjoyed as ultimate goods, which is to say, as temporary flights. Our arts, too, will be measured by a humane criterion. A work of art is enjoyed, not simply as a physical fact, but as a meaning. That is simply to say, in so far as it enriches experience, sharpens vision, widens imagination, and clarifies thought, it will be perpetually refreshing and beautiful. An artist, as Walter Pater (the last one incidentally one would think of in this connection) said, is precisely in the same situation as a scientist inventing a new instrument. He confers a new organ upon the human spirit. It would be senseless to read novels or write them if those romances carried us to a world that did not in some way illuminate and clarify experience. We read Montaigne, not because he is an old essayist, but because his wisdom is perpetually new. We learn to see Dutch landscapes with Ruysdael's eyes, and all spaces and perspectives more deeply from the paintings of Cézanne.

It is shocking to the type of criticism bred upon a romantic notion of the arts to insist that a serious and moving art is an organ of vision, not an ultimate object of it. It gives aesthetic standards a moral tone. That is ultimately what they have and imply. Or, differently stated, those ultimate refinements of taste and judgment which a live connoisseurship implies are a suggestion of what the whole enterprise of intelligence may be, a clarification and organization of experience, a discrimination among possible goods. In a rational society, the free and critical discrimination which marks aesthetic appreciation would be applied to all human concerns. Philosophy itself would be simply the most thoroughgoing discrimination and analysis of values. It would be a criticism whose subject-matter was the whole of experience; it would be a deliberate and considered taste, judgment with consequences, consequences that involved the whole range of human choices and goods. A serious art would be one with significance for all of human interests; a considered criticism would be one that considered, as does a serious philosophy, all human concerns.

DIMENSIONS OF UNIVERSALITY IN RELIGION

Horace L. Friess

THE world has seen many changes in cultus, faith, and morals. And the great diversification in these matters which history witnesses takes place within a still vaster whole of varied and shifting circumstances, including climatic differences, changes in the distribution of peoples, the fertility of crops, the relations of social classes, the state of arts and sciences, together with alternations of war and peace, prosperity and disaster. Yet the faithful in many a cult have affirmed the universal significance of that to which they bear witness. To understand and estimate intelligently these claims to universality, without losing sight of the ramified web of circumstance and its manifold bearing on religion, no less than on other phases of human culture, may well be an endless process. But a beginning may be made by noting that the very complexity and mutability of human circumstances gives point to the desire that things most valued be securely established and widely communicated. And one may continue by exploring some of the different ways and senses in which men have hitherto sought to universalize their religious life, e.g., by associating it with the extension of practical security and dominion, with spiritual enlightenment, inclusive vision and understanding, by contact with sublimity, ceremonial synthesis, and so forth. (Pt. I) The conclusion to which the exploration tends is that man manifests universality in religion, not by possessing the one faith in which all may be led to entire good, but by the character of certain spheres of his interest and activity. (Pt. II)

I

In mediaeval teaching theology figures as the hegemonic science, a keystone in the arch of knowledge. By many of the schoolmen it was regarded also as an architectonic science from which the functions and leading concepts of the other sciences could be derived. But even without making this latter claim, theology enjoyed the distinction of exploring that which was believed to give greatest satisfaction in itself and also to complete the meaning of every other pursuit. Divine truth had the prestige of holiness; it was denied at peril of body and soul; it had autonomous foundations in revelation and inspiration; there was nothing in mundane experience to which it did not, in some sense, apply, and it had a transcendent, eternal reference beyond this experience. It is needless to add that mediaeval social organization corresponded in considerable measure to this way of thinking; far from being merely theoretical, the authority of sacred knowledge was exercised extensively in the law, and in the arts, and even in the market. The chief public monuments of every town proclaimed a theological story. Where religious cultus attains such eminent social status and pervasive influence on culture at large, its claim to possess universal significance involves the function of exercising this influence. In this aspect it may be called a claim to *hegemonic universality,* and perhaps it is one which a religion can modify, but never entirely retract, after once making it.

Theological thinking continues to maintain today that it is dealing with the highest and widest interests, though the actual concerns of thought are scarcely nourished, as in mediaeval days, by its concepts and themes. On the contrary, the number of independent paths is legion by which men pursue their various interests in greater control of nature, more profitable relations with their fellows, and a better management of themselves. And much of theology tends to lean rather heavily upon discoveries in these latter fields, and thus to be invaded by a variety of rival methods. The "rational theology" of the eighteenth century already shows a marked contrast with scholastic theology in this respect. While the latter built very largely upon a special revelation, as its own proper subject-matter, the former tended to reject this and to seek support from the natural sciences, especially at that time from celestial mechanics.[1]

However mediaeval and modern views may differ with respect to the foundations of theology and its relation to culture at large, they have been largely agreed that its aim embraces a kind of *universal vision and comprehension.* Theology, to be sure, has shown less steady interest than her

---

[1] There was already a tendency in this direction in mediaeval Aristotelianism, in Thomas's contention, for instance, that we know God through His creatures rather than by any adequate idea we have of perfection itself. The Platonic schoolmen likewise granted that natural science aided in the recollection of divine truth, but believed a more perfect knowledge could be had of the latter than of the former.

former handmaid, philosophy, in total intellectual orientation, and perhaps less in general intelligibility — though with respect to the latter the honors and the disgraces would seem to be about evenly divided. No less than philosophy, however, probably more strongly, in fact, has theology (with myth and prophecy at her sides [2]) been interested in envisioning the world, and were it not for the challenge and sweep of some of her visions, philosophy would often be left trying to understand the *a, b, c* of things. Today we are perhaps more impressed by the fact that the outlooks for which theology has in the past claimed universality have been found to be in many respects very restricted and erroneous. But the fact that comprehensiveness of vision was claimed need not, on this account, be merely discounted and ignored; it indicates a tendency which might well be carefully cultivated and made to bear all the fruit of which it is capable. When restrictions in a cult's outlook are discovered, the kind of interest which that cult has in mental grasp is put to a test. However dear its original revelations, a cult which genuinely values comprehensive understanding cannot refuse to reconsider them in connection with newly discovered truth. In a society where discoveries of one kind and another are being made along many divergent lines, it follows that the theology of such a cult cannot stand aloof, but must actually cultivate a partial dependence, at least, upon many other branches of knowledge.

When theology thus becomes critical of its original underlying revelations and conscious of its partial dependence upon further knowledge, it will have to reconsider repeatedly the crucial question of what it has to contribute on its own account. What can it still claim to know which other sciences do not know? And with what implications as to its proper rôle? The most obvious answer, of course, is that it claims to know God, but there are other answers that have sometimes been given, which we shall mention in passing. One may say that theology knows how to administer the sacraments of its cult, or that it knows how to make historic experiences of the cult live again. Another answer which we choose to examine at this point is expressed in the very prevalent and important claim that theology knows the spiritual inspiration of the saints and super-

[2] Further analysis at this point suggests a distinction between the more narrative or mythical, the prophetic or imperative, and the more interpretative or strictly theological, elements in religious world-views. The comprehensive narrative span of certain mythologies and the recurrent appropriateness of certain prophetic admonitions have no doubt been as important as any aspects of religious universality we might mention.

eminent men of its cult. Whether this last claim be granted in favor of theology or not, it in any case directs our attention to a mode of universality in which religion has often professed an exceptional interest, namely, *spiritual universality*.

We interpret the spiritual in terms of experiences of supreme intrinsic value, rather than in terms of a non-physical entity. Without claiming to characterize these experiences in the best way possible, we may say that through the having of them men come to know a flawless communion that never disappoints. Such experiences exert a kind of hegemony over us without coercion, simply in virtue of their extraordinary excellence. While they come to most of us but rarely, the record of man would seem to show that they have been and are known in very different contexts, — also that the contexts in which a person may discover them are not altogether limited to those with which he is most familiar. By having these supreme experiences, and perhaps equally by recoil against adverse, divisive, and lacerating experiences, there arises in us the affirmation of a realm in which all conditions of men may communicate to each other a good without blemish. Acquaintance with such a realm and partaking of it is what we mean here by spiritual universality.

Such a spiritual realm has, however, not been merely glimpsed and affirmed; theology has repeatedly claimed to know it fundamentally. It has professed to trace the gleams of perfection, which we have, to their ultimate source, and to say what regions of spiritual life that source has established for us, and on what conditions. We may grant to theology that without some of its teachings on these points the yield of life in spiritual experience would be even more dissipated and submerged than it is; we should lack some of the best aids we have in eliciting choice experiences, and for relating them to each other, so as to attain levels of integration which overlook portions of past and future, and help us to meet what is coming to pass with at least partially concentrated illumination. On the other hand, we find it impossible to concede that theology has ever established its claim to finality of knowledge in the spiritual realm. For taking the world at large, we still perceive too much disagreement over first principles in spiritual matters. The disagreements themselves do not betray theology's weakness in spiritual interpretation so seriously as does the narrowly apologetic attitude of most theologians in the face of them; there has been far too little inclination to explore points at issue with a desire of understanding them. In view of this counsel of patient reflection, we shall not hurriedly press the remaining question of whether theology generally compromises what spiritual insight it has by allowing other interests to thicken its concepts.

The most consistent impulse of theology by and large has not been spiritual; it has been to divine higher powers. While this impulse has often enough run fearfully amuck, and has perhaps never given a thoroughly authentic report of actualities, it has, nevertheless, again and again stirred to some genuine sublimity and has communicated its impress. Theology wishes to emphasize that the sublimity is actual. Hence though it has conceived some of its gods in the light of human ideals, it repudiates the suggestion that they are objects of desire, not yet realized. A divine being must actually possess some surpassing qualities. And where it is held to realize sublimity in every form we have the idea of *divine universality*. Among the various modes of universality in which religion has historically taken an interest this looms up as the primary and paramount one. With rare exceptions in certain instances, the claim which cults make to cultural hegemony, comprehensive understanding, or spiritual enlightenment pales into insignificance alongside of the universality which they claim for their God. It is their relation to his sublimity which most deeply convinces them that they bear witness to something of universal significance.

What moves the majority of men to speak of their several religions as universal is the conviction that only thus do they sufficiently glorify God. But what can be the relation of man to an overarching, inclusive sublimity? Some individuals attain what may be called *mystic universality*, i.e., a sense of being flooded by this sublimity to the exclusion of everything else. In cases where such experience becomes more than incidental, and attains decisive influence over a life-history, it almost always involves unusually severe conflicts and repressions. From these abnormalities of full-fledged mystic experience we need not conclude that mysticism is futile, but the question in how far its essential fruits depend upon an abnormal life cannot well be avoided. For the lives of most men pass with less resistance through a series of half-natural, half-conventional relationships. The divine can attain a large influence in their lives only by being mediated through these more usual human relations. Wherever a religious impulse spreads from the specific center in which it arose through an extensive social milieu, it tends to tie up with an ever greater number of prevailing customs, gradually making connections in some cases with the whole texture of life. This we may designate as a tendency toward *familiar universality* in religion. It is a process entirely indispensable to the attainment of a richly diversified and mellow religious culture, but also one requiring fresh insight and wisdom at every turn if rottenness and disease are not to prevail over mellowness. The sense of discrepancy between human nature and custom, on the one hand, and divinity, on the other, has often resulted in the frightful mutilation of each by the other, rather than in a true sacrament. A flagrant instance is the tendency of religion to feed upon human weakness, which is in a sense so strong, and by looking mistrustfully askance at much of human strength to forego the possibility of qualifying the effect of such weakness as it undoubtedly has.

Something of the familiarization of religion, and in another aspect the conventionalizing of it, may be observed in religious ceremonial and liturgy. Such ceremonial commonly takes shape around familiar facts and situations, being often much engrossed in their details, either actually or imaginatively. At the same time in religious ceremonial there may gather by a kind of collective, super-individual art many converging rays of human continuity, kindredness, peculiar esteem, hope and recollection, common feeling and devotion. So many and such diverse situations have been ceremonialized that a comprehensive list of ritual and liturgical qualities might well-nigh exhaust the ranges of human experience. Worthwhile ceremonial and liturgy generally has as its nucleus a specific purpose, which gives structure and reality, but its synthetic technique makes possible an imaginative expansion of the present over the whole of life. Where this possibility is cultivated we may speak of *ceremonial* or *liturgical universality*. It is interesting to note, in passing, that many Christian theologians have built up their characterizations of God in no small measure upon the imaginative synthesis of all good as found in liturgy. Thus Dionysius the Areopagite, whose book on " Divine Names " exerted great influence upon mediaeval theology, speaks continually of the theologians as celebrants and says: " You will find all their sacred Hymnology, so to speak, arranging the Names of God with a view to make known and praise the beneficent progressions of the Godhead." Again, he speaks of being raised up to the subject of discussion by prayer. A somewhat

similar case of God being known ritually appears to us in the Mohammedan saying: " Verily there are ninety-nine names of God, and whoever
recites them shall enter into Paradise." No small claims have been made
for ritual and liturgy.

But while the theologian in his study may often base his reflections
upon liturgy, the god of whom he undertakes to discourse is likely to be
manifested more actively in other quarters. Ceremonial is, on the whole,
better adapted to conserve and communicate something of the divine than
to give it at first hand. The most celebrated epiphanies are reported to
have occurred, not in temples and services, but in stables and fields, wars
and wanderings, loves and hates. Man's most intense and crucial religious
experiences, whether of triumph or of chastening, have as a background
his exertion of force in some vital interest. Cultus is strongly founded
only where it participates in, or has at least significant continuity with,
such exertions. In testing its practical significance we may, therefore, ask
how it is related to man's efforts to attain security, dominion, healing,
fellowship, love, adventure, and peace. Where cultus is so related to
these human needs that it can be credited with achieving what Moham-
medans sometimes say is the end of religion, namely, making men
" whole," we may ascribe to it a *practical universality*. The doctrine that
" all's right with the world " would seem to be an overdraught on this
sense of being " whole," but it could scarcely gain credit as far as it does
except for some actual experience of perfected well-being.

II

The foregoing paragraphs have distinguished some different phases of
the interest in universality as exhibited by historical religion. They have
not explored the range of any particular religion, but have considered
some categories in terms of which such exploration might be conducted.
Without claiming completeness for our analysis, we suggest that the
above and cognate spheres of interest may be taken to indicate some essential dimensions of the domain of religious universality. Now the pursuit of universality in religion has been widely associated with claims of
particular cults to finality, and sometimes, on the other hand, with the
idea that a universal religion is implicit in a faith common to all cults.
We wish in the following paragraphs to criticize both of these prevalent
conceptions, considering them in relation to present circumstances of

human culture and to the domain of religious universality as we have defined it.

The most virulent of these two conceptions associates universality in religion with the all-sufficiency of a particular cult to prevail and satisfy the entire world. In so far as men have been moved to make such claims for their several religions by the desire to magnify God sufficiently (cf. p. 137), we think it pertinent to emphasize a distinction between divine sufficiency and cultic adequacy. One need not deny that a movement contains something of universal interest and value, nor even that it bears a witness to entire sublimity, in order to reject its claim to be all-sufficient. Under present circumstances of interconnected, yet differentiated human culture the claim of a cult or movement to be all-sufficient, even in a certain sphere of life, whether spiritual, political, or moral, must indicate serious blindness, whatever richness or profundity or purity is there to lend it color. In times of change and distraction there is certainly a place for stabilizing emphasis upon whatever is fundamental in the old. But where the adequacy of established cultus is itself taken as a fundamental, change appears to be prejudged, and its specific effects for good or bad are often lost sight of in the desire to preserve a *status quo* unanalyzed with respect to its bearing upon individuals in new circumstances. Furthermore, besides indicating a disposition unfavorable to the analysis of specific and changing needs, the profession of all-sufficiency on the part of a cult generally betokens an inability to see values independently of cultic associations in an undistorted, innocent fashion. This incapacity in a world bursting with various goods, that cannot possibly be cultivated under one roof and that require man's interested understanding for their consummation, often proves nothing short of tragic. Scripture says: "Give not that which is holy unto the dogs, neither cast your pearls before swine, lest haply they trample them under their feet, and turn and rend you." Now religious history tells us of a species of sacred swine and dogs, consecrated to special gods and goddesses. And we may surmise that were these consecrated animals like human beings, they would probably be exceptionally heedless tramplers and vicious renders, for man when devoted to a particular holiness often excels in being ruthless of divinity in any other form.

The rationalists of the seventeenth and eighteenth centuries were much occupied with this problem of religious intolerance, and put forward a conception of universal religion that was designed to meet it. They had a program of integrating and expurgating religious faith and of redirecting it toward ends of public interest; they regarded it possible and highly desirable for all theists to place subordinate emphasis upon their various special revelations, in order to stress a common devotion to the God of the spacious and orderly firmament who approves a morality of humane citizenship and rewards it in future life. In the eighteenth century a "rational theology" of this type had a footing on ground common to the major religions, Judaism, Christianity, and Islam, which Europeans then took into account; the rationalizing of natural knowledge was in a stage where it seemed possible to trace a simple continuity between the order of nature and the order of God; and finally, the rise of new social classes and political relationships gave a certain commanding and partially unifying interest to questions of civic morality. But all these circumstances have undergone extensive change. We cannot view the different religious groups of which we know today as offshoots of one large theological tree; we see them as giving expression in the religious realm to motives, only in part the same, and conditioned in a thousand ways by the particular circumstances, both inward and outward, under which they function. In this perspective religious conflicts seem to us to arise only secondarily from theological disagreements irrelevant to other interests, and more basically because religious systems may come to enforce manifold tendencies and arrangements that are experienced as threatening and obstructing other interests. And again in the contemporary perspective, if greater unity of interest and effort is wanted in religion, it will have to come basically, we judge, from tendencies and influences creating such unity, rather than by mere selective emphasis on some already existing common factors in the different faiths.[3]

Nevertheless, if we take an inclusive view of mental attitudes in the world today, and do not confine our attention to those of a favored few, we cannot but recognize the continuing pertinence of certain deeper aims which the eighteenth-century thinkers sought to attain through their

[3] Despite the great diversity of religious groups known to us today, it is, of course, possible to frame highly general formulas characterizing salient features possessed by them all; modern "philosophies of religion" abound in such characterizations. They may have value in the universe of discourse or even in that of understanding, but this is a very different matter from serving as an effective symbol and vehicle of common religious interests.

"rational theology." In attacking intolerance and superstition they had the intelligence and prowess to choose undying foes of the very first magnitude. These two, in fact, might well be called forms of *satanic universality* in religion, and a philosopher cannot make peace with them without discredit. However, the question remains in how far the strategy of early modern rationalism in attacking these evils recommends itself to us as wise and adequate. More was accomplished in establishing religious toleration as a political policy than in critically clarifying and cultivating tolerance as a human attitude. The idea of tolerance is still very commonly confused with agreement, while in practice it too often means merely an easy-going attitude in respect to whatever is easy-going toward us. As a virtue, however, we conceive tolerance to lie between generosity as a maximum and fairness as a minimum, and obviously it is a virtue that can only be exercised where disagreements exist. The minimum of this virtue, as we conceive it, is not to overstep even in conflict the bounds of fair treatment.

In its campaign against superstition early modern rationalism enunciated the basic principle that God is honored when nature is understood and appreciated as a source of human benefit. This remains as solid a piece of wisdom as ever, and we personally can agree with the rationalists in wishing that it be taught as a cardinal maxim of civic religion everywhere. The need of passing beyond the confines of their thought, however, becomes apparent as soon as one reflects upon the conditions of making such teaching effective and meaningful. In relying on a supposedly universal "natural" knowledge of God, and in assuming that nature produces human good by a simple mechanism, the rationalists were not minded to sift carefully the historic deposit of culture so as to save genuine inventions and discriminations from the discard of superstition. Just as the first large scale experiments with physical mechanism not only exploited to advantage, but also mutilated large portions of nature, both human and otherwise, so the blunt credo of rationalism did pathetic violence to much of value in religious life. The idea that the most valuable element in any cult is something it has in common with all the rest, pertinent though it was at that time to the problem of mitigating religious controversy, has conspired with other influences to dissipate appreciation of unique values in the differentiated fabric built up through many generations, and has perhaps also been a contributing, if not a fundamental, factor in diluting religious imagination.

The conservative reaction, which began in the early nineteenth century, against " rational religion " thus had its justifying grounds; its exponents were right in thinking that religion had more to give than theistic motives for civic virtue. But in their loyalty to cultic heritage many were moved to reject even the sound principles of criticism which rationalism had provided; they leaned once more on authority, and relied largely on speculation to disinfect the superstitions embedded in the traditions which they cherished. Now speculation may have the virtue of viewing experience from new angles and levels, but it does not in itself supply adequate motives for doing so, nor can it guarantee the relevance of what is thus seen to impinging facts and circumstances. Nineteenth-century metaphysical and theological speculation was in many respects imaginative and profound, but being guided largely by historic loves, it tended to be insufficiently curious and analytic of the great changes taking place in the present. One cannot deny to the nineteenth century a certain inclusive regard: even the defenders of traditionalism in religion did in a measure look out upon the novel relations in business and industry, and clung to the church for relief. They likewise pushed out with scholars and traders to make increased contact with foreign cultures, and in reflecting on alien elements in the religions of these, they at least sought to put their own claims to superiority in a perspective which comprehended variety and change, and undertook an avowed comparison of essentials. Favorite ideas were those of a comprehensive evolution resulting in the production of a highest form, and also the microcosmic idea that while the whole is infinite, a part may serve adequately to reveal the whole. Undoubtedly these ideas contain valuable leads, but it is their weakness to encourage a universality which rests on highly general connections and unstable analogies between part and part, rather than on exact, specific analysis. Thinking in this fashion the nineteenth century could produce such diverse movements as nationalism, socialism, and the Catholic revival, each claiming to be the all in all. On the conviction that absolute being must be in any case, the speculative method was used to argue its full realization in existing cases; change and diversity could be recognized as taking place, and even as a basic feature of things, without disturbing confidence in the adequacy of existing institutions and movements to convey all fundamental values.

Whatever is to have religious value must, of course, convey some sense of adequacy, in fact of super-adequacy. The only question is in what terms this adequacy is to be recognized. If we are not inclined to make such general and comprehensive claims for particular religious cults as did the traditionalists of the nineteenth century, nor to seek religious adequacy as did the eighteenth-century rationalists in a faith which all cults supposedly have in common, are we then reduced to private religious satisfactions and interpretations unrelated to universalizing influences in religion? We cannot answer the question, nor judge whether this would be a welcome or unwelcome consequence, before we know what it means. But the question is clarified for us by the analysis made in the earlier paragraphs of this essay (§1), where we sought to delineate some phases of universality as actually pursued in various historic religions. We were there able to distinguish some of the different ways and senses in which men have hitherto sought to universalize their religious life, e.g., by associating it with the extension of practical security and dominion, with spiritual enlightenment, comprehensive vision, by contact with sublimity, ceremonial synthesis, and so forth. Each of these aspects of religious universality was briefly characterized. We are not prepared to say that by developing the characterization of these various spheres along the lines indicated a final measure of universal significance in religion could be reached. It seems beyond human sense to determine the full range of religious function which a particular item, whether book, prayer, office, person, or sacred relationship, may have in the course of the universe. On the other hand, it is possible for analysis, such as we have suggested, to keep making a net-work of pertinent questions in terms of which the range and character of a thing's religious significance may be more and more comprehensively explored in various directions. A critical answering of the questions raised would no doubt involve many categorical judgments (whereas some orthodoxies have tended to reduce their unconditional requirements to a single maxim of obedience), but it would not assume knowledge of the best possible religion at the outset, nor seek to arrive at it from a consensus of opinion among mankind. Nor would it be obliged, by rejecting such assumptions and methods, to depend on personal intuitions undisciplined by objective considerations.[4]

[4] A simple comparison may help to clarify the general nature of the method which we have sought to use in treating of universality in religion. In order to know and to estimate human characters, it is not necessary to have known all persons or to assume that one has known the best and worst possible of persons, but it is essential to have

In characterizing religious universality through certain spheres of interest discriminated from within historic religion, we neither ignore the levels of excellence attained in past cults, nor make unanalyzed claims for their adequacy. Furthermore, we locate universality in a domain within which it is possible to work for greater agreement and devotion to common essentials, but from which we do not exclude unique values of specific cults by insisting that the common factors are the only ones of general interest. And finally, instead of trying to fix cults and movements as they are within a comprehensive scheme of things, justifying them in toto as last stages of evolution, or letting the light of the Absolute diffuse itself softly over them through the veils of highly general speculative categories, we may interrogate them as to their specific achievements under present circumstances within spheres widely acknowledged to have religious interest. And since present circumstances provide many highly novel conditions of living and thinking, we shall expect to see in present and in future, as well as in bygone periods of history, consummations within the spheres of religious universality, but outside the practice of our traditional cults, and even independent of any recognizable cultus whatever. This expectation, however, does not mean that the importance of cults is denied in some sweeping fashion, but, on the contrary, that their contributions and functions may be estimated in a more specific and differentiated way than heretofore. In questioning whether a particular cult could exhaust any of the spheres of interest which we discriminated from within historic religion, we have not identified religious universality with abstract qualities discovered by analysis and then affirmed to be independent of the contexts in which they are found. Our effort was to characterize rather complex domains in such a way that whatever particular cults or individuals achieved within them might be at once more widely and more specifically appreciated for such religious universality as it actually manifested.

Without embarking extensively upon so many-sided a subject as the functions of religious cults, we shall briefly make one observation related to our main theme. Religion commonly seeks to commit men thoroughly, so that whereas we have analyzed its interest in universality into various

---

known different characters, and helpful to reflect on the implications of their differences. Through such reflection one may gradually fasten on certain dimensions of human life which serve in estimating approximately the spheres and ranges of various characters.

dimensions, we rarely, if ever, find a cult seeking values of one dimension alone, whether practical, intellectual, ceremonial, mystic, or spiritual. The very suggestion reveals its own absurdity. Cults develop historically, not by the planned pursuit of continuous and distinct interests, but through the more or less co-ordinated efforts of certain men in a series of specific situations. Reflection of this obvious fact should warn us against allowing our consideration of universality in religion to terminate in futile abstractions. After all, perhaps the most truly universal feature of religion is that in every case it is a religion of human beings, and traverses its spheres of interest, whatever they are, only under the auspices afforded by human lot.

This consideration leads to a final retrospect upon what has been said, in which we remind ourselves that the efforts of men to universalize their religious life in various ways are compounded of their weaknesses and strengths. What has been written might be misread as implying that the universalizing tendencies in religion are always sheer gain. On the contrary, it is quite evident that in them man magnifies and propagates his vices and limitations as well as his powers and virtues. Nothing illustrates this quite so largely and dramatically as the familiar sight of religion having to qualify, if not indeed to reverse, its own teachings. With one voice religion says: Be ye fruitful and multiply and possess the earth, and in a second it is obliged to add: Come ye out from the evil world and I will heal up your wounds. In one form or other this double rôle of participating in and yet of overcoming the world is grounded in the essentially mixed conditions of life. We neither overlook nor seek to escape the difficulty, but rather to meet it wisely in specific cases. If we have seemed to idealize religion's interest in universality, forgetting its evil aspects and consequences, it is because we should not wish religion to avert its face from the larger spectacle of life, however mixed, and become only a worship of private fetishes in each man's closet. On the other hand, if we have refused to say: Lo, here is the completion of universal religion, it is just because we are mindful of the many shifting contrasts presented by the larger spectacle of the world, and have a certain respect for their generative influence. At least we are hopeful of seeing in the future, as well as in the past, some traces of a large wisdom displayed in the way that new, specific circumstances are met. It would be disappointing indeed if the magnificent revelation of a larger and more

complex world to modern knowledge meant nothing more for religion
than the dissipation of traditional syntheses and the despair of wider
community in a common faith. Or if it were to lead us into a new religious provincialism, complacent and sophisticated, that did not care to
face the larger scene, but took its satisfaction in deliberately gnawing the
bones of a familiar cupboard, then we should almost prefer the old illusion
of cultic all-sufficiency with its seeing in the glass darkly, or even the
misleading dream vision of cultic unification on some simple basis, which
has been dreamed repeatedly despite rude awakenings.

But in place of these forlorn alternatives we have tried to suggest
another way of conceiving religious universality, a way founded on the
recognition of past achievements in this domain, and yet clearly requiring
significant relation to the contemporary world for its further pursuit. By
defining religious universality through certain dimensions of historic religious activity, in which we take a continuing interest, we are prepared
to see both old and new achievements having such dimensions embodied
in the texture of future religious life. In conclusion, we may add that
nothing in our view precludes the possibility of future religious syntheses
comparable to and even exceeding those of the past in their richness and
scope. However, as to the source of such future syntheses, our viewpoint
implies that, if they come to pass, they will result more as the cumulative
product of distinct achievements within various spheres of religious interest than from any single, direct drive toward some all-embracing, hidden
unity. It also indicates some of the ways wherein the religious life of man
may attain universal range without the existence of such syntheses. For
not by possessing the one faith in which all may be led to entire good, but
by the character of the spheres of his interest and activity does man manifest the universality of his religion.

A CRITICISM OF TWO OF KANT'S CRITERIA
OF THE AESTHETIC

KATE GORDON

IN the *Critique of Judgment,* where Kant proposes to distinguish aesthetic pleasure from pleasure in general, he offers several criteria. Among these are "disinterestedness" and "universality." These he regards as holding good of aesthetic feeling, or the pleasantness of beauty, but as being inapplicable to the pleasantness of mere sensation. It is the aim of this paper to show that neither of these distinctions is valid. My argument is that, as regards aesthetic pleasure and sense pleasure, disinterestedness is characteristic of both, and universality is characteristic of neither.

The following passages from the *Critique of Judgment* are concerned with disinterestedness. The translation is that of J. H. Bernard. The German is given at the end of the article.

Book I, sec. 2. "The satisfaction which determines the judgment of taste is disinterested. The satisfaction which we combine with the representation of the existence of an object is called interest. . . . Now when the question is if a thing is beautiful, we do not want to know whether anything depends or can depend on the existence of the thing either for myself or for anyone else, but how we judge it by mere observation (intuition or reflection)." Sec. 3. "The satisfaction in the Pleasant is bound up with interest. . . . Now that a judgment about an object, by which I describe it as pleasant, expresses an interest in it, is plain from the fact that by sensation it excites a desire for objects of that kind. . . ."

These two passages show the difference which Kant seeks to establish between the aesthetic and the merely pleasant. Before discussing them, I wish to add the following line in which a similarity between the two is noted. Sec. 4. "In the case of the pleasant . . . the word always signifies something which pleases immediately. (The same is applicable to what I call beautiful.)"

To resume, then, thus far, for Kant aesthetic feeling is pleasurable, immediate, and disinterested (i.e., nothing depends upon its existence, by which I suppose he means nothing beyond the enjoyment of the experience itself); whereas sense pleasure is pleasurable, immediate, and interested, interested because desire for objects of that kind is excited.

What is the nature of the interest alleged to be present in sense pleasure and not present in aesthetic pleasure? "Interest" may mean merely that pleasure is felt in the presence of the object or in the sensations which the object arouses. If this is Kant's meaning, then, of course, and by definition, sense pleasure is interested pleasure. But in such case, the pleasure felt in the presence of the aesthetic object or as a consequence of the sensations which it arouses is also an interested pleasure. On the other hand "interested" may mean that something else which we desire depends upon the pleasant object. In this case we would find pleasure in it *because* of that something, that is, for some reason or ground. Kant says that sense pleasure excites in us the desire for objects of that kind. Does he mean that when we enjoy the blue color of an object we are wishing for other blue objects, or that the enjoyment of our dinner must include the hope of other dinners? If so I think his introspection is at fault. For myself I can imagine no more immediate and disinterested pleasure than the enjoyment of a simple sensation. I enjoy the fragrance of a flower, and I can enjoy it for no reason in the world. Circumstances are conceivable in which I might enjoy it for reasons. Thus, if I am trying to identify a name, and this odor brings it back by association, I am pleased. Or if I am stocking a shop with perfumes and this suggests a new specimen, I am pleased. Or if I am searching for something to decorate a dinner table and think that this flower will please my guests, again I am pleased. All these would be examples of an interested pleasure in the sensation. But there are surely many times when no such circumstances are present, and when we enjoy a fragrance quite simply for what it is.

Kant is right to insist that the enjoyment of beauty is not a calculation, and that it is not founded upon the desire to promote purposes. I think it worth while to ask at this point whether we have any test by which we may know a disinterested enjoyment, any test, that is, beyond what is already given in saying that we do not consciously like the object for a reason. I think such a test is this: If we ask ourselves whether an exact substitute is possible for the object of our contemplation, the answer will reveal whether the object is looked upon in an interested or a disinterested way. Those things which are valued for a use will give way without causing regret to some different thing provided it forwards that use equally well. A certain advertising slogan says "There is no substitute for music," and we may truly add that there is no substitute for anything which we love for itself. That which we enjoy in its unique character gives us disinterested enjoyment.

On the second point Kant writes as follows: Sec. 7. "As regards the Pleasant every one is content that his judgment, which he bases upon private feeling . . . should be limited merely to his own person. . . . The case is quite different with the beautiful. It would (on the contrary) be laughable if a man who imagined anything to his own taste, thought to justify himself by saying: 'This object (the house we see, the coat that person wears, the concert we hear, the poem submitted to our judgment) is beautiful *for me.*'" Kant then goes on to say that the judgment of taste is not merely empirical, not a judgment of what generally pleases, but is universal, and makes a rightful claim to every man's assent.

It is this distinction between the merely general, and the universal or necessary, to which I take exception. My argument is that unless the judgment of beauty can be shown to be *more nearly* universal in fact than is the judgment of sense pleasure, it cannot claim to be more universal in principle. Do men, then, actually agree better upon a judgment of beauty, than they agree upon a judgment of sense pleasure? This question can be submitted to experimental trial, if fair samples of the two judgments can be agreed upon.

Three tables of judgments are offered below which seem to me to have a bearing on this question. All of this material was gathered for other purposes than the comparisons noted in this paper.

Ten pictures of women's faces were clipped from the pages of *Vanity Fair*. Some of the pictures were of famous actresses and others were of women famous for literary achievements. The selection was made by the writer with the purpose of securing as wide a range between the beautiful and the ugly as possible. (Obviously these pictures cannot be reproduced here.) It is not likely that they represent the greatest possible difference in the world, but only the greatest that I could find in the magazine. The pictures were pasted on a gray ground, and distinguished by number. Two hundred persons each judged the ten pictures for beauty, and wrote down an order of merit for the ten. Table 1 gives the distribution of these judgments. Thus face number One was given first position by 57 judges, second position by 43 judges, third position

TABLE 1

DISTRIBUTION OF JUDGMENTS OF BEAUTY ON PICTURES OF WOMEN'S FACES

Position in Series

FACE No.	1	2	3	4	5	6	7	8	9	10
One . . .	57	43	34	29	13	12	6	2	2	2
Two . . .	41	29	33	24	22	13	9	15	11	3
Three . . .	16	20	30	40	29	31	13	14	6	1
Four . . .	21	24	32	15	29	21	23	11	12	12
Five . . .	24	27	19	17	20	17	14	24	17	21
Six . . .	18	17	18	20	26	24	16	21	19	21
Seven . . .	10	21	11	25	15	26	34	33	16	9
Eight . . .	9	11	11	11	23	22	40	20	31	22
Nine . . .	3	5	6	12	12	18	28	36	34	46
Ten . . .	1	4	5	7	11	16	17	24	52	63

by 34 judges, etc. . . . down to tenth or lowest position by 2 judges. Face number Ten, which averaged lowest, was given first place by 1 judge, second place by 4 judges, etc., to tenth place by 63 judges, this being the highest number of coincident placements which occurs in this table. Now, although every face in the series is judged by some one to belong to every position in the scale, yet this table reveals a very considerable agreement among the judges. The average order of merit reached by the first one hundred judges was compared with the average order reached by the second one hundred judges, and the correlation found to be plus .99, all but an identity of the two series.

The second set of judgments was made on ten geometrical figures, and is summarized in Table 2. The figures used were rectangles cut from gray cardboard and mounted in a row on a white ground. The areas of the rectangles were equal, each containing 100 square contimeters. Their proportions varied and were as follows:

1/1, 6/5, 5/4, 4/3, 29/20, 3/2, 34/21, 23/13, 2/1, 5/2.

These were the ratios used by Fechner [1] in his study of the golden section. The seventh figure in the series, i.e., the ratio 34/21, is the closest approxi-

[1] *Vorschule der Aesthetik.*

mation to the golden section, that is, the relation in which the smaller member is to the larger as the larger is to the sum. Two hundred persons judged these rectangles and listed them in an order of merit for beauty of proportion. Table 2 shows the distribution of these judgments. The

TABLE 2

DISTRIBUTION OF JUDGMENTS OF BEAUTY ON TEN RECTANGLES

Position in Series

RECTANGLE	1	2	3	4	5	6	7	8	9	10
VII . . .	49	27	52	24	13	16	9	6	4	0
VIII . . .	34	46	30	30	14	13	12	12	4	5
VI	29	38	31	23	40	16	13	4	5	1
V	21	31	18	46	29	32	15	5	1	2
IX	34	25	17	19	31	11	14	22	23	4
IV	14	3	14	22	26	36	50	20	11	4
X	11	19	12	19	12	20	10	15	40	42
III	4	6	11	5	19	33	48	51	18	5
II	2	2	8	6	12	13	23	53	60	21
I	4	2	6	6	4	10	6	12	34	116

golden section ranks highest, though it was given first place by 49 judges, second place by 27 and third place by 52. The figure which ranks lowest is the ratio 1/1, that is, the square. This was put last by 116 persons, which is the highest frequency of any placement in the table. As in the case of the women's faces there appears to be a rather wide scatter in the judgments on most of these figures, and yet here too, when groups of judges are compared, the uniformity is marked. The average order of merit for the first one hundred judges and the average order for the second one hundred are correlated by plus .98.

In order to compare these results with some that were found in the field of agreeable and disagreeable sensations Table 3 is given. This represents the distribution of judgments on a series of odors.[2] The odors used were: lemon, cinnamon, peppermint, bergamot, lavender, eucalyptus, tansy, creosote, valerian and asafoetida. These, in liquid form were presented in small bottles, and were arranged in order of pleasantness by each of 200 persons. Table 3 shows that lemon was given first place by

[2] Used in my study " Recollection of Pleasant and of Unpleasant Odors." *Journal Exp. Psy.*, 1925.

TABLE 3

DISTRIBUTION OF PREFERENCES FOR ODORS

Position in Series

ODOR	1	2	3	4	5	6	7	8	9	10
Lemon	84	51	36	12	9	8	0	0	0	0
Cinnamon	47	48	45	30	19	8	1	0	1	1
Peppermint	23	41	47	41	29	13	5	1	0	0
Bergamot	20	28	36	37	44	21	6	7	1	0
Lavender	23	21	21	32	32	32	17	18	4	0
Eucalyptus	3	5	9	24	33	47	51	17	9	2
Tansy	0	3	3	14	19	43	55	47	12	4
Creosote	0	2	2	10	6	15	32	66	47	20
Valerian	0	1	1	0	8	10	30	30	86	34
Asafoetida	0	0	0	0	1	3	3	14	40	139

84 persons, second place by 51 persons, etc., and that it was at no time put lower than sixth place. At the other end of the scale asafoetida, which never ranked higher than fifth place, was put last by 139 persons.

It would be possible to figure standard deviations for each of the items judged in each of these three tables, but it would add nothing to the argument. Inspection shows that the agreeableness of the odors is judged with greater uniformity than is the beauty of the rectangles, or of the women's faces.

The most serious difficulty in making this comparison is, I think, the fact that there is no absolute measure of the range of agreeableness, nor of the range of beauty used in these series. There is no doubt that if, in the series of faces, we could include the most beautiful possible and the ugliest possible, we would find a greater agreement among the judges than is found in Table 1.

In the case of the rectangles we do have a close approximation to the best possible and the worst possible rectangles, but we have no measure of the range of feeling elicited by best and worst in the matter of rectangles. And it may well be that the range of choice is no fair sample of possible aesthetic ranges.

The same criticisms, however, apply also to the judgments on sense pleasure. The difference between lemon and asafoetida may not be the greatest possible difference in agreeableness within the world of odors.

And if we could get the very best and the very worst, then no doubt we would find a still closer agreement among judges than is given in Table 3. Again, if we take into account the whole realm of sensation, and compare the greatest sense pleasure there is with the most exquisite pain, can we doubt that the judgments of mankind would be remarkably uniform? I think it fair to say that the preference of such pleasure to such pain is an all but universal human choice.

I am not arguing that aesthetic judgments are essentially variable: I hold, on the contrary, that they are surprisingly uniform, but I know of no evidence which shows them to be more uniform or necessary than are judgments of sense pleasure.

If, then, aesthetic pleasure is to be distinguished from sense pleasure, the difference must be sought in other characteristics than disinterestedness and universality.

————

First Book, sec. 2. *Kritik der Urheilskraft*. "Das Wohlgefallen, welches das Geschmacksurtheil bestimmt, ist ohne alles Interesse. Interesse wird das Wohlgefallen genannt, das wir mit der Vorstellung der Existenz eines Gegenstandes verbinden. . . . Nun will man aber, wenn die Frage ist, ob etwas schön sey, nicht wissen, ob uns, oder irgend Jemandem, an der Existenz der Sache irgend etwas gelegen sey, oder auch nur gelegen seyn könne, sondern wie wir sie in der blossen Betrachtung (Anschauung oder Reflexion) beurtheilen."

Sec. 3. "Das Wohlgefallen am Angenehmen ist mit Interesse verbunden. Dass nun mein Urtheil über einen Gegenstand, dadurch ich ihn für angenehm erkläre, ein Interesse an demselben ausdrücke, ist daraus schon klar, dass es durch Empfindung eine Begierde nach dergleichen Gegenständen rege macht. . . ."

Sec. 4. ". . . Beim Angenehmen hierüber gar nicht die Frage seyn kann, indem das Wort jederzeit etwas bedeutet, was unmittelbar gefällt. (Eben so ist es auch mit dem, was ich schön nenne, bewandt.) "

Sec. 7. "In Ansehung des Angenehmen bescheidet sich ein Jeder, dass sein Urtheil, welches er auf ein Privatgefühl gründet . . . sich auch blos auf seine Person einschränke, . . . Mit dem Schönen ist es ganz anders bewandt. Es wäre (gerade umgekehrt) lächerlich, wenn Jemand, der sich auf einen Geschmack etwas einbildete (das Gebäude, was wir sehen, das Kleid, das Jener tragt, das Concert, das wir hören, das Gedicht, welches zur Beurtheilung aufgestellt ist) ist *für mich* schön."

A PRAGMATIC CRITIQUE OF THE
HISTORICO–GENETIC METHOD

SIDNEY HOOK

Der Spruch der Vergangenheit ist immer ein Orakelspruch; nur als Baumeister der Zukunft, als Wissende der Gegenwart werdet ihr ihn verstehen.

NIETZSCHE

ALTHOUGH the nineteenth century has been regarded as *the* historical century, it was only towards its close that the historical method itself was subjected to critical examination. Its claim to revolutionize the methodology of the social sciences was revealed to be enormously over-exaggerated, and it gradually became clear that a detailed account of a thing's development could not serve as a substitute for an analysis of its nature. Not that knowledge of a thing's development did not contribute to our understanding of its nature, but rather that such knowledge of the past served at best as a suggestive aid to the *experimental* determination in the present of what the thing really was.[1] Today, however, the historical or genetic method still retains its dominance only in one field, viz., the study of history, under which term we also include anthropology and archaeology. But its strongest roots will be found in popular consciousness, in the curricula of our educational systems, in the verbal by-play, at least, of our courts and legislatures. For example, no notion is more widespread than that knowledge of the past is the key to the present. " How did it *get* that way? " is a question considered by many to be the preliminary indispensable to understanding the state a thing actually is in. Reflection will show that the reverse is true, that knowledge of the present

---

[1] The attack upon the pretensions of the historical method has come from philosophers of the most divergent tendencies, e.g., Bradley, F. H., *The Presuppositions of Critical History*, 1874; Sidgewick, *Mind*, 1886, and *Philosophy — Its Scope and Relations*; Woodbridge, *The Purpose of History*, 1915; Cohen, M. R., " History versus Value," *Journal of Philosophy*, 1914; Dewey, *Journal of Philosophy*, 1915, p. 337 ff.; articles by Dewey and Cohen in *Methods of the Social Sciences*, 1928. For a discussion of a teleological as opposed to a mechanistic historical approach, besides the writings of Windelband and Rickert, see Max Weber's *Gesammelte Aufsätze zur Wissenschaftslehre*, esp. p. 70 ff., p. 135 ff., p. 215 ff.

is the key to the understanding of the past. Or to select a more specific illustration, no amount of knowledge of the mind of primitive man will add one jot to our knowledge of the mind of man today; on the other hand, the more we discover about mental processes going on today — in the illiterate adult, the infantile, the superstitious — the more insight we can win into the intellectual life of the primitive.

The criticism of the historico-genetic method is here undertaken in the light of another method, designated under various names, but which we shall call " pragmatic " or " experimental," since the categories with which it operates — end or purpose or need — exhibit the fundamental qualities of all intelligible explanation as such, contemporaneity, invariance, and relevance.

I

There is no common agreement as to a definition of the historical method. But in its narrow sense, as used by professional historians, it has some definite characteristics. It starts out from the idea that all objects of historical analysis have had a *development* and that this development can be rendered significant, or understood, by tracing the spatio-temporal continuity of its structure — whether it be of an institution, or folk-legend, or tool — as far back as possible. The concept of development is here central and it has been claimed that only those historical methods are scientific which make use of it.[2] And the implication which has generally been drawn from the use of this concept is that every phase of every developing object is just as valuable and irreplaceable, just as indispensable to *what* is developing, as any other. Back of the genetic method, then, is the notion that the series of phases in the history of any object constitute a whole, and that any one of these phases derives whatever meaning it has only in reference to this whole. In conjunction with the use of the comparative method, it has been recommended as the most adequate manner of understanding, " the inner essence of law, morality, language, religion, art, economic, and political life." [3] It is the solitary methodological prop of those who interpret cultural phenomena as survivals. The task then becomes to discover from what remote event and in what direction the institution or practice in question has survived. It confronts

[2] Bernheim, *Lehrbuch der historischen Methode,* 5th ed., 1908, p. 14.
[3] Heinrich Maier, *Das geschichtliche Erkennen,* 1914, p. 14.

us in the unconscious procedure of those who, finding current practices unendurable, e.g., the teaching of dead languages in secondary schools or ceremonial observances in religion, etc., attempt to show that the fact that the practice or institution has had a continuous history is the only reason, or the chief one, that it exists in the form it does. In the theory of cultural diffusion as prevalent in anthropology, we find the logical pendant of the genetic method. Here, too, a cultural fact is "explained" when it is shown when and from where it has been derived or borrowed.

Those who have employed this method have often defended it as eminently scientific on the ground that no appeal is made to factors standing outside of the mechanical causal connection of antecedent and consequent. We shall see that they have thereby mistaken the nature of historical explanation and interpreted a factor which is necessary to a complete explanation into one which is sufficient in itself.

A — Logical Difficulties.

Those who believe that the presentation of a series of spatio-temporal continuities can serve as a solution to an inquiry into the nature of any given institution or event, are guilty of a special form of the fallacy of *ignoratio elenchi*. We ask "why" and are answered as if we had asked "wherefrom" or "what." Suppose we start out to make a study of the system of monogamous marriage. We make extensive researches into its history and lay bare the succession or evolution of similar institutional forms down to the very present. How much illumination does our knowledge of its historical genealogy throw upon its nature? How much of it can we say we understand? Not very much, for this very fact of continuity and development itself calls for an explanation, an explanation which must be given in terms (or categories) other than succession in space and time. In addition, the notion that the present characters of the system of matrimony, or any other "social constellation of forces," can be explained by reducing it to a previous system, overlooks the fact that no matter how far back we go, we must somewhere begin with characters which are not so derivable.[4] Granting, then, that every institution or historical situation has had a development, the most exhaustive knowledge of its development cannot of itself lead to an understanding of (1) why this institution ever originated, (2) why it persisted,

---

[4] Cf. Weber, *loc. cit.*, pp. 173–5; Woodbridge, *op. cit.*, Chap. II.

and (3) why it developed in the direction it did. Although there may not be *absolutely* new beginnings, the fact that novelties arise cannot be disputed nor understood by the genetic method. And although mechanical or social inertia may be *offered* as an explanation for the persistence of institutions, it cannot be accepted as adequate, since if it really were an active force everything which ever came into being would survive, would be retained in some cultural form or other, which is patently not the case.

The fundamental point is that at best historical continuity is a *condition* of survival and not a cause. Historians who have made so much of the genetic method with its emphasis on spatial and temporal succession have done so under the mistaken notion that scientific history is history written in terms of the fundamental categories of the natural sciences. They have converted the necessary conditions of historical existence into real explanations. But an *historical* event, as we shall see, must be understood in categories which are specifically applicable to the activity of men in pursuit of human ends. These ends are different from the ends which natural science takes note of in that they have a definite *efficacy*. Historical activity is understood when reference is introduced to more or less invariant psychological patterns of response — types of motives, desires, and purposes — which take a specific form and expression under the objective compulsions of the environment — character of the soil, method of production, tradition, etc. This is not sinking history into psychology, for the specific expression of interests at a definite moment cannot be derived from any psycho-physical investigation. It is rather making a social science of psychology, since these responses are directed towards certain cultural value invariants — family, state, law, vocation — which confer meaning upon the complex of human activities. But it is always man's *contemporary* social life which gives him the schedule of interests and purposes he applies to the past. And when there is a question as to the plausibility of any historical explanation, *experimental* confirmation in analogous situations plays the determining rôle. Risking a metaphor we may say that an adequate historical method cannot stop with a paleontology of historical forms, but must reveal the physiology of the historical act.

Certain paradoxical consequences seem to follow. How can what is *uniquely* past or historical be understood if the historical act is contemporary and the historical motive invariant? How can we understand out of our own experience, say the activity of an Indian monk or a mediaeval scholar? [5] These and similar questions will be discussed in section II.

Where the genetic method is recommended as the best way to discover a thing's meaning, logical consistency requires that it be used in conjunction with a *theodicy* or some form of externally imposed teleology. Since antecedent continuities extend in all directions, intelligent *selection* can only be made when it is guided by a cosmic plan or super-empirical purpose progressively realized in the serial order of the things selected. Just as the common practice of tracing one's ancestry does not consist in an investigation along all possible lines, but is directed towards some member along *one* of those lines distinguished for some reason or other, so in tracing the history of any institution or object. It is a focus of intersection of many lines which diverge the more the further we go back into the past. The direction we follow, however, is determined by a goal known already in advance. St. Augustine and Hegel are illustrations of this. Even in those whose bias is not so strongly theological wherever we find very sure opinions about the beginnings of things, we can trace it to an unformulated certainty about their ends. Such histories are really apologies and are already finished before they begin in time. The historical construction is undertaken to set the stage for the final act, known by revelation in advance.

The same conclusion follows from another angle. Since the historico-genetic method relies upon cultural inertia and mechanical development to explain the perpetuation of practices and institutions, human purposes, even when their presence is acknowledged, are deprived of active initiating power. They must be so deprived otherwise we would take these human purposes and needs as our causal starting point and not the facts of continuity. But if human purposes are discounted then we have a disguised theodicy which takes one of two forms. Either man is regarded as completely passive and univocally determined by certain processes working themselves out in time towards a preordained goal; or a distinction is introduced between man's apparent will of which he is conscious, and a pre-established harmony of his real will of which he is unconscious. Whatever occurs of significance in the eyes of the person writing the

---

[5] Cf. Eulenberg "Sind historische Gesetze moglich?" in *Erinnerungsgabe für Max Weber*, Vol. I, p. 51, also Simmel, *Das Problem der historischen Zeit*, 1916, p. 5.

theodicy, is an expression of man's real will. Man's temporal destiny is to serve as an illustration of the play of eternal essences.

We shall make a brief aside here to point out the motivation of most of the historically oriented schools of thought in the nineteenth century. In Schelling and the romantic school, in Hegel, in Savigny, we find as a *leit-motif* of their thought, intense opposition to the unhistorical rationalism of the French revolution.[6] The norms of rationalist criticism were either alleged eternal ethical principles or idealizations of present interests. Hence, once the history of institutions is regarded as an *immanent* development, once the evolution of states is interpreted as a preordained unfolding of an inner Spirit or Idea, then with one stroke the ground is removed from every kind of revolutionary criticism. Since only the whole process has meaning, the real significance of any part escapes the radical intelligence which conceives or misconceives things by taking them in abstraction. Projected reform, the creature of the abstract understanding, turns out to be a disturbing intrusion upon the logic of world history.

B — Psychological Difficulties.

It is a philosophical commonplace that knowledge of the order of succession cannot be forthwith identified with knowledge of the order of connection. But the assumption that the knowledge of the successive details in the growth and development of any practice or occurrence is the best way to understand it, expresses just this confusion. Now the fact that the genetic method does make this contribution to our knowledge of succession is important enough. What it gives us, however, is chronicle but not history. Of itself it offers not the slightest insight into historical significance or connection, for otherwise we could not explain the fact that the chronicle of a great many events, established by the genetic method, has remained unchanged while our understanding of the chronicle has varied from time to time. Why do we re-write the history of the past so often even when no new " facts " have been discovered? What are the sources of our new insight into past events and personalities? If we had a complete motion picture of the trial and death of Socrates would we once and for all time understand these events?

[6] Erdmann, *Schmoller's Jahrbuch*, Vol. 30, p. 1. I am indebted to Prof. V. G. Simkhovitch for calling my attention to the importance of Hegel's attitude towards the French revolution as a clue to the development of Hegel's thought, as well as to an interest in the general theme treated here.

Those who believe that historico-genetic inquiries can serve as rational historical explanations are committed to the proposition that the less known, or not so well known, the distant past, can serve as an explanation of the better known, the present. Psychologically, just the opposite is true. The present is the basis from which we determine the kind of interpretation we must apply to the past. It is the source of all our guesses and hypotheses; and it is present uses, purposes, and habits which determine our recognition of the past fact as such. That is to say, even the best of evidence, so-called "material" evidence, is constituted by present interest and activity. We shall illustrate this point at length.

The strongest and most valuable kind of evidence in archaeology is *material* evidence, i.e., the sticks and stones, the very stuff of the past. It is not marked by the bias of the written word or the personal witness. If we allow for the ravaging effects of the natural elements, it still carries the living breath of its creators to other times and other men. It is direct testimony. But how do we come to recognize that something is material evidence, how do we determine its significance? Sometimes an old written record directs our attention to certain objects and we reconstruct its meaning in the light of what we read — a dangerous procedure to be sure. But even in the absence of written accounts we still herald our material discoveries as meaningful, as revealing important cultural activities of the past. On the basis of what? Only on the basis of an assumed identical use which persists in similar forms down to the present. We stumble upon pillars of stone and proclaim we have discovered a *temple of worship,* we unearth an earth-crusted rock and call it a flint fist *hatchet.* The stuff of the past is understood, i.e., becomes meaningful, in the light of contemporary social practices; and the continuity of those practices is established by working backwards from the present, not forwards from the past. What would material at hand be evidence of, if we could find no plausible individual use or social function for it to have served? What would it be *relevant* to, what problem could it decide? Of course we might say that an object which had no conceivable use was a toy, something done in idle fancy, an expression of primitive art. But note what we thereby do. We transfer *our* modern notion of the aesthetic as something which serves no intelligible practical use to the life of man in the past. In using this specific category as an organizing form in anthropology and archaeology, we have again, standing in the present, unconsciously and yet of necessity assumed the invariance of a definite human reaction pattern in the past. It is clear that it is utterly absurd for anyone to maintain that certain sciences have established the fact that the fundamental nature of man has changed from primitive times to the present. Even if it had, the fact could never be known, for no *translation* of the intent of primal human activities could be effected without assuming the presence of certain parameters of meaning, without assimilating the nature of primitive man to our own. True, all explanation presupposes a continuity of some sort, but not the spatio-temporal continuity of the genetic method.

This sounds like a dangerous argument. One might generalize and say that by the same logic it followed that anyone who recognized a person as insane must himself be insane. This is, of course, confusing the external criteria of classification with the psychic state these criteria are a sign of. But what is sound here is just this. If insane people had no lucid intervals and were altogether unable to indicate the meaning complexes which controlled their behavior, and if sane people did not at moments feel the incipient urge of the same sort of meaning complexes, of course, in different contexts, we could never write a psychology of insanity. We might write a description of abnormal meaning behavior other than our own. We could say in what way the behavior was *peculiar,* not in what way it was *confused*. And just as our knowledge of a person's peculiarities first raises the question in our mind, " Is he confused or is there a method in his madness? " so in the analogous case the archaeologist never contents himself with an *inventory* of the material evidence, but is compelled to take it as a sign of some cultural activity. In other words, he must understand it in terms of its meaning.

The kind of continuity which is important in any historical explanation is not the development of similar institutional forms, not parallelisms of structure, not the diffusion of a cultural fact, but rather the exhibition of certain invariant mental and emotional traits directed towards certain cultural *values* which make the acts of human beings intelligible to one another. A visitor from a distant star descending upon the earth might know the chronicle of events down to the slightest detail, might on his way down, since nothing is lost in the ether, discover how everything came to be what it is, but unless his mind-set were similar to ours, unless he had experienced directly or vicariously the chief forms of human interest, he would never understand that history.

C — *Methodological Difficulties.*

The historico-genetic method tends to minimize origins and beginnings, since it confessedly cannot explain them in terms of spatio-temporal continuity. But as we have seen, in delving into the past the geneticist is embarrassed by the fact that nothing can with certainty be claimed as the complete origin of anything else, that his own method impels him to seek for a still earlier stage of the phenomenon in question. That is to say, two historians using the same method rarely arrive at the same results. There is nothing to determine the line or direction in which to go back and where to stop in that line.

Granting, however, that the genetic method results in a single-valued, unambiguous solution, it must forego attempting to explain *specific* occurrences in the series of antecedents it has uncovered. Once questions are asked about any particular member in the series, it is compelled to assign to *accident* a disproportionately major rôle. And where accident is not introduced as an explanatory category, the cultural psychological method is surreptitiously called into play. At some point the genetic method surrenders to another. For example, to trace the form of the American constitution back to earlier constitutional documents is not to explain why that particular kind of constitution was adopted and no other. In fact, no matter what kind of constitution had been adopted, it would always have been possible to trace its historical continuities and relationships back to earlier forms. But the genetic method of itself can never show why *this* constitutional form and not another had been selected, and why at *this* time rather than at another. Explaining everything which might occur in terms of its kinship with other things, it explains nothing which actually did occur in terms of a specific situation. Once we have discovered by the use of a pragmatic socio-psychological method why the American constitution was adopted in 1789, the genetic method might then be able to tell us something about the antecedents of the constitution. In any case, information about formal antecedents is irrelevant when we are seeking to understand how the American constitution arose from the political and social constellation of forces during the Critical period.

Accident, it is true, plays no insignificant part in history. No event can be completely explained without reference to it. But we must look for it in the factors which happen to be present in any situation and not in the manner in which these factors operate. In any historical situation, the historian is justified in taking the invention of a new tool, climatic and telluric conditions, foreign contacts, etc., as accidental. These things may be rationally explained, of course, but not by the historian. What occurs, however, as a result of human activity conditioned by these factors cannot be regarded as accidental by the historian, at least not until he has tried to understand the occurrence by bringing it under the rubric of interests and purposes which enable him to understand the acts of his fellow men in the present.

The theory of cultural diffusion regarded as the mechanism by means of which historical facts are disseminated and survive, is logically in the same boat as the doctrine of historical continuity. Originally it did yeoman service against the idea of *necessary* parallel independent development, but, fascinated by the technique of tracing cultural borrowing, it has resulted in throwing the facts of independent cultural activity into the shadow. Simply stated, rarely, if ever, can diffusion offer a relevant explanation, since it overlooks the process of *active, differential selection*. Its psychological postulate, as Malinowski says, is that man is nothing but an imitative monkey. It assumes that cultural diffusion takes place merely by spatio-temporal contact, that borrowing is a type of social osmosis. But even the most convinced diffusionist will not maintain that culture complexes as a *whole* spread. Only *single* or associated elements of a culture complex (family relationships rarely, aspects of agriculture, art, religion, more often) are adopted. But which elements? Why these elements and not others? Unless we can answer questions of this sort we cannot be said to have understood the process of borrowing. If the mere fact of contact explains why any one element is taken over, then it should explain the acceptance of all other elements, which is never the case. The following illustration will make the point clearer.

When Japan came into contact with western civilization in the nineteenth century, it eagerly adopted certain features of western industrial technique and certain political forms. In all textbooks on history, some form of the principle of diffusion has been offered as an explanation. But can this principle explain why Japan was sensitive to *these* influences and neutral to western art, western religion, and pure science? What we demand in order to make this diffusion intelligible is something which will account for the *selective activity* which followed *upon* contact. What else can explain this selective activity save the needs and interests, the purposes and desires, reflecting contemporary conditions in Japan? Spatial juxtapositions like temporal continuities can only serve as the occasion for borrowing. They may be necessary; in themselves, they are never sufficient. In the present case, it has been conclusively demonstrated that the breakdown of the whole feudal system as a result of the growth of a money economy in Japan, gave rise to certain pressing needs and interests which account not only for the establishment of a semi-constitutional government and the acquisition of the general features of western economic technique, but for the very adoption of the " open door " policy itself.[7] Due to the pressure of economic forces liberated by a change from rice to coin as a medium of exchange, it is quite likely that Japan would have followed in the footsteps of its western neighbors of *itself*. Contact with the latter accelerated tendencies already implicit. For the genetic method it is a mystery why the consequences of the introduction of a money economy in Japan should run *independently parallel* to the developments which took place in Europe when a similar change was effected, e.g., the rise of commercial towns, jurisdictional disputes between the guilds, price-fixing, etc.

In so far as the diffusionists restrict themselves to tracing the spread of a single mechanical element, e.g., a wheel, a button, a match, they are on safe ground. But when the conclusions are generalized to account for the change and growth of institutions we are on a different level entirely. Certain simple tools and practices have a universal relevance only in their instrumental status in a larger cultural whole. Since they are not organically connected with this cultural whole — i.e., do not share its significance, they can be taken over when and where they appear. A savage will not scruple to use the white man's match to destroy the white man's life. His cultural purposes are not changed by the adoption of the match. With institutions expressing the central activities of man, things stand differently. These are not acquired and discarded as readily as a new kind of war-paint or bow and arrow. Here changes take place only with new valuations conditioned in the main by material development.

Where the presence of similarities in institutional forms becomes a

---

[7] See Miss Takizawa's study, *The Penetration of Money Economy in Japan and its Effects upon Social and Political Institutions*, New York, 1927.

problem, the first resort must be to the common needs arising from a similar conditioning environment. This together with Goldenweiser's " principle of limited possibilities " [8] will more plausibly explain the facts of institutional similarity than reference to contact and transference. It is truer, by far, to explain the presence of irrigation in early New Mexico, Egypt, and India as resulting from similar conditions of soil, sources of available water supply, etc., than to fall back upon the " tendency of practices to spread." Can the diffusionist explain without going beyond his own method why irrigation arose in these places and not in Central Europe or New England? No matter how much evidence he unearths to show that the idea was really disseminated by travellers or tradition, ultimately he must introduce *local* determining conditions to explain the lines of direction which the diffusion of irrigation took, the modifications it received, and its final disappearance or survival.

But surely, it will be explained, there are certain unreflective conventional practices which can only be adequately explained by the genetic method. In what other way can we understand practices like tipping one's hat and the wearing of trinkets which do not even serve purposes of adornment, say, like marriage rings, except as inheritances from the past which have persisted by the principle of social inertia? The genetic method claims to reveal where these practices came from and how they were handed down. What is it we understand, however, when we know this? At most why the western woman wears her marriage ring on her finger while her sister in some parts of India wears it on her nose, but hardly why they wear marriage rings at all. The very significance of the practice escapes us when it is approached this way. Tipping one's hat may have arisen from the mediaeval practice of removing one's helmet in the presence of one's friends. This explains perhaps why, when we meet one another, we do not solemnly spit in greeting as do the members of the Masai, a primitive East African tribe. What is of importance in understanding this practice is that the polite white man among the Masai adopts the mannerism and also solemnly spits in greeting. The *greeting* is of importance and not the derivation of the specific form it takes. Neither accident nor inertia can explain the persistence of that greeting. If it is an accident that we use an archaic form of greeting is it also an accident that we no longer eat the dead? Could the inertia of a custom

[8] *Journal of American Folk-Lore,* 1913, Vol. 26.

of itself withstand the attacks made upon it (and what custom has not been attacked), were it not for the presence of some simultaneously operating cause of a cultural psychological nature which sustains it? When the existence of any so-called vestigial social trait is made a problem, more light is thrown upon it by social-psychological analysis than by presenting its problematic historical derivation.

II.

Emphasis on the pragmatic or experimental method in history is not a defence of " pragmatic history " in the traditional sense of the phrase. Pragmatic history of the past was history written to serve a definite purpose or to teach a lesson by indirection. This is a perfectly legitimate thing to do, although it has its dangers, the chief of which is the tendency of the historian to forget that the history can only *illustrate* what he *means,* but can never *prove* the desirability of what he *wants.* From a methodological standpoint pragmatic history enjoys a bad name among historians on the ground that (1) it is too subjective and tendencious, (2) that it underestimates the forces of tradition, general culture, and physical factors, and (3) that it deprives the historian of the possibility of explaining acts by motives and interests other than those exemplified by individuals around him.[9]

The pragmatic or experimental method in history, in the sense in which it is used here, is not interested in teaching anything, but in *understanding* what has happened, no matter what the consequences of that understanding may be. It does not stress the motive of the individual historian — although he always has one — but makes the purposes and needs of the historical subject, be it the individual or community, its central explanatory category. Nor does it see in the cultural values towards which man's purposes are directed a reflection of an ontological scale of ethical norms in the manner of Windelband and Rickert. The first of these objections we need not therefore consider. The other two apply to every kind of teleological approach in history and must be discussed in conjunction with the question, What determines the superiority of one method to another in historical study?

In evaluating the relative superiority of one method to another in

[9] Bernheim, *Lehrbuch der historischen Methode,* 5th ed., pp. 29–30.

history, the only criteria we have to guide us are consistency, comprehensiveness, and relevance or historical plausibility. We have seen that the use of the genetic method, like all investigation into antecedents, gives multiple valued disjunctions mutually inconsistent with one another instead of clear unambiguous results. This has been interpreted as due to the failure of the historian rather than the weakness of his method. But granting that the genetic method *can* give consistent results, the fact that it raises more questions than it answers about the problems it purports to solve, indicates that at some point it must give way to a more inclusive method, that its true function in historical understanding is preparatory and ancillary. This other method we have called the pragmatic method. And were space to permit it could easily be shown that most genetic accounts owe whatever effectiveness they have to the *unconscious* use of the pragmatic method. The first method discovers the material, the second seeks to make it intelligible. The latter therefore is more comprehensive in scope. Not only more comprehensive but more adequate, since of the three possible ways of approaching the study of human activity it does not select categories taken from the level of mechanical cause and effect, or stimulus and response, but of means and end (instrument and purpose). An explanation in terms of mechanical cause and effect is relevant only to a consideration of man as a *body in motion;* in terms of stimulus and response to man as a *biological organism;* the means-end relation alone can apply to man as a *political and social creature* who makes his own history under the limiting conditions of tradition and the forces of production.

The pragmatic method is not a mere attitude towards historical phenomena assumed on personal subjective grounds. It has the same claim to objective validity in its sphere as the methods of the physical sciences in theirs. It is the only historical method conscious of its procedure, conscious of the inevitability of reference to the interests which constitute the empirical norms of historical behavior. That the historian selects certain specific interests of man to guide him in the labyrinth of the past does not vitiate the conclusiveness of his findings so long as he does not pretend that these are man's sole interests and that his account is the whole story. The selection of the interests in terms of which the history is to be told has an objective status, for no historical subject-matter can be handled without some sort of selection. No one impugns the objectivity of a photograph because it has been snapped from a certain point of view. And selection is the point of view from which we see the historical picture. Nor does the fact that partisanship determines the point of view from which we write a history militate against the objectivity of the historical findings.[10] In other words, although the specific selections are not imposed upon us by the subject-matter, the logical structure of organization of the selected subject-matter is not created by the selection. We return to the objections.

To charge the pragmatic method with underestimating the force of tradition, physical factors, and other conditions under which the activity of the historical individual takes place is to forget that it is only by a consideration of their bearing upon human interests that the *strength* of these factors can be determined. Whatever influence race, soil, tradition, forces of production may have, it is one mediated by a reacting organism with a certain schedule of wants and aspirations. Even though the specific forms these wants take may themselves be determined by the factors mentioned, it is the wants — physical and spiritual — with which we must begin and in those terms understand the individual event. But we do not have to stop there. We may want to understand a *series* of historical events, not the individual event. In other words we may want to discover laws in history and write a science of history.

Now history may be scientific, although it does not eventuate in scientific laws. The singular and unique event may be an object of scientific treatment, although we cannot call the results reached a science. To deny this is to forget that necessity (causality) is not identical with regularity. Whether or not there can be a science of history only empirical investigation can show. At any rate the understanding of the historical event, although not altogether uninfluenced by a science of history, is just as essentially independent of it as the understanding of individual characters in a novel of real life is independent of the fact whether or not there is such a thing as the science of human behavior. But the point is that whoever wants to write a science of history, must establish the presence of a definite correlation between the purposes which enable us to understand the historical act and the environment in which those purposes arose. Having discovered what wants are constant in history he must

[10] "Gesinnungslosigkeit und wissenschaftliche Objectivität haben keinerlei innere Verwandschaft," Max Weber, *Wissenschaftslehre*, p. 157.

correlate the changes in their expression with some independent variable. For example, if it can be shown that there is a positive correlation between the productivity of the soil and the different types of socio-political institutions adopted at different times, we may regard this as an historical law and the beginning of a science of history. That does not in the least mean that those types are thereby understood. Knowing what causes their development I no more know what they are, than knowing the bodily changes which condition the development of affection in a human being, I know what that affection is. We understand an institution, a personality, and emotion by relating them to a purpose which defines some *value* or *meaning whole;* we explain them in terms of the structure of value-neutral determinants.

The second objection to the pragmatic method we have already formulated in connection with the emphasis upon the contemporaneity of historical evidence. If we understand the past in terms of the present, how can we understand a past which is *other* than the present? If in our hypothetical analysis of an historic situation we extend present interests and activities, how can we make real to ourselves the life of an Indian monk or an early Christian? At the outset it must be admitted that the approach to the past through the human interests which it expresses is still general. And the individual event as such cannot be completely represented by *any* method which is general. But this does not wipe out the difference, however, between a general method which is teleological and one which is genetic or mechanical. For example, we may approach a man's acts by considering the purpose behind it or its mechanical efficient causes. Both methods are general. But if we want to understand the act, the first is superior to the second because it is more relevant to the direction and significance of our own activities. Now the irreducible uniqueness of an historical situation is not something to be understood, but rather to be felt — to be psychically experienced in a non-cognitive manner. This imaginative projection is not immediate, but takes place *after* we have analyzed a situation in its relevant terms. It cannot be plained, but only indicated as what yields to the various general approaches. Just as the description of a singular object must eventuate in its exhibition, so the analysis of an historical act or personality must be preparatory to an intuitive grasp or imaginative synthesis. The exhibition in one case and the imagination in the other are of the most significance when they follow upon the processes of reflective inquiry. They are, then, subjected to some sort of control. They are the vision which blossoms from understanding.

The presupposition of the imaginative reconstruction of the past is a teleological analysis of the historical situation. But the elements with which the imagination works are given by the present experience of the historian. To know what the life of an early Christian at the time of the Roman terror was like, he must know not only the conditions of life at the time, but what it means to live in the light of a cause, to seek salvation, to suffer in resigned poverty. These things must be known either by personal experience or by the sympathetic understanding of the activities of groups of men who can still be observed. Renan, in order to make it easier for his contemporaries to catch the spirit of the early Christian community, pointed to the sections of the International Workingmen's Association in Paris as its closest embodiment. We feel by analogy as we think by analogy, but behind the extrapolation is the assumption of some kind of identity. Consciousness of this gives rise to the concept of *type* in history as an essential aid in historical exposition. We organize our material with type concepts of the state, industry, man — concepts which may be modified but never derived from genetic research. It is only by imaginatively fusing these type concepts into a concrete picture that we come nearest to reliving the fulness and uniqueness of the past event. The universal confession that it is through the historical *novel* rather than the historical treatise that we sense the life of an age is illustrative of the point. And who uses the genetic method in a novel? True, " one does not have to be Caesar in order to understand him," but one has to have an imagination.

The admission that the uniqueness of an historical event will only yield itself to the imaginative mind may seem to be opening the door to arbitrary subjectivity. Our imaginations do not function alike. The colors and shadows of the picture are sure to be different. It is undeniable that an element of subjectivity must be granted, but it is not arbitrary, for it is limited in two ways. First, by the preliminary objective investigation of leading purposes and conditioning factors in the situation studied. Second, by following the clues suggested by the imaginative synthesis in order to fill out the picture. We check up what we thereby find with the qualitative logic of what we see and feel. Once we use the pragmatic method, the subjectivity or indetermination enters into the process of imagining the past and not in understanding it. As a compensation for not being able to relive the past, we may console ourselves with the thought that in respect to its wider connections we probably understand it better than it did itself.[11] Knowledge of the past varies with the present, insight into the past, with personality.

III

So far we have tried to show that historical understanding is interpretation of events in the light of human purposes expressed in cultural values which are contemporary and invariant. We wish to point out that any study of the past must in analogous fashion, determined by its own concepts of relevance, operate with categories which are themselves experimental and not historical. Facts of the past are not only the subject matter of history but of such sciences as geology, astronomy, biology, linguistics, etc. We wish to close with brief illustrations of the argument in these fields also.

The age of the earth is a special problem in geology. It is an attempt to determine a unique past event which no one ever experienced and which seems to be beyond the scope of verifiability. There are seven independent ways of measuring the life of the earth which, although giving varying results, enable us to fix a probable minimum value of one and one-third billions of years. Two of these methods, of unequal weight, are the methods of radioactivity and denudation.[12] Knowing the rate of disintegration of uranium, we can compute the age of any rock once we have ascertained the quantities of uranium and lead, its emanation product, contained in it. Similarly, assuming that the rate of transport of salt to the sea has remained constant (which it has not) and knowing the total mass of sodium in the sea as well as the average annual deposit, the probable age of the ocean can be computed. What is essential in these methods, as well as in all others employed in historical geology and cosmogony, is the *experimental determination of a natural process which can be directly verified in the present.* In the case in question, they are

11 See Spranger, *Lebensformen,* 2nd ed., Halle, 1921, p. 366. Also *Psychologie des Jugendalters,* Leipzig, 1924, p. 5.

12 See Jeffrey's, *The Earth, its Origin, History and Development,* Cambridge, 1924, p. 61 ff., for a detailed account of these methods.

the laws of radioactive disintegration and the rate of denudation. The other methods involve certain laws of elasticity, heat-conduction, fluid-friction, gravitation, etc., all of which have been established in the laboratory. And what is further necessary is the assumption — as a necessary heuristic principle — that the present laws have remained *invariant* over the whole interval of time in which they are applied.

How is this last assumption to be reconciled with the idea of the evolution of natural laws themselves? Very few are inclined to believe that the natural laws observed today have been constant for all time. The problem is too complicated to be treated here, but this much at any rate is clear. If natural laws are interpreted as essentially statistical, then it is quite probable that the laws we know have had a history. But what this history is can only be discovered by making the same assumptions about a certain rate of statistical variation observed in the present, as we did about the specific laws themselves before the idea that they had a history struck us. Again certain general laws and principles must be regarded as invariant. If, however, scientific laws are regarded as non-temporal natural necessities, then no intelligible question can be raised about their mutability.[13]

In astronomy the choice between the nebular hypothesis, planetesimal hypothesis, and the tidal theory as explanations of the origin of the solar system is determined in the last resort by present observation of the life of history of other stars in the heavens and the application of the conclusions so derived to the sun. In biology, the exact mechanism of organic evolution is still to be established through laboratory experimentation. In linguistics, if the theories as to the social origin of speech or of the manner in which shiftings and blendings have taken place are not purely hypotheses after the fact, they must be checked up by inquiries into linguistic processes of the present.

Only what is regarded as valid evidence in the present can be regarded as having evidential value for the past.

[13] See the interesting study of Max Hartmann, *Sind Naturgesetze Unveränderlich,* Halle, 1926, p. 71 ff., which tries to solve this problem on purely formalistic lines and the much more meaty chapter on "L'Évolution des Lois" in Poincaré's *Dernières Pensées,* 1913, esp. p. 28. Cf. also Nernst "Zum Gültigkeitsbereich der Naturgesetze" in *Die Wissenschaften,* X, 1922, esp. p. 491 ff.

CERTAIN CONFLICTING TENDENCIES WITHIN THE PRESENT-DAY STUDY OF EDUCATION

William H. Kilpatrick

The aim of this paper is to review certain more or less conflicting tendencies of thought observable in the study and practice of education in this country today. In the judgment of the writer advance at certain points is being impeded by failure at co-operation through failure at understanding and agreement, and these in turn appear to be caused, at least in part, by failure to see and appraise the differences at issue. The purpose here is to direct attention to these differences in the hope that further study may bring the issues more surely and prominently into the open where they may receive the attention which they seem to merit.

Leadership in the study of education in this country is largely in the hands of university departments of education. As interesting as it might be to linger over the history and bearing of this fact, we need now only point out that this development of the university study of education is largely both contemporaneous and domestic. We are then not obliged to go far afield in order to find the facts pertinent to our inquiry. Leadership implies a following and exactly this relationship is to be found in the close connection between the university study of education and the actual practice in both administration and teaching in our schools. Herein American practice stands in striking contrast with the typical European. There governmental decree stands in relative independence of immediate public or professional opinion as the source of school procedure, whether administrative or teaching. Here public opinion precedes and determines governmental action, and this public opinion is largely molded by school officers and teachers who are themselves through post-graduate and summer-school work in recent first-hand contact with the university departments of education. As nowhere else on earth the university teaching of education in this country functions as a direct and continuing influence in the actual practice of public education. The university is thus the crux of the problem faced in this paper.

Three distinguishable lines of development in the university study of education principally concern us. First in point of age is the general study of the educative process and the part it should play in promoting the general life process. This oldest line can be traced back in continuous development to Pestalozzi and beyond. To distinguish it from the other two lines we may conveniently call it the *theoretical* interest. Second is the study of concrete administrative experience in its various lines so as to make practical suggestions for improvement. With the variety in American practice arising from our many more or less independent city and state school systems, with the continual necessity for rebuilding and enlargement due to rapid growth of city populations, with the frequent necessity to protect the schools from spoils politicians, there has arisen — partly through the ease of communication in a flexible society — insistent conscious demand that each new venture profit by experience elsewhere. Out of this demand and opportunity — so it would appear — there has arisen the study of the theory and practice of school management and administration, a very distinct and notable achievement of American university study. This line of development we may by distinction call the *practical* interest. More notable still is the third line of development. This is the conscious effort to apply the methods and standards of " exact science " to the study of education. From this has come such characteristic scientific methods as careful observation and experiment, control group procedure, separation of variables, and the application of statistical method. The first problems attacked in this manner were those of the learning process and of the " transfer of training." Later, methods of measurement were studied and practicable measures have been devised or radically improved both for intelligence testing and for ascertaining educational achievement. No other success of the American study of education has seemed so definite as that achieved in the field of measurement, and none has met so clear an acclaim. By distinction, to avoid certain ambiguities in the term " scientific," we may designate this third line of university study by its chief achievement and no less distinguishing procedure feature, and call it thus the *measuring* interest. To ask how these three lines of development and interest interact and conflict is but to state our problem in a further and closer manner.

These three lines of development in the study of education are obviously not accidental. They correspond at least roughly to three apparently fundamental aspects of human endeavor. The problem of *what end* to choose, the problem of *what means* to use and how, and the problem of establishing more *accurate and dependable knowledge.* These three, it would seem, were bound to demand separate consideration so soon as conscious attention should advance much beyond mere custom with its rule of thumb procedure. We may consider these three aspects in the order already followed in the lines of development to which they correspond.

First comes the question of ends. In any situation of conflicting values it becomes necessary to decide what end and goal shall be chosen. " How shall we so conceive our aim as best to conserve the values which contending possibilities now put in jeopardy? " " What is it all about? " " Just what are we trying to do? " " What end or ends shall we choose? " And proposed steps must likewise be reviewed. " How consistent are our proposed steps and means with the approved ends? " The identity of such questions with what is usually called the philosophic interest is at once evident. That they form the principal nucleus of inquiry in what we have called the *theoretic* interest of university study is equally clear. Since the boundaries between philosophy and science are still matters of debate it has seemed better for the present discussion to avoid both these terms and to designate the first development and its correlative interest, as suggested above, by the less provocative term " theoretic."

Second comes the use of means. Granted the aim and goal as no longer in dispute, how then shall we most efficiently attain the desired end? " What means shall we use and how shall we use them? " The substantial identity of this inquiry in the field of education with the general problem of management and administration seems clear. Nor need any question arise as to the aptness of the designative term " practical " to distinguish this interest from the preceding which was called theoretic. It is quite true that some devotee of the theoretical might wish to defend the claim that his interest was just as " practical " as this. However, by common usage, if no more, these two equally essential problem aspects are thus contrasted, the former as *theoretical,* the latter as *practical.*

The third interest and aspect does not stand so clearly distinguished from either of the others as they from each other. Rather does it enter into both. Each of the preceding interests, in order to pursue its inquiry, must use facts and their knowledge relationships. However, while each of these interests may thus incidentally seek a knowledge of facts, such seeking is both logically and consciously subordinate. The primary concern lies elsewhere. With the third interest and inquiry the situation is precisely the opposite. Its primary concern is exactly with the ascertainment of facts and of their relationships, and the concern is to determine both with as much certainty and precision as the wit of man can effect. While to these ends any adequate method of ascertaining facts or their relationship would suffice, it remains true that in the actual development of this study of education in this country it is the methods used with such signal success in the " exact sciences " that have supplied the dominating model. Only small use, for example, has been made of certain approaches which have proved useful in biology. This preference and choice of outlook and method have created a situation to which we must later return. The consequences appear to be capital to our inquiry.

In conclusion of these three aspects of any typical human situation, the inquiry about *ends in dispute,* the inquiry as to the *most efficient ordering of means,* and the inquiry as to *facts and fact relationships,* it stands clear that all three lines of inquiry will be (typically) necessary for the proper control of human experience. The several separate inquiries ought — " ideally " — to co-ordinate their respective results in one consistent ongoing process. Antagonism would certainly seem as unnecessary as its presence would be hurtful.

But antagonisms do actually arise. And human nature and conditions being what they are, antagonisms perhaps in some degree are inevitable. This, however, is no reason why we should not seek to locate and understand any actual antagonisms with the hope and aim of reducing them to the smallest possible degree. This is the purpose of the present inquiry.

For the arising of such antagonisms and conflicts there are both general and particular occasions. Foremost among the general occasions is perhaps the fact of specialization. For the sake of surer and higher success one man will attack only one of these problems. Attention becomes inevitably restricted, with consequent danger of finding criteria of success only within the chosen part. The whole which alone can give adequate criteria is in education unfortunately so prolonged and so complex that testing by it is as yet hardly to be counted feasible. The part that each specialist builds may thus only too easily not fit the parts built by the other two. Each separate worker, however, as he builds his own part must assume more or less adequately the other two parts — the three are in fact but aspects of one whole. Being then specialist only in his own field, his assumptions regarding the other two may fall below the best thought in those fields. Instead of this best he is in danger of assuming what most appeals to him, possibly from his early familiarity, possibly to fit and facilitate the work he is already doing in his own field. Thus since use and satisfied interest build habitude, an outworn answer in one field may actually become entrenched in another, and come thus in fact to partake of the nature of a vested interest. Should this arise a most difficult conflict confronts. A further general occasion of conflict is a sincere difference of opinion as to proper boundary lines between these three interests. At the present time some proponents of the third interest seem to deny a separate *raison d'être* to the theoretic interest as above defined.

In addition to these general occasions of conflict there are other occasions peculiar to each of the three lines of specializations. These may perhaps best be considered as we elaborate more fully the proper content of the three several lines of inquiry.

The theoretic interest was given above as having to do with the educative process and the part it should play in life. When, then, amid conflicting values in this field we try to fix goals and ends for or in education, we face at once the need for as full a grasp as we can achieve of the problem of life itself. This will involve a consideration both of the quality or value aspect of life and of the process of effecting the good life as thus defined. Education is here clearly implicated within life itself. We face thus in the theoretic interest an inquiry into a philosophy of life, into education as a process of self-building, and into the inter-relations of the two.

The outstanding attempt to find satisfactory answers to these questions (as judged by this writer) is the one in connection with which most antagonisms have arisen. It presents several distinct characteristics. Foremost perhaps is an emphasis on life, present actual living or experience, and on persons as the locus of such experiencing. This emphasis is not to be taken in an individualistic sense. Quite the contrary. Life is essentially social experience. Man is man only in and through human association. This is further to be interpreted in the democratic sense of not playing favorites. Each and all are together to share in the highest feasible degree in conducting the joint social process. As we look more closely at life on its value side, desirability seems to inhere in the very process of living. The problem is as to increasing life. The solution seems to lie in the conception of growing or creating, apparently in finding and integrating meanings. Herein seems to lie the identity of " subjective " and " objective " value. To find and integrate meanings is at once to make life more livable from the point of view of consummation and also objectively to make it more defensible as concerns other persons and occasions. When life is thus lived and meanings are thus continually being found and organized, a growing personality is therein being built and integrated, the highest product of intelligent education.

From the wish to build such growing personalities comes the second characteristic of this position. Institutions are to be judged by the degree to which they favor such meaningful growing. If any institution fails to meet this test it stands in so far condemned. That this criterion is thoroughgoing needs no discussion. It is easy to see why tradition and entrenched privilege should not approve the tenets of this formulated position. Even more drastic, if possible, is a third characteristic which nowhere finds permanent existence, but instead everywhere only events more or less prolonged, all inherently undergoing transformations. The contrast between this and certain traditional philosophies is obvious. And again do tradition and entrenched privilege stand jointly opposed.

The implications of these characteristics of the theoretic position for conflict are many and varied, but they can better be taken up as they appear severally in conflict under the discussion of the *practical* and the *measuring* positions. Here it will suffice to call attention to two tendencies frequently alleged against the *theoretic* group. First is the complaint more often raised from their measuring confreres that the theoretic are not as careful to be sure of the fact they use as they might be. For failure of this kind there is, of course, no excuse. It may, however, be questioned whether the better representatives of the theoretic position are more open to this charge than are any other intellectual workers. Much more widespread is the complaint that the theoretic group in its zeal for a better (" ideal ") state of affairs loses touch with the existing state of affairs. It seems probable that there is real danger here just as there is danger that the more *practical*-minded shall become too much entangled within the existing state and not work zealously enough for a better state of affairs. It is with just such failures to come together that this paper is concerned. So far it has not seemed possible to get sufficiently prolonged and patient contacts between the dominant representatives of conflicting groups to reach any common agreement as to which " ideals " are justified and worthy of joint support and which are not. And educational endeavor limps accordingly.

If we approach the *practical* inquiry and consider the university development which has emerged from it we find in general the collection and criticism of varied experience with suggestions for improvement. Efficiency in the management of affairs is perhaps the keynote. No source of possible suggestion has been ruled out, but the two sources outstandingly utilized have perhaps been the third or measuring line of educational development and the practice of efficient business. School management and administration is from one point of view a business, one of the largest we have. In a country where business efficiency has by common consent been carried to the highest levels ever attained, it is but right and proper that school administration should profit by this development. That educational measurement should commend itself to administration is easily seen. Wherever certainty and precision can be substituted for uncertainty and imprecision, management moves more surely to its goal. The emphasis here is on the *practical* aspect of education. But there is another side. In a democratic country no policy is permanently practical which cannot in the end sustain itself with the people. This is not to say derogatorily, " Yes, the school superintendent must be a politician." It is not the politician (in the usual sense) that is demanded by the situation, but rather the statesman. Each school superintendent in this country must be a statesman — on a small scale, if you will, but still in a sense quite true. He must convince his board and his people on any new policy. The necessity for this colors and necessarily must color his whole program. In this respect the superintendent and his necessary psychology are but the inevitable working of a public school system operating within an actual social situation professedly democratic. The superintendent is the point of contact between " theory " and " practice." In him and his success must be decided how far the " theoretically " desirable practice can embody itself in an actual school system located as it is in an actual social milieu. That dangers or difficulties bristle is only too obvious. The chief difficulty arises perhaps in the improper demands of our professedly democratic society upon the social and educational outlook of the school.

In this country, in spite of lip service, most people, particularly most successful business people (who greatly dominate our boards of education) are not great believers in actual democracy. The practical school man, often successfully emergent through his power and interest in controlling others, may thus find his own taste for domination fortified by the prejudices of his board. The personality of both teachers and pupils may thus easily be disregarded. The analogy from success in the business world readily leads toward a like " efficient " system of school supervision with its like insistence upon definite and quantitative educational outcomes. Educational objectives of a quantitative kind, fixed-in-advance curriculum, prescribed methods of teaching, and standardized tests to measure the results, all are congenial with this point of view. If the " theoretic interest " has meanwhile so revised its conceptions of all these things — objectives, curriculum, methods, and criteria of success — as to oppose these procedures, the " practical " interest is tempted in its turn to belittle the " theoretic " findings and reject them as visionary. The danger thus arises that efficiency in school management will be measured in terms of its own standards and in disregard of the validity or lack of validity of these as judged from the point of view of the whole life and of the correlative educative process.

Even greater is the danger of opposition to advance in social and political outlook. While conditions of life are changing, as it were overnight, most people remain more or less traditional in their theoretical outlook. If the school tries to change its approach so as to take better account of changing life conditions, opposition at once arises. Tradition and selfish interest here work in unison. The school, of course, is not to be used for " propaganda " purposes, possibly not even for " good " causes. The idea here advocated by the theoretic interest is to encourage in the growing child such an appropriate study of our changing world as would help him to grow in the power and disposition to think independently of tradition or prejudice about matters of social and public interest. But it is exactly this valid independent thinking which tradition and vested interest do not wish. Since they approach the school management in opposition to such thinking under cover of accustomed terms and ideas, they too often find easy access thus to fix in advance of possible later thinking the desired prejudices against any revision of old notions. In this way, for example, an indefensible nationalism is nourished. In like manner does the Monroe doctrine as a dogma of American infallibility and over-lordship get its perennial lease on life. The intelligent school man will sigh as he sees such forces at work, but he must have a firm grip on better things if he is to resist the narrowing effect on himself. If in his university preparation for the post he holds stress was laid on matters more congenial to public demands he will be but human if he yields to such pressure and avoids trouble by directing his efforts along less controversial lines.

And in this lies perhaps the greatest danger of all. Too often it works out that only the more *practical*-minded can stand the strain of such pressure. There thus tends to grow up in the field of practice a cult of " efficiency " which avoids the more complicated and unpopular issues in education while it seeks success along better approved lines, along lines already accepted by people generally and especially perhaps by " successful " business. We may thus find the emphasis placed on handsome schoolhouses, well located and efficiently built, on excellent accounting systems, on the wider use of the school plant through the platoon plan (for example), on " vocational guidance " (with its practical placement), on segregation by ability, standardized tests in subject-matter (especially the three R's), and on objective supervision. There is, of course, nothing but praise for good school buildings or for good accounting systems, nor should criticism attach to these various new " scientific " educational procedures if or when, all things considered, they were really educative. The condemnation is that attention in all this may be less devoted to education than to its machinery, less devoted to a study of what really makes for educational ends than to improving methods of seeking ends already popularly approved. Instead of adjusting educational machinery to work for the best conceived educational aims, the tendency is too much to omit thinking on education itself and assume instead outworn but popular conceptions in the hope of glorifying the new administration for attaining traditional ends more efficiently. In such ways may conservatism and even reaction masquerade under the guise of " progress." And, sad to say, in this unworthy program a professed " science " of education may lend its unholy sanction. And its aid is powerful. It is when the " practical " interest acquiesces in this virtual refusal to face vital issues that an essential conflict has arisen. "Theory" and "practice" then appear as distinctly opposed.

When we come to the third line of development, inadequately named above as the "measuring interest," we perhaps reach the chief conflict of all. Here is a genuine intellectual interest, one of the finest and most successful that our country has produced. It has definite and outstanding achievements to its credit. It is attracting to its ranks the intellectual flower of our profession. Enthusiasm in difficult work has marked its progress. Tonic breath has followed its insistence upon rooting out sloppy and slipshod thinking wherever found. Its fundamental procedures rightly directed are as sound as anything man has yet devised. All this and more can deservedly be said. But for all that certain questions will not down until they have been faced more frankly and openly than heretofore. Here as everywhere else camp followers and privates are likely to be more reckless than those higher in authority, but some of the questions cut deeper than the behavior of the irresponsible.

A glance at the historic origin of the ideal and spirit of "exact science" may throw an orientating light on its influence in the study of education. It is generally agreed that modern natural science took its practical rise in the Cartesian dualism of mind and matter. In dealing thus with the physical universe measurement and the mathematical treatment achieved such success that till the most recent developments in physics there has been no disposition even to consider the underlying assumptions. *Solvitur ambulando* sufficed to stop questioning before it began. This point of view in an earlier day had said explicitly that "the sole reality that can be accessible to our means of knowledge, matter, nature, appears to us a tissue of properties, precisely ordered, and of which the connection can be expressed in terms of mathematics" (Newton). In later days less perhaps was said in this strain, but the spirit was none the less pervasive. Many indeed, as did Newton himself, had another realm where values were kept, but this was a region not really "accessible to our means of knowledge," and therefore was properly to be ignored in scientific inquiry.

This undiscussed assumption of the body side of the dualism furnished the procedures for "exact science" as seen in the analytic separation of variables, in the control group procedure, and in measurement. It was further assumed that the whole is everywhere equal to the sum of its parts, and that synthesis could properly wait until analysis had done its perfect work. Anything that did not yield to such " scientific " treatment could be disregarded or at least postponed. Explanation of the " higher " and more complex was properly to be made in terms of the lower and simpler. The " effect " might as an available outcome be less than the " cause," but by no means could ever surpass it. Of course as soon as this " exact scientific " method was applied to psychology, the " mind " began to give trouble. In physics mind could be ignored, but in psychology not easily so. The practical solution seems to have pursued the line of least resistance: Follow the successful practice of the " exact sciences," analyze, separate variables, measure; insist on experimental " proof "; be " scientific " at all cost; begin where this procedure will succeed; postpone or ignore all else. Except for ignoring the presuppositions involved in this, such a program to be followed for what it would yield need not provoke criticism. Nor should there be hasty condemnation for ignoring the pre-suppositions. Scientific procedure of the exact kind had to its credit the greatest intellectual achievements mankind could show. To be dazzled by such success was nothing more than being human.

By chance this program as applied to the psychology of learning found waiting in the traditional educational outlook and practice a situation favorable to its processes. From very early times teaching procedure had been on an analytic basis. Reading (by the once universal alphabet method) began with letters and proceeded in succession through syllables, disconnected words, first short and then long, to disconnected sentences, finally to reach the connected whole of orderly discourse. Writing similarly began with the constituents of letters (" pothooks ") and went through an analogous series to end again with connected discourse. It was everywhere the same: parts first, the whole finally to be got by synthesis. True enough the educational reformer had already begun a century and more ago to get away from the extreme of this analytic practice, but the changes had been rather superficial than thoroughgoing. Oral spelling was still common. Wherever school work was taken seriously, teaching by separate subjects with " logical " rather than " psychological " arrangement was the all but universal practice. Subject-matter-set-out-to-be-learned held equal sway, while examinations offered the only available criterion for success at learning. How the measuring emphasis in education has built itself exactly on this traditional basis needs little more discussion than to ask attention to the obvious facts and to point out its further consistent indisposition (or inability) to consider seriously " progressive " programs. How much of the measurer's opposition to " progressive education " is due thus to a vested interest in the traditional is possibly not a fair question. The inquiry, however, is an interesting one.

This traditional procedure found, moreover, a strong ally in the traditional social theory of education as well as in the traditional school system that had grown up about them both. In the prevailing social theory the young must be fitted into the awaiting adult social order. Education, religion, and the penal system were the three main reliances for effecting such adaptation. That resistance should manifest itself in the young was but definite evidence of human depravity. Authoritarianism and the *status quo* were strict correlatives. The corresponding philosophic doctrine was that no change takes place in the " essentials." The school " curriculum " was thus naturally based on existing adult life and was by its very nature made in advance. " Subject-matter " was this adult content arranged best for acquisition (analytically, as we saw just above). Teaching was an apportioning of this content as " lessons " and enforcing its acquisition. " Study " was limited to the activity of acquiring assignments. " Learn " meant such success in acquisition as enabled the learner to give back the assignment on demand (on this is based the scientific term " over-learning "). " Promotion " followed the successful acquisition of the annual or semi-annual quota of subject-matter. These four aspects of tradition hang thus inextricably together: traditional social theory (no significant change to occur in the *status quo*), traditional philosophy (no change thinkable in " essentials "), traditional educational theory (adjustment to unchanging social and religious order by acceptance through " learning " of authoritative subject-matter), traditional educational psychology (acceptance on authority of subject-matter analytically subdivided for unintelligent acquisition, values based on authority and seen not by pupil but by teacher). These exact four by a remarkable chance (if chance it be) furnish precisely the basis on which the modern measuring movement in " scientific " education has reared itself. The parallel is too complete and obvious to require discussion. It is on this basis that " standardization " proceeds. Statistical averages are complacently called " norms." [1] All of these things taken together in connection tend to explain why a line-of-least-resistance administration and the " measuring movement " have so strengthened each other's hands in opposition to a theoretic outlook which definitely calls in question every one of the traditional positions named above. Exactly at this point appears the significant conflict which most of all stimulated this paper. [2]

But we look deeper. That the prevailing " exact science " method in education proceeds analytically needs no discussion. Analysis is its very life breath, as measurement is its bodily structure. And, properly managed and interpreted, there can be no objection urged against either. Objection comes when assumption is made that measurement suffices to care for all values. Whether everything that exists can be measured I for one cannot say. I do not know for sure what " exists " means; but I think I know that measurement cannot adequately care for all we value. To pretend that it does is to distract from what is not measured. The so-called objective studies of class size illustrate this fallacy as well as its bad effects. Objection further comes when the assumption is implicitly made that ultimately the whole where life is involved will be got by a synthesis of separate parts. In education the whole child must always be considered and mere synthesis does not suffice. Further serious objection asserts itself when the added assumption is made that what is separately proved will continue to hold after it is put back into a life whole. The assumption is unwarranted. Methods of teaching reading or spelling, for example, may in a sense be tested by comparing the respective " reading " or " spelling " outcomes resulting from the contrasted methods. But, as we learn from biology (not from physics), the organism responds as a whole, which means that many different learnings are going on simultaneously. It would seem to follow, then, that no finally satisfactory comparison of spelling or reading methods can thus be made till all these simultaneous learning results are taken into account. And these can be weighed only in terms of their bearing on life as a whole. Total and inclusive life values come inevitably into the weighing. So far, at least, no " scientific "

[1] So identified have the two become that the writer has heard students, while admitting that averages do not properly supply standards, still assert they are properly called norms.

[2] In spite of all this, in a recent conference of picked educators, largely " scientific " and " practical," the writer heard man after man in turn deny that any significant conflict exists in contemporary educational theory or practice. Only a small minority thought otherwise.

measuring procedure has even attempted to cope with this full value situation. Whether it ever can need not now be asked. On the face of it these considerations, if admitted, call in question every "proof" based on the analytic procedure. This is not to deny in *a priori* fashion all value to such investigation. Such a position would be clearly unwarranted. But it does seem to indicate that proper validity to any analytic result can be established only by appropriate appeal to the whole from which the part was taken, or better still by appeal to the whole in which the part is to function. The proponents of "exact science" in education must dispose of this contention or admit a severe limitation upon their results. At this point a clear and fundamental issue seems joined.

A further limitation of the "exact science" procedure is its apparent disposition to belittle all "conscious action," as thinking or the part played in conduct by ideas and ideals, with the further disposition to provide little place for deliberation or for the functioning of "values." The why of this is not always clear. It would not be fair to say that all users of the methods of "exact science" in education mean to take this position; but certainly as regards "consciousness" in any form the tendency is to look the other way and to pass by on the other side. Part of this tendency seems to come from the old hurtful body-mind dualism and a choosing of the body to swallow up the mind. How consciously this acts one cannot say. But the net result is a frequent attitude that any "conscious action of the mind" is negligible in the deterministic play of more real "forces." Let no one say in reply that facts, not theories, must control, no matter who is hurt. That is exactly the contention here made: that facts are not being respected, but instead are being reduced to fit the "exact science" presuppositions. In keeping with this, learning is a mere matter of external "conditioning" or of habit formation. Creation has no part in the learning process. The "person" as such is no factor.[3] Meanings tend to be reduced to mere cues. "Responsibility" in any effective sense is an illusion — and is not to be mentioned. "Freedom" belongs to a human only in about the same sense and degree as to a brick. The extreme outcome of all this, especially when construed in the light of a statistical treatment of intelligence, is a definite tendency to belittle human worth and personality. A new authoritarianism — that of the

[3] The writer has heard "integration of personality" bring guffaws as a meaningless term. This was in 1926. Since then the tendency is probably the other way.

" scientific " expert — is to take place of the old; and the incompetent many are to be taught (" conditioned ") robot-like to do their masters' bidding. Deliberation in morals on this basis is infrequent for all and impossible for most. In like manner intelligent action and creation are to be reserved for the higher few. Man as man is distinctly disparaged. While few would go to this extreme, few do not move in this direction.

How these belittling attitudes toward humanity lend themselves to a selfish social and economic exploitation is all too obvious. In the history of social reconstruction the welcome efficiency of a docile science in the service of exploitation is well known. The part that subserviency can play in modern education has less often been considered. Teachers and pupils are alike to take orders. Intelligence descends from above. It is interesting to see how tradition, entrenched privilege, a subservient and narrowly " efficient " administrative outlook, and a narrow and inadequately scientific scheme of educational psychology and measurement play into each other's hands as all together oppose any serious questioning of any of their joint fundamental assumptions. In no essential respect may the older conception of the educative process be revised. " Subject-matter " set out in advance for learning must be safeguarded at all costs as the only feasible end of educational endeavor. To call attention to these things is not to assume that the actual " theoretic " interest is necessarily correct or that any conflict with it points to necessary imperfection elsewhere. The aim is quite different, namely, to get the conflict out in the open so that it can and will be discussed. Only thus may we hope to advance on the road toward improvement. Let the final judgment be what it may, only let it come after consideration and not before it.

One final word lest it appear that an attack is herein made on scientific procedure. No such attack is made or intended. The writer for himself does believe that the methods of " exact " science, founded as they have been on physics (and an apparently indefensible physics at that), do not of themselves suffice for the study of psychology or of education. But it is not necessary to limit " scientific " procedures so narrowly. If we understand by science the determination to test our hypotheses as best we can by observation and experiment, there are other scientific procedures besides physics — biology, for instance. It appears antecedently probable that biology as concerned with life and its conditioning would at least in certain respects furnish more useful suggestions for psychology and education than could physics. And the outcome seems to justify the antecedent hope. Every limitation seen above in the " exact " scientific procedure as applied to education is avoided if biological conceptions be followed. To begin with, behavior and learning seem more fruitfully defined on the theory of biologic organization with life as continued equilibrative process. Further, the necessity of considering organism and environment as one correlative whole will, if intelligently followed, pretty effectually correct the tendency to break up the child's life and learning into separate and unassimilated elements. If this discussion has thus seemed at any point to attack science as such, the effort has belied itself. The hope has rather been to call science to a broader and more adequate approach to education, one truer in every way to science itself. And similarly with administration. The only wish here entertained has been that in its care of practical things it shall not forget the better and, to attaining these, may give its best efforts. What these better things may be and how to get them none knows so well but honest search will find still better.

CAUSALITY

STERLING P. LAMPRECHT

THE controversies of recent years have surrounded the problem of causality with many dialectical difficulties. These controversies have an intrinsic interest to students of history, and good dialectics are always instructive. None the less a metaphysics which aims to be wholeheartedly empirical must begin with a descriptive account of the facts of experience. If we start with some conception of causality derived from the premises of a system of philosophy, we might have to conclude that there were no causes in nature, or we might, finding causes, yet miss some important character of events which an empirical method would disclose. The besetting sin of metaphysical inquiry has been the substitution of some alleged " data " for observable facts; and the outcome has followed that, even when these " data " were not fanciful, all characters of reality have been overlooked, or even denied, that were not included in the selected " data." And so, even at the risk of dwelling on the obvious and of appearing quite trivial, I venture to list a number of situations that are normally regarded as having causal significance. Certainly in the daily course of living we are continually dealing with what we are all accustomed to call causes and effects. And if we begin with such situations, then any term like causality will derive its meaning from the empirical material under observation.

Our normal experiences of the operation of " causes " are of three types. Sometimes we seek to control a " cause " in the interest of obtaining a desired outcome. So a mechanic jacks up the axle of his automobile in order to have easier access to a broken part; a scientist exposes a photographic plate to the heavens in order to get a record of the position of the stars; a cook lights the fire in her oven in order to bake her bread; an invalid swallows the disagreeable potion in his quest for renewed health. At other times we seek to discover and then to remove a cause which has been producing an undesired outcome. So a man eliminates certain foods from his diet in order to hinder the return of a malady; builders adapt the form of their structures to the earthquake disturbances of a certain district in order to mitigate the disastrous effects of the earth's tremors; the cautious man wears his rubbers in rainy weather in order to escape grippe; the owner of property on the sea-front protects his land against the devouring ocean by erecting piers and breakwater. And at still other times, confronted with causes too potent for us to control and destructive of human life or welfare, we step aside and thus endeavor to avoid contact with the dreaded effects. So the soldier hides in the dugout rather than needlessly expose himself to the rain of shrapnel; the Swiss villager hurriedly removes himself and his worldly goods from the path of a prospective landslide; the Iowan farmer jumps into the cyclone-cellar upon the approach of the funnel-shaped cloud; the Sicilian peasant, after first parading his holy images before the menacing lava-flow, is wont to yield his ground if the flow continues. Such a list of what we all, men in the street and philosophers in the cloister, normally regard as causally significant situations could be extended until weariness overtook the most zealous empiricist. We may, indeed we often do, ignore the causal connections with which our life is constantly penetrated; but the most absent-minded of us is jostled into attention by extremes of heat or cold, by fire or flood. Even Socrates, in Alcibiades' account, stood only from one dawn to the next in indifference to the course of nature about him; and perhaps his prayer to the sun at the second dawn was uttered partly in gratitude for protection against attack by hostile causes during his hours of meditation.

Now whether we are seeking to control or eliminate a cause or to absent ourselves altogether from the scene of operation of some causal action, we recognize in all cases alike a genuine compulsion in the course of events. We find ourselves constrained, often against our will; and we must reckon with causality or suffer dire consequences. The literature of all races is full of such maxims as that " whatsoever a man soweth that shall he also reap." And the language is full of terms which designate the urgency of causal connection. We say that one thing *produces* another, that a given remedy is *efficacious,* that a certain outcome is *inevitable* or *necessary,* that one thing *governs* or *regulates* another, etc. These words may be hard to define; but they point to or denote an insistently constant character of experience and a genuinely universal character of events. That we are often mistaken in identifying the cause of a given effect or in estimating the effect of a given cause is no argument against the empirical status of necessity or compulsion in events. For even where our judgments about causality err, they are directed at an analysis of situations in which we are perhaps ourselves put under pressure or are at least aware of forceful determination. In our own persons we shove and are shoved, we push and are pushed, we give and receive blows. And beyond our own bodily impacts we have only to try to unravel the strands by which things are connected, in order to recognize how inextricably things are interrelated and how closely they depend on each other. Both in our ourselves and in objects around us we find active compulsion. There is not merely a fire and then a hot oven; but there is, as we find, a necessary relation between lighting a fire and heat. There is not merely an avalanche and then destruction; but there is an irresistible sweep in which the avalanche destroys whatever is in its path. There is not merely a storm on the coast and then the loss of many feet of property; but there is the inevitable process in which the stormy waters eat away the soft soil. And we use the term " causality " to stand for this compelling character of events. Causality is thus nothing mysterious or recondite or unusual. It is the ever-present character of the existing order in which we play a part and which stretches on far beyond our own immediate scene.

One reason why causality, though dealt with constantly in all other affairs of life, is frequently denied or " explained away " in philosophic discourse, is the fact that we cannot give a satisfactory definition of it. We can indeed point to it; we can designate it by gesture. But from the standpoint of the requirements for a formal definition all our statements about causality are faulty. We can state the genus of causality: it is a relation. But we cannot give the essential difference of the causal relation except in some question-begging synonym. We can say that causality is a *necessary* relation between cause and effect, or that it is the character of the process in which one thing *produces* another, or that it is *efficacious* control of one thing over another. These assertions are true; but they are not adequate as formal definitions. They do not advance the discussion one whit; they would not explain causality to any one who did not already know what we were talking about.

Discovery of the indefinable nature of causality should not lead to erroneous conclusions. It does not imply that we do not know what we mean by causality; much less does it imply that there is really nothing in nature for which the term stands. The indefinability of a term does not distress an empiricist. Formal definition is always impossible where we are dealing with ultimate characters of reality. When we can neither define our terms nor point to the subject-matter the terms stand for, we are probably engaged in sheer nonsense. But where we can point to the type of fact we mean, the accumulation of indefinables is for an empirical philosophy direct evidence of metaphysical thoroughness. In an empirical philosophy discourse must lag behind denotative indication, must be based upon such denotative indication. In the eloquent language of William James: " No one has intelligibly banished the mystery of *fact*. . . . If you are a rationalist you beg a kilogram of being at once, we will say; if you are an empiricist you beg a thousand successive grams; but you beg the same amount in each case, and you are the same beggar whatever you may pretend. . . . For all of us alike, Fact forms a datum, gift, or *Vorgefundenes*, which we cannot burrow under, explain, or get behind." [1] And really the case is not so equally balanced between the rationalist and the empiricist as James generously grants. For in the case of the rationalist the kilogram begged at the outset will not, in a world so full of an indefinitely rich variety of characters, be sufficient for a final metaphysics: something or other will surely be left out and will then either be denied or begged again empirically. We might all find it wiser to beg a bit at a time, since then we can more scrupulously examine what we receive and avoid the mortification of discovering that part of our kilogram is rubbish. But, to leave the metaphor, we are confronted in experience with many a character which is unique or *sui generis;* and here the really humble procedure is to assert such facts dogmatically, because facts assail us with their own dogmatic claims. Dogmatism as a name for a high-strung emotional insistence that will not look at facts (as, for example, that of the professors at Padua who refused to look through Galileo's telescope) may be a rather nasty trait of character. But dogmatism as a name for the ready acceptance of facts and an unwillingness to " reduce " them to something else other than what they are is metaphysical wisdom. Empiricists, in resolutely affirming the reality of all that is experienced, are merely making bold to practise the maxim of Bishop Butler that " a thing is what it is and not another thing."

[1] *Some Problems of Philosophy,* pp. 44, 45, 46.

The evidence for causality in nature is abundant. It is a frequent fact of daily experience. Things beat in upon us and we strike back. We make and use tools; we expend energy and triumph in the achievement of our purposes or are balked by the strength of resisting obstacles. Causality is, of course, not directly observed in most cases, but inferred, as indeed is the case with many qualities and relations in nature. We are not always quick enough to detect it even when it is close before us, even with the aid of our most delicate instruments; and thus nature is for us full of marvels which seem suddenly to come into existence without sufficient warning. We infer a causal connection between the points of light in the heavens and the spots on our photographic plate, or between the medicine we swallow and the health we may recover. But when the mechanic jacks up his car or the unfortunate farmer experiences the cyclonic winds which hurl him and his property about before them, the necessity in nature is surely directly presented and not only inferred. In the use of tools and the resistance of materials, in the hasty erection of barriers and the beat of hostile forces upon them, in the activity of fire and wind and sun, we are handling and being handled by things which obviously have causal connections. As Professor Dewey says: " The first thinker who proclaimed that every event is effect of something and cause of something else, that every particular existence is both conditioned and condition, merely put into words the procedure of the workman, converting a mode of practice into a formula." [2]

Such a " common-sense " theory of causality, if the view here defended may be called by this name, is in striking contrast with most of the ideas expressed by professional philosophers today. One prevalent idea, for example, is that causality is nothing but a certain habit of mind, a kind of expectation built up in us human observers by the uniform sequences in nature. It is said that we observe some thing A and then another thing B in frequent conjunction, that we then eventually come to anticipate B whenever we are confronted with $A,$ and that causality is just this type of psychological association. Now there are implications in this position that are not usually noticed. If habits are built up by uniform sequences in nature, there is at least some kind of operating cause back of habit. In saying that under certain circumstances expectations arise in the mind of the observer of events, we surely mean more than that the psychologist

[2] *Experience and Nature*, p. 84.

has the habit of expecting expectations in other people; we mean that there are causes operating to produce habits in men that would thus justify the perhaps habitual expectation of the psychologist who has an adequate knowledge of human nature. And when we are coerced by dialectic to recognize the causal connection back of the psychologist's habits in interpreting other people, we may then well inquire about the causal connection back of all habits. If the cook expects the lighting of her fire to be followed by a sufficiently hot oven to bake her bread, she is none the less dealing with a situation in which objectively real connections justify her expectations. The Swiss villager would not delay a landslide by sitting still and forming different expectations; rather his habits are built up under genuine compulsion. Causality may indeed operate in producing human habits, ideas, beliefs, volitions, and the like; and if so, the psychologist may, or must, ascertain causal connections as much as the physicist. But the psychologist did not invent the category; psychological analysis did not first reveal causal connections. The category is significantly used by politicians, merchants, and lawyers, and was used by them long before the emergence of psychological science. Causality is a metaphysical category. It designates a character of the events in the world about us, whether these events be explosions, physical impacts, human attitudes, or surgical operations. Unless events had this character before human expectations arose and apart from such expectations, there would be no reason why some expectations are sound while others are silly or only partially correct. There is no reason for supposing that fire became related to heat, that avalanches began to be destructive of whatever lay in their path, that earthquakes first resulted in widespread dislocation of existing materials, only after there appeared animals who are capable of adjusting their lives to the world about them. Causality designates a kind of connection which characterizes natural events whether living beings are present or not, which makes it profitable to human beings to have habits which correspond to the urgency of facts, which probably prevailed on this planet before life occurred and will continue to prevail in case of the extinction of life altogether. What we are talking about in speaking of causes and effects is not primarily a fact in anthropology or any other science of man; rather it is a character of all events and so has metaphysical significance.

The supposition that causality is a matter of human habits or expectations is generally connected with the name of David Hume. Hume did not, however, hold any such view. He was concerned with theory of knowledge, not with metaphysics; he sought to know why we think causes necessary and how experience gives rise to the idea of necessity, and he barely touched on the degree of validity in a causal interpretation of nature. We have the idea of necessity, he tells us; and all ideas arise from antecedent impressions. The impression from which the idea of causality comes is the chief object of his search. He finds it, not in the " external " objects we call cause and effect, but in " a new impression in the mind " which arises after experience has given us many instances of a uniform type of sequence. This impression is of " a determination of the mind " to pass from the perception of an object to the idea of that object's usual attendant.[3] That is, what is central in Hume's theory is that we directly experience causality only in ourselves, that our idea of causality is derived from the operations of our own mind, and that the application of the idea to other events is hazardous.

Even when Hume is interpreted in this way, however, his theory is unsound. Not simply are we not confined to the operations of our own mind for " impressions " of causal connection, but also we detect causal connections less quickly and less easily in ourselves than in things without us.[4] It is from the urgency of events about us, from the way things bang and bump and push and press and clash, that we get our first experience of causality and derive our first idea of causal necessity. In the more or less furious turmoil of interacting events in the physical world, we gradually learn to isolate our own bodies for special attention, we come to know something of our own physical prowess and the extent of our various kinds of skill, and eventually we arrive at an understanding of our own mental powers and the efficacy of our will. Probably we have not yet begun to discover the full extent of our mental power in guiding and controlling bodies. But instead of going from the physical facts of volition to the physical thrusts of things, (so that belief in causality would

---

[3] *Treatise of Human Nature*, Book I, Part III, section 14. (Green & Grose edition, Vol. I, p. 459.)

[4] It is just here that I find myself in disagreement with Professor S. Alexander's position. He writes: " If you wish to discover the nature of causality, look first to your mind. . . . Power is the continuous connection which we observe in ourselves and can more easily and directly observe in ourselves in enjoyment than outside us in contemplated events." (*Space, Time, and Deity*, Vol. I, pp. 8, 290. Cf. also pp. 188, 211.)

be a kind of lingering animistic interpretation of the material world), we begin with the experience of causality in bodily thrusts and only later extend the notion to our own mental life (and the degree to which such extension is legitimate is still to some philosophers an open question). Of course, when we are sufficiently sophisticated, we may distinguish "brute force" and "creative intelligence" as two kinds of causality; but we are aware of the pressing and potent causality of things about us long before we come to distinguish volition, desire, opinion, reason, and inference as special types of cause. Causality is most conspicuously present, for the philosophical theorist as for the hunter and warrior, in the threat of looming dangers in the onward rush of physical events and in the bodily resistance which in our own persons or in the use of tools and barriers we set up to arrest the advance of these dangers. In a sense, of course, it is true of causality as of every other feature of the world that we must begin with our own personal experience; but unless experience is taken as a succession of private "psychical states" instead of an interplay of various bodies (of which the human organism is but one), we are not required to "begin with ourselves." The statement that we must begin with ourselves is an error of fatal consequences for metaphysics if it means more than that we must begin where we are before we can hope to proceed to something more remote. But "where we are" is not inside ourselves: it is a portion of the complex of events which constitutes the course of nature.

Another prevalent idea among professional philosophers is that causality is a name for the uniformity of sequence in the events of nature. This idea has been the resort of those who wished to avoid definition of causality in psychological terms and who yet stood in the Humian tradition which denies direct experience of causality in nature.[5] The fundamental error in this treatment of causality is a confusion of what we mean by causality with the problem whether causality is uniform in its operations. When we discover a causal connection in events we may then

[5] Cf. Karl Pearson: "That a certain sequence has occurred and recurred in the past is a matter of experience to which we give expression in the concept *causation*." (*The Grammar of Science*, third edition, p. 113.) Or cf. Mr. Bertrand Russell: "Events can be collected in groups by their correlations. This is all that is true in the old notion of causality. . . . To say that A is 'necessarily' followed by B is thus to say no more than that there is some general rule, exemplified in a very large number of instances, and falsified in none, according to which events such as A are followed by events such as B." (*Philosophy*, pp. 115, 117.)

go on to discover also that this connection has a certain uniformity of
recurrence. But causality and uniformity are two distinct considerations.[6]
The fact of causality may be the basis for the formulation of general
laws. But the general law would then state that the same cause always
produced under the same circumstances the same effect. Unless each
instance of the general law were a case of causal connection, it is difficult
to see why the general law should be called causal. If avalanches are
always destructive, it is because in each particular instance causality is
involved. If lighting a fire under suitable conditions is always a prelude
to a hot oven, it is because each particular case of such procedure is characterized by necessity. Laws are causal only where the facts they summarize are causal. We can hardly suppose that single events which, taken
separately, lack causal significance, can gain such significance by being
grouped under a general formula. We do not reach through generalization a character which is wholly lacking in the particular facts with which
we start. If all we mean by causality were regularity of sequence or
constant correlation, we should not use the term " causality " at all. But we
do use the term " causality " and know what we mean; and we use it both
for certain generalizations about natural uniformities and for the character of each particular event of all such types as those listed above. And
whether we are applying the term to the generalization or to the specific
character of a single event, we mean something quite different than that
we are able to group a single event with others of a similar sort. We mean
that in each event one thing produces another thing, that one avalanche
causes its consequent widespread destruction, that one exposure of a
photographic plate causes certain specific spots on the plate, that one
carefully regulated diet prevents the continued operation of a harmful
cause. Causality is basically a matter of a kind of connection between
elements within single events. If there were a thoroughly unique event

---

[6] This point has been ably made in recent writings by both Professor C. J. Ducasse in
Causation and the Types of Necessity, Chapter VI, and by Mr. H. W. B. Joseph in *Introduction to Logic*, p. 404. And it should be noticed that we really have no such general
rules " exemplified in a very large number of instances and falsified in none " which Mr.
Russell would substitute for the fact of particular causal connections. We have rules of an
ideal nature which are in a sense the norm from which all particular instances more or less
depart. The general rules isolate a single feature of a mass of instances, ignore the rest,
and state the selected feature in a precise form in which it is never, or at least very seldom,
actually found. The supposition that events then have no characters except what the ideal
laws specify is decidedly naïve.

(and every event is to a certain extent unique), we would still know what we mean in calling it causal. And if there were a group of events of exactly the same nature (and any such group is probably never encountered), we would still use the term " causality " for the nature of each event in the group separately. What we group in classes and describe in causal laws is events similar in their causal characters; and unless they had severally such character, we could never reach a causal law. Regularity of sequence may be taken as indicative of causal connection, though it is not always such. Yet even where it really is such, it is not the source of the causality therein affirmed of the separate events.

The idea that causality is but a name for uniformity of sequence is due to a misunderstanding of scientific method. In spite of the deference which contemporary philosophy, in fact the whole of modern philosophy, pays to science, philosophical writers have often failed to recognize the function and purpose of science. Two features of science are relevant to the present point. One feature is the selective character of scientific analysis. Science always chooses some phase or aspect of the existing world for detailed examination, and so selects, for its data, certain qualities or relations which are to be found in the welter of cosmic events. But it does not deny the existence of the complex world from which the selection was made. Science is not photographic; it is analytical. Whereas no metaphysics can afford to neglect the discoveries of science, it is also true that no metaphysics can hope to be adequate that merely pieces together the results of scientific work. Only the enthusiastic scientist or philosopher would take some intriguing or favorite set of scientific data and theories as equivalent to the whole of reality. The other feature of at least a good deal of science in our day is that it is interested, and with perfect propriety, in translating cosmic events so far as possible into formulae of functional correlations and into mathematical equations. That is, science is concerned with what Aristotle called the formal cause and is mostly unconcerned with what he called the efficient cause; and Aristotle's formal cause is, in our contemporary usage of language, not a cause at all, but an essence or form or universal.

We need have no quarrel with scientific procedure for either of these features; we need only resist the attempts of overly zealous partisans who deny other features of our complex world than those reflected in the selective formulae of science. The concrete events of nature make pos-

sible many an analysis: there are always more aspects of events than any
series of scientific and philosophical analyses can exhaustively list and
describe. [The unnoticed is not the non-existent,] especially when it is
merely unnoticed by one human enterprise and fully recognized in the
more ordinary affairs of life. Against the " vicious intellectualism " which
equates some set of scientific formulae with the whole of reality we may
well protest in the words of William James. " The original form in
which fact comes," he wrote, " is the perceptual *durcheinander*, holding
terms as well as relations in solution, or interfused and cemented. . . .
Our reflective mind abstracts divers aspects in the muchness, as a man
by looking through a tube may limit his attention to one part after another of a landscape. But abstraction is not insulation; and it no more
breaks reality than the tube breaks the landscape." [7] And among the
aspects of the concrete whole that James accuses academic philosophers
of most frequently neglecting are the relationships denoted by the prepo-
sitions and conjunctions of ordinary speech — *in, on, of, with, but, and, if,
for, because*. To emphasize the inclusion of these empirically given elements of the course of events, elements that classic empiricisms had overlooked or denied, James coined the term " radical empiricism." To a
radical empiricist the attempted sublimation of causality into uniformity
of sequence is the height of vicious intellectualism.

Aside from neglecting the particular urgency of events the doctrine
that causality is but a name for regularity of sequence has two further
erroneous consequences. One of these is the failure to distinguish causal
efficacy and its absence. We are accustomed to say, not merely that the
exploding of gasoline in the cylinders causes the automobile to move
down the street, but also that the absence of gasoline in the tank causes
the automobile to stop moving. The latter statement is innocent, but
quite inexact. There is strictly no causal connection between the absence —
of something and the failure of an event to happen. Rather in such cases —
there is no such causal connection as we are perhaps looking for. The
lack of gasoline may well be called a " reason " for the stoppage of motion; for it points out to us what to do in order to remedy a distressing
situation. But if we adopt such language, we have not resolved causality
into mere uniformity of sequence. Lack of gasoline is as uniform an
antecedent of cessation of motion as the proper supply of gasoline is an an-

[7] *Some Problems of Philosophy*, p. 199.

tecedent of motion. And the method by which we establish the fact of causal connection between cause and effect may be the same by which we establish the non-causal connection between withdrawal of a cause and the non-occurrence of an effect. Doubtless there are causal connections in all events; and the event of the cessation of motion of an automobile will through analysis reveal that the friction of the moving car with the surrounding air and the road down which it was proceeding caused the car to come to a stop. But we can surely distinguish clearly between uniformities that are causal and those that are not.[8]

The other erroneous consequence of regarding causality as a name for uniformity of sequence is inability to distinguish between the cause and the " conditions " of an effect. Thus John Stuart Mill is led to say that the cause, e.g., of death after a person eats of a particular dish, is " the set of antecedents . . . but for which it would not have happened." That is, " the real Cause is the whole of these antecedents; and we have, philosophically speaking, no right to give the name " cause " to one of them, exclusively of the others." [9] And then we would have to say that a man's having a stomach was as much a cause of his death as the poisonous food, that the presence of villages in the path of a lava-flow was as much a cause of their destruction as the advancing lava-flow, that the lens of a camera was as much a cause of the spots on a photographic plate as the rays of light from the distant stars. Now if we wish to alter the usage of the term " cause " to include all conditions within which the causal connections are operating, we can do so; but there is a distinction between cause and condition, as the terms are normally used, that we should then have to designate by some other terms. It seems wiser to follow customary lan-

---

[8] It is just at this point that I am compelled to differ with the otherwise satisfactory treatment of causality by Professor C. J. Ducasse in his *Causation and the Types of Necessity*. He defines causality thus: " A state or change X of an object is said to have been the cause of a state or change Y of another object, if the factuality of X was *sufficient to* the factuality of Y." But in explaining what he means by *sufficient to* he drops out all reference to that natural necessity that is the essence of causality. He writes: " The change from not-X to X of object O was *sufficient to* the change from not-Y to Y of the object Q, if (1) the object Q in circumstances not-X, a, b, c, d, . . . was in the state not-Y, (2) the single change not-X to X of the object O in these circumstances occurred, and (3) the change not-Y to Y of the object Q then occurred " (pp. 55–56). This statement seems to me an admirable formulation of the experimental method of ascertaining causal connections and non-causal connections alike. But it also seems to ignore the essential difference between operation of a cause and the cessation of operation of a cause, and so fails to distinguish the nature of the very fact it aims to designate.

[9] *Logic,* Book III, Chapter V. section 3. (Harper's edition, New York, p. 237.)

guage practice where possible; and it is at least quite indefensible to ignore
a clear distinction in case we alter such practice. What we normally mean
by the conditions are all those circumstances without which the entrance
of a new element into the situation would not have the influence it does
have; and what we normally mean by cause is that new element which
enters the situation so as to alter what would otherwise have been the
outcome of the situation. This statement does not ignore the fact of
composition of causes for many, perhaps for all, effects; for whatever our
situation may be, the disturbance of the situation is, in such a complex
and interrelated world as ours, likely to be multiple and various. The
term " causality " does not designate the undisturbed development of a situation (if there be such situations), nor that part of the development of the
situation which is accounted for and understood in terms of the elements
that were present prior to some intrusion. Causality is essentially the
interference of new elements in existing situations. And if we extend the
meaning of the term to include all the connections in nature (coexistence,
sequence, distance, inclusion, etc.), we have not abrogated the specific
type of connection which the term has traditionally served to point out.

Some ancient mariner may have been guiding his ship across the seas
by the light of the stars. And if he met shipwreck at some definite point
through violent seas or coral reef, we could not completely describe his
shipwreck without reference to the stars by the guidance of which he
chanced to follow the particular route which brought him to the scene
of disaster. Yet it would be absurd to speak of the light of the stars as
one of the " contributing causes " of the shipwreck. And the absurdity
here is not merely due to the fact that many ships meet disaster where no
attention is being paid to the stars. Even if ships had always been guided
by the light of the stars, so that such guidance was an invariable antecedent of shipwreck, it would still be a non-causal condition of the result
we are dealing with. Similarly the earlier part of the uniform motion
of an object in a straight line would not be the cause of the later part of
that motion; for there is no new element to modify the uninterrupted
development of a " closed " situation.

Of course, it is true that causality is always mutually determining. And
nothing in the distinction between causes and conditions imperils recognition of this further fact. If the lava-flow causes the destruction of the
village, the village also causes the deflection or delay of the progress of

the lava-flow. If the star-light causes the spots on the photographic plate, the photographic plate causes the reflection or absorption of the light-rays. If the food causes the person's death, the person's body has been actively transforming the food. But we could not legitimately say that the presence of the villages on the hillside was one of the causes of their destruction, that the lava-flow was one of the causes of its deflection, that the photographic plate was one of the causes of its sensitivity to light-waves. Causal connection is always between two (or more) elements that affect each other, differently but specifically, so that neither element continues on in the process it would otherwise have exhibited. But the reciprocal causality of two elements does in no way imply that all the elements in a causal situation, however relevant to the outcome, are connected as " causes " with a specific result.[10]

In conclusion a word of warning may be added against an old misunderstanding of the idea of causality, a misunderstanding that has perhaps been responsible for the entire rejection of the idea by some thinkers. Causality is not a force or power. The recent endeavor to assist in the resurrection of the idea of causality from the limbo to which it has often been assigned (and this essay aims to assist in that endeavor) is not dependent upon any hypostatization of an abstract term. Causality is a name for a certain quality of events; it is not a name for the agency behind the events. The agency is there, to be sure: it is the lava-flow, the medicine, the light-rays, the mechanic's muscles, the tossing waves. There is no other " force," there is no other cause, than just these specific things. But these things are force*ful;* they operate; they produce. And they are forceful and operate and produce in that specific way we call necessary. Causality names that kind of necessary operation. Things, then, things in the sense of particular substances or concrete individual objects, are the causes which through analysis we always reach. But these things are not causes when taken in abstraction from the temporal passage in which

[10] Professor S. Alexander is only protesting against an extreme form of this mistaken notion when he attacks the supposition that the cause of any event is ultimately the whole universe. He writes: " If this were true the idea of cause would indeed retain a certain usefulness in practice, but as a theoretical basis of procedure in science it would be useless. But the objection rests on a misconception. It assumes that the operation of the stars is a motion which interferes with the causal act by which a man knocks another down; and does so because there is direct or indirect connection between all parts of the universe, throughout Space-Time. The question rather is whether the intimate causal relation mentioned is interfered with by the rest of the universe which undoubtedly sustains it." (*Space, Time, and Deity,* Vol. I, p. 229.)

they occur. They are causes when taken (as indeed they alone exist) in their efficacious activity. Or, to phrase the point differently, we do not find both things and causality in nature: rather we find causally active things. There has been considerable discussion between those who maintain that only *events* are causes and effects and those who maintain that *things* are causes and effects. It is like the battle between Tweedledum and Tweedledee. These two ways of conceiving the matter are, in spite of the logical battle fought over them, almost indistinguishable twins. For we can hardly say that in this world of ours we have, first, things and, secondly, events; but we have temporally-occurring things. And in such a world, it is not surprising that, no matter how much technical philosophers discard the idea of causality or resolve it into " nothing but " something else which is not causality at all, we all continue to be concerned with the compelling and necessary connections in which we stand to objects about us and find they also stand to one another.

EXTERNALISM IN AMERICAN LIFE

M. T. McClure

The conflict between Plato and the Sophists was over the rival claims of being and seeming to be. The Sophists were specialists in the art of keeping up appearances. What troubled Plato was not what they did not know any mathematics, but that they could talk in such a way as to make people think they did. Plato hated them because they were untrue to the Greek spirit. The essence of this spirit was fidelity to nature. The lines of division that separate one thing from another and form the bases of classification, order, and even of social distinctions, are lines of cleavage inwrought in the very structure of things. Nature was for Plato the model of all excellence and the pattern of all perfection. This metaphysical view finds expression on the moral side in the virtue of sincerity, a frank acknowledgment that we *are* where nature intended we should be. To cross the border lines of nature was the cardinal vice. Effrontery, pretense, over-stepping your limits, getting out of your element were immoral because they were unnatural.

As one grows older he feels less inclined to trust himself, and more inclined to put his confidence in the objective order of things. He feels, or perhaps would like to feel, that his ideals have some sort of cosmic validity. But when we are young we think that the energies flowing through our veins are products of our own creation. Quietism, submission, and renunciation seem confessions of weakness. Activity, achievement, prestige are the things that move us. Now it is doubtful whether Plato with all of his greatness had any real sympathy with youth. When Protagoras was in Athens the young man Hippocrates was so eager to see him and to make fresh intellectual contacts that he got up before daylight in order to enlist the aid of Socrates. But by the time Socrates had got through talking to him about his soul, surrounding him with cautions and warnings and inhibitions, all the boy's enthusiasm had gone.

The Sophists were much more in sympathy with the ambitions of youth. When they appeared Greek life was at its zenith, at least in outward form. Quick to take advantage of the opportunities afforded for personal glory, the Sophists turned philosophy into the art of rising in life. They sought to attain a specious greatness for the many that would compare favorably with the natural greatness of the few. Their aim in education was a sort of democratization of nobility. For the realization of this end a skillful artistry was more effective than formal discipline. What counts is not what you are but what you can succeed in making yourself seem to be. The metaphysical distinction between reality and appearance becomes a moral distinction between sincerity and pretense.

History never quite repeats itself. But the spirit of contemporary America is in many respects very like the spirit of the Sophists. Of course no sweeping formula will hold. Generalizations are usually untrue except where they are unimportant. But, for the most part, American life is an exhibition of appearances. We have not yet attained a firm hold on reality, if by reality we mean the inner, more subtle, and spiritual values of civilization. It is not too much to say that pretense is one of the dominant traits in American life.

We are not animated by what we are, but by what we wish we were. We do not make our homes expressions of our personality. With the aid of interior decorators we make them expressions of the personality we would like to have. Pretension is the chief factor in the psychology of our advertising. The appeal is not to the intrinsic merit of the object, but to the social ambition of the purchaser. In Europe one sees in the advertisement of a stove, for example, an ordinary stove with a contented man sitting in a comfortable chair remarking on the excellence of the heat. In America we design something resembling a musical instrument, call it a Heatrola, and display it in a spacious room filled with sophisticated people. The man who reads the advertisement thinks if he can just have that stove he will be like the people in the picture. We make the stove look like something that it is not, and we make the man feel that if he had the stove he would be like something he is not.

St. Augustine found the patterns for progress in the form of ideas in the mind of God. Exemplarism exists for us in more accessible form. We find our ideal world in *House Beautiful* and the *Ladies' Home Journal*. The fact is significant that nowhere except in America do we find such a wealth of popular magazines devoted to the external forms of refined living. Nowhere except in America are the appearances of culture made so accessible to the masses of the people. And what is even more significant, nowhere else in the world does there exist a people so eager to grasp what seem to them to be the marks of the ideal. The shop girl who confessed that she did not read the *Saturday Evening Post* as much as she *ought* to was expressing a moral idealism wholly suitable to her experience.

Every one knows that American hotels are the most luxurious in the world. There is no one who cannot for a day or for a week pretend to be a millionaire. The pages in our moving picture theaters are not there to show us our seats. They are there to create atmosphere. After the day's work the washerwomen have their entrances and their exits as ladies of the court. American life is so organized that every one can, in one form or another and at periodic intervals, pretend to be what he knows he is not. The criticism that our civilization is external, and that too often our manners are characterized by bluster and pose, describes a partial fact. Let us seek to understand it.

In Plato's *Republic* only soldiers and philosophers had social position. The Middle Ages added lawyers, doctors, and theologians. In modern times we have added men of business, industry, and the applied arts. The democratic ideal of equality has penetrated to the core of our national life. The result has been a leveling of values. If we are to trust our most recent historians our good men have been no better and our bad men have been no worse than the general run of us. Americans take their ideals seriously. When values cannot be equalized in reality they are equalized in appearance. We dignify the commonplace in the interest of social self-respect. Our fireside literature is devoted largely to the task of imputing a dignity to domestic service that we know very well is not there. It is easier to equalize things in outward show than in inner content. Striving after the ideal has this much of virtue, it affords a motive for effort and results in a gain in morale. For an undertaker to call himself a " mortician," perhaps because, as Mr. Aldous Huxley suggests, the word rhymes with mathematician and academician, may be a falsification of values, but it is also something more. To interpret what we are doing in terms of something better is to take the first step in the direction of the ideal. If the undertaker does not realize his scientific pretensions it is almost certain that his son will.

William James's *Will To Believe* formulated for us a philosophy of pretense. If you are unable to believe in God, act as if you believed, and the action will help to make the belief a reality. If you are unable to feel an emotion, go through the bodily movements that appear to accompany it. If you are unable to grasp reality in the fulness of its content, lay hold on the appearances; a firm grasp of them may help you to see what lies behind. This philosophy of pretense is partially applicable to our conduct. We seem to say to ourselves: If we are not sophisticated, let us act like people who are; if we are unable to appreciate art, let us pretend. Although we mistake appearance for reality, if we continue to imitate we are likely to acquire something of the spirit of the original.

Pretense is a bridge between an ideal and a failure. It is a compromise between dissatisfaction with what we are and inability to be all that we wish to become. Consciousness of limitation and pursuit of the ideal exist in American life to a degree not found elsewhere in the world, with the possible exception of Japan, and perhaps the young nationalists of China.

We are aware of our faults. We seem to be always analyzing ourselves in the efforts to discover them. We are conscious of the obvious limitations that come from isolation, frontier life, and preoccupation with material development. Our bluster is in part an honest effort to conceal our inexperience and in part mere whistling to keep up our courage. We have little of the self-assurance of the young debutante who, after a violation of convention, exclaimed: " I am so common that everybody knows I am nice."

Self-criticism, ambition, and vigor are characteristic of America. With a gift for progress unprecedented and unparalleled in the history of any people, we set about to improve ourselves. Our eyes are always fixed on the ideal. When we look at the ideal the obvious things we see are the appearances. They are all, it may be, that we are able to see. We lay hold of them thinking we are grasping the ideal in its entirety. In outward appearance we make ourselves like the models we admire. Our pretense is sincere although our judgment is immature.

In a general way what we have accomplished so far has been to appropriate the outward marks and visible appearances of the ideal. We have succeeded in making America in external form the best equipped nation in the world. But we are not yet satisfied with ourselves. We are discovering that there is still something we lack. The man who bought the Heatrola finds that after all he is not like the people in the picture.

When we discover that externalism falls short of the ideal, it is natural that criticism should first express itself in a rebellion against form and convention, and that it should emphasize the more direct appeal to the inner spirit of culture. It is not, however, that we have been going in the wrong direction, it is rather that we have not gone far enough in the direction we are already moving. We have changed the log cabin into the salon. It remains for us to discover the spirit that goes with it. It remains for us to see the inner significance and ideal possibilities involved in our material development. What the critics of externalism fail to see is that it has taken much experimentation in living to devise our social conventions and practical institutions and that more of the wisdom of the ages is embodied in them than is first apparent to the intellectually provincial. In accomplishing what we have already done, we have created a favorable material environment for the development of a rich and expanding inner life.

I believe profoundly that the same ambition, the same vigor, the same self-criticism that has led us to seek appearances will lead us beyond them. Already we are beginning to ask what our outward achievement means in the way of inner value. We are beginning to look for the spiritual equivalents of our material prosperity. When business corporations maintain scientific laboratories where co-operative research is bound to accomplish more than scattered individual effort, industrialism is setting an end for itself that transcends its medium. This is merely an example of what one may expect when America turns her genius in the direction of intellectual things. Of course, no one can predict the future of American life, but it seems reasonable to believe that when America turns her energies in the direction of art and the inner values of life she will produce a civilization that is no mere imitation of foreign culture, but something germane to her genius. It would not be surprising to find America applying her methods of organization and of wholesale production to the life of the spirit.

It is in the spirit of the foregoing analysis that our achievements and our mistakes are to be understood. It is inevitable that an age capable of apprehending the ideal only in the guise of appearance should over-evaluate the significance of outward form. That we have done this in many ways cannot be denied. We tinker with the external forms of living in the hope of improving the inner quality of life. In public affairs we have been led to an exaggerated trust in organization and excessive legislation. Plato said long ago: " Are not those the most amusing creatures in the world who think that by their everlasting enactment of laws they can make men good? "

Another mistake we have made, traceable in part to our limited conception of the ideal and in part to our passion for equality, has been to suppose that moral values can be produced by industrial reform. Now it is true that many of us are either too busy or too poor to do the things we ought to do. If only we were idle and rich how easily we might behave ourselves! So the economic reformer with a generous and opulent gesture would scatter wealth and leisure among a hundred million people, changing a famous and not altogether fallacious maxim into " the greatest idleness for the greatest number."

Aristotle said that the trouble with the Spartans was that they did not know what to do with their leisure time. Now leisure like grace is a dangerous thing. Grace is dangerous in a world that is prone to error. Leisure is dangerous in a world that is prone to idleness. And just as there are moral parasites who live on grace the devil will find work for idle hands to do. Leisure is effective only in a state of society that is civilized enough to know how to enjoy it. In so far as economic reform creates leisure it affords the condition of culture, but it is only the condition.

Even our educational practice has not been entirely free from the charge of externalism. The quarrel between Plato and the Sophists reappears. Plato emphasized the discipline that comes from training one's mind to the subject. He recommended rigorous training in science as the best preparation for a political career. The Sophists emphasized methods of presentation. Statesmen, they thought, were likely to find rhetoric more useful than metaphysics. Our emphasis on methodology, our teaching of teachers, our indefatigable energies expended on the modification of curricula, are more Sophistic than Platonic. In a few cases, although the instances are rare, our imitation of the German method of research has enabled mediocrity to pose in the guise of scholarship.

Notwithstanding our mistakes I believe our progress toward the ideal has been in accordance with a sound philosophy of ideals. No one quite so clearly and so forcibly as Professor Dewey has rightly evaluated the relative significance of the outer form and inner meaning. They are related to each other as means to ends. Living does not go on in a vacuum. Insistence on a spiritual ideal apart from the concrete conditions available for its realization ends in vain and vacuous abstraction. The worth of every institution is measured by what it contributes toward improvement in the inner quality of life. From Professor Dewey we have learned two things about ideals. One is that development of inner meaning comes through appropriation and criticism of outward form. To be effective ideals must project in fuller, freer, and safer form a value already experienced. As Aristotle says, one must live before one can live well. History everywhere illustrates the development of the inner through participation in the outer. The ideal of holiness came to the Jews only after long training in externalism, ceremonialism, and blood sacrifices. In the second place, ideals must be germane to the medium in which they function. Exotic ideals soon wither and fade.

Excessive preoccupation with ideals divorced from their material basis, the abstract manipulation of meanings severed from the subject-matter they are devised to interpret, gives rise to intellectualism. Intellectualism is a philosophy for the very young or for the very old. It begins in innocence and ends in detachment and impotence. Children are almost always rationalists. With little experience of the checks and frustrations of actual living, they see no reason why things should not be ideal. Innocence coupled with an exaggerated trust in reason is characteristic of all Utopias. The political and economic theories of early American life were conceived in intellectual terms. The " contract " theory of government and the doctrine of " abstract " rights are typical of intellectualism. Liberty, fraternity, and equality are ideal virtues which loom large in colonial periods, but they are met with as actualities only among men who have had experience enough to be generous, mellow, and urbane. The theory of enlightened self-interest was based on the belief that men were civilized enough to be discriminating in their interests and wise enough to pursue them intelligently. But this was a childish fallacy. When we pushed our civilization beyond the Alleghanies we ceased to be English children and became adolescent Americans. Abstractions had little use in Trans-Appalachia.

Professor Gilbert Murray has characterized the spirit of post-Aristotelian philosophy as a " failure of nerve." The turning of the spirit inward upon itself, the inordinate preoccupation with spiritual values, the renunciation of the world characteristic of the moral and religious life of the period is an example of old age and impotence. The same thing may be seen in India today. Hindu civilization is very old and very spiritual. In outward form, except for what England has contributed, there is little but degeneration and decrepitude. The Bengali clamor for self-government and exalt the ideal of freedom. If England were to withdraw from India, her civilization would collapse because there is no material framework for the support of her ideals.

The *Education of Henry Adams* is a remarkable example of individual disillusionment and impotence. It is the record of a man who had no control over the forces which were shaping his life. From his youth up he could never make contact with the civilization of which he was a part. He was startled at every turn by the play of a power which he could not comprehend and was bewildered by the surprises for which he had not been prepared. There was nothing in common between his ideals and the world in which he lived.

Human nature is a model of patience and will sometimes support an ideal that is alien to its being. At other times it institutes an instantaneous revolt. The Ameer of Afghanistan has just lost his throne by attempting to graft a foreign ideal on a people wholly unprepared to receive it. It is not likely that America will borrow her culture. We have advanced far enough for one to see that the trend of our civilization is indigenous. Our ideals are " conditioned " by the actualities with which we are confronted. It is in part the business of philosophy to take an inventory of resources, to interpret their meaning, and to project ideals that envisage in fuller and more enduring form those turns in experience that we have found to be good.

As a nation we are growing up. With infancy behind us, and with old age ahead, we are passing from adolescence to maturity, a period usually fraught with fervency, danger, and doubt. The dominant traits in our national life are for the most part transition traits and are to be understood as passing phases of growth. But development is not always even. Much of the dogmatism in current thinking, and a good deal pertaining to discipline, standardization, and rules of practice is evidence that our age is still very young. We should, I think, view our era of order and organization, of standardization and legislation, as affording opportunity for an apprenticeship suitable to our years, and as promising much for a comprehensive enlargement of mind when we shall have grown up.

Much of the complacent scepticism that is rampant in morals, in letters, and in art is typical of the adolescent mind striving to free itself from parental control. Here perhaps belong the literary *intelligencia*. These clever, multiform gentlemen who annihilate clergymen, statesmen, and philosophers have all the complacency with none of the humor of Jack the Giant Killer. When you find a spirited young man expressing his views in a violent reaction to what he believes to be the weight of authority and the burden of tradition, it should be said in his defense that his agitation is more the measure of the limitation of his experience than a wilful disposition to disbelieve. Complacency is characteristic of a certain immaturity of mind.

Even the current cynicism that finds occasional expression is no more than youth becoming conscious of itself. After all, intellectualism was no philosophy for an age of adolescence. Psychoanalysis, though far less imposing, was more germane to the incipient strivings of our latent energies. Unlike Adam, Freud was born and not created. It was natural, therefore, that he should have been more sensitive to the forces which produced him, a fact which he never seemed to forget. We can never be innocent again, now that we have uncovered the roots of our being. The discovery of the body came as a shock to dreaming youth. It undermined his idealism and entailed a re-interpretation of values. What shall it profit a man if he gain the world and lose his larynx? The historian, with his tongue in his cheek, tells us that the real George Washington was the man unclothed and in his right impulses. The collapse of intellectualism was bound to create surprise. It marks, however, no philosophical tragedy, but a stage in growth.

On the more strictly intellectual side, the development of contemporary psychology is an example of externalism, immaturity, and the passion for equality. With an experimental gesture the psychologist cut loose from philosophy. He was eager to establish himself as a scientist. Now science meant for him the achievements of chemistry and physics. Instead of investigating mental life in terms of its own subject-matter, and working out a set of psychological concepts germane to the nature of mental existence, the psychologist took over the already existing concepts of the mechanical sciences. In equipment and apparatus his workshop has all the appearance of a physical laboratory. Now that he has trained himself in the discipline of science, perhaps he will tell us something about the nature of our minds.

Mechanism is a philosophy which has great fascination for the young. It is so beautifully simple, so rational, so comprehensive in its explanatory value. It gives unity to all science and intelligibility to all experience. It is difficult to convince one who loves a shining formula that there is no one end capable of expressing the entire burden of free intellectual inquiry. Moreover, it is an observation quite familiar that concepts often outlive their usefulness and continue to operate in allied sciences after they have been abandoned or modified in the field in which they first arose. If we turn to the field of physical science we shall see that the concept of mechanism is steadily losing ground. In no other department of human thinking is a change in intellectual temper more observable. In 1903 the catalogue of one of the leading American universities made the statement that the future of physics was to be sought in the sixth decimal point. This meant that physics at least on its theoretical side was a closed subject. Its hypotheses had been experimentally verified, its basal concepts had been established on a firm foundation, all that was left to do was to refine its measurements. In 1915 the leading physicist of the country, in addressing the national association of physicists, said to the young men of the association: " Go back to your laboratories and try every fool experiment you can think of; nobody knows what may come of it."

The present uncertainty in science may be disconcerting, but it is far more promising than the smug statement that the future of physics lies in the sixth decimal point. There is good reason for thinking that the downfall of dogmatic science is the outstanding intellectual revolution of our time. Although uncertain, science is at least sincere. It may be that a formula is all that the scientist has been able to extract from his analysis of matter, but he is no longer deceived; he knows the formula is not the reality. The shell of externalism is broken in science. With our initiative, our love of experimentation, our tendency to be scientific, it is reasonable to suppose that it will also be broken in the sphere of practical conduct.

THE EMPIRICIST AND EXPERIMENTALIST TEMPER IN THE MIDDLE AGES

A PROLEGOMENON TO THE STUDY OF MEDIAEVAL SCIENCE

RICHARD McKEON

NOT a few changes which have occurred recently in inquiries into mediaeval phases of thought are to be traced to events and opinions long posterior to the end of the middle ages. Histories, no less than the doctrines they record, evolve in the evolution of the ages in which they are written; and the evolution of histories of thought becomes itself a decisive factor, though usually unstated, in the history of ideas stated and restated. Successive and differing interpretations of past philosophies and past sciences, consequently, are no less frequently expressions of contemporary theories of philosophy and science than vehicles for new knowledge of the past. Until recently it would have been proper to find the beginnings of modern philosophy in the seventeenth or the sixteenth century. If the neglect of the middle ages in the history of philosophy, which would have been good history two centuries ago, is bad history now, if mediaeval studies during the past few decades have succeeded in returning mediaeval philosophy to some dignity, the doubts that have been raised concerning what philosophy is, have played no less a part than have historical studies in determining where philosophy, or modern philosophy, may be said to begin.[1] As proper caution, therefore, preliminary to further inquiry into mediaeval science in particular, something of the theory of science should be stated before the remains of science in the middle ages are studied.

Usually a mechanistic science based on observation is intended when the traces of science are sought by inquirers into the middle ages. With difficulty a little that resembles science by such criteria has been discovered. Part of the middle ages, it seems, got along with no physics, and then the

---

[1] See R. McKeon, "Thomas Aquinas' Doctrine of Knowledge and its Historical Setting," *Speculum*, III, particularly 425 f. and 442 f.

physics of Aristotle, which was a false physics, was translated from the Arabic and the Greek. Against that Aristotelian physics the *moderni* of the fourteenth century and Galileo some centuries later formulated objections which constituted the initiation of modern physics. If this interpretation may be pushed a little further, the moment may have arrived to return, at present when modern physics is in turn discovering insufficiencies, to an inquiry into the principles of Aristotelian science which have been in bad repute for nearly three hundred years. It is even possible that the history of a science so different from modern sciences in manner and consequences may yet reveal fundamental points of likeness which might be of theoretic value in the study of later scientific developments. In any case, the opponents of the Ockhamites and of Galileo expressed a rival estimation of the aims and methods of science. Their writings, none the less, have seldom been examined for a contribution to the theory of science, for only such contributions are usually sought as will be harmonious and directly relevant to the inquiries and discussions of modern science. Abundant materials suggest that the difference between competent Aristotelians and Buridan or Galileo was not a difference between the false and the true, but rather in large part, a difference in problems discussed. The problems and the solutions of Aristotelian science were not the problems which modern science poses. If the study of the developments of fourteenth- and sixteenth-century science is to make estimation of what had gone before and what resulted, more is needed than just the statement of beliefs and conclusions. The practices and results of science cannot be judged finally or completely without its theory and purpose.[2]

---

[2] The judgments concerning whether or not there were sciences in the middle ages, and the judgments with respect to when science may be said to have begun, are all in terms of the science of the present. Pierre Duhem, in his monumental works, *Le Système du Monde* and *Etudes sur Léonard de Vinci*, pushes the beginnings of modern science two centuries earlier than had been possible before his studies. He finds precursors of Galileo and Copernicus in John Buridan, Albert of Saxony, Nicholas Oresme and their followers. "Si l'on voulait, par une ligne précise, séparer le règne de la Science antique du règne de la Science moderne, il la faudrait tracer, croyon-nous, à l'instant où Jean Buridan a conçu cette théorie [theory of impetus], à l'instant où l'on a cessé de regarder les astres comme mus par des êtres divins, où l'on a admis que les mouvements célestes et les mouvements sublunaires dépendaient d'une même Mécanique." (P. Duhem, *Etudes sur Léonard de Vinci*, 3ème série, Paris, Hermann, 1913, ix-x.) C. H. Haskins looks for the history of mediaeval science in the translations from the Arabic and the Greek by which the science of antiquity was recovered and assimilated, and in the extension of knowledge by experimentation and observation, by the treatment of disease, by geographical exploration, by observation of plants and animals, and in sum by the growth of the experimental method.

When it is said that there was no science during the middle ages or when the beginnings of science are sought, whether in the middle ages or later, both the opinion and the inquiry rest on the supposition that a point in history may be discovered at which the observation of nature, experimentation under proper controls and conditions, and finally the manipulation of the forces of nature by man may in some sense be said to have begun. There is a primary improbability in the supposition that during any considerable period of time man should have ceased utterly to observe and to attempt to control nature. At no time, of course, has the control of nature been complete or the interpretation of nature satisfactory in all details; during times of famine, war, disease, and distracting hardships it is usually difficult to recognize the results of human observation and control. To be sure, the devices of one age may be useless to accomplish the purposes of the succeeding age, and judgments are therefore not improperly passed on the purposes and wisdom of peoples and periods. Not only has it been supposed that during the middle ages interest in science and nature was at a low ebb, but reasons have been furnished abundantly to account for that state. Thirteen centuries of stagnation in the natural sciences could, until recently, be referred as effects to the " otherworldliness," the contempt for material things which attended the

---

It is science, not modern science that he seeks, but the traits by which he recognizes science indicate implicitly much the same notion of what science is and much the same departure from Aristotelianism. His judgment, therefore, of work done according to an Aristotelian method is usually without reference to the Aristotelian aims; for example, " Abelard would probably have said that what he acquired from the Arabs on the subject of physics was not so much facts or theories as a rationalistic habit of mind and a secular philosophy. The recourse to observation and experiment, already evident in the *De eodem,* appears likewise in the *Questiones,* in spite of its reliance for the most part on *a priori* reasoning." (C. H. Haskins, *Studies in the History of Mediaeval Science,* Cambridge, Harvard University Press, 1924, 39.) Lynn Thorndike studies the evolution and separation of science from its admixtures of magic, folk-lore, and religion. In the tracing of such an evolution, the estimation of previous science is referred to the last stages of science. For example, Roger Bacon's experimental method is discussed under the marginal title *Lack of Method*. " His explanation of the rainbow, which is his longest illustration of the value of experimental science, is based merely on ordinary intelligent observation and reasoning, although he adds at the close that tests with instruments are needed and that consequently he will not assert that he has reached the full truth of the matter. . . . Of laboratory equipment, of scientific instruments, of exact measurements, he has no more notion than his contemporaries." (Lynn Thorndike, *A History of Magic and Experimental Science During the First Thirteen Centuries of Our Era,* New York, Macmillan, 1923, II, 652–653.) Despite, therefore, the excellent studies which have so recently made available materials on the history of mediaeval science, the estimation of what science was intended to be prior to and other than what modern science became, has not been attempted.

advance of Christianity. Parallel with the beginnings of Christianity were traced a decline of reason and a decline of interest in experience of the world and nature. Recently the causes for the situation have been extended: the decline of reason is recognized, not merely in Christianity, but in the social, moral, and intellectual degradation of the Roman world; the degradation is seen manifested in Stoicism, Platonism, and the mystery religions no less than in Christianity itself.[3] If this decline and its causes are carried over to the middle ages, many influences can be found operating against science, the interest in theology which is destructive of naturalistic philosophical conceptions, a human fondness for the fallacious, and not least Aristotle.

There is, notwithstanding this history of the decline of interest in observation, and notwithstanding the excellent reasons which can be made to account for it, a mass of facts and observations recorded in the literature, pagan as well as Christian, of the first centuries of Christianity. Moreover, strange facts and observations are fitted, during that period and during the later middle ages, into an elaborate system of theory and explanation which give them an interpretative significance comparable with that of the facts of later science. Clearly, since facts do not exist separate from the system of thought to which they are proper, these facts are not the facts of the modern world. Like the facts of physics which are impossible to conceive without the theories of physics, the facts observed during the first thirteen centuries of Christianity cannot be taken in isolation; yet in isolation from the system of thought proper to them they have been read as evidence of an antirationalism and distaste for observation which has then been made the characteristic of the period. The letters, the controversies, the rhetorical interpretations, if they are conceived on the analogy of a later period, depart from all of a variety of facts attested by observation. Yet the startling quality, to modern minds, of the facts observed during the period of early Christianity and the middle ages may be explained by the circumstances that observation depends on thought no less than thought depends on observation. Mediaeval philosophers and some modern philosophers have treated specifically the theory of this relation of thought and observation. Though we have forgotten many of the mediaeval truths, the methods and interpretations of

[3] See, for example, W. R. Halliday, *The Pagan Background of Early Christianity* (Liverpool, University Press, 1925), especially Lecture VI, on " The Decline of Rationalism."

what might be called mediaeval science can be examined only after some statement of the relation of experience and principles has been made.

The instances which have been taken to indicate an absence of interest in the things of nature during the early period of Christianity can be balanced and rectified by examining what the contemporary observer did see when he looked about him. Thus, the comparative rarity of descriptions of nature in the literature of the time, often insisted on, is significant only if one consider, too, records like those of travelers to the Holy Lands during the fourth and fifth centuries. These record in detail what a Christian saw on journey. Among such travelers of the time, two of the companions of Jerome, Paula and Eustochium, her daughter, preceded him to Jerusalem. They wrote, about the year 386, to urge their friend Marcella to join them. Their persuasions are fortified with frequent quotations from the Bible concerning those who were advised to leave their homelands and concerning the spiritual advantages of this place. For all the symbolism and scriptural quotation one reads the passage with the unweakened recognition that this is the description of Judea. The letter continues,

This land, mountainous and raised up on a height, delights the spirit the more the further it is removed from the delights of the world . . . In this city, and particularly in this place, Adam is said to have lived and to have died. Therefore the place in which our Lord was crucified is called Calvary, namely, because the skull [*calvaria*] of ancient man was preserved there, so that the second Adam, that is, the blood of Christ dripping from the cross, might wash away the sins of the first Adam and the first man lying there and that the word of the Apostle might then be fulfilled, " Awake, thou that sleepest, and arise from the dead, and Christ shall shine upon thee." (*Ephes.* 5, 14.) It is long to review how many prophets, how many holy men this city sent forth. The name of the province, of the city, is the whole of our mystery. It demonstrates the faith of the Trinity in three names, *Jebus,* and *Salem,* and *Jerusalem.* The first is *trodden under foot;* the second, *peace;* the third, *vision of peace.* For by degrees we come to the end and after the treading under foot we are raised up to the vision of peace: from which peace Solomon, that is, *he who was pacified,* was born in peace, *and His place was made in peace.* (*Psal.* 75.) And in the figure of Christ, under the etymology of the city, the Lord of those who rule and the King of kings takes his name. What shall I say of David and of all his progeny, which ruled in this city? As Judea is more sublime than other provinces, to that degree is this city more sublime than all Judea. And (to state it very briefly) the glory of the whole province is vindicated in the metropolis, and whatsoever is of praise in the members is referred entire to the head.[4]

There is a great deal of description of this sort, and the manner of its narration makes clear that the description is of the relics and memorials of Christ, left in the country in which the miracles of the faith were enacted. The land is the sum of the mysteries of Christianity, and if there are few attempts in contemporary writings to describe the externals of the countryside, there are on the contrary frequent attempts to state the very essence which is, for example, the truth of the Trinity embodied among many truths in Jerusalem and conveyed by the name " Jerusalem." Paula and Eustochium saw in Jerusalem this embodiment of the truths of Christianity. To much the same end Bonaventura, centuries later, trav- elled to Mount Alverna to write his *Itinerary of the Mind to God* on the spot at which St. Francis received the stigmata; yet if the document is read literally it is difficult to find the description of the place and the process which Bonaventura had undertaken to relate. The place and the event are described in the statement of the truth they contain. The marks of truth are scattered throughout nature and literature. The very letters of the Hebrew alphabet have hidden and profound significances; the proper names of the Bible, too, have meanings which help express the truths of the holy writings, as the name of Solomon, *he who was pacified,* fits the interpretation of the meaning of Jerusalem; finally, all names of places, no less than the name of Jerusalem, have their meanings. There was in the various ancient tongues a developed science of names, as little known and as little sympathetic to us as the Pythagorean science of numbers. The Christian interpretations of the Scriptures follow in an old tradition and contribute to it only a small part of its lore, the *onomastica sacra,* lists of meanings of names which occur in the Scriptures, such as Jerome was anxious to translate from the Greek of Origen that they might be available to the Latins. The science of names in turn is only a small part of the elaborate system of analogy and etymology by which the truths of sacred books might be known. When the Christian of those days accepted the Bible and found not only all wisdom but the beginnings of all sciences there, or when he saw God manifested about him on all sides, his discovery was made by such means and aids.

[4] *Epistola* XLVI (*Patr. Lat.* XXII, 484–485).

The system of these analogies is, of course, the structure of the superstition which has so frequently been found in the writings of the Church
Fathers and the Doctors of the middle ages. Even so considered, however, the analogies and etymologies are not disposed of finally and adequately. They were devices of thought widely spread in ancient systems
of science and philosophy, not peculiarities introduced with the beginnings of Christianity or the decline of the Roman Empire, and the subtlety
and effectiveness they developed cannot be swept aside in the assumption
that logic was at the time in its infancy and that these were the vagaries
that attended its early developments and false starts. Symbolism, reasoning by etymology, the logic of essences and internal relations were common in pagan Greek and Latin writers and even in writers in the Semitic
languages. Plato, Varro, Philo Judaeus had speculated on the philosophy
of etymology before Origen and Jerome. The pseudo-Plutarch found the
beginnings and the sum of the sciences, history, philosophy, politics, the
seven arts, medicine, the art of war and gymnastics in Homer as readily
as the Christian philosopher found the same wisdom in the Bible. Contemporaries of these writers, like Cicero and Plutarch, were sometimes
violent in their condemnation of the effort to find in the ancient poets
the whole of later sects and opinions, of which the poets themselves must
have been, save in anticipation, unaware. From our vantage point in the
present age, since we assume that the legitimate basis of reason is different
from this formal, non-genetic, non-historical approach, the tendency is to
agree with Cicero and brand such thinking primitive vagaries, undisciplined and wholly lacking in historical sense. This, however, is to
ignore that it did not involve theories of history, but theories of knowledge.
Ancient philosophy furnished for this manner and mechanism of thought
an excellent speculative foundation; since our own theories of knowledge
are in confusion there is little speculative ground for condemning the
manner of thought because its products are not found to be in conformity
with what we sometimes hold to be the truths of science. Doubtless it
has in the course of history led into absurdities; doubtless there have been
quacks who practised it; but the ancestry of science is involved in its
speculations no less than in the practices of the technological tradition
or in the advances of machines, and it is not impossible that the logic of
modern science operates on a system of similar analogies.

If the observations and the experimentalist knowledge in the middle ages are to be examined in full, there is, to be sure, the tradition of the technologies as well as this tradition of analogical interpretation to be examined. The advances in the crafts, particularly in the art of building during the twelfth and thirteenth centuries, the changes in methods of planning, geometric drawing, projections, stereotomy, systems of traction and leverage, empirical calculation of thrusts, strains, loads, the use of architectural materials, particularly stone and glass, might be studied for the rich details of precise observation which each of the alterations involved. In the tradition of the technologies and the crafts was perpetuated the expert knowledge of how things are made, and in that tradition the explanations of things are, therefore, in terms of their efficient causes. The tradition of analogical explanation from which poetry, theology, magic, and astrology grew, differed from the tradition of the technologies in that it sought to explain the qualities of a thing by the essence of the thing and sought therefore to know forms, not to produce objects. The analogies of the one tradition and the efficiencies of the other were, of course, brought together eventually, and the explanations and the magic of modern science resulted. But the efforts of the great thinkers of the middle ages were exerted in varying ways to prevent the confusion of the two traditions, for it was everywhere the conviction that things and even events could not be explained by external and efficient causes. The circular movement of the stars, the attraction at a distance evident in the fall of a heavy body or in the movement of iron to a magnet, the transmission of light, the effects observed in medicine and alchemy, the hidden life and power of animals, plants, and even minerals, all require for their explanation, not forces external to the thing, but the adequate statement of the nature of the thing itself. These were the occult forces which were at work no less than the obvious external causes.

The opposition of the two traditions of observation is not the opposition simply of science to superstition, nor is it the opposition of a tradition of reasonable systematic explanation to a tradition of collected strange facts. Rather there are two traditions of science based respectively on different types of causes, efficient causes and formal or final causes. Sometimes the two sciences have been kept separate in single systems: probably the anomalous positions of Kepler, of Ockham, and of some of the Ockhamites might be explained through their success in distinguishing formal from efficient causes and recognizing the place of both. In the mathematical and rationalist (or in the theological) traditions, the formal cause tends to absorb the efficient, while in the empiricist tradition the formal cause is foresworn and introduced surreptitiously and unexamined among efficient causes. It is significant of the place which observation occupied in the science of formal causes that the terms " experimental " and " experimentator " and, if the literature is to be credited, the fact of experimentation occurred first in the tradition of magic. In the twelfth century (and earlier periods had their equivalent preferences) a magical formula usually laid claim to ancient authority, preferably the authority of Rasis or Galen, but it always owed its place in any particular collection of formulae to the circumstance that the collector had personally experimented and found the formula efficacious. Usually included in such collections of observations, illustrating the irreducibly non-mechanical nature of the occult influences with which magic operates, are statements of the manner of the transmission of light, electro-magnetic phenomena and examples of actions performed at a distance. That these are among the phenomena that have proved least amenable to later mechanistic physics may be passed by. But the observation is unavoidable that the manner in which the magician and the craftsman tested his knowledge, modified it when necessary, or attributed unsuccess to faulty arrangements of material or the intrusion of an uncalculated element, would be the same. If there is therefore a difference in the observations, in the experiments and facts of the two, and if both are different from the observations of later science, that difference should be examined not in experimentation, but in the theories which motivated and directed the experimentation.

So far as there was a theory of scientific knowledge prior to the twelfth century (and whether the expression of the theory was Platonic or Aristotelian in emphasis) it was a theory of knowledge by analogy and by formal causes. The logic was Aristotelian based on the surviving books of the *Organon* and on scattered bits of information concerning the rest of the Aristotelian philosophy. From the end of the twelfth century through the speculations of the *moderni* of the fourteenth century, the theory of science was in detail and accurately Aristotelian even among the opponents of the dominican Aristotelianism. In the relation of experience to science there is no great alteration from the doctrines of the Aristotelians of the twelfth century through Albertus Magnus, Thomas Aquinas, Duns Scotus, William of Ockham. There are many and detailed disputes concerning the details of the relation, concerning the steps of the transition from experience to science and from science to experience, concerning the source and the warrant of knowledge of first principles.   But the fundamental relations are stated as definitely in John of Salisbury, Abailard, Hugo of Saint-Victor as in the writings of any of the two hundred years of philosophers who succeeded them.   John of Salisbury quotes Aristotle to the effect that all art or science must draw its origin from the senses.[5] But that doctrine does not lead him to suppose that the things of experience are either the subject-matter or the test of science. To the contrary, despite the repeatedly avowed empirical origin of knowledge, nothing occurs in fact as it is understood truly.[6] Between the two statements there is no contradiction except in seeming. They return properly to the Aristotelian paradox that demonstrative knowledge depends on first principles, "common conceptions," which are prior in the mind and which are known through themselves. Only demonstrative knowledge is certain, for it alone proceeds from the true to the true by syllogism. Yet first principles, known *per se,* are arrived at by induction, as Aristotle understood induction. Without experience, without the senses, principles cannot be known.[7] Reason has the power to transcend sensation although it begins with the materials of sensation; in knowledge reason contemplates all things in their eternal causes.

This is an accurate statement of Aristotelianism, although it was written before the translation of the *De Anima* or the *Metaphysics*. The disturbing knowledge of Avicenna and Averroes and the speculations concerning the active intellect did not enter in John of Salisbury's Aristotelianism, but the disputes of Aristotelians can be ignored for the moment in the recognition that the varying statements of science and of method from the time of Boethius, but especially after the twelfth century, reflect something of this Aristotelian background. If the science of the period is read with its Aristotelian tendency in mind, some of the paradoxes found in it by later readers disappear. It is not longer surprising, for example, that a trained experimentalist should insist on deductive demonstration of the knowledge which his experience opened to him. Nor is the extreme im-

---

[5] quia, ut ait Aristoteles: *Ars sive scientia originem trahit a sensu. Metalogicus,* IV, xx (*Patr. Lat.* CXCIX, 928).

[6] "Nihil enim tale in rebus occurrit, tale quid tamen fideliter intelligitur." *Meta.,* II, xx (*Patr. Lat.* CXCIX, 886).

[7] *Meta.,* IV, viii (*Patr. Lat.* CXCIX, 920–921).

portance which John of Salisbury, Richard of Saint-Victor, Descartes, and dozens of other philosophers saw for science in self-consciousness an unexplained confusion of the nature of thought.[8] And finally, the place at which modern science emerges from the double tradition of magic and the technologies, interpreted in the light of this much of the Aristotelian doctrine of knowledge, becomes rather less the fortunate accident it figures as in another interpretation.

The place of experimentation and the meaning of observation indicated in the doctrines of these men are doubtless sufficiently strange to modern conceptions to justify, by way of clarification, their detailed examination in the writings of one of the mediaeval philosophers who stated them definitely. Roger Bacon has suffered unduly from the exaggerated importance that has been given to his espousal of the experimental method and experimental science. Read partially, his account seems to anticipate much that is thought of as modern; read more fully it disappoints the further expectations of a modern inquirer. Expositions of his philosophy have rarely touched the medium ground between proclaiming him a genius three centuries ahead of his time and berating him a carping critic and unoriginal borrower of the ideas of men he criticized. Yet his statement of the Aristotelian sense of experimental science is clear and not unsubtle. His fundamental judgment of the value of experimental science is that without experience nothing can be known truly. Reason may lead to a conclusion and may even induce the acceptance of the conclusion; but only when the conclusion is discovered in experience is doubt removed, and the mind rests then in the perception of truth. Even in a mathematical demonstration the mind will not cleave to the conclusion without experience. Experience, to be sure, is of two kinds, one by way of the external senses, the other by interior and divine illumination, but even that more human experience has three prerogatives other than sciences. First, it investigates by experiments the conclusions of other sciences; second, it delivers to us truths within the confines of those sciences which the sciences could not have discovered in any other way; third, it opens to us an unexcelled knowledge of past, present, and future.

---

[8] See John of Salisbury, Meta., IV, xl (*Patr. Lat.* CXCIX, 943), "Nam *se nosse,* sicut ait Apollo, *fere summa sapientia est."* Or Richard of St. Vicar (*Patr. Lat.* CXCVI, 116), "Nihil recte aestimat, qui seipsum ignorat."

These statements, taken together with the pretentious reiterations of a needed and new instauration of the sciences, sound new enough and are, in fact, reminiscent of the program of the other buccinator of new sciences, three centuries later, who bore the same surname. Before the heralded science is taken in the present sense of experimental science, however, further aspects of science and method remain to be examined. The separation of the experimental science from other sciences, even from mathematics, is at the outset suggestive, if this is, as it has been interpreted to be, the announcement of the laboratory technique. Fortunately, Bacon gives examples of each of the prerogatives he attributes to experimental science. His most significant and longest illustration is of the first prerogative, that experimental science investigates the conclusions of other sciences. Other sciences, he says, derive their principles from experience, but their conclusions are arrived at by deduction from principles so established. What experimentation supplies for them is a particular and a complete experience of their conclusions. In great detail the rainbow is examined to illustrate the principles of science and experimentation. The many ways in which the rainbow, or the phenomena of the spectrum, may be produced are stated; its colors, shape, its position and elevation relative to the sun, its size, time and place of formation are examined; the question is raised concerning whether it is produced by reflection or refraction; its motion relative to the observer is discoursed on; whether the colors are real or only apparent, and whether or not they are the consequence of a defect of vision, is discussed. Much of this is good enough observation, though to be sure, much of it falls beyond merely empirical determination. But the type of contribution which experimental science can make is clear: where alternative explanations are possible, observation may single out traits in the phenomenon which fit it to one explanation better than to the other.[9] Reason cannot determine such a choice between explanations, but experimentation on a large scale with instruments and with the various necessary means can. Bacon concludes modestly therefore, among other conclusions, that he has not grasped the whole truth since he has not made all the necessary experiments.

The proper estimation of the place of experimental science, however, cannot be made from this appeal to experience alone. The conclusions

[9] See, for example, Bacon's explanation of the corona, *Opus Majus* (ed. Bridges, London, Williams and Norgate, 1900), II, 198–200.

which experimentation undertakes to prove are the conclusions of other sciences, and those sciences have their own principles, based on experience, to be sure, but independent of this experimental science. Fortunately, we have Bacon's statement of the contribution which another science can make to our knowledge of the rainbow. It is seldom read in connection with the constatations of the experimental science, yet it is their necessary other half. In the Second Part of the *Opus Majus* Bacon is concerned to show the affinity of philosophy with theology and particularly to show that the whole of philosophy and science is contained in the sacred Scriptures. He illustrates, in the eighth chapter of that section, how the Scriptures may be the source of knowledge of the rainbow.[10]

But the whole intention of philosophy is only to work out the natures and properties of things, wherefore the power of all philosophy is contained in the sacred writings; and this is especially apparent in that the Scripture deals with creatures far more surely and far better and more truly than philosophic labor is able to work out. This may be shown, out of infinite examples, for the present in the rainbow. The philosopher Aristotle disturbs us with his obscurities, nor are we able to understand through him anything that is proper; nor is that surprising since Avicenna, his chief imitator, the prince and leader of philosophers after him, confesses (as the commentator says in connection with Aristotle's chapter on the rainbow in the third book of the Meteors) that he does not understand the nature of the rainbow very well. The cause of this is that philosophers did not know the final cause of the rainbow; and having ignored the end they do not know the things which lead to the end, because the end imposes a necessity on those things which are ordered to the end, as Aristotle holds in the second book of the Physics. But the final cause of the rainbow is the dissipation of aqueous vapor, as is manifest from the book of Genesis, whence in the apparition of the rainbow there is always a resolution of clouds into an infinity of drops. And the aqueous vapors are consumed in the air and in the sea and in the land, for one part of the rainbow falls into the spheres of water and earth. Moreover, the consumption of the aqueous vapor cannot be through the rainbow except as the rays of the sun accomplish it, for by various reflections and refractions an infinity of rays are congregated, and the congregation of rays is the cause of the resolution and consumption of the waters, and for that reason the rainbow is generated by multiple reflections. For the rays cannot be congregated except by fraction and reflection, as will be shown later in its place. From the Scripture, then, when it is said in Genesis, " I shall place my bow in the clouds of heaven, that there may no more be a deluge over the earth," the final cause of the rainbow itself is given, from which can be investigated the efficient cause and the mode of generating

[10] *Opus Majus,* II, 8; III, 52–53.

the rainbow. This mode is not sufficiently known to philosophers, as their books make manifest to us. And so it is with every creature. In fact, it is impossible for man to know the ultimate truth of the creature as it is employed in the Scripture, unless he shall have been especially illuminated by God. For creatures are employed there to bring forth the truths of grace and of glory, concerning which philosophers were ignorant, and therefore they did not attain to the most exalted power of the wisdom of creatures, such as the sacred Scripture contains in its bowels. Whence all the excellence of philosophy reposes in the literal sense ornamented with the sacred mysteries of grace and of glory, as if wreathed in a manner of paintings and of most noble colors.

All philosophy and all sciences were revealed to the patriarchs and were stated in the Scriptures, but the relation of that revelation to the experimental science is laid bare in the circumstance that the patriarchs were given their exceptionally long lives that they might fill in from experience the details of the sciences. The frame and form of the conclusions of the sciences are in the Bible, but if one is to have a particular and complete experience of those conclusions, experimental science must be invoked. Many of the apparent contradictions of Bacon's position arise from his double mission: his is the position at once of the prophet and the scientist; he is announcing the old truths and revelations and at the same time the new discoveries which are the fruit of his experimentation and yet fit the old truths. The laws long known were to be seen in particular detail and exemplification. It is not improper for him, therefore, when he has shown by observation five colors in the rainbow, to attempt to justify his experimental results *a priori*.

For the number five is better than all other numbers, as Aristotle says in the Book of Secrets, and this is true with respect to distinguishing the number of things truly, although the number three is better with respect to the numeral property found in anything. For we derive the latter number from the nature of things, as Aristotle says in the first book on the Heavens and the World, because in everything there is a trinity, as Aristotle shows in that work, in Creator as well as in creature. Wherefore nature intends five colors in preference, because the number five distinguishes things more certainly and better. Therefore these five colors are in the rainbow rather than any others, in accordance with the general ordination of nature which carries into effect and intends that which is best.[11]

The enterprise is avowedly a search for final causes, and since it is no longer proper to speak of purpose explicitly in science, it is not difficult

[11] *Opus Majus,* VI, 12; II, 197.

to condemn as unscientific the teleological explanation which results. The nature of purpose in the sense in which Bacon seeks it may be made clearer from the remaining two prerogatives of experimental science. The second prerogative is that experimental science is able to give us important truths within the confines of the other sciences which they could not have learned in any other way. This circumstance leads Bacon to suggest a wise caution to those who would learn from experience, namely, that prior to experience one must not seek first a reason by which to understand, for the reason will come after the experience. Therefore one should go to the experiment prepared to believe until after the experience, and then reason may function. This Bacon illustrates by the example of the magnet, which is ubiquitous in magical treatises. Before seeing the operation of the magnet, the description of an object which attracts iron to it from a distance is hardly credible; after the experience it can be made credible and can be interpreted in systems of reasons. Or again mathematics can produce the spherical astrolabe on which astronomical phenomena may be described according to latitude and longitude. But that the measurements should apply precisely to the diurnal movement of the earth is not to be determined by mathematics, but by experience. In the same way, medicine cannot teach the means of prolonging human life, but experimentation can. The third prerogative of experimental science is another instance of this distinctness of reason and experience: experience affords particular knowledge of past, present, and future, and the experimental science can itself perform wonderful works, for it knows what can happen in nature and what can be effected in art.

Bacon's expression of the theory of science may be taken to apply excellently to science and magic as they were practised throughout the middle ages. There are, of course, a great many other contemporary theories of the relation of experience and knowledge. Bacon's theory, however, although it is not unique, is a subtly conceived and very effective theory; the objections which have been raised against it are directed for the most part against the facts it accepted, the hypotheses it elaborated, or the laboratory means it employed, not against the relation it stated beween experience and knowledge, between fact and theory. It is safe to say that Bacon would have recognized no facts in isolation from theories, for the scientific generalities to be found in the Bible and the first principles of metaphysics can be classified in this respect with scientific theories. In the estimation, then, of the scientific achievement of the middle ages, in the statement of the corpus of mediaeval observations of nature, it is a needed precaution that the facts be stated only in the environment of the theory to which they are fitted. Such a precaution is not to the end of discovering truths in every statement of centuries of voluminous writers, but to the end of understanding the truth which is stated before it is estimated and rejected. There was quackery, ignorance, charlatanry in the middle ages as there is now; much that was written was without adequate ground of experience or proof; much of the inquiry was directed to ends which we should today judge to be chimerical or unattainable. But the historian of science need not be limited to hunting the records of the past for instances of the predilections of his own age. It is interesting to note that much of the magic of the middle ages would be called superstition now; it is interesting too that present-day pharmaceutical manufactories have found valuable specifics against diseases by delving among magical formulae. But there remains besides either interest the question of what was conceived to be the nature of things which was implied in these formulae and practices, and what knowledge was conceived to be, and what methods were thought to be effective in the search for laws of natures and things.

When the history of science is examined from this point of view, the formulation of methods in modern science is seen as an evolution from the magical tradition. The magical formulae expressed first the recognition of the importance of experience for the discrimination between the good and bad among magical practices. Roger Bacon's experimental lore is so closely related to this magical wisdom, that much of the *Opus Majus* reads like magical formulae; scarcely any specific bit of information is advanced there without the specification that Bede or Aristotle or Galen is authority for it and that we know it from experience. When Bacon criticizes magic he disavows the illusions of magic, the incantations, sacrifices, invocations, conjurations, and cults, but many of the magical experiments he repeats, and he finds their foundation in the nature of things. Frequently the influences that move things are mysterious and occult, but mystery is the mark of much that the experimental method handles. The fourteenth century is prolific of attacks on astrology and alchemy that, like Bacon's attack on magic, inveigh against magical spells and extreme superstitious practices, but yet retain a great deal of the

sciences they condemn. Today these criticisms are judged most usually
to be the works of men in revolt against a superstition from which they
were only partially freed. Yet they are works unusually explicit in the
statement of the purposes of their authors: in the place of astrology is to
be expounded a science of final and formal causes freed from the myths
with which earlier writers had encumbered it. The relation of things to
the changeless principles of things, no less than the separation of principles and things, was in this manner clear in the mind of Paracelsus;
the logical background of the theory of induction and the materialism of
Telesio and Campanella was clearly expressed. Yet in the history of
modern science the one is seldom more than a bumptious, mystifying,
though occasionally shrewd charlatan; the others are omitted as if they
contributed nothing relevant to the discussion of science. Confusion was
introduced into their ideas after their time in the philosophy of another
man, but notwithstanding, the figure of Francis Bacon, who borrowed
much of his science and his facts from Paracelsus and who took over a
garbled version of induction and the doctrine of ideas from Telesio,
looms still massively among the beginners of scientific method. Boyle is
separated in the story of the growth of science from Paracelsus to whom
he owes so much, and that Newton was an alchemist is forgotten in the
generalization that science, of course, evolved from magic by shedding
its superstition and retaining its truth.

The changes by which it was possible for modern science to emerge
from magic need further, if they are to be understood, the elaboration
of the history of the techniques. Progress in the crafts, in building, and
navigation had introduced a body of material, constantly increasing, to
which the generalizations of theology, alchemy, and magic might be
applied. One has only to read the opening pages of the *Two New
Sciences* to see the bustle of commercial Venice in the background of the
science of Galileo, and it is not impossible to see the speculations of John
Buridan on impetus and mass bolstered on observations of a similar commercial background in the fourteenth century. At present the first stir-
rings of modern science are customarily sought in the works of John
Buridan, Albert of Saxony, Nicholas Oresme, Peter d'Ailly, and other
speculators who followed in their steps. That these writers and their
contemporaries discussed earnestly the problems of local motion, particularly uniformly accelerated motion, and the problems of the position of

the earth in the universe, constitutes clearly the beginnings in question of modern science; during this period, too, were formulated such conceptions as inertia, mass, center of gravity, the devices of analytical geometry, the rotation of the earth, the laws of motion. But besides the contrast of this science to a science in which problems such as these did not occupy a central place, there is the problem of what had happened in method and in the conception of the universe to make such a change possible.

The progress of the techniques is only one out of many approaches to this problem. There is the same problem in the peculiar place that mathematics occupies in the evolution of science. Mathematics had an important rôle in the sciences of final and formal causes; it had a place of no less importance, though totally different, in the formulation of the laws of mechanistic physics. But here again latterday estimations of the movements of the evolution are somewhat biased, for the Neo-pythagorean speculations of, say, the Alexanderians are labeled most usually (when contrasted to the formulae of modern physics which are labeled science) superstition. Mathematical terms were early attached to practitioners in both the magical and the technological traditions: during the middle ages the *mathematici* were magicians, the geometers were architects, or perhaps more properly engineers or stonecutters. With the progress of each tradition mathematics came to have in each a more and more interpretative function. However, to present the mathematics of the Platonic tradition or the Pythagorean tradition, or the mathematics of astrology or magic would be as difficult, not to say impossible, at the present stage of research and of scientific sympathies, as to present satisfactorily the symbolism which held in words no less than in numbers. Yet the symbolism of modern mathematics might be stated more easily if its nature and its similarity to what has gone before were more apparent.

Moreover, the shift to the science of efficient causes and the successive advances in it, which can perhaps be correlated with changes in technology, are interdependent step by step with changes in mathematics. The greater number of scientists in the fourteenth century were good mathematicians no less than good logicians, and it would not be a meaningless explanation of the formulation Galileo made of the science of mechanics to derive it from his discovery that time might be represented graphically as the side of a triangle of which distance and velocity are the other two sides rather more than from any experimental discovery. In any case what happened in the beginnings of modern mechanistic science could after such investigation be told as somewhat other than a turning from a false and inaccurate science, or even a turning from the biological science, which Aristotle's malign authority had foisted on the middle ages, to a science which permitted a mathematical formulation. Then, still other anomalies in the history of science disappear. Not only does Francis Bacon's program become a somewhat less miraculous occurrence, not only is the place of the Ockamites in history to be explained, but one is tempted to speculate, at least pending satisfactory editions of Ockham's physics, on the position of Ockham himself. For it was from his followers that the formulation of modern mechanics very directly derived, yet such notions as impetus and inertia are not to be found so treated in his works. This has been read as the mark of weakness in a great mind, but one may be permitted to suspect that what Ockham's disciples derived from him would be formulated differently in his own works, that the Aristotelian physics, which he stated and criticized excellently, might, if his statement of an almost modern version of it were known, be saved the indignities to which later commentators on Galileo submit it, and that finally the puzzled theoricians of the method of modern science may find suggestions in the forgotten logic of a physics in which efficient causes were one of the four kinds of causes and local motion one of the six kinds of motion to be studied.

THE NATURE OF THE PAST

George H. Mead

The present is not the past and the future. The distinction which we make between them is evidently fundamental. If we spread a specious present so that it covers more events, as Whitehead suggests, taking in some of the past and conceivably some of the future, the events so included would belong, not to the past and the future, but to the present. It is true that in this present there is something going on. There is passage within the duration, but that is a present passage. The past arises with memory. We attach to the backward limit of the present the memory images of what has just taken place. In the same fashion we have images of the words which we are going to speak. We build out at both limits. But the images are in the present. Whitehead's suggestion that rendering these images sufficiently vivid would spread the specious present is quite beside the mark. No memory image, however vivid, would be anything but a memory image, which is a surrogate merely for what was or will be spoken.

The actual passage of reality is in the passage of one present into another, where alone is reality, and a present which has merged in another is not a past. Its reality is always that of a present. The past as it appears is in terms of representations of various sorts, typically in memory images, which are themselves present. It is not true that what has passed is in the past, for the early stages of a motion lying within a specious present are not past. They belong to something that is going on. The distinction between the present and the past evidently involves more than passage. An essential condition is its inclusion in some present in this representational form. Passage as it takes place in experience is an overlapping of one specious present by another. There is continuity of experience, which is a continuity of presents. In this continuity of experience there is distinction of happening. There is direction. There is dependence or conditioning. What is taking place flows out of that which is taking place. Not only does succession take place, but there is a succession of contents. What is going on would be otherwise if the earlier stage of the occurrence had been of a different character. It is always a passage of something. There is always a character which connects different phases of the passage, and the earlier stage of the happening is the condition of the later stage. Otherwise there would be no passage. Mere juxtaposition of events, if this is conceivable, would not constitute passage. The connection involves both identity and difference, and it involves that in the identity which makes the condition for that which follows. The immediate position of a moving body is conditioned by that which preceded it. Continuity is involved as a presupposition in passage in experience.

Although apparently sudden dislocations take place, back of these we imply continuities within which these dislocations could be resolved into continuities. The spatio-temporal connections which these continuities express involve the conditioning of any spatio-temporal position by a previous set of positions. This conditioning is not complete determination, but the conditions that are involved in the continuity of passage are necessary. That which is novel can emerge, but conditions of the emergence are there. It is this conditioning which is the qualitative character of the past as distinguished from mere passage. Mere passage signifies disappearance and is negative. The conditioning, spatio-temporally considered, is the necessity of continuity of relationship in space-time and of characters which are dependent upon space and time, such as velocities and momenta. The discontinuous is the novel. When a force is applied which is responsible for an acceleration, the moment at which that force is applied may be as respects its appearance an emergence from a continuous past, but the spatio-temporal continuities set conditions for the accelerations which result from the application of the force.

There are other continuities which we look for besides those of space-time. These are those of the so-called uniformities of nature. The embedding of any two successive events and their characters, however fortuitous they may seem, within a continuity of happening registers itself as carrying some conditioning of their happening in the succession within which they have appeared. The physical sciences push this conditioning into spatio-temporal form as far as it is possible. They attempt so to state the two happenings that the mere fact that one occurs at a certain place and time determines in some degree that which follows upon it. The ideal of this presentation is an equation between a situation at one moment and that at the next. We seek such a statement that the mere

passage of experience will determine that which takes place. Where this
can rigorously be carried out we reach what Whitehead calls the Aristotelian adjectives of events, but where it is impossible to so present the
happenings that the continuity of passage determines what will take place
we have in his terms pseudo-adjectives of events. But that the continuities of space-time do carry with them conditions of that which takes place
is a fundamental presupposition of experience. The order within which
things happen and appear conditions that which will happen and appear.

It is here that we find the function of the past as it arises in memory
and the records of the past. Imagery is not past but present. It rests with
what we call our mental processes to place these images in a temporal
order. We are engaged in spreading backward what is going on so that
the steps we are taking will be a continuity in the advance to the goals of
our conduct. That memory imagery has in it characters which tend to
identify it as belonging to the past is undoubtedly true, and these characters seem to be frequently independent of its place in a continuous order.
A face or a landscape may flash upon the inward eye with seemingly
intrinsic evidence of past experience, although we may have great difficulty in placing them. The evidence is not nceessarily of an immediate
character. There are certain sorts of images which belong to our pasts and
we are confident of them because they fit in. And there are sorts of images
which betray the operation of the imagination. A memory may be recognized as such by a method of exclusion, because it has not the fashion of
the fancy — because we cannot otherwise account for it. The assurances
which we give to a remembered occurrence come from the structures with
which they accord.

What is, then, the immediate occasion for this building out of specious
presents into a past? These presents themselves pass into each other by an
overlapping process. There is no break except under what may be called
pathological conditions. We do not build out into the past to preserve
mere continuity, i.e., to fill out breaks in reality. But it is evident that we
need to complete something that is lacking in that which is going on.
The span of that which occupies us is greater than the span of the specious
present. The " what it is " has a temporal spread which transcends our
experience. This is very evident in the pasts which we carry around with
us. They are in great part thought constructs of what the present by its
nature involves, into which very slight material of memory imagery is

fitted. This memory in a manner tests and verifies the structure. We must have arisen and eaten our breakfasts and taken the car, to be where we are. The sense of this past is there as in implication and bits of imperfect scenes come in at call — and sometimes refuse to arise. But even in this latter case we do not feel that the past is lost.

It may be said that the existence in experience of affairs that transcend our presents is the very past under discussion, and this is true, and what I am endeavoring to make evident. The past is an overflow of the present. It is oriented from the present. It is akin on the one side to our escape fancies, those in which we rebuild the world according to our hearts' desires, and on the other to the selection of what is significant in the immediate situation, the significant that must be held and reconstructed, but its decisive character is the pushing back of the conditioning continuities of the present. The past is what must have been before it is present in experience as a past. A past triumph is indefinitely superior to an escape fancy, and will be worn threadbare before we take refuge in the realm of the imagination, but more particularly the past is the sure extension which the continuities of the present demand.

The picture which Bergson gives of it seems to me to belie both its character in experience and its functional character — the picture of an enormous incessantly accreting accumulation of " images " against which our nervous systems defend us by their selective mechanisms. The present does not carry any such burden with it. It passes into another present with the effects of the past in its textures, not with the burden of its events upon its back. And whatever account we give of our exiguous imagery, it is marked by what Bergson has himself emphasized, its function of filling out present perceptions. It bears no evidence of the richness of material which Bergson predicates. It is hard to recover and disappointing in its detail. Imagery plays the same rôle in the past that it plays in the present, that of supplying some element of detail that makes the construction possible.

The inevitability of existence is betrayed in its continuity. What follows flows from what was. If there is continuity, then what follows is conditioned by what was. A complete break between events would remove the character of inevitability. The elimination of continuity is the gist of Hume's attack upon causality. While the recovery of continuity in passage is the gist of Kant's second deduction of the categories. If there were bare replacement of one experience by another, the experience would not be that of passage. They would be different experiences each wrapped up in itself, but with no connection, no way of passing from one to the other. Even a geometrical demonstration involves passage from situation to situation. The final structure is a timeless affair in the sense that it is a completed structure which is now irrelevant to the passage by which it has arisen. Any passage is in so far inevitable as earlier stages condition later achievements, and the demonstration is the exhibition of the continuity of the passage. One route when it is once taken is as inevitable as another. The child's whimsical movements of the men upon the chessboard is as inevitable as the play of the expert. In the one case its inevitability is displayed by the psychologist and in the other by the logician. Continuity in the passage of events is what we mean by the inevitable.

But bare continuity could not be experienced. There is a tang of novelty in each moment of experience. Kant reached this by the *Mannigfaltigkeit der Empfindungen,* an unordered sensuous content which becomes experience when it is placed within the forms of the understanding. Without this break within continuity, continuity would be inexperienceable. The content alone is blind, and the form alone is empty, and experience in either case is impossible. Still Kant's chasm between the two is illusory. The continuity is always of some quality, but as present passes into present there is always some break in the continuity — within the continuity, not of the continuity. The break reveals the continuity, while the continuity is the background for the novelty.

The memory of the unexpected appearance of a supposedly far distant friend, or the memory of an earthquake can never recover the peculiar tang of the experience. I remember that there was a break which is now connected with just the phases of the experience which were unconnected. We recall the joy or the terror, but it is over against a background of a continuum whose discontinuity has been healed. Something was going on — the rising anger of a titan or the adjustment of the earth's internal pressures which resulted in that which was unexpected, but this was not the original experience, when there was no connection between the events before the occurrence and the sudden emergence. Even if no qualitative causal connection appears in the memory, the spatio-temporal connection is there to be developed as thought or imagination may refashion it.

Redintegration of the past can never bring back the unexpected. This is just the character of the past as distinguished from the passage of presents into each other. The primal break of novelty in passage is gone and the problem of bridging the contingent factors is before the mind, though it may go no further than the oppressive sense of chance or fate. The character of the past is that it connects what is unconnected in the merging of one present into another.

The corresponding character of the future is still more evident. The novel is already there in the present and introduced breaks into the continuity which we must repair to attain an approach to certainty in the future. The emergent future has therefore a hypothetical character. We can trace the spatio-temporal continuities into it and the less rigorous continuities of other uniformities, but the particular aspects they will assume depend upon the adjustments which the present with its novelties will call out. Imagery from past continuities, such as the concluding words in the sentence we are speaking, or the house around the corner which we are nearing, approach the inevitable, but we may break the discourse and an explosion may send us down another road. The inevitable continuities belong to the structure of the hypothetical plans of action before us.

What is now to be said of these pasts and futures, when we seek them outside of human experience in terms of which we have been considering them? In the first place we can say that the only pasts and futures of which we are cognizant arise in human experience. They have also the extreme variability which attaches to human undertakings. Every generation rewrites its history — and its history is the only history it has of the world. While scientific data maintain a certain uniformity within these histories, so that we can identify them as data, their meaning is dependent upon the structure of the history as each generation writes it. There is no texture of data. Data are abstractions from things and must be given their places in the constructive pasts of human communities before they can become events. It is tempting to illustrate this in the shifting histories which our present generation has constructed of its habitat — including the whole universe, so far as it has been able to survey it, but the phenomenon is too evident and striking to call for illustration. Every advance in the interpretation of spectroscopic observations of the stars, every advance in the theory of the atoms opens the door to new accounts of the millenia of stellar history. They rival at present the rapidly changing histories of human communities. The immutable and incorruptible heavens exist only in rhetoric. Minute shifts in the lines of the spectrum or the readings of the spectroscope may add or subtract billions of years to the life of the stars.

The validity of these pasts depend upon the continuities which constitute their structure. These continuities in passage are the essence of inevitability, and when we feel the continuity we have reached the security we seek. It is an error to assume that the security depends upon the form of the continuity. For the Psalmist the only form of continuity that gave security was that of the Everlasting Hills and for the Greeks it was the Unchangeable Heavens. We find greater security in the laws of stellar evolution because it knits the continuities of the atoms with the continuities of the stars. The continuities of process are more universal than those of structure. More particularly we have swept away the cosmical and metaphysical chasm between the changeless heavens and the contingent earth. Ancient metaphysics divorced the two inseparable components of passage — the continuous and the emergent. The doctrine of evolution has obliterated the scandal from the union out of which arise all objects in experience. There is no more striking contrast in the history of thought than the gathering security with which we control events by rapidly reconstructing our histories, which reveal our dependable continuities when we stretch them out into their implied pasts; and the helplessness of ancient and mediaeval thought that found continuity only in a changeless order and an irrevocable past.

The conclusion is that there is no history of presents that merge into each other with their emergent novelties. The past which we construct from the standpoint of the new problem of today is based upon continuities which we discover in that which has arisen, and it serves us until the rising novelty of tomorrow necessitates a new history which interprets the new future. All that emerges has continuity, but not until it does so emerge. If we could string together the presents as presents we would present the conditions under which the novel could arise but we would not deduce that which arose. Out of the discovered continuities of that which has arisen with all that has gone before we can reconstruct it — in the future, and we obtain the field for this reconstruction by stretching backward in history the new-found continuities. Within our narrow presents our histories give us the elbow room to cope with the everchanging stream of reality.

If the novel emerges, there can be no history of a continuity of which it is a constituent part, though when it has emerged the continuities which it exhibits may enable us to state a succession of events within which it appears. Let us assume that life has emerged. In a genuine sense the conditions which allow of this emergence determine its appearance. It could not have appeared earlier than these events. The history of life will relate it to these events, which have now become its conditions, but previously were not its conditions, for there was no life to constitute those events the conditions of life. The setting up of the relation between the events which have become conditions and the emerging life is an establishment of continuity between the world before life and life itself, which was inconceivable before life appeared, as one establishes in his memory a continuity between the moment before the earthquake happened and the earthquake, which in its unexpectedness permitted in its happening no such connection. The past thus belongs to a generalized form of experience. It is the arising of relations between an emergent and a conditioning world. Any organism, taken in its widest Whiteheadean sense, maintains itself by means of relationships which, extended backward as well as forward, constitute a history of the world, but evidently it arises only after the appearance of that which gives to the world this value. The past consists of the relations of the earlier world to an emergent affair — relations which have therefore emerged with the affair.

A FUNCTIONAL VIEW OF MORALS

S. F. MacLennan

The general presuppositions of this essay are two. *First*, it is assumed that the moralities (and immoralities) of men can — and should — be studied in a distinctly scientific manner. The facts of the moral life are to be sought wherever they may be found. These facts must then be accurately described: theories as to their origin, function, and development must be elaborated; finally, these theories must be tested by further reference to the facts themselves. *Second,* it is assumed that the moralities and immoralities of men vary concomitantly in their origin, modes, and development with the social organization and life of the race. In this correlation of social activity and life, morality is regarded as the dependent variable and social activity as the independent variable.

It is with the second assumption that we, at present, propose to deal in detail; the first assumption expresses the general standpoint and method of the enquiry and will be exemplified throughout by the argument.

If the contention that the moralities and immoralities of mankind are functions of the social organization and life, be justified, it is essential that this social activity upon which man's moral behavior is conditioned be in some measure understood. We shall proceed, therefore, to note the main genetic phases of man's social organization and culture. After so doing we shall characterize each phase briefly, and, lastly, we shall trace in outline the features of the morality conditioned thereon.

The history of mankind exhibits four emphatic phases in its development. The four are these: — the Kinship Group, the Nation, the Sovereign Individual, the Democratic Social Order. In each of these stages, successively, society has been centered. There have been many partial, subordinate, connective phases, but the outstanding dominant ones that have been mentioned are the centers in and through which the human race has achieved its measure of development.

I A

The simplest form of organization that we know is that of the Kinship Group. It does not represent the very first in human affairs, but merely the earliest form of which we have accurate information.

When we characterize the primitive social life as that of a kinship group it is to be observed that both terms of the description are to be taken as emphatic. Primitive social organization is distinctively a *group* form, and the group is ever a group of *kinsmen*. In man's " earliest " life and culture the individual counts for nothing; the group counts for everything. Primitive interests are group interests. Privileges and responsibilities are of all, not of each. Land and other forms of property are possessed in common. Individuals respond spontaneously to the call of the group; private interests in the modern sense there are none. For this reason primitive group life has been described as having an essential element of solidarity about it. But again, the group is an organization of kinsmen. The ties which hold the group together are a common life, belief in a common descent, and the possession of a common blood. Friendliness of individual toward individual goes only as far as the blood goes. To be of the same blood means, in primitive life, to be friends; to be of different blood means to be enemies. For this reason the primitive group is *exclusive* as well as *solid*. Put concretely each one of the numerous social organizations of humankind is an enemy to every other, except in so far as this attitude is reversed by the claims of a common blood.

Now wherever primitive life undergoes continuous development, the kinship group exhibits centrally three distinct types of growth — the totem-kins, the clan, and the patriarchal family. On its periphery it passes through the phratry to the more inclusive tribal organization.

Totem-kins consist of individuals — whether living together or not — who believe themselves to be possessed of a common blood through descent from some common animal, bird, plant, heavenly body, or some other natural object. Clans consist of individuals who live in a common center and claim descent from an original common ancestor who is represented by the hereditary chieftain in whom the kin " blood " is condensed, and in whom, accordingly, all authority resides. The patriarchal family exhibits the latest and last internal development of the kinship group. It consists of a body of nearest Kinsmen dwelling under the authority and power of a living ancestor or father.

The phratry is an organization of at least two totem-kindreds or clans whose function (somewhat uncertain) appears to have been that of regulating the intermarriage of exogamous groups and the performance of certain rites and ceremonies. It exhibits a wider organization of near kin than the totem-kins or clans, and paves the way to the emergence of tribal organization. The tribe marks the farthest circumference of kinship. It embraces families, clans, and phratries. All whose blood relations fall within the bounds of the tribe are friends; all those whose ties fall without are enemies. As the tribe grows and its head secures greater power and authority to himself, the phratry dies out and the clan relations become direct to the tribe. The family, however, maintains its patriarchal authority far beyond the organization of the Kinship Group.

Once upon a time it was assumed that the life of primitive man was almost altogether untrammeled and free. Modern anthropology, however, has disabused our minds of this notion. On the contrary, it has pointed out to us that primitive life is enmeshed in rules and regulations to which those of our day appear simple and innocuous. From birth to death, in life and in death, in everyday affairs, in worship and in all other situations in life, there is a way in which everything must be done. This governance of the behavior of primitive peoples functions positively as *custom,* negatively as *taboo.* Custom and taboo are not single, but multiple. We should speak indeed of customs and taboos. These are the masses of authoritative folk-ways which regulate the conduct of kinship groups, and which each individual group inherits from its own past. The authority and sanctions of these customs and taboos are those of superstition, antiquity, present communal sentiment, and actual physical force. Thus in natural kinship groups the " yeas " and " nays " of custom and taboo are rarely challenged, whether the totem-kins, the clans, the patriarchal family, phratry, or the tribe be concerned.

I B

From this general description of the Kinship Group we now turn to the examination of the morality characteristic of that group.

According to our second assumption the moralities and immoralities of primitive life must vary concomitantly with the structure, organization, and growth of the Kinship Group. It is our present purpose to show that this assumption is correct. First, however, we must state what our general assumption with reference to the field of morality is. Concerning this it may be said that morality and immorality have to do with the conduct or behavior of men one with another in any given society, as this conduct is measured by the standards of that society.

How, then, do primitive men, living in some form of kinship group, conceive of morality and immorality? The answer that must be made in the light of anthropological and ethnological research is that morality consists of loyalty to group life and custom, and that immorality consists of disloyalty thereto. He who respects the requirements of custom and taboo and embodies them in his everyday life is a good man. He who contemns the customs of his group and is disobedient to their dictates is a bad man. Virtue, as the primitive good man sees it, involves an interest in his group such that man is willing not only to inconvenience himself or to bear discomfort or pain for it, but even to die willingly for the group. Furthermore, the virtuous man recognizes the rôles of custom and taboo in life, and accepts them as authoritative and sacred. Vice, on the contrary, involves lack of a dominating interest in the group, a disrespect for customary folk-ways, and a refusal to recognize, practically, the sacred authority of custom and taboo.

Thus primitive morality is a function of primitive life and social organization. It varies concomitantly with them and shows forth the organization, regulation, and valuation of human conduct as that conduct is conditioned by the circumstances of primitive life, and is governed by the regulation of group custom.

This general result is reached by several other lines of approach. First, it is to be noted that there is a parallelism between the solidarity of the kinship group and the communal character of its moral estimates. Individuals have no function *as individuals* within the kinship group; they are what they are because of the group, and not because of themselves. In like manner, primitive morality (and immorality) is communal. Land and other forms of property are held in common; marriage, in its many forms, is a concern of the group, not of the individual; justice functions in the name of the group. To take the life of any member of a kindred is to offend against the entire body of kinsmen. Thus, if the murderer and the murdered are of different groups, war between the two groups breaks out unless — as in the practice of a later day — compensation, monetary or otherwise, is made. If the murdered and the murderer are of the same kin the entire group turn upon the murderer and punish him.

This communal aspect of primitive morality is well illustrated by the case of Achan, as it is set forth in the Old Testament. Achan defies the war-taboo and takes to himself from the spoils a wedge of silver and a goodly Babylonish garment. On its being found out, he and all that belonged to him were destroyed. Achan had sinned — but his family had sinned with him.

Again, the kinship groups are mutually exclusive. Beyond each group are those who are different in blood: the stranger, the alien, the enemy. To injure such, in any form, is not immoral and reprehensible, but moral and praiseworthy. Only as groups are slowly unified and are thus assumed to be of the same blood, can moral relations and responsibilities be established. Within the group virtue and vice, morality and immorality, are matters of custom and taboo — of primitive folk-ways. As the kinship group evolves through totem-kin, clan, and patriarchal family, morality and immorality differentiate also. In totem-kindreds, morality consists of being loyal to one's totem-kin, of aiding and defending them, and of following the traditional folk-ways of the group, especially the ceremonials of the totem. He who fails in these respects and is disloyal to his totem-kindred or to the rules and regulations of his group is vicious and evil. When clans develop, with their patriarchal chieftains, morality and immorality are functions of the common life. In clan-morality, loyalty to the chief and to inherited customs stands above everything else. The authority and honor of the group are centered in the chief. The common customs he interprets and administers either with or without councilors. Similarly, in the patriarchal family, morality and immorality, virtue and vice, are measured in terms of loyalty or disloyalty to the family, to the family honor, to its patriarchal (or matriarchal) head, and to its traditions. In China, where the patriarchal family is the social unit even today, morality and immorality are defined in terms of family loyalty, supreme respect for the father, honor to the wife and mother, obedience of children to parents, deference of younger children to older, and deference of women to men. Confucius summarized patriarchal family morality thus: " To serve my father as I would require my son to serve me; to serve my older brother as I would require my younger brother to serve me; to behave to a friend as I would require a friend to behave toward me." "The virtue of a woman consists in obedience to her father while he is alive, to her husband while she is married, and to her sons when she is a widow."

II A

The second outstanding phase in which the evolution of society centers is the Nation, in the form of the autocratic state. I say "autocratic" for the reason that we shall meet later a form of "democratic" state radically different in its organization from that of the early nation. When first the Nation appears in history, it is a thorough-going autocracy. The growth of human society is slowly displacing autocracy by democracy, but throughout the long ages of what we call antiquity autocracy prevailed. In isolated instances in antiquity, small and favored states have for a time achieved democratic modes of government and of life. But as a general observation, we say that not until the modern period of western culture came did democracy organize itself effectively and progressively. Even now democracy to many peoples is no more than a catch word of propaganda, a hope, or an aspiration.

What, then, are the chief characteristics of the ancient Nation-State? And how is it distinguished from the Kinship Group? We conclude that:

(1) The nation as we observe it throughout its long course, is a much more comprehensive thing than the Kinship Group. In its most complex form the group included patriarchal families, clans, or phratries united more or less closely as a tribe or as a group of tribes, but the families persisted and formed material for all later organization.

(2) The cement which holds the nation together is patriotism, and not blood — loyalty to the nation-state or to the kindred. Loyalty to kin — to family, clan, and phratry — remained, but as subordinate to the claims of patriotism. The process of subordinating the ties of blood to the claims of patriotism was long, slow, and in many cases imperfectly accomplished. But in stronger and better-organized states, the claims of all organizations contained within the nation were thoroughly subordinated to its requirements.

(3) The Nation differs further from the group in that it is a highly organized society with a sovereign head. The Group was governed by traditional customs of an unreflective order; on the other hand the nation, under the aegis of its sovereign head, builds, upon the basis of custom, laws and institutions to meet its own actual needs. The sovereign combines in himself the dignity and power of the nation. The nation is himself and he the nation. From his sovereignty flows, without question, the authority and sanctions which give power and efficiency to the institutions and laws by which the nation is governed. As the source of law and the embodiment of sovereignty, the head of the state is an autocrat whose will is supreme and whose person is sacred.

(4) Whereas in the kinship group the individual was swamped in the solidarity of the social order, in the autocratic nation-state the individual slowly emerges into view. The way of the individual's emergence was after this fashion: the sovereign of the autocratic state was desirous of binding his subjects to himself and to the state in the closest ties of loyalty, and so, because of the fact that under the kinship group organization an individual's loyalty was to the family, the clan, the tribe, division was made in the loyalty offered to the state. To build up a feeling of nationality, and to wean away his subjects from the older loyalties, the sovereign granted to the individual rights to " life, liberty, and the pursuit of happiness." These rights were not conceived as belonging inherently to the individual. They were a grant of the sovereign and were to be enjoyed and lived out in active loyalty to the nation, to its sovereign head, to its institutions, and to its laws.

(5) As individuals differ in temperament, so also do nations. The temperament of the Greek was cultural; of the Hebrews and Hindus it was religious; of the Romans, political; of the Carthaginians, industrial and commercial.[1]

II B

The morality which fashioned itself in the medium of the autocratic nation-state corresponds point for point with the determining features of

---

[1] The feudal system has not been taken into consideration as it embodies not a main but a subordinate type of social organization. It is but a transitional stage in building up the consolidated nation. It is, as it were, a first step in the development of that unified structure which is the true state. The feudal system has been truly described as a centralized-decentralized totality. When true nationality appears, the feudal system disappears.

that state; i.e., it is a functional expression of the new social order. To explain: Nation-State morality (and immorality) is conceived of, fundamentally, as loyalty (or disloyalty) to the state, to its sovereign head, to its institutions, to its laws, and to its ideals. This loyalty is to be expressed in one's everyday life and behavior. The morality of the patriarchal family, with its attendant ancestor worship and clan-tribe morality, remained in operation, but was subordinated to, and in time absorbed by, the morality of the new organization.

Now that we have enunciated this general principle, we may pass to detail. The code of nation-state morality (and immorality) involves supreme respect for, and absolute obedience to, the head of the state. Respect for the sovereign frequently rises to worship and to the willing sacrifice of life. The great institutions — religious, military, etc., — and their leaders, demand a similar respect and obedience. This is notably true of law and its institutes. As custom and taboo embodied the corporate will of the group as expressed in the organized behavior of its members, so law expresses the will of the sovereign, operative in terms of authoritative rules for the interaction of the life and conduct of men within the nation-state. Law is to be revered and obeyed because it is the will of the sovereign: i.e., that of the state. Respect for public law and order is therefore an integral and fundamental part of nation-state morality.

We have maintained that nations exhibit differences of temperament in their lives, just as individuals do. This characteristic of the culture of nation-states expresses itself in their conception of morality (and immorality). For example: to the Greek, morality was conceived of as all-round, harmonious good citizenship; to the Roman, virtue was essentially political — "to die for the fatherland is a good and noble thing"; to the Hebrew, whose social organization was religious, morality was pictured as loyalty to the sovereign god, Jehovah — "the fear of the Lord is the beginning of wisdom," "and what doth the Lord require of thee but to do justly and to love mercy and to walk humbly with thy God?" To the Hindu, incurably religious, morality consists of obedience to the sacred rules of caste.

III A

In the period in which the kinship-group was in operation the individual was swamped in the solidarity of the group, or, to put it otherwise, the individual had not yet emerged from the communal continuity of the social order. During the régime of the autocratic nation-state, as we have observed, the individual began to be a factor of privilege and responsibility in the social order. He began in other words to possess in the eyes of his sovereign and in his own eyes, rights and duties, which were a grant from the sovereign to the subject and were strictly limited and defined by sovereign law. Theoretically these grants under the law could be revoked at any moment. However, as time passed and the social organization became more complex and differentiated, the individual achieved for himself an ever-wider and self-dependent sphere of action, until the privileges and responsibilities which, originally, had been sovereign grants, were assumed to be rights and duties inherent in the individual. With the passage of time, wider and wider circles of individuals came to conceive of themselves as social factors possessing intrinsic value, until finally the general belief that individuals are sovereign units in themselves, with rights to self-determination individually and socially, arose. Thus democracy came into being as an active political and social belief. Its effective emergence in the social order represented a complete shift of the center for society. In the kinship group and in the autocratic nation-state, the individual existed essentially for the group or state. In a democracy, society and the state exist for individuals. Democracy is indeed " of the people, for the people, and by the people." In the ancient world, Greece approximated most closely a democracy, but not for long. Among other peoples — among the Hebrews, for instance — men arrived at a belief in the sovereign value of individuals. But democracy, as a continuously effective dynamic agency, is a thing of the modern western world alone. Democracy first began to become self-conscious, to define itself and to take practical, effective form in Europe. From Europe it spread to the new world, to the islands of the seas, and since the great war, especially, to older nations and people as a resurgent interest in self-determined nationality. To bring democracy to the status of a practical, reconstructive social agency required at least fifteen centuries of struggle; from the days of the Reformation and the Renaissance, when individualistic democracy burst forth with transforming power, to the present time, is some five centuries; and today, democracy has defined and shaped itself so effectively that to have it has become the abiding satisfaction of those nations in which it has long been established and the great hope of the whole world outside democracy. How long a time will elapse until democracy has perfected its principle and has established itself throughout the world no one may say, but however slow or fast its movement is, the future rests with democracy.

In its historical development democracy has exhibited two distinct phases, individualistic democracy and socialized democracy. They agree in the belief that the individual is the sovereign center of the social order; they differ in their conceptions of the nature of the individual. To the one the individual is an exclusive, self-centered, non-social being; to the other he is by nature a social being.

Of the two phases individualistic democracy developed first. Whereas ancient individualism was satisfied with tearing down the old structure, modern individualism has been concerned with rebuilding the old and constructing the new. In this reconstructive-constructive movement two factors soon made their presence felt, fundamentally. The first was the belief that the individual, as individual, is a unit of sovereign value. From this central belief individualistic democracy drew the following conclusions:

(1) All authority, intellectual, aesthetic, moral, political, religious, and social, rests in individuals. Reason, conscience, good taste, and other individual functions, must determine belief. Other and extraneous authority there is none.

(2) All individuals the world over and without regard to differences of color, caste, poverty and riches, nationality, religious or other beliefs, etc., are units of sovereign value and heirs to all that mankind has found of worth in the world. Thus, individualistic democracy is a positive humanitarian principle as broad as the race. Its effectiveness is seen in all the changes which during the past five centuries have made this world a better place in which to live.

The second factor in individualistic democracy is the belief that every individual is an exclusive non-social unit. Accordingly, all social structures — political, religious, etc., are contractual in nature. Institutions, of whatever order, are man-made and are revocable. They arose out of the composite needs of men in the past; they may be challenged, reconstructed, or abolished as current needs require or seem to require. In our day monarchy on the continent of Europe has given place widely to republicanism, and, in Russia, Bolshevism has superseded Czarism.

But not only is the social order contractual and relativistic; the question has been raised whether any social order is possible in a world of exclusive sovereign units. Individualistic democracy would seem to lead logically to anarchism. This, however, is a problem for the latest phase of human evolution-socialized democracy.

III B

As the individual, in modern democracy, came to conceive himself to be the sovereign center of political and social life, so he came to believe that man's moral life also centered in him. As a center of ultimate authority the individual became a center of ultimate value. In the ancient world this conception had been reached in Greece, among the Israelites, and in India, representing the views of a few advanced thinkers, but it was in the religion of Jesus that the belief first became aggressive and constructive. Jesus said " What shall it profit a man if he gain the whole world and lose his own soul, or what shall a man give in exchange for his soul? " These words embody the emphatic belief that there is nothing in the whole system of things for which one may, profitably, trade his individual self-respect or honor. To attempt so to do is to endeavor to exchange for a lesser good that which gives value to all things. Throughout the dark and middle ages the belief was kept alive to emerge as an effective leaven in the Renaissance, the Reformation, in Romanticism, and in all other movements by which society was being gradually and progressively individualized. Kant contends that the fundamentum of morality is to " act so as to use humanity whether in your own person or in the person of another always as an end, never merely as a means." Similarly Hegel said " Be a person, and respect all others as persons."

This individualistic conception soon proved itself to be thoroughly dynamic and constructive. Through its pragmatic influence the individualized morality was gradually freed from the limiting control of sex, class, color, race, and nationality, and established firmly on the basis of sovereign individuality. As an individual man is intrinsically a being of ultimate moral values. His duty is to respect himself and to respect other persons the world over, regardless of color, creed, or other adventitious circumstance. Thus individualism has resulted in a humanitarianism as broad as the race. Today it is a gospel acted upon to the ends of the earth. With the preaching of this gospel the tide of respect of individuals one for another is steadily rising, and the idea of a human brotherhood has become something more than a catch word.

But if individualistic democracy is an attractive, broad humanitarianism, of individuals mutually loyal to their best selves, it also expresses itself in a moral philosophy which time has shown to be much less desirable and tenable.

To individualistic democracy the individual is conceived on one hand as a positive dynamic agent of sovereign worth. On the other hand each individual is thought of as an exclusive non-social unit. On such a basis social relations, with all that they have meant to moral life in other days and still mean to us, become illogical, meaningless, and destined to be set aside. Complementary to this exclusive non-social nature of the individual is the belief that each is essentially self-centered. The only interests that human individuals can feel and act upon are self-centered, i.e., selfish; altruistic interests in others are illusory and non-existent. This situation has given rise to a paradox. It is this. Altruism has been believed to be the heart of morality and yet men are by nature egoistic. Men *should* have an interest in one another, but they *can* have interest only in themselves. Many and fierce have been the intellectual battles fought over this issue. Nor did they cease until it was perceived that the problem was factitious and arose out of a mistaken notion of the individual. The individual is not an exclusive unit, but a social factor.

With this result we pass to the fourth stage of social evolution and its characteristic morality. Further correlations between the social organization and the moral life might be wrought out. The fundamental principles, however, have been shown, and a larger treatment would over-run the bounds of space assigned to this essay.

IV A

Long centuries ago Aristotle enunciated the well-known dictum that " man is by nature a social animal." The early modern world overlooked the saying and at any rate was not interested in what it stood for. The early modern world was in fact too much concerned about saving the individual soul, or in cultivating it, or in some other individual concern to bother about what the word " social " really connoted. To them society was the product of a contract, and itself an artifact. Now and then men like

Vico thought of the social tie as natural and organic and of society as the matrix of individuals. It was not until the middle of the nineteenth century that the idea got well under way. Since then, however, the social conception of the individual has advanced by leaps and bounds. Today individualist democracy is waning rapidly, and socializing democracy is taking its place. The latter, indeed, has become the watchword of human progress.

In characterizing socializing democracy two things must be kept in mind. First, individuals are the functional organs of the social order. Society, at any given moment, " lives, moves, and has its being " in individuals. They are the agents of its life. Second, society is more than the individual's action at any given time. The organic unity of individuals operates from moment to moment, as well as at any particular moment of time. To this connective unity of group, nation, race, etc., we give the name " society." It embodies the corporate life of group or nation or other human organization, and conserves the values and methods of living achieved by group or nation in the past. These values and methods so organized constitute the regulating institutions of society.

Concerning individuals, as viewed by socializing democracy, we may therefore say that they are the active sovereign centers of any social organization and the final courts of appeal concerning the values and methods of living.

Concerning institutions, as viewed also by socializing democracy, it may be said that they embody in organized form the gains made by any social order in the values of life and methods of living. They are conservative and regulative, but not creative. In this natural function they are ever open to question and criticism by individuals whose privilege and responsibility it is to demand that the values and methods of living shall serve the present circumstances of individuals whose servants they are.

IV B

Socializing democracy, we have asserted, is the watchword of social progress. In the main it has to do with a society which is not yet, but which is yet to be. Similarly the morality of this latest phase of social life and organization is a hope, a prophecy, and a program of constructive work. Its centers of interest are two: an interest in the individual and an interest in the social order. As an interest in the individual it maintains not only the unique and ultimate value of each individual, but it seeks also to capitalize for each the corporate values and methods wrought out in the past. This phase of moral procedure, accordingly, fills out and gives content to the formal principles of individualistic morality.

As an interest in the social order the morality of socializing democracy maintains that the idea of the common good and not private interest should govern all debate and decision in matters moral. The sweep of this principle of the common good is as wide as human society and is as deep as the interests of mankind. It seeks the common welfare of parties to every debate, without regard to nationality or creed or color or race or sex. It allows private advantage, but private advantage only within the limits of justice, as the expression of the common good. Further, socializing morality would dedicate all institutions to the service of the common good. An excellent illustration of the fulfilment of this moral desire is to be found in our public school systems as they are organized from kindergarten to university. Whatever may have been the motive which gave birth to our schools, it is beyond question that now their reason for existence in all their marvelous growth is democratic service — the common good. There are evidences that other institutions, such as the church, the law, medicine, etc., are responding to the new urge which, like a leaven, is at work actively within our social organization. It is indeed the belief of this type of moralist that the day is coming, however distant it may be, when all institutions will directly, efficiently, and justly serve the common good.

Thus the maintaining of a loyalty to the common good of all sovereign individuals, and the establishing of societies which will serve this common good, is the principle of socializing democracy. It is spreading its influence far and wide, not simply as a militant faith, but as a constructive idealism in the communities of men the world over, wherever democracy has gone. To summarize:

Morality and immorality vary with social organization. The organization known as the *kinship-group* produces custom morality; the *autocratic state-nation* produces authoritative institutional morality; *individualized democracy* makes for individualistic morality; and *socialized democracy* results in the morality of the common good.

A MATERIALISTIC THEORY OF EMERGENT EVOLUTION

WILLIAM PEPPERELL MONTAGUE

IN this paper I shall explain and defend three propositions:

(1) That a *living being* is an individual whose reactions to the present environment are controlled primarily by its actual past history and secondarily by its potential future history.

(2) That a *person* is that higher kind of living being in whom the vital power to react to his present in the light of his past and future is not restricted to the preservation of the physical organism and its species — so that for the first time in evolution individuals become ends in themselves rather than means to the perpetuation of their type; and the life of the body becomes secondary and instrumental to the life of the spirit.

(3) Lastly, I shall argue that " Emergent Evolution," which means the temporally continuous development of qualitatively discontinuous levels of being, can be explained by a special adaptation of physical categories, and to that extent " materialistically."

From Newton to Einstein, scientists have agreed that the behavior of inanimate bodies can be described in terms of motions, actual or potential; and that these motions are determined in their intensity, direction, and acceleration by the spatial relations between the bodies concerned. Molecular, atomic, and electronic theories serve the purpose of reducing to external or spatial relations of particles what would otherwise figure as the internal or occult nature of the wholes which those particles compose. But while scientists generally are agreed that this mechanistic conception suffices for the description, prediction, and control of inorganic nature, there is no such unanimity in the belief that mechanism applies equally well to the realm of organisms.

Wherever there is *life,* a new factor appears to be involved in the determination of behavior; and this new factor can, I think, be described as the determination of a body's movements, not only by the spatial relations of its mass and velocity to other moving masses, but also by its temporal relations to its own past and future. External neighborhood is supplemented and dominated by internal history as the controlling factor; and time replaces space as the primary *milieu* of all that lives.

This description of the nature of life in general may be given more clarity and plausibility by a consideration of the three specific types of life that are revealed in our experience — viz: Plants, Animals, and Persons. For in an ideal definition, the *principium definitionis* should be capable of serving also as a *principium definitionis;* and if the essence of life consists, as we have stated, in duration or extension in time, the three stages in the hierarchy of life-forms should be describable as the successively higher manifestations of this " temporal extension."

In vegetative or plant life, we find that the protoplasmic individual is content to objectify the history which makes up its heredity in the series of material forms that constitute its growth from the comparatively amorphous seed to the comparatively differentiated and articulated system of interacting members composing the adult organism. The typical plant seems to dedicate its individual efforts to the realization of a material structure and to the reproduction of other instances of that material structure. Such activity of *function* as it displays is secondary and instrumental to the building of its *structure*. And in keeping with this subordination of *doing* to *being,* we find its effective intercourse with the environment mainly confined to the domain of immediate contact, and its own locus usually stationary rather than mobile.

The general truth of this description of the vegetative type of life is, I think, quite compatible with the atypical and border-line cases in which plants may dispense with chlorophyl, or devour insects, or react to the presence of water or other nutrient substances not in contact with them, or even move from one part of space to another.

Now in the animal type of life, we find most of the vegetative powers and then something different and more advanced. The chick in the egg, and the calf in the uterus express the history embodied in their heredity by transforming a comparatively amorphous germ into a comparatively differentiated organism. During gestation, the vital functions of an animal are dedicated like those of a plant to the building up of a material structure. And even in its post-embryonic life its assimilative functions, though more extended and elaborate than those of the plant, are directed largely to the growth and maintenance of a physical organism. But supervening upon these essentially vegetative activities we find at the typically animal stage of life, a power of the living being to control its reactions to the present environment, not merely by an *inherited* past, but by an *individually acquired* past. The animal uses two histories where the plant uses but one. The nervous system characteristic of the animal provides for the retention and accumulation of traces of its past reactions. And these traces of past experience, constituting what we call memory and the capacity to learn by experience, make the animal far more of an individual than the plant. It has an acquired private life over and above the inherited life common to its species. It reacts to things not merely in virtue of their general nutrient value, but in virtue of their individual bearing upon its individual history. How a dog will react to the visual stimulus of a whip or to the auditory stimulus of his master's voice will depend upon what his own past experience has been. There are, moreover, certain secondary concomitants of this primary capacity for developing an individual history, which are so often found at the level of animal life that we come to think of them as in themselves definitive. I refer particularly to the capacity to be effected specifically by spatially distant objects, which we call " perception," and the affiliated capacity for selective and self-directed motions of the whole organism with reference to such distant objects, which we can call " volition."

Now, of the two kinds of vital capacities present in animal life, which is the more important, the old capacity to grow, preserve, and reproduce the material structure common to its species, or the new capacity to accumulate and utilize an individuated system of functional activities relevant to its private history? The first-named capacity it shares in common with the plant, the second differentiates it from the plant. Which is the controlling influence in its life? The two factors are, I think, of about *equal* importance. They exist reciprocally, each for the sake of the other. On the one hand the vegetative process by which the brute's organism is built up in its ontogeny is obviously subordinate to and determined by the distinctively animal functions of his post-embryonic life. The *anabolism* primary in the foetus or in the plant is directed to the formation of organs adapted to the *katabolism* which is the primary and distinctive feature of an adult animal. Energy is accumulated in organic structures to the end that it may be expended in functional activity. But, on the other hand, while vegetative growth is determined by, and preparatory to, animal function, those animal functions are themselves, apparently, determined by, and adapted to, the preservation and reproduction of the physical organism. The animal develops a private and individual history, but he can use it only or mainly for the public good: i.e., for the perpetuation of the species which he shares in common with his fellows. The animal has a mind or mirror image of the world outside him, an organism within his organism, consisting of the traces of his past by which he controls his present and anticipates his future; but his " mind," as thus constituted, is an organ of his body, and restricted in its scope to the serving of bodily needs. If we say that an animal remembers, perceives, and imagines, we must say also that these psychic activities are not emancipated from the material interests which they serve. They are not an end in themselves, but a means. The brute is not a vegetable, but he is a slave to his vegetable nature, which is the soil from which his intelligence grows, and by which it is nourished and directed.

Now, when we pass from the Animal to the Person, we enter upon a level that is not only higher but easier to analyze, for our external observation of the behavior of others can be supplemented by the internal experience which we have of ourselves. On this third level of life, we discover at once that, as the brute includes most of what the plant can do, so the person includes, in his complex life, the two earlier forms from which he has evolved. In the first place man is a plant in that his organism develops vegetally from the parental seed; and throughout his life he will be largely occupied with activities instrumental to the nourishing of his body and the procreating of his species. In the second place man is not only plant, but an animal in that he acquires an individual or private history, through which he learns by experience. He has perception of distant objects and the volitional power of self-directed motion. But in the third place man is something more than either plant or animal; and it is my contention that this increment of vitality in which man differs from the lower forms of life is adequately traceable to a *reversal* of the relative potencies: first of the physical and the psychical; second of the public history of the species, given in heredity, and the private history acquired by the individual.

The traces of individual experience constituting the memory in an animal seem only strong enough to modify his conduct at any moment to the extent that they are relevant to the practical needs and the physical situation of his organism at that moment. It is only in man that the brain has passed the critical point, and evolved in retentiveness and complexity to a stage in which memory ceases to be a mere slave of perception and attains autonomy and self-determination. Images of absent objects, which, in the waking life of the brute occur only as parasites of the present situation, in man become preoccupations, with reference to which the present situation is subservient or altogether disregarded. In the animal, there are no images of absent objects that occur spontaneously and apart from perceptual bidding except those dream-images which come when the senses are closed and perception itself is in abeyance. Man alone can dream without sleeping, for only in him are the images of memory and imagination strong enough to endure the rivalry of perception. Man's thoughts are waking dreams. They are like stars so steadfast and bright that not even daylight can pale them.

It is this critical *excess* in the strength of his memories that makes man capable of living more in the past and future than in the present. He is the absent-minded animal, and his thinking is lyrical and abstract in contrast with the brute, whose consciousness is so pathetically concrete and practical. Between the two types of life the difference is infinite; and the old theologians who talked of the animal and vegetable " kingdoms " apart from the " kingdom " of man were nearer the truth than we, who, having discovered the descent of man from the animal, have forgotten the abyss that that genealogy has bridged. We may put the matter in the form of a question: How can a spatio-temporally continuous process give rise to qualitatively discontinuous types of life?

The answer is to be found in recognizing, first, that one and the same pair of factors can give opposite products according to whether one or the other factor *predominates;* and, secondly, that *this change of one* *product into its opposite can be brought about by the gradual increase* *of one of the factors until the critical point is reached in which it just* *exceeds the strength of its former superior.* Consider the " evolution " of water into steam. In each of these contrasting states of matter, there are the same factors of molecular attraction and molecular repulsion. In the liquid state, the attraction exceeds the repulsion. As the application of heat is increased, the agitation among the molecules becomes greater, until the critical point is attained at which the repulsion of the molecules for one another becomes just greater than their attraction. The water *boils* and we have the " emergent evolution " of a gas from a liquid. A qualitative discontinuity has been generated through the medium of a quantitatively continuous change. Now, the ape-like and the man-like brains are each of them vehicles of the same pair of factors. In each there is first the interest in the perceptually present pertaining to the spatial body, and second the interest in the conceptually absent pertaining to the mind or temporal history of the individual. Let the cells of the simian cortex, in which the physical interest in the present dominates the psychical interest in the absent, increase in number and connectivity as slowly and gradually as you please through any number of generations, and there will come a time when a " boiling point " will be reached — interest in the absent will overtop interest in the present and the *man* will have emerged from the *animal*.

May I guard here against a possible misunderstanding? I do not mean to imply by the illustration just used, or by anything said before, that the sharp distinction in *essence* between the higher and lower levels of life carries with it a correspondingly sharp separation in *existence*. All that the experts may say as to the blend of plant and animal functions in creatures below man, I am, of course, ready to accept. While, as to the inextricable shifting and blending of personal and animal traits, in the individuals of the human species, not only in the days of Pithecanthropus Erectus, but in our own time and country — it is too sadly obvious to require telling. The coming of personal life is like the coming of the tide or the change from winter to spring. It consists of waves of advance and recession. The water boils, but the steam lapses back into the liquid state. Winter has days of spring warmth, and conversely. Animals at their best will sometimes manifest more truly personal living than men.

Let us note once more that an essential phase of the new type of life is the new level of *individuality* which it involves. The dominance of the memory system over the perceptual system brings with it the emancipation of the creature's *private* history from the history of his *species*. The mind and spirit which he *acquires* as an individual count for more than the organs and instincts which he *inherits* from his species. Persons will unite into families, tribes, and nations, and into all sorts of less permanent and more specialized organizations. But in each case the group will, or should, exist for the good of its members rather than the members for the sake of the group. The value of even the Beloved Community will consist, not in itself, but in its ministry to the persons who compose it, and in the opportunities which it presents for individual creativeness and reciprocal affection.

In my paper, thus far, I have been mainly concerned with a schematic description of the three levels of life; and I have in addition already attempted something in the way of that quantitative or materialistic explanation of their successive appearance which is the goal of my inquiry. I wish now to proceed to a more definite and extended explanation of emergent evolution; and to that end I shall offer a hypothesis as to the nature of life and its relation to the material matrix with which it is so intimately associated.

But before presenting my own theory, I will state the three other conceptions which have been applied to the problem, and give in a few words my reasons for rejecting them.

First of all, there is the conception of the Mechanist who holds that the peculiar behavior of living beings can be adequately explained as the outcome of a system whose laws differ only in their degree of complication from the laws obtaining in the inorganic world. I cannot accept this answer to the question, because, in agreement with Driesch, McDougall, and Bergson, I cannot conceive of any way in which a mere aggregate of material particles, no matter how complex, could provide for that preservation of the past along with the present which we directly experience in what we call *duration*. One configuration of molecules could give place to another, but it would seem impossible for the earlier and later configurations of the same particles to exist and act together at the same time.

Secondly, there is the conception of the Vitalist or Dualist, according to which the essence of life and mind is incommensurably and inexplicably different from matter, and at least potentially separable from it, though capable of interacting causally with it. I cannot accept this view as satisfactory, because it seems to me to leave a bigger problem than it takes away — the difficulty of understanding how an " entelechy " or " animistic factor," not spatial and not located in space, can be conceived as interacting with the brain, or even as existing concretely at all.

Thirdly, there is the view of the Emergent Evolutionists, who agree with the Dualists as to the hopelessly inexplicable contrast in essence between life or mind on the one hand and mere matter on the other, but differ from them in that they admit that the contrasts have come about as the result of natural evolution. They say that when the arrangement of the particles of a material system attains a certain stage of complexity, new properties are manifested, and new laws of behavior emerge, which cannot be made homogeneous or commensurable with the older and simpler laws of mechanics. They plead for the autonomy of biology and psychology, and for the irreducibility and ultimacy of such categories as organicity and mentality; and they demand that we rest satisfied with this methodological pluralism and accept with " natural piety " the emergence of the new and higher levels of being. I cannot accept this theory as final, because, in spite of its advantages over Mechanism and Dualism, it seems to me to substitute a statement of the problem for its solution. The emergence of new properties and laws constitutes a question rather than an answer; and it should act as a stimulant rather than a sedative. *The history of science is the history of replacing empirically given emergence by rational etiology.*

Ice emerges into water, and motion emerges into heat, but it is the molecular theory that gives us an understanding of how in each case the transition is possible. When we pass from the intra-molar to the intra-molecular or inter-atomic we find in the minds of all chemists the methodological ideal of explaining the emergence of the new qualities of chemical compounds in terms of the quantitative relations of the atoms composing the molecule. And when we pass from the chemical realm of the intra-molecular to the intra-atomic or inter-electronic domain of radio-active phenomena, do we not find an analogous faith in the possibility of explaining such specific properties as those of hydrogen and helium and of uranium, radium, and lead in terms of the quantitative relations of the protons and electrons composing the atoms? If there should be a step beyond this to an intra-electronic domain, we should again expect to find that the new elements (Schroedinger waves or whatever they might be) would explain through their relational structure the protons and electrons which were their emergent resultants. In short, throughout the entire hierarchy of successively larger wholes, from the lowest sub-electronic elements up to the colloidal and crystalline masses that are visible to our eyes, we can expect to find (as in large and promising measure we have already found), a series of structures each of which will possess a nature different from the parts which compose it, but explainable in terms of the relations between those parts. The successive levels of being will indeed be different, but the difference will be commensurable and intelligible, rather than ultimate and unanalyzable.

Whenever we are confronted with the emergence of a novel form we never rest content with an attitude of " natural piety." " Natural piety " is scientific treason, a betrayal of the faith that has generated progress and enabled us to replace the helpless acceptance of novelties as brute facts with an increasingly satisfactory understanding and mastery of their genesis.

Now I wish to guard against an exaggeration of this doctrine of Rational Etiology, which would be fatal to its utility and even to its truth. In explaining the novelties of Emergent Evolution, we do not explain them away. The solid condition of matter remains just as different from the liquid condition, after the change is explained in terms of molecular inter-relationships, as before that explanation was attained. There is the new kind of behavior after the fluid has frozen, and there is the new and unique quality or immediacy which we call solidity, and which we contrast with the antecedent quality of liquidity. More than this we should not desire. It would indeed be the greatest of pities if the Helmholzian analysis of a clang into its constituent tones were to deprive us of the clang itself.

There is, moreover, a second aspect of the situation which we must not lose sight of. The analysis of a thing into its parts not only fails to destroy its immediate quality as such, it fails also to touch the attributes that pertain to it in virtue of the larger wholes of which it is itself a part. The analytic explanation of a mental state, for example, must be supplemented by its configurational or synthetic interpretation in terms of the *Gestalt* within which it is contained, and from which it receives its meaning and value. On the mental and on the vital levels of being this configurational aspect of a thing may in fact be of more importance than the other or analytic aspect. And even on the inorganic plane the qualities of a phenomenon that are contributed by its context must not be neglected.

Now if we have been right in holding that the properties of inorganic nature (within the limits just noted) can be explained analytically in terms of the parts of which the structure is composed, may we not hope that the greater gap between the inorganic on the one hand and the vital and mental on the other can, at least to some extent, be similarly explained? It is in the faith that this question should be answered affirmatively that I am proposing the hypothesis which apart from any claim which it may have for final validity, seems to be the kind of hypothesis for which we should look.

In the beginning of our discussion we noted that the fundamental property of a living being was its possession and use of a history. Now everything, living or dead, possesses a history; but only a living thing uses its history to determine its conduct. It not only has a past, but it has a past that is present and operative.

That this is so is obvious and undeniable. *How* it is so is the great problem. To explain life would be to explain how the material structure called protoplasm can retain and operate with events that have been, but are no longer, members of the physical world.

There is one and only one physically definable situation in which a sequence of past events can be present and causally operative with their specificities undestroyed. This is the situation in which a series of motions or kinetic energies have been successively transformed into modes of stress or potential energy, and superimposed upon one and the same material system. A simple illustration of this super-position of energies is afforded by a rope which is first twisted, then folded upon itself, then twisted and folded again, and so on. A rope treated in this fashion will, when released, regurgitate more or less the same series of overt motions which were imposed upon it, thus revealing the fact that the past has been present in the present. If protoplasm were a structure capable of retaining in an intensive or potential form the energies given to it by the environment, it would possess what as a matter of fact it does possess, *viz.,* the capacity to respond to the present in the light of its accumulated and retained past history. Its reactions would be of the trigger-type in which the response bears no fixed and measurable relation to the stimulus that releases it. Any system such as a twisted rope in which potential energy is stored up, betrays " irritability " when teased. There is more to it than appears to an external observer. Its actions cannot be explained in terms of its contemporary environment (which alone is externally visible), but only in relation to its past environments, the contacts with which constitute its history.

If the reader will be kind enough to grant that my twisted rope is strikingly analogous to protoplasm in respect to the primary property of *preserving the past,* and the resultant secondary property of *irritability,*

I will at once reciprocate the kindness by confessing that there the analogy ends. The case of the rope and similar cases of potential energy in the inorganic world lack the property which next to history itself is the most important characteristic of life-system; I refer to *anabolism* and its climactic phase which is *reproduction*.

A quality as pattern of any kind may pass from one place to another in two ways by *conduction* and by *induction*. The curse that rests upon most accumulations of potential energy in the inorganic realm is that they tend to waste themselves in motions which conduct and dissipate their accumulated energies over the environment. The Increase of Entropy or the Second Law of Thermo-dynamics is the name given to the one-way tendency of energy to flow from the more concentrated, differentiated, and organized conditions to the more dissipated, more uniform, and more random conditions. The intense waves caused by the stone dropped in the pool spread out over the water. The hot stove in the warm room never sucks up the warmth and grows hotter and thus more differentiated, but diffuses its heat to the cooler environment until thermal differentiation is gone and thermal equilibrium is attained. Humpty Dumpty falls from the wall and his exquisite organization is irremediably lost in the squash.

Now if we turn from death and the ways of dead things to life and the ways of growth, we find the opposite to all this. Protoplasm presents us with concentration rather than dissipation of energies and their patterns, and with an increase of differentiation and organization and thus with at least temporary and local decreases of entropy. Instead of waiting for the wind to blow Humpty Dumpty from the wall, let us gently replace him in the warm nest on which the mother hen is sitting. We shall then see the fertilized germ impose its primary energy patterns upon the comparatively amorphous material of the egg. The latter, as food for the growing embryo, will gradually be transformed by a miraculous ontogenetic anabolism into the lungs and liver, wings and beak and brain of the chick. Like the acorn and elm seed planted in the same soil the life-system amplifies and reproduces its pattern at the expense of the environing food. To describe this anabolism as " the interaction of organism and environment " is the sorriest and most mischievous of truisms for it masks the infinite prepotency of the living member of the partnership. Vital growth is transposition of the organism's pattern to the food around and within it. And this transfer of pattern takes place by *induction* rather than by *conduction*. I would illustrate this by another analogy. Instead of the twisted rope, let us take a group of electrifiable bodies insulated from their environment except with respect to the wires through which we shall charge them with current. When charged, we leave them suspended near each other in a viscous fluid, and then " feed " them with other electrifiable particles placed among them. We shall expect to find the electro-static force pattern of the system imposing itself upon the new particles by inducing in them charges appropriate to their position in the field. Similarly chargeable particles added from time to time would in their turn receive charges determined by their positions and by the increasingly complex pattern of the whole. Nor would it be beyond the possibilities of arrangement to create a situation in which the entire pattern or a portion of it would by induction duplicate or " reproduce " itself. The point is that with induction in contrast to conduction fields of potential energy or force can be transferred from one material system to another without loss of specificity, and that the new and more complex system that results contains more rather than less organization. There is, at least locally and temporarily, the same sort of reversal of the principle of entropy that a life system seems to exhibit in the anabolism by which it builds up or synthesizes the comparatively less organized food-molecules into its own comparatively more organized tissues.

If we knew with sufficient detail the fine structure of protoplasmic units, molecules or molecule-clusters, we might expect to understand just how this quasi-induction with the accompanying growth of the organism takes place. To discover this would be to discover how a material system storing up a history in the form of potential energy (which is the only physically possible form in which the past can be present in the present) amplifies and reproduces that strange intensive pattern. Life once started would ramify and spread over the fortunate earth; its varied forms sometimes perpetuating themselves unchanged, sometimes simplifying or degenerating, and sometimes evolving into more diverse and more complex or higher types.

It seems to me that it is a great mistake to measure vital excellence by degree of adjustment to environment. If life be at all as we have described it, its business is not to adjust itself to the environment, but to adjust the environment to it, to impose its pattern upon its surroundings and increasingly inform them. It is the inorganic systems that tend toward conformity and orthodoxy and approximate in their increase of entropy more and more to undifferentiation and equilibrium, thermo-dynamic or otherwise, with their environment. The deader a thing is the more stable its adaptation to its *milieu*. A block of granite, a diatom, a clam, an ape, a Socrates, embody in increasing measure an aggressive and rebellious power to impose their retrospective and impliedly prospective patterns upon a neutral or more or less hostile world. This invasive, insurgent and heterodox temper of life does not, of course, preclude— on the contrary it necessitates—a certain modicum of adaptation. Life must stoop to conquer; but unending conquest, not conformity, is its goal.

And now, did space permit, we could formulate again and with more precision, in terms of our theory, the main ascending steps in evolution. As it is, we shall content ourselves with a summary outline of the three successively emerging levels of Plant, Animal, and Person, interpreted materialistically in the sense already defined. That is to say, we shall endeavor to show that there are the same two factors in any pair of successive levels, and that the transition from one to the other, momentous though it be, is adequately explained by a continuous *quantitative* growth of the lower factor until the critical point is reached when it gains ascendancy over its former superior and there *emerges* a novel quality of being seemingly discontinuous with that which gave it birth.

(1) *From the Inorganic to the Organic.* — In the domain of dead matter and in the domain of life we find the same two factors: *first,* the factor of kinetic energy with its tendency to diffuse and run down by *conduction;* and *second,* the factor of potential energy with its tendency to perpetuate and reproduce by polaric *induction* the past history which it invisibly embodies. But in the domain of the inorganic, the visible and primarily spatial energy of motion predominates. Energy is, to be sure, accumulated and concentrated in electric, magnetic, and gravitational fields and in the explosive combinations of atomic systems; but in the main it tends to dissipate and diffuse into motion. It is saved only to be spent. It is not until the coming of the type of carbon-compound called *protoplasm* that we find a material system that is capable not only of storing in potential form and specific pattern the energies that impinge upon it, but also of propagating them or imposing them by a kind of induction upon new

matter. This capacity of a thing for preserving *and reproducing* its past history is the definitive property of a living being. Once started it tends to spread and inform more and more of the environment. It tends also to increase the richness of its own organization, and so to evolve new and higher types of itself. It is definitely anti-entropic, if not in physical literalness, at least in intent and significance. It is a level of being on which the temporal dominates the spatial, and history ceasing to be external and factitious, becomes internal and causally operative as such.

(2) *From Plant Life or Mere Life to Animal Life.* — On each of these levels of the evolutionary process, we find the same two vital factors: *first,* the factor or capacity for receiving, retaining, and organizing the energies that are bound up with matter as food; and *second,* the factor or capacity for receiving, retaining, and organizing energies not bound up with matter. Thus the plant not only anabolizes the soil that feeds it, but by its chlorophyll mechanism receives and stores up the radiant energy of light-waves. And the animal, also, not only takes in food and builds it up into the specific tissues of his bodily structure, but through his nervous system (or through those diffused and less differentiated receptors which in the lowest animals are the evolutionary ancestors of the nervous system) he retains and organizes the impinging energies of light, of sound, of mechanical or molar contacts, and of those molecular contacts which when dissolved in liquid constitute taste and when in volatile or gaseous form constitute smell. But whereas the chlorophyll mechanism in the plant resembles the animal nervous system in the single point of being an energy-receptor rather than a food-receptor, the nervous system differs from the chlorophyll system in these two all-important respects: it receives and retains the impinging energies in such a way as to preserve their individual specificities; and secondly and relatedly, it preserves the energy-traces distinct from one another and distinct in their entirety from the growth-system of the organism. The plant uses up the free energy which it receives from the environment in its business of structural growth. The animal uses the free energies which it receives to build up a cerebral memory-system which enjoys a certain autonomy and insulation, so that it does not go into structure, but into function or behavior. And the fact that the different energy-impacts are not fused into an undifferentiated mass, but are retained with something of their incoming

distinctness, gives to the animal a particularized internal record of the extra-organic objects that are relevant to his weal and woe. This internal record constitutes a secondary organism within the primary organism. It embodies a private history by which he guides his behavior. He learns by experience which means that he reacts to the present in the light of his individual past. His life is not like that of the plant, entirely occupied with preserving and amplifying his material structure. He is a *doer* and not merely a *grower*. We are not to construe the emergence of animal life from mere life as indicating a descent of animals from plants. The chlorophyll mechanism is the brother or cousin rather than the ancestor of the nervous system. The brute and the vegetable are, as Bergson has pointed out, divergent alternative developments from the undifferentiated protista, who were the common ancestors both of the protozoa and the prototypes. But, whereas the chlorophyll receptor merely provides a new and richer means of extending that anabolism or structure-building (which is the generic character of mere life as such), by utilizing sunlight as well as food, the acquirement of a nervous system results in a new and higher level of life, on which, over and above the capacity to build a body in the ancestral form, there is the added capacity to build a private and individual history and an internal and individual replica of the objects in the outside world. This secondary organism is both the cause and the effect of the self-directive and increasingly adaptive motions by which life begins its conquest of the extra-organic environment.

(3) *From the Animal to the Person.* — In both the animal and the person there are the same two factors: *first,* the vegetal and inherited factor of body-building anabolism; *second,* the private history of the organism's own adventures with the surrounding world. And in the early part of our study we set forth with some care the manner in which the gradual increase of the second factor to the point of emancipation from the mere service of the first factor resulted in the emergence of the rational or personal type of life. We need now only to restate the conclusion, in terms of our hypothesis, as to the identity of the history embodied as an operative factor in a life-system with the pattern of energies stored up in potential form. It is when the potential energies constituting the memory-system or secondary organism become sufficiently strong to be capable of functioning autonomously and independently of the sensory

solicitations of the environment that the individual becomes freed from the *here* and *now* of his body and life becomes spirit.

(4) *From the Personal to the Divine.* — No one can discuss Emergent Evolution without having in mind the great book of S. Alexander on *Space, Time, and Deity.* And although the present essay is a protest against one aspect of that work and a plea that when confronted with the emergence of new levels of being we should substitute the search for a rational etiology in place of the attitude of " natural piety," yet it is Alexander's treatment of Deity as the not yet achieved stage of evolution that suggests the question as to whether our own theory provides a basis for conceiving of a level that is higher, not merely in degree, but in kind than personal life at its best.

Man like other animals extends his vital power of organization beyond the limits of his organism. Beehives, birds'-nests, and human dwelling houses, are examples of the animal ability to objectify in extra-organic material the needs for bodily shelter and procreation. It is, however, in his laboratories and churches and in such quasi-physical institutions as government and school that man objectifies his distinctively human capacities, and by a kind of sublimated anabolism makes carnate in his culture the ideals of his spirit. These cultural embodiments of the human spirit are not themselves alive. They differ from the physical offspring and the body-cells which are the living creatures of a living being. These latter are, however, embodiments only of the organism and not of the mind or spirit. *If man were able to give actual life to the children of his spirit and to endow them with the same independence and capacity for self-preservation and reproduction as that possessed by the fruits of his body, he would have attained the next higher level of evolution, which, following Alexander, we may denominate the level of Deity.* We should need, in short, to be like Pygmalion and bring into existence living Galateas, who would incarnate our needs and aspirations and at the same time share with us the boon of independent and self-perpetuating existence. Then we should be as Gods. As it is, our cultural creatures are but shadows and images, transitory reflections of spirit in the flux of matter, precarious adjectives of a substance not their own. Whether we are to attain to the higher level which we can now only vaguely imagine and whether the Macrocosm has already attained or from the beginning possessed it, we have no sure means of knowing. Deity may be only an essence, destined never to emerge into existence. Or, if it exists, it may be only as a prerogative of the universe as a whole. But there is also the possibility that even finite beings may in time achieve it.

In conclusion I would advert to the question which each writer in this volume will, I suppose, have put to himself: What relevance has the essay which he has been privileged to tender as a tribute of affection and admiration for John Dewey to the philosophy of John Dewey himself? " A materialistic theory of Emergent Evolution," even if well-founded, might at first hearing sound alien to the temper of Dewey's own work, which has so consistently expressed a distrust of old and conventional labels. I am sensitive to the defect in this respect not only of my title, but of my whole discussion. I am, however, to some extent consoled by the reflection that while the founder of Instrumentalism has protested against the older categories and captions by which philosophers have separated themselves from one another and from the reality which they sought to interpret, he has supplemented that protest by much concrete and positive insistence upon the pluralistic, the contingent, and the discontinuous phases of experience. And furthermore, he has accompanied his plea for a due recognition of the discrete with an equally positive demand that the heterogeneities and pluralities of experience be included in the one homogeneous continuum of nature.

If my paper has to any degree mitigated the conflict between the earlier concept of a continuous evolution and the more recent concept of an emergence of successive discontinuities, it will in so far forth, I hope, have been in harmony with the philosophy of " Experience and Nature."

WHAT IS MEANT BY SOCIAL ACTIVITY?

ERNEST C. MOORE

Is society a precondition or an achievement? It is both, and if not both, it is neither. Society is human beings associating. Clearly there never was a time when such beings abandoned a previous isolation and said to themselves and to each other henceforth we shall associate. Association brought them into being and association safe-guarded them in infancy; indeed, associating safe-guarded them through life. To ask why this should be so is to ask why nature is as it is. " He who says development says germ."

The first reflective account of society is found in Plato's *Republic*. There its essence is correctly stated to be co-operation. We are not alike at birth. There are diversities of nature which are adapted to different occupations. Having recognized them Plato does not make very adequate provision for these diverse natures. He lumps them together in three classes and trains his citizens for but three occupations. That was because the working state was as yet but a thing of simple outlines. Not all the differences of men could be used in it. Nevertheless, the discovery is a momentous one — that we are tied to each other by our differences and that what we call society is just folks working together. When Plato came to write the *Laws* he gave an historical rather than a functional account of group life, an account which anticipated Darwin's in the *Descent of Man*.[1] " Did not the eldest rule among them because with them government originated in the authority of a father and a mother whom like a flock of birds they followed, forming one troop under the patriarchal rule and sovereignty of their parents which of all sovereigns is the most just? " [2]

" The state," said Aristotle, " is a creation of nature. . . ." The word he used was *physis*. That word Professor Myres warns us is not properly rendered by the Roman word " *natura*" which means " the act of being

[1] Part I, chapter IV.
[2] *Laws*, p. 680.

born." [3] Jowett has it that the *physis* of anything is its fulfilment of perfection, that which it was intended to become,[4] but *physis,* as Professor Myres has explained, is to early Greeks " the way things grow." Man is by growth, not by birth, a social animal. It is the growth process which makes him responsive to his fellows. The same is true of language. We do not bring it with us at birth, but being the kind of creatures we are we grow it as a part of the process of living.

If we turn to the sociologists and inquire of them what kind of a process social activity is we find that their answers are many and various. In the great morning of physical science when astronomy, physics, and mathematics began to reveal their power men said the same forces operate in human affairs and the same kind of study will reveal them. Individuals influence each other just as the constituent parts of an astronomical system. Some they attract, others they repel, and that attraction and repulsion tells the whole story. Man is a machine started and stopped by the forces which play upon him. The interpreters who took that view expounded a mechanistic theory of society in chapters devoted to social statics, social dynamics, social energetics, etc. All that is social in the give and take of human beings is left out of these interpretations. They do not explain social action as something added to physical action nor as physical action with a difference. They disregard the very thing they are trying to explain. There is no satisfactory account of what social action means to be had from them.

That society is an organism is an ancient teaching. It became an authoritative doctrine when Herbert Spencer espoused it and announced that he had made it his own. His reasoning is analogical. Biological organisms grow, so does society. Structure changes and function changes in both. The parts are interdependent in both; the biological organism is composed of cells, the social of individuals. Within limits a destroyed part is renewed in both. Society has the analogue of an alimentary, a distributing, and a nervous system. It is not quite clear just how literally Spencer intended to be taken. Others have announced that they held the doctrine, but they seem to employ it for illustration rather than as a statement of fact. It is one thing to say that social action is based on biological action, it is quite another thing to say that it is nothing but biological

[3] Myres' *The Political Ideas of the Greeks*. The Abingdon Press, p. 385.
[4] *The Politics of Aristotle*, Jowett. Part I, Vol. II, p. 7.

action. Each organ of the body has its special place and function. Each cell is a very limited portion of its organ. If separate individuals are cells their sphere of operations is fixed and unchanging. The unities of social action are reached by processes which are essentially different from the combining of the cells to constitute the body.

The sociologistic school makes social interaction the mother of language, mind, morals, and every other phase of human efficiency. "The individual is rather a product than an author of a society," writes Espinas. The soul reflects the society which shapes its being. Even the greatest geniuses are but social products of their times. Durkheim goes farther than that. To distinguish social facts from psychological facts he proposes the criteria of exteriority and constraint. There is a social mind independent of individual minds and different from them. "Being placed outside of and above individual and local contingencies it sees things only in their permanent and essential aspects, which it crystallizes into communicable ideas. . . . Society sees farther and better than individuals." (Durkheim, *The Elementary Forms of Religious Life,* as quoted by Sorokin, *Contemporary Sociological Theories,* p. 465.) Gumplowicz carries the doctrine to its extreme. " It is not man himself who thinks but his social community." Commenting sarcastically upon this statement Sorokin wishes he could see how " not a man but a community thinks." The sociologistic school he believes is right in making social interaction a factor in the growth of mind and in pointing to a correlation between social and psychological processes and in insisting upon the social origin of language, logic, religion, science, morals, etc. But is social interaction alone a sufficient explanation? He holds that it is not. There is social interaction without mental stimulation as well as with it. Prolonged social interaction does not guarantee the maintaining of an achieved level of thought, much less a development beyond it. The factor of interaction does not explain the origin and development of thought or the processes of thinking. In short, the facts do not confirm the theory.

There is a fourth school which is philosophical rather than sociological, though institutional sociology is derived from it. According to this school it is not " the social mind," much less the minds of individuals, it is the Absolute Mind which manifests itself in social order and determines the progress of mankind. In this view the *Weltgeist* is responsible for most that is done, indeed for all that is worth considering. It is finely disdainful of " subjective opinions " accounting them as nothing in the presence of " the work on which reason has been engaged for more than a thousand years." (Hegel, *Preface to the Philosophy of Right*.) " In relation to it [the ethical system] individuals are merely accidental and whether the individual exists or not is a matter of indifference to the objective ethical order which alone is steadfast. It is the power by which the life of individuals is ruled. . . . It has an absolute authority or force, infinitely more sure than that of natural objects." (*Philosophy of Right,* Dyde, pp. 145–6.) It is sometimes said that these strong statements were made by Hegel to emphasize the importance of the other in human development. If so, they overshoot the mark for they destroy the self.

From each of these four theories it would seem that nature has perhaps made a mistake in not casting human society in one piece, for they each agree with Napoleon that it is not really men who live but institutions. Yet it is unlikely that diversity of existence has no value in a world which is made upon its principle. If we start with our bodies, and psychology in its recent development advises us to do that, there can be no doubt that they are many. Our sense organs and action systems are individual and separate. Now generalization concerns itself with identities by overlooking differences, that is, it does not consider individuals in their entirety, and failing to do that it cannot do justice to a world in which they function together in their entirety. Just as there are no eyes or hands that are not the eyes or hands of some body just so there are no brains or nervous systems which are not the brains or nervous systems of particular individuals. It is from the movements of these same hands, eyes, and other parts of human bodies that we infer that the individual whose they are, is suffering pain, experiencing joy, is hungry, angry, confused, alert, sick, devout, friendly, disdainful, thinking, observing, idling, cooperating, loyal, patriotic, criminal, or saintly.

Individuality consists precisely in this: that we cannot exchange our feelings, our awarenesses, our thoughts, our resolves, our acts, any more than we can our hands or eyes. Each one always has his own and only his own and in all his affairs, intellectual as well as physical, he must proceed under his own power. This, to be sure, is what is called " the formal separateness of individual centers of experience " and it is said that this separateness is overcome, transfused, sublimated in experiences which are identical and universal, but our contention must be that just because experiences are not interchangeable they never can be contentually identical, though functionally identical they may be. "If we were," says Mr. Bosanquet in a much-quoted passage,[5] " to base our theories on what human beings are when they sing together, or fight on the same side, or sacrifice themselves for those dear to them or for a cause, or think with the full power of their intelligence, the difference in our attitude would not be one of idle sentiment alone, but would be a logical and metaphysical difference of immense significance." But in what sense is individuality overcome or sublimated in any of these operations? Do players in an orchestra become more or less conscious of their parts and realize their skill more or less clearly when the undertaking is a public rendering of, say, Beethoven's Fifth Symphony under a renowned leader than when they play alone? Does the orator become more or less conscious of his power when he attempts a great theme upon a solemn occasion? Do the soldiers who make a last stand in a lost battle realize their individuality while they yield their lives for the cause they have made their own? In all these cases the sense of power grows with the cause. We do not forget ourselves, we find ourselves when heavy demands are made upon us. The separateness of individuality is not sublimated or wiped out. It is heightened. "Upon me, upon me, O Lord, is the salvation of the city"; and unless there is a summoning of resources not in general, but mine and mine only, on the part of each man defending it, the city cannot be saved.

The argument of Professor Fite in his valuable discussion of Individualism [6] is immensely clarified by his use of the illustration of the driverless engines to make evident the nature of mechanical action. I have wondered why he did not use engines with engineers at the throttle to show what social action is. I shall take a more complicated illustration. The daily miracle of ten thousand automobiles keeping their distance and position and accomplishing their several errands almost without bloodshed upon the highways of every section of the forty-eight commonwealths is to me the truest and most convincing clarification of the reality of social action which I know. Let no one say that ours is but a negative undertaking — that of keeping from running over a pedestrian or smashing into my neighbor's machine. It is a positive effort to body forth or bring to being that degree of consideration and skill which will safeguard

[5] *The Principles of Individuality and Value,* p. 272.
[6] *Individualism,* by Warner Fite, Longmans, Green, and Co.

my well-being and that of my fellow man and these terms are reciprocal. The action is social. There is response in it, for both in initiative and consequence it must be his as well as mine. And it is individual as well as social; there is an individual at the wheel of each car and he must do his part, for if he is unskilled or drunk or insists upon driving at seventy miles an hour, his act is plainly unsocial. Clearly one does not lose his individuality in trying to guide his car safely through the maze of traffic; the more exacting the road becomes the more conscious must he be of the demands upon his skill and his responsibility for meeting them. And he does not lose his individuality by trying to do what increasing millions of his neighbors are trying to do. Uniformly safe driving does not abolish individuality, it creates it.

Now, if my illustration is worth anything, it seems to warrant certain conclusions. First, that society is a very unsatisfactory word to use to describe what exists here. It is a noun for which there is *no thing*. The thing which exists calls for an adjective, an adverb, or a verb. Folks exist. They act and their acts are social or unsocial, that is, they act socially or unsocially, they socialize or unsocialize themselves and each other. There are folk ways and ways which destroy folks and which if any cluster of folks allow will speedily destroy that folk. That is what I think Professor Sumner had in mind. But I am not so clear that he applied his term to all the interactions of men or saved it merely for those forms of interacting which had become crystallized and so thoroughly established that the moss of antiquity had begun to grow upon them. My point is that the centers of initiation, the wells of energy, the existent beings are always individuals. They make tools, they fight, they make peace, they converse, they traffic, they make inventions, they build institutions, they form states, they organize sciences and they develop and cherish ways of life which they teach their children and these their children after them, but these things are their handiwork and are less and other than they. Second, there would seem to be but little sense in talking about an automobile-driving mind. If invented, that term would be far more compromising than enlightening, far more harmful than helpful, for though it might be employed to designate merely those common features of mind which the practice of driving an automobile is apt to emphasize in each and all individuals who drive one, yet the mere existence of such a term in the language would certainly constrain some to forget the wholesome principle of William of Ockham.

Third, we might get a certain speculative comfort and seeming enlargement of thought by denominating the automobile and automobile driving
an " institution." Then we would doubtless be moved to go farther and
point out how the institution of the automobile between the years 1910 and
1930 assumed great power to shape and mold the human race so that
having tended hitherto to build their houses on level ground men strangely
enough now under this new influence began to build them on mountains;
some being without possessions were nevertheless constrained — such was
the amazing power of this institution — to sell themselves into slavery to
deferred payments for its sake, and more strangely still, the very shape of
the human body changed to conform to its relentless demands.

Just as the institution of slavery mastered the master as well as the
slave, just so any widely used practice or discovery is bound to change
the lives of those who discharge their energy through its channeling.
But does that in any sense make it a being co-ordinate with the folks who
use it? It is easy to talk of the family, the school, the university, the
church, the state, language, art, science, philosophy as existent reals, easier
perhaps than to think of them as activities of men just as it seems to have
been easier for Plato's interpreters throughout history to have understood
the letters of his alphabet of courage, temperance, wisdom, and justice as
separate metaphysical archetypes rather than building blocks with which
to make a world — easier, but how much less satisfying! One longs for
that rebellious quietist to come again who shocked his generation by
asking: " Is it this pile of brick and mortar — these dead floors, windows,
rails — you call the church? Why this is not the church at all — the
church is living, ever living souls."

Institutions are functionings of men. They are real only as minds
make them, no matter how much heaping up of wood or stone or printer's
ink they may have occasioned. Unless living, breathing folks enact them
now they are as dead as the Egypt of the Ptolemies or the empire of
Nebuchadnezzar. To use such terms as the church, the family, the city,
the state, and society is always to invite the mind to regard as separate
and static entities certain specific human relations which are dynamic and
functional. Our relations to our fellows in each one of these groupings
are very much like our relations to the other drivers of automobiles upon
the highway. When we say that the family is one of the constituent
institutions of society we tend to think of it as a once-for-all relation

instead of a long journey full of ever changing hazards with a little band of road partners. When we think of the school it is only by the greatest straining of the imagination that we can bring ourselves to remember that that is a name for the incessant interaction of some hundreds of thousands of eager, struggling young people each working out his own interpretation of certain activities which all are invited to master. When we talk of the church it is next to impossible to see it as a voluntary partnership of folks perpetually engaged in assisting each other to live after a chosen way. And the state we are apt to picture to ourselves as anything but just all of us trying to march forward together through the years with something like due regard for the orderliness of the line. One gives and takes with the other members of his family, of his business, his club, his church, his community, his state, by incessant re-relating, very much as he gives and takes with his fellow drivers upon the crowded road. He never succeeds in being a good husband, a good father, a good teacher, a good business man, a good member of his community to the extent of being able to say: Now the thing is accomplished, henceforth I need take no thought for that. If he should make the mistake of saying as he drives his car in traffic: My relations to my neighbors are all arranged; I need henceforth consider them no further — the result would be disastrous. It is not otherwise in the other cases. A man's relation to society is not a relation to a fixed thing. It is not a fixable relation. It is only when institutions are taken as entities instead of conjoined and co-operating folks that misunderstanding is certain. The relations are moving; they are discussed as though they were static.

But, it will be said, this self, this soul, this individual to which you attach such importance in social relations, what of it? Is it not a product also? Wherein is it more real than institutions? The individual is indeed a product, but he is also a maker. It is not necessary to answer Hume's " I desire that it may be produced " with the demonstration of the existence of a substantial self; it is enough that there are centers in which experience grows, in which awareness is continuous and unified. The individual appears in time; he inherits something from his parents. He is born an animal, but a peculiar animal. Other young animals are sent nearly ready made into existence. All that is human he must learn — except the capacity of learning itself. He comes of a stock whose members survived, whose variations both preserved and were preserved because they were not ruthlessly self-centered but co-operative. It would simplify matters greatly if we could say that instincts do the work of socializing them. But instincts would account for both too little and too much to constitute social action. Instincts are mental mechanisms which have a one to one correspondence with the acts they occasion. The variety of acts which the children of men perform is too chaotic a repertory to be instinct-occasioned. The young human is too plastic to be geared down to instincts. His mental mechanisms are not so completely assembled yet. He gets his full complement of nerve cells by the end of the fifth month of embryonic life, but it takes a long time for him to grow connective fibers between them. He has few fixed co-ordinations at first, but is instead a bundle of impulses, an energetic center of movements, random, inchoate, and meaningless for the most part. Always he is tended by adults who feed him, wash him, change his position for him, pet him, take notice of him, come when he cries, relieve his pain, rock and soothe him to sleep, play with him, repeat after him with delight the first sounds that he makes and invite him on to other sounds slightly different which seem to them better. It takes but a single sentence, though a long one, to indicate this earliest form of human give and take, but in that sentence we have the matrix of all social relations.

It is under these influences that unordered native activities are gently guided into preferred human regularities. Nature which sends us into the world so unformed and helpless provides each of us with a guardian, a companion, and a model. Professor Baldwin believes that the child distinguishes his mother's or his nurse's touch in the dark as early as his second month. The tones of voice, the expressions of features, the attitudes of feeling that go along with them are copied from the mother; with her help mind, or better, since it is a process, *minding* begins, not relying upon itself, but guided and assisted by another at first, just as walking is.

We do not start as atomic individuals. The inchoate and scattered impulses of the infant co-ordinate into serviceable activities only through shaping by the environment which is of folks and things. At first we might almost say of folks alone, for the meanings of things are all interpreted to the infant by the ministering folks who attend him in his first responses. By them his hands are lifted to contacts to which he is invited and gently put aside from others not desirable. Objects are pointed out to him and he is showered with encouragement when he begins to make approved responses and is discouraged from the other kind. The environment of folks is so solicitously about him that all his doings get meaning from their doings. He grows up the reciprocal of his mother, of his family, of his village or neighborhood, of his school and his country. What he takes he takes from them and what he gives he gives to them. It is by folks that our impulses are guided as they form themselves into attitudes and habits of belief and judgment. Incessantly folks make demands upon us. We learn their language, word by word, making it our own; we learn their scheme of values and their classifications of things and men. The concrete demands which they put upon us constrain us to admire and hate in keeping with the texture of our place and time.

Since folks play so large a part in determining what we are and shall be it would perhaps be helpful if they influenced us immediately. Do they do that? The evidences for telepathy are not clear,[7] and if it existed it could hardly be rated as a social force. Professor Boodin thinks we must " presuppose an immediate protopathic sense of social presence (however overlaid and difficult to disentangle) as the background of our life and of social relations." [8] He is a strong anti-behaviorist regarding social relations as immediate deliverances, as sense experiences. But this immediate protopathic sense is not an observable factor in human equipment.[9] It is a postulate, perhaps a desirable one, but not an inevitable one.

The speculations of Mr. C. Delisle Burns [10] as to the nature of the contact between minds is equally engaging, but seems equally not proven. Mr. Burns defends the metaphysical hypothesis " that ' other minds ' are enjoyed in the same sense as ' my own ' mind is enjoyed," employing Alexander's terminology in which enjoyment is that experience which distinguishes awareness of the mental process from awareness of an object in or through that process; the experience which is enjoyed by A and B being that each is a mental process. The enjoyment is not after the fact

---

[7] Sir Ray Lankester, *Great and Small Things*, p. 131.

[8] Boodin, *Cosmic Evolution*, p. 204.

[9] Trotter and Davies: "Experimental Studies in the Innervation of the Skin," *Journal of Physiology*, 1909, Vol. 38, pp. 134–246.

Franz: "On Sensation Following Nerve Division," *Journal of Comparative Neurology and Psychology*, 1909, Vol. 19, pp. 107–124, 215–236.

Boring: "Cutaneous Sensations After Nerve Division," *Quarterly Journal of Experimental Physiology*, 1916, Vol. 10, pp. 1–95.

[10] *The Contact Between Minds*, Macmillan & Co., 1923.

or retrospective as all introspection is. It is contemporaneous and immediate and it does not erect the other mind so enjoyed into an object. One can behold bodies, he cannot see another mind, but according to this hypothesis he can enjoy it. The theory calls for a degree of introversion far greater than that with which nature has provided man. The human species seems to have been equipped to struggle with an external environment rather than to note the processes it employs in that struggle. Behaviorism would have no warrant if we were immediately aware of minds, our own and our neighbor's. It is only by its results that my mind reveals itself to me. Apart from the reports which it makes about objects its existence is as unknown as was the circulation of the blood before Harvey observed it. If it is said that the baby must enjoy his mother's mind, is it not equally evident that he enjoys the mind of his feeding bottle? And that the primitive man enjoys the mind of his fetish as certainly as the mind of his fellow? Again the immediate awareness of the presence of another mind should make it unnecessary for one to look under the bed to see if a man is hiding there or for an army to employ scouts to detect the presence of the enemy or perhaps even for one to call in an alienist to determine the sanity of a neighbor who is acting strangely. Again if we were immediately aware of the existence of another mind would not the Golden Rule be the easiest instead of the hardest of moral injunctions to obey? If the reply is that it is only when we contemplate another's body that we enjoy his mind, the process has at least some of the marks of inference. It is not clear what survival value such " enjoying of other minds " could have. If it is offered as the explanation of social action is it not an explanation akin to that of the soporific quality of opium?

What is the social process? The young child and his mother are not one, but two — two centers of experience, two memory systems. No matter how much unity there may be between them, it can never be the unity of a single consciousness. And their separateness is of like kind, though perhaps not of like degree, with the separateness of all individuals. No matter how vague that difference is at first the day will come when the infant discovers that his hurts are his and not another's, no matter how sympathetic that other may be about them. The locus of all experience is individual, all perceptions, all wants, all understandings, all deliberations, all choosings, all actions proceed from single human beings.

There is no alternative to the acts of individuals, for the only action systems which nature has made are of individuals. But individuals do not act alone, they interact, they grow up together, they communicate, they influence each other, they agree, they co-operate; but always individuals are the centers of energy, the carriers of the forces which are generated and released.

Their first concerns are with objects; they point them out to each other and as they point them out they make sounds which are intended to designate the objects, to symbolize them, so that when an object is absent it can be brought to mind by some one mentioning its name. That, of course, is possible only when both parties to the conversation have already had sense experience of that object, for if only the person who speaks the name knows to what it refers, the hearing of that name will not call up its significant image in the mind of the hearer. Communication has been called the most wonderful of human affairs. In lauding it we are apt to overlook how essentially difficult it is and how far it falls short of producing that unity of separate understanding which is its aim. To be sure, the pointing out of objects does not guarantee similar perception of them unless the objects are both very simple and very familiar. For example, let two persons, one an automobile mechanic and the other the owner of the car together look at the defective engine of the owner's car. Under what conditions can they possibly see with equal clearness what is before them? Illustrations might be multiplied. The very existence of experimental science is a monument to the fact that fruitful observation is one of the most difficult of man's undertakings. But the difficulties of seeing objects eye to eye are slight in comparison with the difficulty of arriving at an identity of experience by means of words. Objects are particular, words are universal. We talk glibly of the identities of thought which the use of the same words occasion. There would be far fewer suits for breach of contract than there are if every seeming meeting of minds in offer and acceptance for a consideration were indeed a real meeting of minds. There is a passage in Brander Matthews' *These Many Years* which seems to me to be so rich in implication that I should like to appeal to it here. In a private dining room of the Savile Edmund Gosse had gathered a group of his friends to do honor to W. D. Howells. They talked first of the disappearance of revenge as a motive in fiction. Their second topic " was a definition of the image called up in our several minds by the word *forest*. Until that evening I had never thought of forest as clothing itself in different colors and taking on different forms in the eyes of different men; but I then discerned that even the most innocent word may don strange disguises. To Hardy, forest suggested the sturdy oaks to be assaulted by the woodlanders of Wessex, and to Du Maurier it evoked the trim and tidy avenues of the national domain of France. To Black, the wood naturally brought to mind the low scrub of the so-called deer forests of Scotland; and to Gosse it summoned up a view of the green-clad mountains that towered up from the Scandinavian fiords. To Howells, it recalled the thick woods that in his youth fringed the rivers of Ohio and to me there came back swiftly the memory of the wild growths bristling up unrestrained by man in the Chippewa reservation which I had crossed fourteen years before in my canoe trip from Lake Superior to the Mississippi." And is not Professor Brander Matthews right when he says that even the most innocent word may assume strange disguises? Take the words *home, school, church, mother, child, war, work, duty, love, truth, character,* or any other word and ask what kind of an agreement of minds exists when men use it? Clearly their minds have not been reduced to a common denominator of content or meaning.

Language is not a device for thought transference. It is a signaling system and far from a perfect one. When we speak to another or write for another to read, we invite, stimulate, challenge, demand, provoke, require him to make meanings to fit our words, but the meanings which he makes are his meanings, not ours, though if he is a skilled interpreter and we are careful in selecting the signals which we give him we may measurably succeed in making him aware of our purposes. But he is limited to the reading of our signals and we are limited to the reading of his. We do not send our thoughts to him. If the man in the car in front of mine stretches out his arm at a right angle as we approach a cross street, I infer that he intends to turn to the left and drive my car between him and the curb that I may turn to the right. But he intended to turn to the right and made the mistake of giving the wrong signal. Did I read his thought or his signal? And what could I read? When Hamlet says to Ophelia, " I did love you once," Ophelia replies, " Indeed, my lord, you made me believe so." Then Hamlet says, " I loved you not." What is Ophelia to make out of such a conversation? Yet it is from signals nearly as conflicting as these that each one of us must work out his accords with his fellow men.

How do these signal systems attain such effectiveness as they have? The process of learning the signs is at the same time the process of defining the experiences which the signs signalize. It is the lifelong process of discovering what features of our experience are negotiable in give and take with our associates. Sir Henry Jones somewhere reminds us that if a teacher gives a class of boys a problem on their first day in school the chances are that he will get a different answer from each boy in the class. Let him then teach them arithmetic for a term and at its end he will receive the same answer to that problem from each boy. This in epitome is the process of socializing individuals. It is not different when what is in question is our perception of objects. The infant reaches for the moon; his mother explains why he does not succeed in touching it. "When ten men look at the moon," said Ried, "they all see the same individual object." "Not so," said Hamilton, "the truth is that each of these persons sees a different object." If each of the ten in locating his experienced object persisted in pointing to a different quarter of the heavens, they would never arrive at the conviction that their minds were in agreement. The one moon of their common reference is made by the oneness of their referring. No such oneness obtains in the judgments which a group of critics indulge in upon a musical event, though the time may come when even musical critics will learn to point in the same direction and to hear and report the same experiences. The question is not: How does the one object make such different impressions upon different minds; the question is: How do individual centers out of widely different experiences construct a world which is so nearly common to them that it can serve as a basis of all their giving and taking together, for construct it they do after they come here at birth and without the aid of innate ideas. They construct it out of common actions, pointings, namings, declarings, invitings, promisings, avowings. They think in the same way, but they discover that they think in the same way through the confirmation of common doings. The meeting of minds in the making of a contract is revealed or disproven by the subsequent actions of the contracting parties. The fact of agreement as to meanings in general can be established in no other way. The proof of the unity of a family, a group or a nation is their behavior in time of ordeal. Miss Follet, in her valuable book, *The New State,* convincingly uses the procedure of a committee in arriving at a decision with respect to a difficult matter before it as typical of the process by which collective ideas may be evolved. The ideas of the members are not added; they are interactively developed. *A* says something. What *A* says causes a thought to rise in *B*'s mind, which he utters. *B*'s reaction to *A*'s idea invites *A* to a slightly new point of view. *C, D,* and *E* enter into this process of give and take until an idea is created which is owned by each of them and belongs to them all. If one of them now says, *I think this,* he speaks for the committee and not for himself alone. But can he be sure that what the committee has merely agreed to do it will do and stand by and defend? Is not the test of the reality of this union of minds a pragmatic test also?

There is no implication of self-sufficiency in this teaching. The doctrine of individual human infallibility finds no encouragement from man's greatest effort to integrate experience. Thinking is an individual matter as certainly as digesting is, but as Professor Minot pointed out, "Science consists in the discoveries made by individuals, afterward confirmed and correlated by others. . . ." These others are always individuals too and each one confirms his own idea and never any idea but his own, yet these individuals believe that their ideas refer to a common event and confirm each other. "Though I cared in the highest degree for the approbation of such men as Lyell and Hooker, who were my friends, I did not care much about the general public," Darwin writes. The unity must be worked out. The confirmation can come only from those who by their works give evidence of a pre-occupation similar to mine and by their words of a critical solicitude concerning my results. Those who can and do test my processes by repeating them and my formulations by analyzing them qualify to communicate approval or disapproval. Our agreement is subject to revision, however, as long as we are separate gatherers of experience. We seem then to arrive at a threefold conclusion:

(1) Individuals add their forces to those of other individuals through co-operation. (2) They aim at and arrive at what is outwardly a mutuality of understanding through participation in similar or inter-related undertakings. This mutuality of understanding they evidence to each other by their acts, but by their acts they also reveal to each other that that mutuality of understanding is full of rifts and discords, that it can be

a harmony only by persistent harmonizing. (3) But is there no closer relation? There is. There are in that process moments in which a nearly perfect harmony of understanding appears to exist. Sensitiveness responds to sensitiveness in an accord so penetrating that mutuality of comprehending is unmistakable. It was of moments such as these that Wordsworth could write in the first draft of the Prelude:

> When strongly breathed upon
> By this sensation, whencesoe'er it comes
> Of union or communion doth the soul
> Rejoice as in her highest joy; for there,
> There chiefly, hath she feeling whence she is
> And, passing through all nature rests with God.

Such a supreme moment came to Darwin when to his "I shall be *intensely* curious to hear what effect the book produces upon you," Huxley, having examined his advance copy, answered on the day before the publication of *The Origin of Species* that he was "prepared to go to the stake if requisite in support" of the evidence therein for evolution. Every administrative officer in the land, whether his office is a large or a small one, has for his portion the carrying on of a nearly ceaseless ministry of reconciliation between men whose views must be adjusted to the demands which are made upon them. The surface observer, with repertorial aloofness from the human struggle, and social theorists are too often such remote observers, does not discern the endless effort to bring about a working unity of minds which goes on and must go on. He takes the unity for an original datum and regards it as a point of departure. It is in fact nothing of the sort. It is a product, the result of an intense friction and as momentary and unlasting as ripened fruits upon an orchard tree. Not without reason did Professor Royce make perpetual interpretation the means to the community.

It is folks who make society. It exists, as arithmetic and music and morality exist, nowhere but in the minds of men. It is there, too, that institutions have their being. Their outward forms have all been arranged by men who went before us and are like the roads which we find here when we come, only facilities for our going. All that is really objective about these activities of folks is that harmony of operation which their interactions reveal. It is true that language is social, religion is social, ethics is social, commerce is social, but that does not at all mean that these are molds that we are pressed into as we grow, but rather that they are like walking, talking, stone-throwing, etc., activities into which we pour our energy and which we keep alive by doing them. Do the individual and society grow together? No, if by that you mean two related existences, two entities developing side by side. Yes, if you mean one subject and its activities. The individuals relate themselves to each other. Their relating or organizing or combining is the society. Their acts are social and they exist as individuals only in the degree that they maintain these interactions with their fellows. But there is no social force except that which operates through persons and no social equilibrium but that which interacting individuals embody. " There can," [11] to borrow Thomas Hill Green's words, " be nothing in a nation however exalted its mission, or in a society, however perfectly organized, which is not in the persons composing the nation or the society."

[11] *Prolegomena to Ethics,* section 184.

THE CULT OF CHRONOLOGY

Helen Huss Parkhurst

Mankind is ill at ease in the passing moment, and ever seeks refuge out of it, through the gates of anticipation and of memory. To this rule are only two exceptions: the aesthete, oblivious of both past and future by excess of absorption in the present; and the saint, blind to the temporal altogether in his intoxication with eternity. All others, far from deploring, rather exult in their escape from the common light of today into the fading sunset of yesterday or the dawning vision of tomorrow. We of the twentieth century being, alas, whole-hearted lovers neither of beauty nor holiness, are distinguished more than commonly by the prospective and the restrospective posture. Nor must this excessive concern of ours with time that is yet to come and times that are over be supposed a token of our inferiority. If it marks us as notably deficient in mystical and artistic consciousness, it serves also to set us in flattering contrast with the brute and the savage. For whereas it is upon the eternal that the saintly mind is fixed, and upon a present moment insulated from intrusion by the temporal stream of cause and consequence that the mind of the artist is intent, primitive thought, though engrossed with a segment of true time, is restricted to a much abbreviated segment. Widening of the temporal range of an individual's preoccupations should connote then loss of savagery. And serious general concern with the happenings of a distant past or of a remote future should serve as an index as good as any other of the degree of civilization achieved.

On this basis, we of the twentieth century might be diagnosed as rather markedly civilized. For it is to an astonishingly enlarged world that our minds are habituated — a world of swifter motions, farther journeys, and retrospections and hopes that comprehend hitherto undreamed of periods. Individually and selfishly obsessed as we frequently are with petty desires and regrets that belong to a mere hour or day or year, vistas are opened for us incessantly upon profounder abysses of time. An Egyptian tomb yields up its treasures and straightway the accumulated shadows of five thousand years roll back and we feel ourselves in the presence of things whose date makes all ordinary historical antiquities appear absurdly recent. A pre-historic jaw-bone is unearthed, and the scene is shifted to yet remoter reaches of time in comparison with which the entire length of recorded history is but the last leaf of a prodigious cosmic calendar. Not rare scholars only but quite ordinary people are aware that our earth has lasted already perhaps more than a billion years, and that our sun, with a past it may be of five trillion earthly years, has a fair prospect of continuing ten, or a hundred, or five hundred times that unthinkable duration. The span of frequent if not quite everyday attention thus for multitudes passes the limits, not simply of twenty years of Europe or of a cycle of Cathay or even of the long reach of geologic ages, but attains proportions commensurate with the slow gestation and final death of worlds. Along with these extensions backward and forward of our consciousness of time there goes a corresponding stretching of our notions of space. But so immense are the sizes and distances which the astronomer proposes that to become intelligible they need to be translated into the language of time; and the distance traveled by light in one year is taken as the foot-rule for these gigantic measurings. Thus it is that the constantly augmented spatial estimates of the physical universe turn out to contribute no small part of our increased acquaintance with time. We tell ourselves how wide and deep the inter-stellar spaces are, not in terms of miles, but of light-years. A mere 2,000 of these is all we need to postulate for the diameter of our local star cloud, but 100,000 for that of the spiral in which our solar system, with our earth, is contained. There must be envisaged 850,000 light-years as the temporal measure of the distance from ourselves of the very nearest spiral nebula, and anywhere from 200,000,000 to 200,000,000,000, on present estimates, for the diameter of the entire physical universe. As a new measure of time — a single pendulum swing, as it were, of a clock of sufficient proportions to mark the rhythmic pulse of worlds thus generously interpreted — we may use the calculated period of rotation of our own galaxy: a single revolution in 300,000,000 years! Nothing comparable to this in the way of a temporal unit has perhaps ever been entertained by the wondering mind of man, at least in the midst of its soberer scientific investigations. We may, indeed, if we turn from modern calculations to the extravagant fabrications of the Orient, encounter imagined magnitudes which cause even our colossal astronomical quantities to dwindle. The Hindoo concept of a Kalpa is an invention of this kind. " If there were a lofty rock, sixteen miles in each dimension, and one touched it once in a hundred years with a bit of the finest Benares linen, it would be reduced to the size of a wango-stone before a fourth of one of these *Kalpas* had rolled by."

But we are here concerned with temporal fact not fancy — or at least with supposed fact; and with contemporary experience of it. That experience, that increased pervasive awareness of time as a super-sensible medium or container, as a stream, or an infinitely extended warp upon which the woof of human happenings is woven, is without question a notable characteristic of present-day consciousness. The dazzled but hospitable mind of twentieth-century man is offered a vast array of new discoveries, new theories, new intuitions having to do with the temporal in all its aspects. By the psychologist he is presented with laboratory researches into such things as the experience of the specious present; by the Freudian, he is asked to believe in an indefinite prolongation of the past into the present by way of continued functioning of remote post-natal and even pre-natal experience; by the mathematician he is initiated into such problems as those of durationless instants and an infinite divisibility of the temporal continuum. On the one hand the semi-mystical Bergsonian concept of pure duration as distinguished from spatialized time is pressed upon him, and on the other he is made aware of the austere mysteries of Einsteinian time with its entanglement with space, its innocence of simultaneities at diverse positions, its strange absolute measure in terms of the speed of light.

Since the dawn of speculation time has, of course, been an object of much theoretical concern. The logical puzzles implicit in it, together with those of space and motion, were immortalized in the ancient antinomies of Zeno. Even earlier, the problem of temporal measurement, for its practical and still more for its religious uses, commanded the talents of the ingenious; and the day, the week, the lunar month, the year, and thereafter hours and minutes and seconds were gradually projected. But not until the present era does there seem to have converged upon the problem in all its ramifications such varied and intense interest — philosophical, psychological, logical, and scientific. This is in part due to the fact that never before has man been in possession of such masses of facts, and of sequences of events macrocosmic and microcosmic. Temporal occurrences have rendered us aware of time; but awareness of time has reacted also to stimulate increased interest in temporal occurrences. As Professor Shotwell has remarked, " The sense of Time is really a sense of times, and that is not a sense at all, but the slow product of developing intelligence." And in the last analysis it has to be admitted that ". . . we mark Time by events rather than events by Time." It must then really be time as implicated in happenings rather than time as a pure abstraction, emptied of its sensory content, that the average mind, even in this time-conscious period, is aware of.

What, accordingly, under the cloak of the phrase " Cult of Chronology " we want here to consider are the peculiarities of latterday thought and theory in so far as they are invested with temporal emphases and implications. We want to determine some of the meanings and the prospects of the passion of chronology — the insistent historicism — with which our age is indisputably infected. It is not, of course, our mere possession of huge historical interest that is here in question, although that interest at the present moment has attained almost the proportions of a cult, of a priestless and a godless religion. Not the extensiveness of our historical obsession, nor the variety of its forms, nor its vehemence and solemnity is what calls for especial comment. We moderns are notable for the making of histories without number, histories of heaven and earth, and of the myriad varieties of human achievement, histories even of history itself; but it is because of another phenomenon, partly perhaps a by-product, partly also a cause, of this voluminous chronicling that the matter of twentieth-century historical activity is here broached. Our objective is of the nature of a quarrel with the historian, a complaint as to the misuse of history — an indictment even of historicism as in certain respects a vice. But before stating our case we shall delay a little, and indulge in a few observations designed to clarify somewhat the meaning of the term " history."

The present moment being a vanishing thing not seizable in speech, it would seem that if we deal with things temporal it must be either the past or the future that we must address ourselves to. All discourse that is not prophecy might appear therefore to fall under the large concept of the historical. For those records that are in this wider sense of the term history we have, however, for greater accuracy devised a variety of names. Only when a record is of the stream of outward occurrences primarily human and social in character do we commonly call it history proper. James Harvey Robinson quotes Professor Seeley as calling history nothing but a ". . . residuum which has been left when one group of facts after another has been taken possession of by some science," and as adding, ". . . that residuum which now exists must go the way of the rest, and that time is not very distant when a science will take possession of the facts which are still the undisputed property of the historian." This is reminiscent of an equally gloomy prognostication for philosophy; that it is destined to vanish from the earth as the hitherto unanswered questions constituting its subject-matter are one by one appropriated and answered by the various sciences. But for the moment at least history and philosophy as distinctive enterprises are still with us, and we shall shortly have occasion to note certain recent mutual encroachments of their respective domains. Regarding their earlier stages one interesting point of resemblance between them may at once be mentioned. According to Robinson it was only the " startling and exceptional " that attracted the older historians. " They were like a geologist who should deal only with earth quakes and volcanoes, or better still, a zoologist who should have no use for any thing smaller than an elephant or less picturesque in its habits than a phoenix or a basilisk." Somewhat similarly the more primitive philosophic generalizations were notably picturesque in character, and excitingly antagonistic to the testimony of common sense — to the effect, for example, that number is the stuff of the universe, or that all is water, all is fire, or all is sheer illusion. But startling transcendence of appearance and obstinate indulgence in paradox, is a characteristic of the philosopher even to the present day. And, correspondingly, history down to our own time has, in the words of Robinson, functioned " to gratify a natural curiosity in regard to the achievements and fate of conspicuous persons, the rise and decay of monarchies, and the signal commotions and disasters which have repeatedly afflicted humanity." Philosopher and historian alike at their most characteristic appear to be imbued with an almost childlike weakness for the bizarre, the grandiose, and the sensational.

But with the increase and spread of yellow journalism, cheap fiction, and the cinema there has come to be less excuse for a catering to the human lust for excitement by makers of chronicles and cosmologies purporting to be true. Popular sensational philosophy and semi-imaginative biography still thrive, and in greater abundance perhaps than ever before. However, a soberer, more scientifically conscientious type both of philosophic theory and of reconstruction of the past is now in the ascendant. Commerce, agriculture, exploration, manufacture, art, and invention — all the products of the less picturesque but more fertile periods of peace — are at last claiming the major share of the historian's attention. This is one metamorphosis which the historical enterprise has undergone. Another is its adjustment to the concept of evolution which has been gradually pervading the entire intellectual world.

The beginnings of this second reconstruction must, of course, be dated some distance back. With the first startled discovery that things change, giving birth at length to things of different sort, the past became at once prodigiously inflated and the subject-matter of history increased correspondingly in range and magnitude. In place of an original fiat, a state of innocence, a fall from grace, and the glorious deeds of a few ancestors, the nineteenth-century historian found confronting him the spectacle of a long process of innumerable stages. And gradually he came to realize that if he would exhaust the contents of primeval periods he must detail the growth not of man only, but likewise of the brute, and before that of the vegetable, and yet before that of the mineral. But once the hypothesis of evolution was adopted, the tale of humanity alone proved to be capable of an almost limitless expansion. Relinquish the belief that fire dates from Prometheus, curiosity and maternity from the Garden of Eden, and diversity of tongues from the tower of Babel, and the lengthy search into origins is initiated. First developed and applied in the theory of the nebular beginnings of our world, the concept of evolution with its demand for vast stretches of time and leisurely processes of transformation has been gradually introduced into the account of all the important institutions and activities of man. Thus has been expanded into an epic the statement of what would otherwise have been treated as practically instantaneous events — the occurrence upon the earth of marriage and the family, government and the church, battle-formations, the various industries, speech and the alphabet, fine art, and the body of the law. Now the building up of genetic accounts of all these things has demanded the long labor, the careful research, the attention to detail, and the faithful amassing of instances, characteristic of the worker in the laboratory. It has indeed conferred upon the enterprise of historical chronicling something of a scientific status. And the historian is fully aware of his promotion. He wears nowadays almost dramatically an aspect of soberness, a little self-righteous, perhaps, in his consciousness of deliberate and total abstaining from the spectacular rôle of necromancer, intimate of kings, and privileged dispenser of the more lurid blasphemies, atrocities, and perversions of an earlier generation. And this sober outlook of the up-to-date chronicler which he denominates a *sense of fact* — this appreciation, as Robinson phrases it, " of the overwhelming significance of the small, the common, and the obscure," is hailed as both a symptom and a guarantee of his scholarliness. In so far as it is in truth a token of a new worship of accuracy it should no doubt receive the highest commendation. For what, one may ask, could be more laudable than intentness upon fidelity to nature alike in the scientist's description of the world and the historian's reproduction of the long panorama of the past? A hint of doubt as to the importance of this scientific attitude might well be felt to savor of the blasphemous. And of course no serious dispraise of the contemporary passion for fact, is here contemplated. At most a slight tempering of the unqualified approbation of it will shortly be suggested. For the moment a different sort of comment upon it may be indulged in. The present high regard for " the small, the common, and the obscure " appears certainly to indicate an increased sobriety, but is it not perhaps rather to be taken as evidence of a new fanaticism attended by the taboos, fastings, and excesses characteristic of all unbridled idolatries?

This second interpretation is undoubtedly borne out less by the realistic outlook of the scientist and the historian than by that of the artist. For rather surprisingly there flourishes just at present, even among artists, an interest in the unspectacular, the mean, and the lowly so excessive as to deserve the title of " the cult of the commonplace." In painting and sculpture, in poetry and drama and fiction are to be found strains of the same curious obsession for the ugly, the trivial, the drab, and the dreary as somehow more *real* than anything else. The uncouth and monstrous forms offered us by Rouault and Picasso, are among the examples that may be cited, and the heavy corpulencies of Lachaise. In a thousand ways also the devices of modern fiction testify to the obsession for a hitherto unimagined degree of representational accuracy. Conversation is staccato and interrupted, as in life, and reverie disconnected and propositionally incomplete. But most notable is the frequent choice of characters determined seemingly by the criterion of maximum dullness and vulgarity. A depressingly large number of the men and women in the modern novel are themselves bored and disillusioned; they are likewise unromantic and inarticulate, spiteful and unpleasant. The narrative of their lives mediates a sense of the omnipresence and exclusive reality of monotony and dreariness, and of the stale and unprofitable character of the world. Even in contemporary poetry is manifested something of the same prejudice in favor of the soot and mire and dung of life, as if because swans, rainbows, and daffodils are rarer than less lovely things they are, therefore, less factual. Now the foregoing complaint is by no means intended to suggest that treatment of the ugly, mean or disagreeable is inappropriate to the aims of the highest art. The work of Rembrandt and of Flaubert would alone be sufficient to refute any such interpretation. All that is here desired is to emphasize the fact that in artistic creation no less than in intellectual pursuits there is abroad a spirit of distorted realism which is clearly responsible for what may be called the " cold gravy " school in fiction, and for the cult of the ugly in painting and poetry.

It is not, however, with these aberrations and idiosyncrasies of contemporary art that we are now concerned, but with those of current historicism. And what we set out to consider is whether the addiction to chronology, admirable in many respects as it may be, is not perhaps also in others, deplorable.

In the first place let us get clearly before us that liking for truth for its own sake should be held a thing beyond reproach, as is the love of beauty or passion for disputation or weakness for athletics. It is a very human and quite innocent trait. All of us on occasion have experienced the peculiar fascination exerted by little shining nuggets of allegedly pure truth, guaranteed free from admixture with any doubtful man-made theory. Not all cases, of course, of such nuggets are equally alluring. As Bertrand Russell once remarked; if you want as large chunks as possible of perfectly incontrovertible truth you can't do better than turn to a railroad time table. Such turning would probably dampen much uncritical ardor for truth for its own sake. On the other hand prolonged excursions into that compendium of unrelated facts, the World Almanac, promise many and varied delights. For most people it is not necessary to seek out startling and far-fetched items such as are retailed in that volume of modern wonders, *Believe It or Not.* Freakish and unplausible discoveries are always welcome, but to satiate the inquisitive mind of man almost any humble bit of information will serve. Statistics, particularly if they involve superlatives or anything in the way of records — whether of speed, size, age, or whatnot — meet a surprisingly prevalent need. An example of this is the figures with which the weather bureau regales us. For some unknown reason it affords deep satisfaction to know that it has been the coldest or the warmest, the wettest or the dryest January first ever recorded. Knowledge even of the average wind velocity for the state of Oklahoma, of average annual rainfall for the kingdom of Monaco or for the earth, is not without its queer benefits in the way of pleasure.

Such pleasure should not be, and probably seldom is, deplored. At worst it is felt to be devoid of significance. Delight derived from information might be said to acquire a status of dignity only when that information is ordered and organized into transverse or longitudinal sections through the fabric of historical fact. Otherwise it smacks too much of the unselectiveness of a dictionary or of the over-selectiveness of catalogues. When, or if, however, the question of justification for knowledge, particularly knowledge about the past, is raised, there are two chief points that would be made in its defence. First, there is the increased understanding of mankind and of the world as a basis for future behavior that such knowledge is supposed to make possible; and second, there is the juster evaluation of all things that is supposed to follow upon it.

Regarding the first of these pragmatic defences of history no special comment is necessary. It is beyond question that knowledge of the past is indispensable for full realization of the meaning of the present and for intelligent preparation for the future. But a defence of history as a means to better values is a more complicated issue.

Now it is certainly true that a raising or lowering of present appraisals has sometimes been not merely the accidental by-product, but the deliberately sought consequence, of a genetic account of the valued object. A maximum glorification of the human race is sometimes looked for from the flattering account of its almost immaculate conception, even though that entails an admission of a subsequent very heavy fall from grace. Correspondingly, the theory of man's animal beginnings is regarded by many as involving a subversion of his present claims to significance. But as William James observed in connection with his own researches into the genesis of religion, it is time we got over the ". . . assumption that spiritual value is undone if lowly origin be asserted." Indeed perhaps quite as good a case may be made for man's present and future glory by emphasizing the distance upward that he may have climbed as by pointing out the distance downward that he must have fallen.

Other sorts of doubtful or deplorable uses of historical research are to be found in the attempts to determine what our present judgments should be on the basis of the judgments of the past. We have long been familiar with this, the case method, in the study of law and medicine. To some extent the method as employed in both these fields is defensible. Medical diagnosis is, however, not so properly a matter of valuation as of assertion of causes and cures; and provided one may postulate uniformity of nature, new instances of symptoms should in general tend to yield to the same treatment as did the old. On the other hand the interpretation of the law as merely a body of precedents to be adhered to as closely as possible is in most respects unfortunate. The greatest jurists, indeed, attempt as far as possible to free new judgments as to crime and punishment from a mere slavish copying of those of the past. As for education, religion, and ethics, it might actually be said that ignorance rather than knowledge of the past would favor the achieving in these of the highest standards and ideals. The attempt recently made by G. C. Cox in his book, *The Public Conscience,* to initiate a true science of ethics by application of the case method is unquestionably interesting, but yet perhaps to be denounced as misguided. Only if the nature of the good and the means to its attainment is invariable from age to age could it be desirable to model present ethical judgments upon those of our forefathers. And only if majority opinion either past or present is to be taken as a sound criterion of right and wrong could accumulation of its pronouncements help in the discovery of the good. The conception of value as unvarying directly runs counter, of course, to the entire evolutionary conception of things. Many of those seemingly imbued with the spirit and outlook of the true evolutionist nevertheless fail to apply its philosophy when it is a question of concrete human situations — educational, marital, governmental, or religious. Professor Dewey, in whose honor the present volume has been executed, is the outstanding example of an evolutionist who has stood by his guns with regard to precisely those issues where the evolutionary viewpoint is most fruitful, but most demanding also of sanity and courage.

He, himself one of the most important promoters of the geneticist point of view, has everywhere in his writings and teachings emphasized the importance of refusing to let the past, and knowledge of the past, stereotype present judgments, mold present standards, determine present methods of attaining goodness and truth.

One of the very significant expressions of this protest of his against the misuses of historicism, has been his theories of education. Neither the training of the child nor of the adult, he has insisted, should be decided on the basis of what in a different age, and under different conditions, was found to serve past purposes.

But mere knowledge of the past — there can be no question about it — acts as something of a coercion upon the feelings and judgments of living individuals. When incorporated in quite dispassionate records the ways of our ancestors — except to the young and very adventurous — tend to seem on the whole good ways. Still more is this the case when the recorded past has gained the sanction of religion or the glamour of art. It is conceivable, for example, that a thorough emancipation of woman, a really fair trial of her equality with men, would be impossible unless the entire body of our romantic literature, written in an opposite, anti-feminist tradition, were destroyed. The emotional current set up by that tradition constitutes an obstacle too great for the majority even of women themselves altogether successfully to withstand. Similarly it is a question whether the imperial ideal of Divinity which persists in many minds otherwise democratically inclined, could be completely exchanged for an ideal more consistent with modern notions of fraternity so long as historical record preserves and so perpetuates the ancient superstition of the glory of kings. Certainly historical information as to the content and methods of university study approved by earlier generations, has until very recently thwarted serious innovations in the college curriculum. The lecture as the method of instruction, and the classics, logic, and geometry as among the important subjects of study may well be really commendable. But awareness of their long and impressive history as part of the learned tradition has militated against an unbiased judgment as to their true worth.

Knowledge of the truth about the past may then often hamper us in our efforts to transcend that past, by holding before us with fatal vividness ways of feeling and of doing, once approved, and still all too natural and easy, but also, alas, too barbaric. Not that one would therefore recommend, precisely, the suppression of those portions or aspects of history that contain insidious suggestions — any more than we find it on the whole desirable to suppress newspaper reports of contemporary happenings even when such reports operate upon the innately imitative human animal as a direct incitement to crime. In both cases alike the way of safety probably lies in trying for more truth rather than less.

More subversive than any deploring of the possible evil effects of historical knowledge upon our contemporary outlook, is the query whether, despite any pleasure the knowledge may bring, knowledge of mere fact is after all much of a good at all. To this effect is the comment of Guglielmo Ferrero in his book on Symbolism that: " facts, important as they may be, have not really any value in themselves, but borrow their significance from the theories for which they serve as a foundation." In the foregoing discussion we have limited our attention to the present widespread and multiform craving for fact; but in this era worshipful of the concrete and factual there is an emphatic and noteworthy craving for theory as well. Very few persons expend much emotion upon mere facts. What more frequently arouses feeling is a large and high-sounding generalization drawn out of or based upon facts, and in particular a generalization involving the notion of causality. For the craving for causal explanation is one of the most basic elements in our intelligence. If we go back through the history of the search for causes to its first appearance among men we encounter, to be sure, nothing better than those primitive rationalizings which we call superstitions — a superstition being but an ill-considered and unverified faith in some far-fetched causal connection. But even in the most preposterous early interpretations of rainbows, comets, and eclipses as omens of human weal and woe, we ought to be able to trace a genuine effort on the part of the progenitors of our Newtons and Einsteins to bring order and harmony out of chaos.

Not only has there been, perhaps always, and is still, in human nature, an inborn propensity toward the speculative, but in the present as in the past it has found abundant chance for gratification in the products both of scholarly and of popular theorizing. Recent cases of these have ranged all the way from affirmation of the origin of some insignificant particular phenomenon to that of the entire physical universe, including explanations of the weather in terms of sunspots, of personality by glandular secretions, and of the various human institutions as in one way or another derivatives of the Oedipus Complex. But it is perhaps in its application to the problem of human motivation that causal explanations have been most productive of excited interest. Among these are to be numbered the many formulations — of Nietzsche, Marx, Freud, Trotter, Crile, Veblen, and the rest — which exalt one or another of the major " instincts " or drives as the crucial one for the interpretation of man's behavior. Perhaps not even history written in terms of theories such as these, with their judicious blend of empirical data and picturesque generalization would still the protest of any to whom mere fact is everywhere and utterly devoid of significance. But with such extreme addiction to theory as this protest would imply we need really have nothing to do. There is a sufficiently obvious need, as well as a liking and a use in the world for fact as well as theory. What we do want to consider as the final qualification of the praise of historicism for which we have been preparing is the charge that chronology, admirable as it may be, tends to over-reach the limits of its proper domain and to crowd out other interests and activities. Chronology, as the name indicates, is the science of the temporal. The proper domain of the historian is that of time. If he be conscientious he will limit his inquiry to those things and events which did actually at least once have position in the space-time world. But over and above the myriads upon myriads of items enjoying membership in the world of the actual there is the whole huge universe of the merely possible; and after that even of the impossible; with besides those universes of discourse with which notions of spatiality and temporality have no intelligible relation whatever. The grave danger at the present moment would seem to be that our preoccupation with time and the temporal, combined with a new and vigorous empiricism, should lead us to an undue neglect of those domains which lie outside the field of the historical and to which the methods of experimentation or even of empirical observation are wholly inapplicable. The world of time and space is inhabited by items concrete and particular, and these are being ever more extensively subjugated, the more distant and elusive and obscure among them falling one by one into the traps set by the historian and the natural scientist. These traps not being adapted to ensnare the other sort of knowledge there is the danger already mentioned of a misplaced historicism: a crowding out of questions of goodness, beauty, and validity by a too insistent employment of the his-torical method. In particular this consists of the intrusion of questions of antecedents and origins where they are not appropriate, which has been called the genetic fallacy.

Now in every type of inquiry into which the theory of the good, the beautiful, and the truth might enter, this ultra-empiricist substitution is to be found. Professor Whitehead complains of one instance of it in his comment: " The nineteenth century exaggerated the power of the histori-cal method, and assumed as a matter of course that every character should be studied only in its embryonic stage. Thus, for example, ' Love ' has been studied among the savages and latterly among the morons." We have already noted the recent attempt to derive a " scientific " ethics through a review of the actual moral judgments passed by law-courts as supposedly pointing the way to a knowledge of what moral judgments should be. This is presumably the genetic fallacy in ethics. Similarly, as pointed out by Professor Montague in the *Ways of Knowing,* there is a widespread tendency in logic and metaphysics to substitute for a search into the nature of the true a search into what people have said that truth was like, but even more particularly why and under what circumstances they have said it. Even into aesthetic inquiry this procedure born of experimental technique and exaggerated stress upon empirical findings is being introduced. More and more we are warned to study the great art of the past in the full context of its social setting. We are supposed to refrain as far as possible from the allegedly rationalistic approach with its attempt to evaluate art *an sich* and *überhaupt*. Instead, a knowledge of the artistic creations of earlier ages is recommended as contributing to the history of culture and not as possessing intrinsic lasting values independent of the particular purposes and prejudices in relation to which they were originally devised.

It is a good thing, of course, to know where things come from, how they started, and why. In its proper place even such a question as whether Shakespeare or Bacon wrote Hamlet may be not altogether worthy of de-rision. But the disproportion in significance between the two questions of the authorship of the play and of its value tends to make the solemn mulling of the historical issue rather ludicrous. So in other cases of a choice between determination of genealogy on the one hand and of value or validity on the other, the chronological question appears of comparative unimportance. But the two kinds of matter need not, do not, occur always as rivals. And when they do not we may bless our good fortune in living in an age in which the cult of chronology has not entirely supplanted enthusiasm for hypotheses and generalizations.

DUALISM IN METAPHYSICS AND PRACTICAL PHILOSOPHY

John Herman Randall, Jr.

I

ANY naturalistic philosophy finds itself primarily opposed to a dualistic interpretation of reality. It is a protest against digging a bottomless chasm across the world, and then attempting to bridge the gulf by dialectic. It may be the logical and biological naturalism of Aristotle, protesting at the fissure introduced by the Platonists of his day between a world of existent objects and a world of logical, moral, and aesthetic Ideas. It may be the logical naturalism of Spinoza, revolting against the mathematical physicists who split Nature into a realm of extended bodies in time and space and a world of minds capable of logical thought. It may be the physical naturalism of Whitehead, decrying the bifurcation of Nature into an apparent world that is not real and a causal world that is not apparent. It may be the empirical naturalism of Dewey, condemning all absolute dualisms at once, between subject and object, between the objects of thought and the objects of feeling, between a realm of existence and a realm of values. In every case, the naturalist has maintained that such divisions, however valid they may be as important practical distinctions within a more inclusive Nature, are after all metaphysically and ontologically the products of analysis, selections made from a larger context to serve human ends, and not an antecedent and rigid fracture in Nature itself.

Various motives have lain behind these critical attempts to insist on the common texture of experience and the continuity of Nature. At bottom, however, they have all been inspired by the same desire, at once theoretical and practical, to find reality accessible to human thought in all its parts, and amenable to the operation of human intelligence in all its processes. Certainly the naturalism of the present day is bred of the hope that the intellectual methods so successful in the so-called " natural sciences " may be brought to bear upon all problems of human interest. In designating their naturalistic interpretation " empirical " in contrast with past naturalisms, its proponents are insisting that all human experience reveals a Nature possessed of the common quality of amenability to the " empirical method " of science, with its harmonious and effective combination of observation, hypothesis, reason and calculation, and experimental verification.

Such naturalism thus finds itself drawn to the Aristotelian tradition with its insistence that the world is by nature intelligible and that thinking is itself a natural event. It welcomes also the biological setting of intelligence in the behavior of living beings adjusting themselves to their natural environment and manipulating the materials they find. It conceives thought and beliefs, even the elaborate techniques of scientific method and the complex conclusions thus reached, in the anthropological sense as parts of group culture, functioning in specified ways in a cultural whole that is itself a purely natural and objective process of interaction between men and their environment. It even has great sympathy for the idealists, of both the Greek and the German traditions, who have found man inhabiting an intelligible universe rich in human values, although it criticizes the customary failure of idealism to deal with its complex values by the empirical methods found effective in science. Contemporary naturalism, in fact, has its immediate origins in the bringing of scientific methods to bear upon a universe conceived broadly as the total subject-matter of idealistic metaphysics.

Naturalism has traditionally protested against several types of metaphysical dualism. It has denied the religious supernaturalism that has set up God as a supreme Reality or First Cause. It has opposed that form of Platonism, not, to be sure, discoverable in any unbiased reading of the Platonic dialogues, which divides the world into an ideal Reality and an illusory appearance, into separate realms of logical essences and eternal values on the one hand, and of unintelligible and base existence on the other. During the course of so-called " modern philosophy " it has arisen in criticism of the bifurcation of Nature into an internal world that is knowable and the seat of values, and an external world that is in itself naked of all value and radically unknowable. Hence naturalism today finds itself opposed to certain contemporary interpretations that have themselves at times claimed and enjoyed the epithet of " naturalistic." It reads the present philosophy of Santayana, for example, as radically dualistic and non-naturalistic in both the Platonic and the epistemological sense; his realm of essence it sees as a supernatural realm divorced from Nature, and his animal faith it finds to be a denial of the intelligibility of Nature. It realizes that Bertrand Russell is still caught in the episte-mological dualism between internal data and the external world that has permeated modern philosophy.

In the light of its basic opposition to such ontological dualisms, con-temporary empirical naturalism views as less significant the traditional division between monistic and pluralistic systems. Dualism insists that there is the one thing needful, the supreme Reality, the certain and un-changing; and then besides there is everything else. It is the product of a loyal devotion to certain aspects or parts of Nature, so exclusive that those elements singled out for praise and worship are elevated above the rest of Nature and cut off from it. Both monism and pluralism escape such an exclusive emphasis. Nature can be read in its systematic aspects, or it can be read with an eye upon the many natural objects and processes that go to make it up. No unbiased observer can fail to recognize the wealth of individual objects, events, and processes which any reasonably empirical method discovers in Nature. Similarly, no unbiased observer can help admitting that in significant ways all that is discovered of Nature has a relevance for man, and possesses a certain unification in the light of that relevance. All the wealth of pluralistic detail pointed to by the most radical pluralist is *ipso facto* an object of human experience; it *is* pointed to. And philosophers concerned with knowing the universe have traditionally asserted that for thought it is a universe, that it can be talked about, enter rational discourse, and be manifest to man in intelligible fashion. The very basic insistence of the empirical naturalist is that certain common intellectual methods can deal with whatever is experienced of Nature, be it geologic epochs or the poetry of music.

Yet it has historically been true that a too exclusive emphasis on the systematic and unified character of Nature has tended to give rise to dualisms, ever bred of exclusive emphasis. Monism is the father of dual-ism, in that the One is always in danger of being set apart from the world of which it is the systematic unity. For Plotinos, the whole world was ultimately comprehended in a unity of thought and value; but the One of Neo-Platonic metaphysics passed easily, in Moslem, Jewish, and Chris-tian theology, into a supernatural deity apart from the world. So impressed was Spinoza by the systematic character of Nature that for him the one Substance, the one logical order, was split into two attributes which, while ultimately the same order, were yet different; and it was the logical order of thought that was important. To speak in other terms, Spinoza was so intoxicated by the discovery that the whole of Nature could be understood, that he made intelligibility the essence of Nature, and showed little concern for extending man's knowledge of particular natural processes. And the vastly richer unified system in which Hegel caught up the whole realm of human society and human history easily became an Absolute Mind divorced from human knowledge and from the natural realm of mere appearance. It is with such examples in view that empirical naturalism is apt to emphasize the pluralistic aspects of Nature, fearful lest an undue dwelling on the unity that exists should blind it to the plurality that is also an insistent fact. Yet an empirical method, content to record what it finds, need not hesitate to point to both unification and plurality in Nature.

An empirical naturalism does not object to the distinctions which have been made in Nature by dualistic philosophies, so long as they are consciously offered as distinctions made within a larger context for a definite purpose. Such selective emphasis, it recognizes, is the nature of thought; to condemn it is to deny that intelligence can function practically. It does not object on general grounds to such distinctions as the basis of a practical philosophy of life, though it reserves the right to criticize such proposed aims in detail. Spinoza's ethics, as an *ethics,* was certainly valid for Spinoza, and has proved a worthy guide for many who have shared his ideal. Naturalism opposes dualisms only when they represent an unavowed and hence uncritical choice, and read their practical acceptance and rejection of certain elements in Nature as the metaphysical assertion of a gulf dividing Nature, or separating it from a realm of more ultimate Reality. The needs of a given age, or, for that matter, of a given individual, may well lead him to set certain goods before him as supremely valuable. What naturalism denies is his privilege to regard those goods as alone ultimately real, in a metaphysical and ontological sense, whether they be electrons, logical essences, or God. It insists that all things found in experience are alike natural and real. Their precise relation to other objects is to be discovered, not in the practical needs they satisfy, but by an unbiased examination of their context.

Empirical naturalism is thus pre-eminently a critical attitude, in the widest sense of the term. It realizes that all thinking is selective of certain objects, and necessarily rejects others; it is an affair of choices. It does not seek to eliminate choice in practice; it tries to make it less arbitrary and more significant by insisting on the wider context in which choice is made. By pointing out the ultimate purpose of choices, it reveals the ends for which they were made, and in terms of the attainment or non-attainment of which they can be objectively tested. It points to other goods that Nature offers that may have been overlooked, and that in any final reckoning should be at least considered. Above all, it insists that any enumeration of the general features of Nature, any intellectual map of the world in which practical choice is to be made — in a word, any metaphysics of reality — must be not selective but comprehensive, not exclusive but inclusive. In this sense of the term " critical," the philosophies of Kant and the Romantic Idealists who followed him were in their day performing the same function in criticizing the narrow, one-sided, and dialectical " empiricism " of the eighteenth century by appealing to a wider experience of the world in which man lives, even when they did not succeed in bringing under the operation of one intellectual method the physical experience and the non-scientific experience of men.

The natural tendency of thought in interpreting the universe is to read it in terms of some dominant interest, some outstanding characteristic. It is only as an afterthought, when perhaps other needs have arisen, that men are brought to recognize that Nature contains more than was dreamt of in their philosophies. " Naturalism " thus arises as a sophisticated and critical attitude, not as a spontaneous reaction to the face of Nature. Men come into a world whose categories and traits have been determined for them in advance, by the accumulated wisdom of their ancestors. Grown reflective, they do not discover afresh what Nature is like; they discover that it is not really what they had been taught it was. Their very protests are made in the name of some vital concern; like the Sophists, they are surprised to find that Nature does not sanction the ancestral laws. The most reflective men become aware that Nature responds to their insistent desire to know; they are in turn intoxicated by the discovery that Nature is intelligible, is really a logical system. It is a work of patient toil and disillusionment to realize that Nature comprehends far more than any man has thought of. In slowly appealing to Nature as it is more fully experienced, men come to criticize their earlier extravagant hopes and baseless fears; they find a larger context in which to set them.

Historically, " naturalism " has been achieved after a selective " idealism " has dominated men's minds. Aristotle followed Plato; and again and again, in the maturing wisdom of individuals and races, Aristotelianism has succeeded Platonism. The gaining of Aristotelian sobriety after the youthful exuberance of Platonic theology marked the intellectual coming of the age of the Western peoples in the thirteenth century. The humanistic naturalism of the Renaissance signified the welcome of a wider variety of goods than the narrow if intense religious devotion of the Middle Ages. Nor was the great Romantic Movement of a hundred years ago any exception; for what was the rationalism of the Age of Reason but an idealistic enthusiasm for a newly discovered intellectual method, and what was the purport of the Romantic protest but an insistence on a broader world than that of Newtonian science, a world to be found in the realm actually experienced by men?

II

Naturalism as a metaphysic is thus a protest, against views maintaining the supreme reality of certain aspects of Nature, that all experienced aspects are equally real. Naturalism as a theory of values is a protest, against the dominance of codes emphasizing certain goods to the exclusion of others, that immediately and in themselves all goods are on the same level. This democratic insistence on the equal reality and value of all objects of experience is obviously not in itself an adequate or completed metaphysics or ethics. It is an incident in a process of criticism, not a goal. All experienced facts are experienced facts, and all have implications as to the nature of reality; but ghosts, growing pains, gorillas, gravitation, and God are obviously entangled in different ways in the complex structures of Nature. Naturalism insists that they *are* all entangled; it also insists that intelligence must discover how. As against views that would disregard either gravitation or God, it maintains that both must be somehow fitted into the Nature that experience reveals; but it may well turn out that gravitation is not an occult force, that God is not a first cause, and that the natural status of the two is quite different.

Similarly, push-pin, poetry, peanuts, and Platonic love are all goods, and as such entitled to consideration as possible components of the good life. Yet for no conceivable society or individual could they all ultimately turn out to have the same place. It is for intelligence to assign them their proper status, in the light of its examination of the means necessary to procure them and their effects upon other goods. There is this obvious difference, however, between the two cases: while it is quite possible that a good life might be led without ever having tasted the savor of peanuts or the magic of poetry, it is impossible to arrive at an adequate knowledge of the traits of Nature without making some place for ghosts as well as gravitation, for gorillas as well as God. A practical philosophy of life need not be all-comprehensive; a metaphysic neglects any aspect of experience only at its peril.

Naturalism as a metaphysical method, therefore, demands that all the traits found in experience, and not merely some selected set, shall be taken into account in formulating an adequate philosophic theory of Nature. Nature reveals itself to man as truly in poetry, in self-sacrifice, in religious adoration, as in physics or biology. If Nature lends itself to physical or biological analysis, it lends itself also to lyrical expression, to moral devotion, and to selective and idealizing worship. All these activities of men have definite implications for the character and structure of the Nature that sustains them.

Naturalism as a practical method, as a theory of the criticism of values, similarly insists that all things found by any man to be good are found by him to be good, and as such are entitled to a position on a comprehensive list of possible human goods. But it does not insist that every man shall find every such possible good to be actually good, or that he shall seek to incorporate into his life all those activities which he finds immediately good in themselves. If he is deaf to the appeal of music, and finds nothing in the playing of bridge or dancing, it may point out to him that others do relish them; it may even maintain that his failure to include them makes his life in so far illiberal and inhumane. A life that rejects goods it can transform from a mere blind ignorance to a reasoned and intelligent choice. A man may take great joy in the lust of combat; an empirical naturalism can point out the cost in the sacrifice of other goods which a gory career will entail, it can direct his aggressiveness into a respectable if not entirely harmless channel, like playing football. It can even persuade him to renounce physical combat entirely.

Naturalism can, indeed, on occasion, counsel more than this. It can advocate another choice, the choice of making no choices. It can bid men search for the richest possible variety of goods; it can urge them to incorporate in their lives all that human experience has tasted and judged worthy of inclusion, and it can label the rejection of any values narrow and illiberal. In a word, it can proceed from its insistence that immediately nothing is better or worse than anything else, to the added advice to seek the utmost of variety in experience. It can stand for a Romantic ideal of multiplying experiences *ad infinitum*. When confronted by the apparent necessity of choice, it can insist that both possible courses are desirable, and it can impel an active and aggressive manipulation of conditions until both can be made compatible.

Such a Romantic ideal of life is assuredly one valid ideal. It is a natural consequence of rebellion against a narrow and constricting code; historically it is in ages of the disintegration of such codes, as in the Renaissance and again in Romantic Germany, that such an ideal has been advanced. In our own escape from the repression of traditional Protestant Puritanism, something of the sort has gained considerable vogue today. As a critical protest against too narrow a range of envisaged goods, it has served a useful function in the past and is serving such a function in the present. Already there are indications, however, that such an ideal has begun to lose its utility. Those who have not in their own lives been compelled to break away from rigid mores are beginning to seek a more definitely ordered notion of a possible good life.

But there is nothing in the naturalistic insistence that all goods are worthy of consideration to imply that all goods should be chosen. Any particular choice, to be intelligent, must be made with a realization of the values that are being rejected. But to choose to make no choice is not to refrain from choosing; it is not even to avoid rejection. If experience points to any values that have been widely found to be good, it is to the values of concentrating on certain values to the inevitable exclusion of others. And it is precisely these values of selection that Romanticism rejects, in life as in art.

It may indeed turn out that further consideration of these values of selection would reveal them as unnecessarily restrictive, as excluding many goods which their advocates are not prepared to discard. But the basic contention of empirical method, that all values are immediately and in themselves just what they are, and that intelligence is concerned with the conditions of their attainment and their harmonious organization, must surely lead to a recognition of the *prima facie* value of selective emphasis, of rejection, of concentration. In a word, the implications of naturalism as a theory of the criticism of values is not the preference for a Romantic over a Puritan ideal of life; it is a recognition of the real values that have been found in both positions, and a challenge to examine the goods that are obtained and those that are renounced in each case. It is the reminder that whatever choice is made, certain goods are selected from a larger context of possible goods; and that the goods excluded in practical choice are still in their own right good.

The essentially critical insistence of empirical naturalism that all the dualisms introduced by past philosophies into Nature have been practical in intent, aiming at securing certain selected values in view of the felt needs of particular situations, is obviously a primary recognition that practice has found such selection to be a good. What naturalism contends is that such practical choices should not be confused with a statement of the actual structure and traits of Nature, but should be made with a knowledge of the broader background of action. It is perhaps to be expected that certain naturalists, decrying one-sided selection in metaphysics, should proceed to sympathize with practical aims that also seek for the values of an inclusive organization of human goods, rather than those of intensive concentration. Such a practical choice must justify itself to intelligent criticism; in situations where the practice of men needs enlarging and enhancement, it can indeed make out a plausible case. But the naturalist should not forget that all practice does ultimately demand choice, and that his choice of the Romantic ideal of the utmost enhancement of life through a multiplication of goods is itself a choice made from a still larger group of possible goods.

In other words, naturalism maintains that every dualism introduced in practice is a distinction made within the Nature to which an empirical method points. It is the task of practice to make such distinctions; it is the task of metaphysics to point to the whole in which they are made. What it decries is the tendency to read into metaphysics distinctions made for a practical purpose, to identify a metaphysical theory of Nature with the demands of a practical philosophy of life. In protesting against the one confusion, it is assuredly no gain to fall into the opposite confusion, and to identify the aims of a practical philosophy with the necessary inclusiveness of metaphysics. To take such a position is to recur to the traditional fallacy of proclaiming that the Real and the Good are co-extensive, that the subject-matters of metaphysics and ethics are the same. It is to incur the charge that naturalistic metaphysics, also, is a reading in cosmic terms of what it finds in human life to be valuable and worth attaining.

In contrast to this confusion of metaphysics and practice, empirical naturalism insists that metaphysics is the account of what experience finds in Nature, and that practical philosophy is the account of what experience finds in Nature to be good and sought for, to be bad and avoided. The goods of experience all fall within the totality of Nature; but the totality of Nature is not of itself good. Metaphysics must supply the context of all dualisms; practice must draw a dualistic distinction between the better and the worse.

III

In describing the place and function of knowledge in Nature, an empirical method points out that as objectively found and analyzed, knowledge is an instrument whereby men reorganize parts of Nature by seizing on its structural aspects. In its own procedure, knowledge is a disinterested attempt to discover what these structural aspects actually are; and the contemplation of the structure of Nature may, indeed, be for many the highest good. But to insist on the intrinsic value of the process of acquiring knowledge, and of the contemplation of knowledge when it is attained, is not to define the proper objects of knowledge. As contrasted with the objects of other human activities, the objects of knowing are those enduring structural aspects of Nature which condition the appearance of the goods that are immediately craved and enjoyed, and which make possible the prediction of other events to be experienced and their practical manipulation. Knowledge is a grasp of the instrumental aspects of Nature, of those processes that lead to other events and objects; it functions itself as an instrument in the manipulation of Nature, it is a tool whereby natural events are transformed into the means of attaining goods and avoiding evils.

In this sense, metaphysical knowledge, in pointing out the generic traits of the Nature within which structural relations are found to obtain, is the most generalized instrument of all; it maps the field of human activity, and catalogues the means and ends that are there to be found. To be an effective instrument, such metaphysical knowledge cannot be selective; it cannot leave out any means or ends. As an intellectual tool, it must be wholly disinterested and unbiased.

Yet, ironically enough, critics of empirical naturalism habitually complain that such a metaphysics is too disinterested, and not instrumental enough; it is too impractical. With one breath, they cry out that knowledge must never, never be conceived in functional terms; that it is a kind of magical addition to Nature, a further supernatural mirroring of the world that is. Its function is to mirror the world; miraculously, such a mirroring can be turned to practical account. With the next breath, such critics protest that to describe the traits of Nature impartially, to point to the context of practical dualisms, is to cut the nerve of those activities in whose interest dualistic distinctions are made. Naturalism points out that to be an effective instrument in practice, knowledge must envisage the total setting of practical distinctions; it must realize their instrumental functions and their selective nature. It has been shown, by sad experience, that there is no means of ascertaining whether or not knowledge mirrors Nature; while there is a ready means of verifying the success of knowledge in fulfilling its instrumental function. It has also proved again and again that the identification of the objects of science with Reality has led to the reading of Nature in purely intellectual and structural terms, to the ultimate denial of the many other aspects it reveals to experience. Just because knowledge properly seizes on the instrumental processes of Nature, it has repeatedly found itself, in traditional metaphysics, with much of the experienced world left over.

Thus men whose practical concern is scientific investigation have refused to admit that the truth they are seeking is an instrumental quality that attaches to beliefs that are verifiable in experience; they have insisted that truth is not thus relative to a particular function of beliefs, to a particular investigation and set of tests, but that it is a Truth all naked and alone, quite independent of any natural function. They point ·to the practical value of assuming that there is an absolute Truth that can be sought after and discovered, even while they admit that investigation can reveal only relative truths. Bertrand Russell has well expressed this practical value of refusing to view truth in its natural context. " If the instrumental theory of knowledge prevails, and theoretical problems are put to one side as merely scholastic, the inspiration to fundamental discoveries will fail. I am not arguing that the instrumental theory is false; on the contrary, I incline to think that it is true. But I am arguing that it does not afford a sufficient incentive to the precarious labor of serious thinking. . . . A false belief may be an essential ingredient in discovery, and perhaps the progress of science will cease on the day when men of science become completely scientific." [1]

This is a characteristic rejoinder to the empirical naturalist, though it is rarely made with such engaging frankness. The criticism does not concern itself with whether the setting of science and truth in Nature can be justified by pointing to their natural occurrence or not; it maintains the practical disadvantages of admitting it. It may or may not be true that science is a natural event, with a natural function; it is not advisable to mention it. Empirical naturalism may even be recognized, as by Russell, to be a sound metaphysics; the contention is that it is not an adequate philosophy of life. Surely this position of the critic of naturalism is a capricious and arbitrary pragmatism, if there ever was one! We must not be scientific and disinterested; we must delude ourselves with false beliefs in the interests of practice!

Or the moral idealist replies to the naturalist that to regard man as a purely natural being, the natural product of natural processes, is to make him a mere animal whose interests can have no claim on others. Men must be set apart from Nature, to retain their own self-respect and to win the respect and consideration of others. Man must be regarded as a spiritual being, a dweller in another transcendental realm, if his good is to be taken as of paramount importance. Nor can the aims men set up be conceived as the natural organization of the ends of human activity; there must be a Right, quite distinct from all that is humanly desired, which imposes its obligation upon men in the face of natural impulse and all that is merely experienced satisfaction.

Thus the scientist is quite willing to admit that the aims of practical activity, of artistic creation, and of religious worship, included within Nature, are important because of their function in man's experience; but Truth, the intelligible structure of the universe, must dwell in a realm of pure essence apart. It is true because it is true; and though it is discovered by experience, it is not made true by its fitting into that experience. The moral prophet will also admit that science, art, and religion are all natural

[1] "Science," by Bertrand Russell, in *Whither Mankind,* ed. by C. S. Beard, p. 80.

activities of man; but there must be an absolute Good and Right immune to criticism, a realm of ends and values elevated above Nature. The artist similarly maintains that the significant form of beauty he is striving to shadow forth can have no instrumental function in experience, and no empirical tests; beauty is beauty, is immediately perceived by the initiate, and that ends the matter. The religious man has preëminently insisted that the object of his worship is supernatural, a Deity transcending Nature even when his hand is discernible within it.

Every man, in a word, can be brought to admit the truth of the naturalist's contention in those activities that are not his own primary concern. Where his own practical interests are deeply involved, however, he insists that there is a gulf dividing the object of his devotion and endeavors from the rest of Nature. The True, the Beautiful, the Good, or God must dwell as Platonic Ideas in a heaven apart; there must be an absolute truth for the scientist to pursue, absolute moral standards for the prophet to proclaim, pure and unchanging beauty for the artist to incorporate, an eternal God for the faithful to worship and obey. To conceive these supreme realities functionally, to assign them their appropriate place in the natural processes of human life lived in its environment, to narrate their natural history, to subject them to the criticism of intelligence in terms of their actual functioning in human experience, is to lay sacrilegious hands on things most holy and untouchable.

The dualist, in a word, insists on making his distinctions metaphysical and absolute for pragmatic reasons. He is so impressed by the importance of distinguishing in practice between what he is seeking and the rest of Nature, that he endeavors to strengthen his selective emphasis by placing its objects in a separate realm of reality — often by insisting that they alone are ultimately Real. The naturalist counters to this pragmatic metaphysics by pointing out that an empirical method simply cannot find such absolute gulfs in Nature. The dualist maintains that it is essential for his own concerns to read all Nature in terms of the practical distinctions he makes. The naturalist points out that in the interest of the sum total of human activities, it is still more essential to recognize all such distinctions as practical, functional, and instrumental. The dualist is convinced that what he finds good to believe must be true. The naturalist holds that what experience reveals as true must be ultimately good to believe.

IV

It has been pointed out that the naturalistic position is essentially critical. In emphasizing the continuity and homogeneity of Nature, in insisting on the functional and instrumental nature of all distinctions, it is denying that there are realities and values exempt from intelligent criticism. To maintain that all distinctions are instrumental, and function in experience in definite ways, is to provide a means for testing their validity. To point out that moral standards are instruments for the organization of the experienced goods that Nature affords, is to set a means for objectively verifying whether they do organize those goods. Empirical naturalism thus makes all distinctions and values amenable to the type of intellectual method that has proved successful in disciplining the beliefs of science. In the hope of rendering practical choice less arbitrary and more significant, it has placed all distinctions and goods on the same level, all equally subject to empirical testing. The dualist has protested that in practice some distinctions and goods are immensely more important than others; and he has reinforced them by assigning them a peculiar metaphysical reality.

In the light of this situation, it is clear that where most naturalists have been at fault is in not recognizing the practical and instrumental values of the recurring philosophic dualisms. They have allowed their interest in criticism to blind them to the practical importance of establishing certain goods in a position of relative immunity to chance and capricious criticism. Before the dualist will recognize that his dualisms are instrumental in function, he must be assured that their practical value will be appreciated and not lightly disregarded. He will surrender transcendentalism in metaphysics only if it be accorded its proper place in practice. He will admit that all objects and values are metaphysically of equal reality, all equally involved in Nature, only if it be at the same time recognized that some are of transcendent importance. And any unbiased empirical method must in fact find both that all goods have a natural status in a larger context, and that of the goods that are found, those of selective emphasis, concentration, and single-minded devotion do justify themselves to critical analysis. Intelligence discovers that immediate goods when viewed in the light of their conditions and consequences are by no means of equal value in practice. Error and evil are indeed as real as truth and good; they have equal implications for a theory of Nature. But the whole life of the scientist and the moralist consists in cherishing the latter and overcoming the former.

The contention that an empirical method, while finding no transcendentalism in metaphysics, does find it in practice, can be illustrated from any activity. Human conduct will serve as well as another. The voice of the moralist has ever proclaimed that certain moral principles are of transcendent importance. Human societies have through long ages acquired certain ways of performing their activities, certain mores and customs embodying standards of conduct that have served to guide and direct men's actions. To the unreflective, all mores have perhaps seemed equally obligatory; but to the discerning, there has always been a distinction between fundamental principles and inessential forms. The prophet has again and again called the spirit to witness against the latter, until even for the average man there has been achieved a certain organization of goods, the conviction of certain ideal ends and standards in terms of which lesser goods are to be judged. The moral life, like the process of scientific investigation, has come to rely on ultimate principles. Those who have first formally enunciated them, or contributed to their revision, the great ethical geniuses of the race, have usually spoken as prophets of the Lord. Men have looked on them as divine, and on their messages as revelation. In the past, the authority of these principles has been buttressed by supernatural sanctions. They have been the commands of God, the ultimate law of the universe, the supreme Reality in the midst of appearance. In listening to them, men have felt themselves in the presence of a voice from eternity.

The naturalist can disclaim all such metaphysical interpretations. He can explain the prestige of such ultimate moral principles as due to their unique instrumental value in organizing human conduct to the attainment of cherished goods. But he cannot deny that prestige or that instrumental value. He cannot bid men discard these moral convictions and start afresh with a clean slate to build a new organization of the moral life from the ground up. He cannot urge an experimental attitude toward conduct that takes no account of the principles of moral verification by which alone moral experimentation can prove anything.

There is indeed need of such ultimate postulates in the moral life. It is no more possible to appeal to immediate and uncriticized experience to determine whether a certain action is ultimately good, than it is to appeal to such experience to decide whether a certain belief is true. Men have found sexual excess to be good; they have observed ghosts and witches. Such immediate observation can prove nothing. Scientific experimentation can only decide which of several rival hypotheses equally consistent with established scientific principles is true; moral experiment can only determine whether or not a proposed action results in the kind of good that is recognized as being ultimately good. The final values of the moral life are as exempt from experimental proof or disproof as are the postulates of scientific method. No marvelous event can shake the scientist's faith in the uniformity of Nature. His ultimate conviction the laboratory can neither verify nor deny, for it is the faith in laboratory proof itself. Similarly, no experienced good can appear really good if it involves the violation of another human personality. Such convictions are not the fruits of experiment, they are its premises. They are the postulates by which men ultimately judge.

To be sure, such postulates may admit of exceptions. The scientist may be convinced of the uniformity of Nature; but as a good Catholic he may also recognize the immediate hand of God in the miraculous cures of Lourdes. Similarly, men may be convinced of the worth of human personality, and yet as good patriots recognize the righteousness of warfare. Such exceptions cannot, indeed, directly overthrow basic convictions; but when they grow too numerous they can force reconstruction. An empirical method can point to slow modifications of the basic principles of scientific proof; it can also point to the gradual re-adaptation of the fundamental moral principles of a civilization. When a system of scientific postulates leaves too many observations unintelligible, it is modified to provide an intelligible place for what is immediately experienced. When a system of moral postulates gives rise to too many tensions and conflicts, it too is extended to provide a more satisfactory organization of conduct. History records that even these basic convictions are not wholly immune to criticism; that they are slowly reconstructed and broadened to serve better their instrumental function in experience. But it also makes clear that they are not mere ordinary hypotheses which experiment can confirm or reject; they operate at a much more fundamental level than that. In a very real sense, they are, with reference to the experience they serve to organize, transcendent; they are instrumentally absolute. Men do not abandon their scientific standards because they observe something that seems to violate them; they do not reject a moral faith in the equal worth of every human personality because intelligence tests show that brains are unequally distributed. Even when such ultimate principles are modified, they are not merely discarded; they are revised, re-adapted, expanded, and enlarged. Mathematics, for example, plays a more important part in present-day science than ever it played in the rational methods of the seventeenth century; but it has been supplemented by a more elaborate safe-guarding of its foundation and culmination in observation.

Such final standards of testing are enshrined in cumulative traditions. They are handed on from generation to generation, for they do not grow spontaneously in every human heart. Scientific procedure has been built up for centuries; the convictions of the moral life have an even longer history. It is only by authority that they propagate themselves, the authority of successfully functioning enterprises. They are parts of a group culture; once written into a civilization, they remain, slowly undergoing reconstruction as the conditions of their functioning are modified. Circumstances may cause them to be overlooked for a time, but they are rarely dislodged. They are there to be rediscovered and employed again. Greek thought has never been completely obliterated; it has enjoyed one rebirth after another. Even the Gospel of Jesus has survived the centuries of Christianity.

It is such systems of values that the dualist finds to be so important that he reads them as absolute, immutable, eternal, and above the rest of Nature. His metaphysics may be faulty, but his practical philosophy is sound. They are important, and any empirical method must recognize this insistent and patent fact. Faith in the principles of scientific investigation, or faith in the final standards of conduct, may indeed turn out to be so essential to the pursuit of truth and the living of life, that men must make them absolute in Nature as well as in practice. But the naturalist refuses the fruits of such a beneficent illusion. He believes that, after all, truth is a more potent instrument than delusion, and that only by recognizing it can intelligence perform its full service in human life. It is admittedly a difficult practical problem to combine devotion to the transcendent values of science, art, morals, or religion, with a readiness to revise them in the light of their actual functioning in human experience. Men need both faith and intelligence; whatever their activities, they need a critically held faith. But the way to attain it is not to deny the necessity of either faith or intelligence. The naturalist may well ponder whether he should not give greater weight to the values of faith, whether he should not insist more strongly on dualisms and choice in practice. But, after all, the import of empirical naturalism is to point out that knowledge is knowledge, and not faith; and that faith is faith, and not knowledge. As opposed to all metaphysical dualists and supernaturalists and pragmatists, the naturalist maintains that what is true is true because it is verified as truth, and that what is important is important because intelligent criticism recognizes its importance.

PROLEGOMENA TO A POLITICAL ETHICS

A. K. ROGERS

THERE are two sorts of consideration that enter into political debate about whose standing a difference of opinion may exist. The politician who sets out aggressively to be a realist is commonly disposed to confine relevant discussion to utilitarian or economic values. To this the idealist will object; politics is for him a moral issue, and he aims to raise it from a mere dispute about expediencies into the nobler realm of universal principles and emotional enthusiasms.

This difference of approach has had a corollary of some practical importance. Utilitarianism historically has been the natural ally of democracy. To interpret conduct in terms of motives to which everyone yields assent is to render it more difficult to find a ground for those intrinsic differences between man and man which any form of aristocracy has need to presuppose. By emphasizing sentiments which in the nature of the case are less widely and securely held the idealist is not in so good a position to make a general appeal. Morality gravitates naturally toward censure and intolerance, and however this may be held in check it is almost certain to inject an element of dogmatic self-complacency which hampers democratic reason.

It will be my general contention that the case for realism is a good one and that it is well to subordinate moral enthusiasms pretty sharply to expediency or self-interest in politics. I do not altogether like the state of mind which frequently keeps company with such a thesis. Along with political realism there has been very apt to go an impatience with the moral preoccupation generally, and this has put unnecessary difficulties in the way of its acceptance. I share with the idealist his ultimate prejudice in favor of moral distinctions. But while politics, too, comes under the head presumably of moral action it is moral action under conditions of its own, and it is a fair question to what extent the larger conclusions of an ethical inquiry may need to be modified in view of the special character of the political situation.

The radical peculiarity of a political ethics lies in the fact that here we are dealing in the first instance, not with personal conduct, but with methods of argumentative persuasion. This follows, that is to say, unless we choose to think of politics merely as a struggle for arbitrary power. On such an alternative Machiavellianism is the logical issue and politics in consequence, like war, will have to stop talking about right and wrong. The objection to this is that as a practical philosophy it will not really work. As a matter of self-interest no man can afford to make too evident his belief that might — his own might — makes right for the reason that, since his neighbors cannot be expected to agree with him, he has thereby deprived himself of any hold upon them except a physical ascendancy which he is unable permanently to make good.

The foundation, accordingly, of any general formula which can serve as a method of political procedure is the necessity a man is under to recognize and cater to the interests of other men before he can have a rational ground for thinking his own ends will be secure. And this will mean that in two senses a political ethics goes back to self-interest; self-interest represents the motive a given man will have in resorting to political reason, and also the principles in particular which reason can lay down rest on an understanding of the methods which a successful appeal to interests other than his own will find it necessary to adopt. But these two aspects do not have the same ethical significance and they will need therefore to be taken separately.

The motive that leads a man or class of men to resort to political persuasion might, of course, be a relatively disinterested or " moral " one. But it is equally possible, and considerably more likely, that it will be a motive of self-interest in the narrower sense. A politician may now and then be found who places human good ahead of that of class or party, but the group for which he speaks will rarely if ever follow him to this height of disinterestedness. It will talk fluently about the common welfare, but it will instinctively identify this with its own advantage, and historically it has almost never been found feasible to change its conviction by moral exhortation. The difference between intelligent and unintelligent partisan policy lies not in getting away from class interests, but in bringing home to men the chance that these may be themselves endangered unless they find a place for the ambitions of other classes which have the ability to make trouble. A landowning aristocracy, for example — I do not speak of individual landowners — has invariably been unwilling to admit any defect in its title; effective political reason addressed to it will get its force only from a recognition that it is better to concede a little than to run the risk of losing more.

Meanwhile it may be granted that in so far this leaves us still outside the field of ethics in any proper sense. The self-interested motives of groups of men are data that a rational politics will need to face, but they do not constitute a rational or moral standard. It is when we turn to the second aspect of self-interest — the interests of other men which political reasoning has to take into its account — that the possibility first arises of finding rational principles to govern political conduct.

Even here at first sight it may not seem apparent that we have any more excuse for talking about ethics than we had before. The moralist still may say that to shift from the interest of one class to that of others is to leave discussion on the same non-moral plane; it only becomes in the true sense ethical when we cease appealing to private notions of the good and substitute principles that have a universal authority. But this is to confuse two things both relevant in their proper place. The penalty of ignoring self-interest is that we then are left without a motive power sufficient for getting political results. We might like to think that men in the mass can be approached from the side of disinterested principle or a love for the human race, but we know that as a matter of fact the chance for this is very small indeed. Self-interest is not morality, but morality will never move men generally if self-interest is disregarded. Meanwhile if we set out to establish moral principles it is not enough to assume that such principles exist; we have to determine what they are in particular and on what their authority depends. And all I am saying is that the most obvious source for this authority in the political field is the fact, which experience reveals, that one can expect to gain his own ends in the long run not by brute force, but by agreement after rational discussion, and that discussion presupposes not only a consideration of appropriate means and instruments but also, if it is not to remain forever at cross purposes, a common end on which the disputants agree. It is from the necessity for this common basis of agreement that there emerges the possibility of general principles to furnish a vantage ground beyond the private interest of any particular man or party; and it does this, not in terms of a special ideal based on some speculative superiority to other ends, much less an ideal that dispenses with self-interest, but by supplying the logical conditions which discussion is compelled to recognize if it is to retain its standing as a practicable method of co-operation.   Such a method, to repeat, does not presuppose any one accepted basis of agreement beyond the reach of moral scepticism.   But it does assume the possibility of *some* common end on which men can meet in argument, and it supplies a way of testing such an end in so far as this must needs be of a sort not to exclude the chance of finding common ground.

It follows that politics as a form of intelligence will derive its authority in the first instance from reason rather than moral sentiment — not in the sense that its principles are intuitively perceived by reason, but in the sense that they are involved in the possibility of rational debate.   The most fundamental political virtues, accordingly, are intellectual virtues, and in essence they may be reduced to two virtues in particular — openmindedness or realism on the one hand and consistency on the other.   An appeal to reason has no meaning unless to begin with it is prepared to admit the evidence apart from which reason is an empty name; and it is not the least weighty objection to emotional exhortation as a political device that its natural effect is to inhibit the readiness to acknowledge uncongenial facts.   No instructed person would, for example, turn to the Anti-Saloon League for an unprejudiced survey of the working of the prohibitory amendment.   But facts do not cease being facts because we refuse to look at them, and arguments that in the long run only convince fellow partisans are scarcely worth their trouble.

With facts recognized, the other demand of argument is that we accept the conclusions to which logically they point.   In detail this belongs to the technique of reasoning, and as such it leaves the way still open to legitimate diversities of judgment.   But it has one general aspect to which the word " ought " can be applied.   Men may differ honestly in their conclusions, but this is subject to one limitation; at least it is their duty to avoid self-contradiction.   I cannot claim authority for my opinions unless I am prepared to apply exactly the same reasoning to myself that I ask others to accept; if the arguments I enlist against opponents condemn equally conclusions of my own, such arguments cease automatically to carry political weight, and this irrespective of the question as to where the truth really lies.   Thus it may be no easy matter to determine the soundness of a given method of agricultural relief, but this does not excuse the statesman when he is found accepting for the industrialist or the ship owner the same policy which he indignantly repudiates as an economic heresy when it is put forward by the farmer.

I perhaps ought to stop here to explain that I do not mean, of course, that political controversy cannot be carried on without living up to the claims of self consistency. A man may have reason to suppose that he can influence the judgment of other men while evading facts and slurring over contradictions; this is indeed the principle on which the propagandist systematically proceeds, and frequently he gets away with it. Nor is it of much use to appeal to him in the name of intellectual honesty, about which he will very likely be quite indifferent. But while in the short run such pseudo-reasoning often serves its end, and while a man may have faith in his continued ability to fool a sufficient number of the people all the time, at least his procedure is one which he is debarred from setting out explicitly to justify in principle. Inconsistency is effective only so long as it is covered up. And since its exposure is not so very difficult in any state of society where the means of enlightenment are at hand it is apt in the end to prove self-defeating.

That the rational virtues are of very large importance for a political ethics I assume needs no further proof; but it still may not seem obvious that they are its peculiar or exclusive virtues. I have been saying that persuasion is impossible without common premises, which means, for politics, the existence of common social ends. And the justification of the rational virtues lies in the demands set up by such a need; *any* common purpose will involve the acceptance of the logical conditions made necessary if we are to reap the fruits at which rational discussion aims. But in practice the common end will be more than a methodological abstraction, and there is no reason to suppose that human preferences backed by moral sentiment will not be present in its actual content. Why should we not use these, then, as standards in political debate?

It will simplify the question I am raising if we first stop a moment on the alternative possibility. It is evident that with human nature what it is there is bound to be an effort made in some fashion to recommend to others the standards of conduct which we ourselves approve. There are ways of doing this, however, which are not political in their nature. The preacher and the moralist have always occupied a position which sets them apart from the politician, and there are certain advantages that follow from this separation. Politics in the last resort is after all a method of compulsion. But compulsion has drawbacks when exercised upon a man who does not admit the excellence of the end proposed. It is very unlikely to convince him; he remains a rebel constrained by superior force. It is not hopeless to think of bringing him to a better state of mind. But the way to do this is not by resorting to compulsion, but by making as persuasive as possible the motives to which our own unforced emotional response is due. If this last is in truth a response native to the human constitution there is always a chance that we may be successful; but the chance is not made better by the natural obstinacy which compulsion rouses. Feelings need extremely delicate handling and it is seldom safe to try to commandeer them.

At the present moment there is an object lesson which illustrates this disability. The prohibition of intoxicants has in America always been approached primarily as a moral question, and as such it has been accomplished largely by the entrance of organized religion into politics. The reply most often made to those who object to this alliance is not without some force; the church, it will be said, cannot stay silent where moral issues are involved unless religion is to be divorced from conduct. But there is, of course, an easy distinction here; it is one thing to urge that temperance is the better way and quite another to enlist religious zeal to legalize some particular method of repression. I am not saying that the liquor traffic may not properly become a political problem; it has aspects which lend themselves to argument along lines on which reasonable men might hope to come to terms. But the attempt to identify reform with direct political action has plainly had results that are not particularly happy, not the least of which is the growing disposition on the part of moral leaders to substitute loyalty to a legal gesture for an honest concern with concrete moral consequences.

The issue to which such considerations tend is that so long as widespread differences of value judgment continue to exist the first need is for agitation and for education rather than for attempts at political compulsion. If a moral ideal is relatively unpopular this usually is evident; laws in advance of a settled public opinion are notoriously futile even if by some fluke they find themselves upon the statute books. The case is not the same, of course, when a majority opinion on some moral question has attained a strength that enables it if it so chooses to force itself on a minority; but the expediency of this will still be an open question. No realist can fail to be aware that danger always lurks in moral catchwords, and this risk is not abated by the fact that their general acceptance may seem to render it less necessary to define them. Patriotism has been a constant and fertile source of international anarchy; religious and moral idealisms pass naturally into fanaticism and intolerance; loyalty and law-abidingness are among the most powerful weapons of class dominance and class injustice. Not that any of these qualities in themselves are bad; presumably they all will find a place in any social end. But in emphasizing their emotional or moral rather than their utilitarian claims we are relaxing the safeguards of a sound political reason; so long as people disagree about their meaning and authority — and they would not be resorted to were it not for the need to overbear recalcitrants — we are abandoning argument for declamation plus coercion. To get a reasoned basis for agreement we shall need to abate our claims and fall back on the premises which men can more safely be presumed to have in common; and it is difficult to see where these are to be found unless it be in the familiar terms of everday self-interest.

And of the two rejoinders that can most readily be made to this conclusion neither seems quite sufficient. In the first place it may be said that self-interests also clash; they constitute in fact the major source of political dissensions. But I have had no intention of denying this. My point is not that self-interest constitutes in any unambiguous way a common ground of action but only that it affords a common ground of *argument*. My own self-interest as I conceive it may seem to be opposed to that of others; undoubtedly it does often so appear. There is no concrete form of co-operative good which we can presuppose as a universally accepted premise; if this were so politics would be a far simpler business than it is. Any possible basis of agreement has to be laboriously discovered rather than taken as a starting point. But I *can* assume that whenever I am able to point out the relevance of some consideration to a man's self-interest, however, it may be conceived he will be disposed to accept it as a working motive. And consequently, in so far as I am in a position to convince him that his goal cannot be attained unless he is willing to find a place in it for what other people want, I have a rational chance of overcoming the defects of self-interest when short-sightedly interpreted — a chance not equally present when the end is determined by feelings that themselves are in dispute. It may be no such way can be found for reconciling interests. Nevertheless politics will have to presuppose its possibility or give up any ambition to be rational.

The second objection returns to the more fundamental query I have previously raised. Among the ingredients of such a common interest as political discussion aims to arrive at there are bound to be considerations that we have naturally to call moral. No one wants simply food and drink and selfish pleasures; he wants as well a field for the human affections, free play for his enthusiasms, an escape from things that offend his sense of decency and fairness. These, too, it may be presumed, are part of a generic human nature which the search for a concrete basis of co-operation cannot afford to disregard; and it may seem captious therefore to persist in excluding them from the field of politics and turn them over simply to the moralist and reformer.

Now there are, it may be granted to begin with, certain moral judgments so universal and unequivocal that it might appear no reasonable ground exists for refusing to resort to them. Even here the case is not, however, unambiguous, and it is easy at any rate to exaggerate their political importance. If there is any judgment about which it apparently is safe to presuppose a general consensus it is the condemnation of plain dishonesty in office, and it would doubtless argue a low state of political morality were the public to be aroused to no resentment when it is betrayed by its representatives. At the same time one is forced to recognize that in practice the motive works very inefficiently. Even when party spirit does not interfere to dull its edge the public is apt to be surprisingly indifferent toward corruption unless it can be made to see that it has an obvious personal stake, and when powerful interests happen to be tied up with the practices in question the disposition is strong to feel that moral fervor is out of place. Only recently we have seen a political scandal of the first magnitude slurred over or condoned by almost the entire articulate body of public opinion in the nation because its repudiation was thought to be inimical to party success and the continuance of an industrial situation with which the mass of the voters were measurably content. And if it is difficult to stir the average mind to indignation against admitted wrongdoing without the lever provided by a sense of private grievance there is a good deal to be said for recognizing this frankly and leaving the moral feelings to emerge of their own accord from the adverse effects upon self-interest instead of resting too heavily on the direct appeal to a disinterested moral conscience so uncertain in its action. Apart from being precarious, too, political attacks upon the wickedness of individuals offer too many opportunities for moralistic prejudice and partisan hypocrisy to be altogether profitable. And in particular they have the disadvantage that they are apt to switch attention from more fundamental issues. For while individuals may be subjected and in the public interest should, of course, be subjected to criticism when they violate plain standards of honesty or decency, the problems of politics that are most significant are of a sort that cannot be met by any such simplified application of a moral truism. It is a superstition to suppose that honesty in government is the one political desideratum. A statesman may be honest in his way and yet be committed conscientiously to a thoroughly vicious program. It is the expediency of this program rather than the morality of its defenders that sets the ultimate task of government, and in a dispute about policies as distinct from personalities a primary concern with moral virtues essentially personal in their nature can only be misleading.

And one other point may help relieve difficulties that might be felt by the zealous moralist. Doubtless it remains the case that after all is said political discussion cannot be kept apart from moral sentiment; the common good at which politics must aim will be a moral good if morality is to have any concrete meaning, and so inevitably will have its connection with feeling as well as with utility. But there still are alternative methods of procedure, and this brings me back to my previous results.

There are, that is to say, two ways in which any element in the content of a general human good which comes home to us as a value may enter into social discussion. I may make this the premise from which my reasoning starts, and then, as I have pointed out, I have no way of logical co-operation in case my neighbor sees fit not to grant it. And in that last event three alternatives are open. I may cease trying to persuade him and undertake instead to kill him or put him in jail unless he gives up his opposition. Or I may turn to exhortation and try thus to elicit the assent which he denies to force or logic. Or, finally, I may reserve such a disputed value as a part of my own ideal while leaving others to a similar freedom, and may be content to look for political agreement in terms only of those more obvious and tangible forms of good which *can* safely be taken as a premise.

To this last course the general drift of the present argument has tended, and it still seems to me that it must constitute the main reliance of the statesman. Politics, because it needs to sway men in large masses, has in the nature of the case to move on a relatively low level. It does not follow that there is no more generous strain in human nature which at times can be successfully appealed to provided self-interest does not actively intervene; still less does it follow that those who profess to be our leaders ought themselves to be guided by no higher standards. But it is arguable that a statesman will be best serving the cause of morality if he refrains from the methods of the preacher and relies instead on the surer sentiments that attach to economic welfare, using his own better insight mainly to separate sound and lasting interests from trivial or mistaken ones.

But now this does not exclude all reference to those subtler constituents of human good which cannot be reduced to merely economic values; there is a way in which these also become amenable to logic. No man can be forced to assent to them against his will; that, once more, is why their value for political debate is so equivocal. Nevertheless if they are in fact congenial to the human constitution we presumably shall find them present among the implicit presuppositions on which men are wont to reason, and when brought into the open they are capable of being used in consequence to clarify and unify opinion. But for such a purpose moral suasion is not the only tool. As a method of debate the more direct way to get a man to accept the logic of his own implicit premises is not to bombard his feelings, but to ask him to be self-consistent; and consistency thus reappears as the virtue peculiarly relevant to politics. I think it is scarcely necessary to dwell on the argumentative possibilities that are present in a clear-sighted recognition that no moral premise has a logical footing so long as it is limited to any special class — a principle independent of the moral fervor that may accompany partisan controversy. Quasi-ethical appeals to the rights of the public which grow spontaneously out of an industrial dispute that threatens general inconvenience and which really mean that railwaymen and miners ought in equity to put up with any treatment of themselves provided the remedy brings temporary discomfort to the traveller or the householder; insistence on the sacredness of property rights in behalf of a business order which leaves the small investor with a minimum of protection where it does not actively encourage him to lose his money; patriotism which comes to flower in the killing of other patriots who happen to have been born outside certain geographical limits; resentment at an interference with the freedom of the powerful and successful to restrict the freedom of less important people; the enforcement of respect for law by over-riding constitutional guarantees — in all such cases, and they are legion, political argument has resources which have never been adequately exploited.

In the interest of realism I shall have to repeat one qualifying observation. Whatever its claim in theory any attempt to confine political reasoning to the limits here proposed will no doubt meet with obstacles. The normal human mind is not content merely to be logical and realistic. It craves food for its emotions also; and given the human material we have to work upon, these cannot easily be kept from taking on defective forms. Allegiance to large principles of truth and reason is a desideratum, but it calls for an intellectual enlightenment and grasp of which the average man falls short. Ideas are too abstract for him. To become real his ideals have to be attached to more limited objectives with their identifying catchwords; he needs intermediate pegs on which to hang his half-understood feelings for the good — country, party, sect, heroic figures to arouse his loyalty, exciting events to stir him from the lethargy which everyday life induces. But while such relatively unintelligent ideals furnish in consequence instruments for moving men which the politician naturally will not hesitate to employ, they set problems rather than offer a solution; they are data and not themselves principles of politics. It is not with them, therefore, that a political ethics is primarily concerned; the business of the enlightened statesman is not to identify himself with them as authoritative premises but to subject them to the rational scrutiny apart from which they will almost certainly be used for purposes that obscure and frustrate reason. No doubt there will be occasions when he will find it expedient to make his own appeal to the feelings which he can rationally approve, if only that he may not leave so powerful a weapon entirely in the hands of the unscrupulous. But he will do this cautiously and not until he has good empirical reasons for thinking it will be effective in the particular case; and one of the first conditions of effectiveness is that the method should be given very sparing use, since there is no more certain way to dull the emotional life alike in its sensitiveness and its precision than to keep it continually under pressure.

As a final remark I return to a qualifying consideration of a different sort which, if my aim had been less limited, I might well have made more prominent. For there is one form of moral feeling which if we approach it critically enough, not only does not come in conflict with the demands of utilitarian reason, but will follow from them as a corollary. The emotional sentiment which belongs to politics most closely is that which goes under the name of justice. Now justice may be interpreted in a way to leave it equally with other moral sentiments open to the strictures I have noted; if it means, as it has very often meant, our moral right to the benefits which through law and custom have come to form the *status quo* it may very well be the source of political evils rather than their solvent. But justice has a simpler and less dubious sense. It may stand for the denial of any man's right to what he is not prepared to grant to every other man; and as such it represents the distinctive emotional backing which self interest within the limits of argumentative consistency calls to its own support. There still may be some doubt as to the expediency of too direct and unqualified an appeal to the emotional feeling of grievance that is natural to any social class when it sees itself handicapped by special privileges that other men enjoy, since the effect of this appeal may sometimes be to arouse unreasoning prejudice and postpone enlightenment. Neverless the emotional revulsion that accompanies the perception of injustice is a motive without which no such thing as social progress toward equality could very well take place; it is the pure essence of sentiment in politics. And because it does not need to be confined to those who suffer from the grievance but has a universal field, it is the source of a moral value which, in so far as it is thus universalized, is free from the intolerance that moral sentiment in general is apt to foster; and it goes a long way in consequence toward meeting the customary charge of sordid and materialistic greed which is supposed by its philosophical opponents to lie against a doctrine of economic realism.

RADICAL EMPIRICISM AND RELIGION

HERBERT W. SCHNEIDER

I

THERE are at least three common approaches to the scientific study of religion; the theological or philosophical, which undertakes a critique of religious beliefs in the interest of reconstructing them into a body of knowledge consistent with the approved science of the day; the historical or genetic method, which aims to discover the origins of religion and the causes governing its evolutions and varieties; and the empirical or psychological method, which analyzes the motivations and functions of religion in human experience. This last method is at present in the hands of either academic or therapeutic psychologists, who are notoriously interested in the sentimental aspects or the fantastic forms of religion. The sociologists and anthropologists, on the other hand, who approach the subject more objectively, are still too largely pre-occupied with theories of the origin of religion to give us an empirical account of the significance of our own religious institutions and behavior. Presumably their accounts of so-called primitive religion are empirical, but the mere fact that they are pre-occupied with primitive peoples and the mere fact that they call them " primitive " bears witness to the genetic or historical motivations of their science. Primitive man still bears the burden of being forced to testify for general social theories, which cannot be substantiated by an appeal to modern cultures directly. Certainly there is a practical advantage in starting the empirical account of religion with our own religious institutions and traditions instead of with our more ancient and " primitive " contemporaries, where distance lends enchantment and ignorance lends learning.

There is, of course, much talk of a radically empirical, social, and behavioristic psychology of religion, but a little perusal of the literature in this field is sufficient to convince an innocent amateur that only a small area of religious experience really interests these professed empiricists. William James, the most religiously empirical of them all, was catholic in his sympathies precisely because he was protestant in his interests. Having himself achieved an irreligious " healthy-mindedness " after years of struggle, he was free to extend the broadest sympathy to " sick souls." His *Varieties of Religious Experience* is therefore not an objective account of religion, but a clinical diagnosis of religious diseases.   The sicker the soul the better it suited him, for such cases admirably illustrated his philosophy of consciousness.   *Varieties of consciousness* was his real interest.   James was quite aware of this fact, and would have been the last to claim that his psychology of religion was intended as an empirical account of religion in general; it was material for the psychological laboratory taken from the field of religion.   Hence, James, as a psychologist, was interested in the immediate and private aspects of religious experience, and ignored the social and institutional aspects.   His protestant background and environment led him in the same direction: the most conspicuous factors of religion in New England were those connected with conversion, salvation, revivals, theological controversy, and similar fundamentals in evangelical and sentimental religion.   Pre-occupation with this kind of subject-matter has continued to characterize the psychology of religion since James.   The psycho-analysts have, of course, simply exaggerated this tendency.

There is, to be sure, no sense in complaining because psychology is psychology and not everything else.   But the preponderance of the psychological interest in religion is really symptomatic of a puritan distaste for the other aspects of religion and ought therefore to put us on our guard. A whole philosophy of religion is presupposed by these psychological " empiricists." or example, James says quite frankly: " I speak not now of your ordinary religious believer, who follows the conventional observances of his country. . . .   His religion has been made for him by others, communicated to him by tradition, determined to fixed forms by imitation, and retained by habit.   It would profit us little to study this second-hand religious life." [1]   " In one sense at least the personal religion will prove itself more fundamental than either theology or ecclesiasticism. Churches, when once established, live at second-hand upon tradition; but the *founders* of every church owed their power originally to the fact of their direct personal communion with the divine." [2]   Here James com-

---

[1] *Varieties of Religious Experience*, p. 6.
[2] *Varieties of Religious Experience*, p. 30.

mits himself definitely to the naïve protestant belief that religions are really founded by their "founders" and that institutional religion is "second-hand." Even if this should be granted from the psychological point of view (though more recent psychology would certainly not grant this), from the historical point of view it is certainly not true. For "founders" are themselves ecclesiastical creations, reared in institutional imagination and erected for social functions. Jesus was obviously not a Christian and as Christ, the "founder," he was created by his church. Furthermore, is it intelligible to abstract Jesus' personal religious experience from its environment, to regard it as primary, and to call the traditions of Hellenistic-Judaism in which he lived "second-hand"? In Lecture XIX on "Other Characteristics," James assigns churches to their proper place: he regards them as satisfying those people whom naked truth does not satisfy and who demand aesthetic "richness." His treatment of the aesthetic aspects of religion is clearly ironical, if not sarcastic. The same might be said of his treatment of religious acts and forms — sacrifice, confession, and prayer. Though he admits that prayer "is the very soul and essence of religion," [3] he dismisses prayer and other religious practices with a few courteous, perfunctory remarks. On the inner emotional side he maintains that only experiences of "solemnity" and "enthusiasm" can be properly called religious. All this reflects James's own philosophical temperament, his individualism, his spontaneity, his hatred of the conventional, and his radical Protestantism.

What is more surprising in James's treatment of religious experience is the cursory way in which he dismisses what he calls "medical materialism" and with it the whole problem of the physical basis and motivation of religion. He discounts the importance of sex and the analysis of physiological functions in general. He does not deny the physical basis, but he regards it as a truism and as insignificant for an interpretation and evaluation of religious experience. More recent psychology has changed all this and has centered its attention on the external motivation rather than the inner content of emotional states. As a result even the science of personal religious experience has been revolutionized since James delivered his Gifford lectures.

There is a significant and neglected passage, however, in which James

[3] P. 464.

himself points out a quite different approach to the whole subject-matter of religious experience. I quote it in full:

The moment we are willing to treat the term " religious sentiment " as a collective name for the many sentiments which religious objects may arouse in alternation, we see that it probably contains nothing whatever of a psychologically specific nature. There is religious fear, religious love, religious awe, religious joy, and so forth. But religious love is only man's natural emotion of love directed to a religious object; religious fear is only the ordinary fear of commerce, so to speak, the common quaking of the human breast, in so far as the notion of divine retribution may arouse it; religious awe is the same organic thrill which we feel in a forest at twilight, or in a mountain gorge; only this time it comes over us at the thought of our supernatural relations; and similarly of all the various sentiments which may be called into play in the lives of religious persons. As concrete states of mind, made up of a feeling *plus* a specific sort of object, religious emotions of course are psychic entities distinguishable from other concrete emotions; but there is no ground for assuming a simple abstract " religious emotion " to exist as a distinct elementary mental affection by itself, present in every religious experience without exception.

As there thus seems to be no one elementary religious emotion, but only a common storehouse of emotions upon which religious objects may draw, so there might conceivably also prove to be no one specific and essential kind of religious object, and no one specific and essential kind of religious act.[4]

Here James definitely applies the term " religious " to *objects* of experience, not to any immediate content; but he leaves us with only the vaguest notions of what constitutes a religious object. He talks vaguely about " supernatural relations " and he evidently is thinking of God, but he does not even attempt to analyze the meaning of " religious " when applied to an object and not to an emotional state. My thesis, in brief, is that James is right in asserting that religion contains " nothing whatever of a psychologically specific nature," but that what James here called " religious objects " turn out to be, on analysis, specific techniques or social patterns by means of which almost any experience may find expression and in terms of which religion may be distinguished and defined.

Such an approach to the study of religion received its first theoretical formulation in the writings of William James. In his famous essay, " Reflex Action and Theism," he developed the thesis that the intellectual and theological aspect of religion represents an intermediate phase of expe-

4 *Varieties of Religious Experience*, pp. 27–28.

rience, and that it can be understood only in terms of its non-intellectual antecedents and consequences. This analysis was characteristically couched in physiological terms — in terms of the reflex-arc concept, of stimulus and response — which have since become the commonplaces of psychological methodology. Nevertheless it was with the intermediate, conscious, cognitive phase of experience that James was primarily concerned and hence he regarded the task of making an empirical analysis of the other phases as not a psychologist's business. Since then, psychology has become much more empirical: it takes the whole of human experience and all forms of human behavior into consideration. It is needless to mention the significance of Dewey's writings in giving us a better understanding of the biological and social setting of conscious experience; and it is impossible to mention the various schools of psychology which have contributed in recent years to our concrete knowledge of why we behave as we do. But I can select a few sentences from James's *Reflex Action and Theism* to serve as a text for what more recently psychology has illustrated abundantly.

God may be called the normal object of the mind's belief. Whether over and above this he be really the living truth is another question. . . . The conceiving or theorizing faculty — the mind's middle department — functions *exclusively for the sake of ends* that do not exist at all in the world of impressions we receive by way of our senses, but are set by our emotional and practical subjectivity altogether. It is a transformer of the world of our impressions into a totally different world — the world of our conception; and the transformation is effected in the interests of our volitional nature, and for no other purpose whatsoever. . . . The theological does no more. And the reflex doctrine of the mind's structure, though all theology should as yet have failed of its endeavor, could but confess that the endeavor itself at least obeyed in form the mind's most necessary law. . . . Man's chief difference from the brutes lies in the exuberant excess of his subjective propensities . . . and in the fantastic and unnecessary character of his wants, physical, moral, aesthetic, and intellectual. . . . And from the consciousness of this he should draw the lesson that his wants are to be trusted; that even when their gratification seems farthest off, the uneasiness they occasion is still the best guide of his life.

By putting together these scattered bits of the essay, I have given a different direction to the argument than James did. He developed the argument along Kantian lines. I have purposely selected certain passages which point away from Kant, and towards Dewey; and I aim in the present essay merely to call attention to certain empirical aspects of religion, implied in the foregoing citation from James, but neglected by him and other empiricists.

II

To an irreligious observer the most obvious characteristic of a religious person must be the fact that he engages in certain practices in which others do not: he goes to church or prays or sacrifices or reads sacred scriptures, in short, he performs acts which are known to everyone as religious. Just what acts are regarded as religious depends upon the particular culture and religion of the people; what is religious to some is not to others, but within any culture there is usually a fairly distinct and generally recognized group of religious activities. Engaging in these activities, unless they are practised perfunctorily or for some ulterior motive, marks a person as religious. Merely to have certain beliefs is obviously not enough. Theological beliefs are religious only in so far as they lead to the above-named practices.

Even the devil believes in God, but he does not fall on his knees. And, vice versa, even atheism is often a religious cult. No doubt beliefs of one sort or another function in religious practices, but there is no specific belief which brands the believer as either religious or irreligious apart from the acts with which that belief is associated. Nor is there any one set of acts which is universally characteristic of all religions. Religion can be defined only relatively; relatively, that is, to the culture of which it is a part. But within any given culture certain acts are conventionally known as religious. In order to engage in these practices, a person is forced more or less to participate in a social institution and in conventional forms and symbols. To be sure, there may be privacy in religion, but a purely private religion is a physical impossibility. At least a few of the elements of a socially recognized cult are necessary: the prayers may be private and unconventional, but prayer is conventional; the particular god may be an innovation, but to have a god is conventional; or, in case there is neither prayer nor god, there is always some other conventional form or symbol (meditation, meeting, sermon, celebration, or what not). Without these a religion would be unrecognizable. Nor can each man have his own religion; there must be a minimum of discipleship, communion, or sharing of common rites and ideas. A religion, like a language or a dance, even in its private aspects, employs social patterns. It is, therefore, something which can be studied objectively, like any other cultural institution.

Such an objective study naturally begins with the question, why people engage in these practices; that is to say, not what the historical origin of these practices is, nor what reason people give when asked why they engage in them, but what they actually get out of them. For the discovery that these practices are established by custom and performed by habit may be true enough, but it does not answer our question. We want to know what satisfactions or burdens such customs entail now. A habit is not based on habit, but on some continuous function or motive which it serves. Of course, the *original* function or motive may long have been lost; but the question we are now raising is not historical, but psychological: what does the participant get out of it here and now? To say that he prays because his ancestors practised magic makes sense only to an historian. On the other hand, it will not do to ask him who prays and take for granted that his answer is correct; he may not know and may merely repeat a conventional answer to the question. It is plainly a case for experimental observation such as any natural science must employ.

Of the many answers which may be given to this question we list a few — enough to serve as illustrations of the variety of facts and inquiries which are relevant to an empirical study of religion. First of all, we might mention that religion serves as a means of expression. It is a kind of language or art whereby we can give social and intelligible expression to our ideas, feelings, needs, and hopes. A community of farmers, for example, is in the midst of a drought; the crops are burning and every one thinks only of rain. They come together and pray for rain, or they publicly assert their confidence in Providence, or they fast, or in some other conventional and mutually intelligible way they give vent to their common anxiety. There are, of course, non-religious ways of doing this; and in the long run, the religious methods must compete with the secular on the basis of their effectiveness as mediums of expression. From this point of view rain-rituals are essentially art-techniques. Of course, they may in addition be devices for securing rain; but that is another question. Let us suppose, for the present, that the farmers know all about the causes of the weather. Nevertheless they continue to pray for rain, not all of them, perhaps, not so industriously perhaps, but nevertheless the need of rain prompts prayers for rain. The way in which this is done will naturally reflect the tension and the tastes of the community; it may be a simple " Lord have mercy upon us! " or it may be an elaborate fast or a dance or an imitation shower. In China, I believe, there was an ancient custom prescribing more and more elaborate sacrifices until the rain came; and when it finally *did* come, it was a religious duty to stand still and be drenched — theoretically, in order not to offend the rain; psychologically, no doubt, in order to enjoy the longed-for drenching. I have chosen a simple, elemental religious rite to illustrate the way religion gives expression to needs and desires. The reader can easily supply his own illustrations for the expression of sorrow, rejoicing, love, fear, rest, remorse, hope, loyalty, victory, truth, error — practically anything that enters the human mind and heart. Whatever else it is, then, religion is at least an art of expression, a form of celebration, an established technique for symbolizing and publishing human experience.

But it goes beyond this function of expression to one of sheer imaginative creation. Compensation phenomena and techniques for escaping from reality into a world of the imagination are found in all the arts — from drinking to painting. The religious techniques of this sort are not so much new and distinctive as they are a synthesis of various secular devices. Classic rituals of salvation have embodied in one form or another, in one combination or another, ecstatic dancing, drunkenness, visions, hysteria, myth, poetry, music, hypnotism, etc. Indeed one chief reason why religion is so powerful is because it compounds the powers of these various devices into an unusually effective stimulant. Few utopias can vie with the classic religious heavens; few dramas have the power of the cosmic tragedy of sin and salvation; few orgies are so ravishing as a wholehearted revival camp-meeting; few romances equal that of St. Catherine, the bride of Christ. Though this type of imaginative stimulation is enjoyable, it is not necessarily pleasurable. Man freely tortures himself and others and gets certain satisfactions in the tragedy. Both penance and salvation have their intrinsic values and the cross is as powerful as the crown in commanding affection and obedience.

Another function which religion commonly serves is that of offering the opportunity for participation in the life of a public group. Membership in a family or in a corporation is not enough to lift an ordinary private person to an active sense of his membership in the public, and the opportunities for political action are too circumscribed even in a democ-

racy. But public worship immediately conveys to the participant the sense
of his social dignity and the feeling of membership with " the Lord's
people." The communion may be silent, the process of sharing may not
be articulate, but the effect is achieved in spite of, perhaps even because of,
the fact that it operates sub-consciously. In addition to conducting public
worship, the churches, of course, carry on any number of other social
activities which may or may not be recognized as religious; but it may
be doubted whether the so-called social work of the churches is half as
social, either in motivation or in effect, as is their public worship. But
this is a matter of taste. Some prefer religious sociability to the more
subtle and imaginative forms of public worship. They deliver sermons
to *their* worshipers, or they chat genially after church or in Sunday
School. Even prayer tends to become a conversation; and many evidently
prefer communication with the saints to the communion of the saints.
The way in which religion satisfies this conversational need is best illustrated in spiritualism, where a simple and effective device has been
invented for enabling the bereaved to talk with their departed, and lovers
to meet with their " spirit-mates "; where all sorts and conditions of men
(mostly women) who seek concrete and practical guidance, but are deprived of trustworthy friends, can get " spiritual " advice for all their
daily troubles, their business deals, their health, and their future.

The mention of one more function of religion must suffice for the
present: a religion provides a faith. Having a creed or a faith is not like
having beliefs; it is, as St. Paul said, more like fighting a good fight. A
creed is the analogue of a flag or banner; its literal value may be negligible, but as a symbol of one's willingness to fight, it is invaluable. Most
creeds which are actually in operation, irrespective of their origins, are
not formulations of beliefs actually held, nor even of beliefs which it is
thought ought to be held; they are sanctified slogans. They serve as
badges by which the faithful are known and as banners under which the
faithful fight. They represent the " secret doctrine " of the initiate, the
esoteric wisdom of the elect. To have such symbols, to be one of the faithful, is a luxury with which few persons can dispense. To " keep the
faith," to believe *in* God, is quite different from believing *that* God exists;
it is to be convinced that in pursuing one's interests one is also fighting for
ideals. It puts a halo on the drab routine of life; it lends " spiritual significance " to what might else be merely a struggle for existence. It

fortifies one against doubt, keeps one on the alert for enemies, and comforts one in defeat. Faith is by nature indomitable. Faith is not necessarily religious, witness salesmen and senators; but it tends to become religious if it meets sufficient obstacles. Certainly religion is notoriously faithful.

III

It would be an endless and thankless task to continue to map out the domain of religion in human experience in all its detail; we proceed, therefore, to the theoretical points which the foregoing considerations raise.

(1) Religion is an institutionalized form of behavior rather than a kind of experience. Or, to put it in other words, it is not the inner contents, but the social forms, which determine whether an experience is religious or not. The few illustrations given above were intended to suggest that any conceivable emotion or idea can be put into a religious form. Religion, apart from the limitations of any particular religion, is as broad as human experience. The whole gamut of needs, aspirations, pleasures, sorrows, loves, and hates may receive religious treatment, just as it may receive musical or dramatic treatment. Or, if I may be permitted to use another analogy, so-called religious experience is logically on the same plane with cognitive, linguistic, or aesthetic experience, and must be defined in terms of its formal structure, not in terms of its possible content. Almost anything may be known, said, or put to music; even more, if possible, may be expressed religiously.

Epistemology is gradually freeing itself from the question: what can I know? and attempting to answer the question: how do I know? But the would-be sciences of aesthetics and religion, for motives which the reader may suspect, are still engaged in the desperate task of locating their distinctive realms of experience. Such terms as the "numinous," the sacred, the holy, the supernatural, and "the religious thrill" are supposed to describe a concrete inner content of a particular kind of experience. In reality, I suspect, their popularity is due to the fact that they have given metaphysical apologists a fresh category to exploit; they are convenient methodological devices and are not really descriptive of any empirical content whatsoever — except that perhaps these terms roughly indicate the state of mind in which scientists now approach religion, a

state, so to speak, of taking off their intellectual shoes when they touch
" holy " ground.   But supposing for the present that the psychologist can
find this " numinous " quality in experience, we can readily infer from
the above illustrations, if not from our own experience, that such a quality
must play a comparatively minor rôle in religion.   For, unless we take
an ultra-puritanical and narrow view of religious experience, the behavior
which is known as religious reflects all the varying moods of the seasons
and fortunes of mankind.   And this is true not only of the ecclesiastical
rites, but of the more private devotions of mystics.   Any good mystic can
get more varieties of religious experience than a " numinous " psychologist can talk about.

If we abandon all this attempt to locate *the* religious experience, and
turn to the distinctive *forms* or techniques of religion, we are confronted
with a limited number of readily observable and socially conventional
patterns, the discovery of which is neither difficult nor profound.   We are
confronted with a number of institutions, theologies, and customs, functioning as integral parts of a culture, whose features they reflect and whose
fortunes they share.   But here again scientists have spoiled the picture by
pretending to find a single, essential *social function* for religion.   Most
famous, perhaps, is the theory of the Positivists who assign to religion the
essential task of maintaining social solidarity; more recently, Malinowski
has proclaimed a somewhat similar theory to the effect that the essential
function of religion is to impress the individual with the power and value
of tradition.   Freud's theory that religion is essentially a sublimation of
the sex-complexes arising out of family life is another variant of the same
general attempt to find *the* social function of religion.   That these are all
over-simplifications becomes quite evident when one faces the bewildering
variety of cults, each with its own variety of functions.   Religion may
unite or it may divide a society; it may maintain conventional standards
or it may break them; it may keep the masses under or it may incite them
to revolt.   Religion can serve God or Mammon or both.   And who are
we to decide which is *true* religion!

For the functions of religion must not be confused with its values.
Whether or not it is good that religion should do the things it does is
another question entirely.   The present account is purely descriptive.
But obviously the question of value is not apt to make much progress until
there is more light on the question of empirical functions.

(2) Religion is an art, not an inquiry. This is really but a corollary of what has just been said. Since religion is identified by its techniques or forms, it is obvious that these must vary with the material and intellectual cultures of which they are a part. They must express local needs and varying tastes. The functions and values of religious techniques must therefore be estimated in their interactions with the other arts of a particular culture; their scientific status or naked truth is irrelevant. A negro " spiritual " loses its spirituality in a night-club and God loses his religious value in the hands of an epistemologist. Puritanism is unintelligible apart from its historical and geographical locus; Shintoism could not be a religion in Germany; a crucifix is not sacred to a Latter-day Saint, nor is the Book of Mormon sacred to a Catholic priest. There are a few religions which enjoy a specious universality, like Christianity, but the universal name really conceals many different cults. Christianity in Haiti is hardly to be identified with Christianity in Havana, nor, for that matter, in Palm Beach. This social relativity of religion makes it possible to criticize it intelligibly. Were religion a search for the Absolute, one might throw stones at it or pity it; but since it is a human art, expressive of human themes in terms of standardized artistic techniques, it is subject to the same canons of criticism that apply to any other art. There is no excuse for it, if it is not done well. It can be cultivated, not as an intellectual necessity or a moral obligation, but as an opportunity for creative, imaginative art.

This applies not only to religion as an art of expression, but to its other functions as well. The arts of salvation, comfort, anaesthesia, loyalty, conflict, celebration, and contemplation, to mention only a few at random, are all subject to the ordinary canons of criticism. And what is more, as secular arts performing these same functions increase in power and in perfection of technique, the corresponding religious arts feel the keen competition. There was a time when religion had almost a monopoly in this field. At present, however, almost all the great religions are decadent, lamely hobbling along with outworn techniques, vulgar standards, and mediocre talents. It remains to be seen whether or not they can bear up under the competition. If not, it is more probable that new cults will take their places than that the secular arts will crowd out religion entirely.

(3) Theology is not primarily a science, but a religious technique. We are now back where we started — back with James and his thesis that theology is an intermediate phase of experience. But the social interpre-

tation of this pragmatic thesis, I hope, throws it into a different light. It suggests that God is not the *object* of religious experience, but a part of its *apparatus*. Whatever use scientists and metaphysicians may be able to put theology to, the religious use it serves is that of a mythology. To insist that theology is a mythology would seem to be a celebration of the commonplace, were the fact not so generally overlooked. Philosophers especially seem to dread mythology — (probably a defence mechanism). But in religion mythology is very useful; in fact, without a mythology a religion could hardly operate. For the materials taken from mythology are usually the most effective instruments of religious expression. The biblical stories of the creation and fall of man, of the Mosaic legislation, of the divine government of the world and the day of judgment; the doctrine of the Trinity, the lives of the saints, and the love of God — all this religious material forms the very heart of the practical devices by which the Christian religion operates. Take away the use of the mythology and you take away the religion. Take away the *belief* in the truth of mythology, and you begin to understand the religion for what it really is. The theological ideas are neither the cause nor end of religion — they are means. By them faith is symbolized, hopes are dramatized, needs are made explicit, and joys are celebrated. Religion is not merely a system of magic, nor is theology mere rationalization; theology is a religious instrument in the imaginative representation of the fruits of experience.

To illustrate: when a man prays, the reason for his prayer is not found in the object to which he prays. He may be a monotheist or a polytheist, he may practise idolatry or he may believe in the guidance of the Holy Spirit; he may light a candle, use a rug, tell beads, or lock himself in his closet. All these factors are technical or formal. The efficient cause of stimulus of his praying is to be found in *what* he prays *for;* the prayer is a device for making his wants explicit. Take the farmers we spoke of before, who gather to pray for rain. It is the need of rain that is uppermost in their minds; acts of prayer, church, God, and all the rest are so much ready technique or apparatus for expressing this need. Probably they have no option as to how and to whom they pray; they must use the forms and objects of prayer which happen to be available in their community. As part of the act of prayer, to be sure, it is important to address God, but the conception of God, the hearer of prayer, is a means, not a cause of prayer. The cause is to be sought in the contents of the petition.

Now, to complicate matters, let us suppose that our farmers pray not merely because they seek an outlet for their anxiety, but because they believe that by praying they might possibly get rain sooner than otherwise. In this case, the premium is put on praying as well as possible, or, as they would put it, making their prayers acceptable to the Lord. This would call into play their standards of worship, of propriety, and in general of the best way to behave under the circumstances. How to pray effectively would be the uppermost question. Now, to change the case, let us suppose that they realize that it makes no practical difference whether they pray or not, and that hence if they pray they do so in order thus to express their need for rain. In this case, they would use or devise whatever techniques most adequately expressed their needs. This would put their conventional religious practices to the test. In either case (whether prayer is believed to have magical efficacy or not), the problem on which the worshiper focuses his attention tends to shift from the original problem of the drought to the technical problem of *how* to pray well. This sublimation of the anxiety for rain into an aesthetic problem of expression is presumably the cause for the relief from tension which prayer usually brings with it. But whatever the psychology of prayer may be, the logical point is that the practical preoccupation with technique in the act of prayer, misleads both the worshiper and the observer into believing that he prays in order to worship God when as a matter of fact the motive which drove him to prayer was his anxiety over the drought. Such a misplacement of means and end is but another illustration of a common fallacy in the analysis of experience, to which the writings of Dewey have called our attention.

Now, to return to the farmer, if the technique of prayer should be completely standardized for him by a fixed and satisfactory ritual, and hence no technical problem be presented by his engaging in prayer, his mind remains focused on the anxiety for rain which the ritual expresses, but the form or technique of the ritual transforms that anxiety into a calm, dignified feeling of dependence or into a hilarious excitement, according to the nature of the ritual. Here we have a case where the intellectual and moral structure of the experience remains true to its original intent; means and end are not confused. Perhaps an analogy may be useful to clear up the logical point at issue here. The act of prayer may be likened unto an automobile ride. The driver may become so pre-occupied with his engine that he actually drives for the sake of running his engine, whereas his original intention was probably either to enjoy the scenery or get somewhere or both. Traditional theology, being the product of religious conflicts, is so pre-occupied with the technique of prayer that it forgets its empirical occasions and foundations: God, the technical object of prayer, is transformed by the theologian into the psychological object or goal of prayer. A more disinterested observer of religious experience is able to see the techniques of religion in their proper, empirical functions and perspectives.

The foregoing analysis applies to what might be called primary, naïve, or unreflective religious behavior. It obviously does not apply to the theologian, to whom God is an end and not a means. To infer from this that theologians are irreligious, would be a *reductio ad absurdum* of the whole argument, though many an illustrious theologue might lend support to such a conclusion by his personal habits, if not by his sermons. The aim of the argument is rather to put theology in its proper religious setting. Gods exist for the reasons we have given, but once created, God may be consciously sought as the object of a real need. St. Augustine and St. Anselm, to say nothing of the mystics, are notoriously seekers after God. But this type of religious experience is derivative, not primary. It may be generated by inner conflict, doubt, and confusion, or by the rivalry of Gods for the kingdoms of this world. Under such circumstances the search for " the True God " or for the infallible proof for God may become a direct need of the human soul expressing itself in theology. This need, however, is not the origin of religion, but one of its incidental products. It is introspective, introverted, and, in extreme cases, inversive religion. It is not necessarily pathological, but it is always a secondary, reflective form of religious experience produced by conflicts within a religious order. If space permitted, it would be easy to prove by historical illustration that theology thrives in an atmosphere of contention, not in what is usually known as a religious atmosphere; and that, in other words, attention is centered on God, when conventional religion ceases to satisfy. Men consciously believe in God only after they have begun to doubt him. Theology is the beginning of the end for any religion. The prophet of God imagines he is doing his Lord a service by defending him in the face of his enemies, but eventually a God who relies on prophets is doomed.

Whether or not this introverted form of religion is better than the more overt forms, is, of course, a matter of religious taste which this essay does not presume to discuss. Religion may find its euthanasia in giving birth to theology, and the love of God may be higher than the earthly loves out of which it grows. It is enough for the present argument that the empirical relationship between the two be established; that the search of the soul for God, when it is definitely religious and not merely a scientific or metaphysical enquiry, be understood in terms of those more primary forms of religion which take sacred beings for granted and use them in the expression or satisfaction of the varieties of human experience. Images and symbols are religiously useful and may also be beautiful, but when some professional priest exploits the symbolism, he transforms religion into idolatry. And theism is but artless idolatry.

In one sense idolatry is harmless, and there is sufficient room in the world for a variety of things, even for theology. Morally and intellectually, too, the search for God is not necessarily fruitless. The chief harm done by theology is neither to science nor to society, but to religion. It robs religion of its spontaneity and humaneness. The so-called " minister " or priest, like his secular analogue, the " servant-of-the-people," is too apt to forget his servitude and sincerely imagines that he and his symbols are the crown of all culture. Thus religion becomes self-centered and forgets its dependence on that mother-sea of human experience whom it must serve in order to survive. By dint of increasing hardships, theology itself is now half-heartedly recognizing these obligations and resigning itself to its instrumental functions. The theologian is turning from his quarrel with science to learn something about civilized life and how it can be served by religious art. If I may paraphrase Professor Whitehead, who says "religion is tending to degenerate into a decent formula wherewith to embellish a comfortable life," [5] I could sum up my contentions by saying, if religion ever again becomes a decent formula wherewith to embellish a comfortable life, it will cease to be degenerate.

IV

Now, to return from this critical digression to religion itself. In the long run religious institutions and practices adapt themselves to the actual needs and satisfactions of the participants. I know that generation after generation may take up its religious cross and bear its religious burden

[5] *Science and the Modern World*, p. 262.

out of a sheer sense of duty or a tenacious faith in its literal efficacy, but even the bearing of this burden has an intrinsic tragic fascination which makes it seem plausible and empirical. Sooner or later, however, the merely obligatory and the pseudo-utilitarian aspects of a religion are sloughed off, though theology may not discover the change until much later.

A closer examination of living rituals and rites would demonstrate, I believe, that few practices maintain themselves out of sheer social inertia, or sheer theological belief in their utility. They have in them something intrinsically enjoyable. Also, I think it would be found that few theological ideas live or die because of their truth or falsity; their religious vitality depends on their usefulness in religious practices, and religious practices follow the wanderings of human experience, not the dialectics of theology. To take an illustration: there is among spiritualists today a definite demand for more specific and concrete guidance than the traditional forms of prayer offer and consequently they patronize " message services," mediums, and other devices for connecting them with spirits who know them intimately. In this sort of religious technique the spirits displace God in practice. And in their theology, though God still presides over the spiritual world, he is definitely receding into the background. He is still called in whenever ultimate metaphysical explanations of the structure and machinery of the spirit world are needed, but He is of practically no value in the actual operation of the cult. If the practices continue to be popular, the theology will probably revert to a frank spiritism such as our " primitive " neighbors employ. The Great God, meanwhile, is passing from religion to metaphysics. In general, metaphysics might be pictured as picking up religious discards — but that is another story.

To conceive religion in terms of social techniques may seem like conceiving art in terms of paints and brushes. And in a sense the analogy is just. It is academic nonsense to pretend that art can be explained by " aesthetic impulses "; and it is a false empiricism that bases religion on *religious* experience. The method of departmentalizing experience is too easy to be informative. Civilization consists of particular ways of achieving particular ends, but no particular instrument of civilization can monopolize a particular realm of human nature. Business, sport, art, religion, and science are not distinguished by the wants they satisfy, but by their *methods* of satisfying wants. A radical empiricism will, therefore, insist on judging particular cults, practices, and beliefs by their effectiveness as specialized instruments in the service of whatever varieties of human experience may care to use them.

Of course, civilization does not exist independently of civilized human beings; nor can religion be divorced from the individuals who practise it. The thesis that religion and other institutions are instrumental would be meaningless if one overlooked the persons whom they serve. An empiricist can ill afford to forget experience. But neither can he afford to regard the institutions of society as " second-hand." Society is but a name for certain ways in which individuals behave and does not exist as an independent reality. To be understood, a social institution must be seen at work, living in persons.

Hence religion, though social, is none the less personal and vital. Music is not less intimate because it needs physical instruments nor is thought less personal because it is expressed in social symbols. Human wants, hopes, emotions, and ideals are not robbed of their power nor of their sincerity by being religiously expressed and cultivated. But particular religions may petrify and particular gods may die. They become not only " second-hand," but useless. They may linger to haunt the living, but their forms are empty and their strength gone. With them we have no quarrel; they have had their day. In general, as empiricists, we have no quarrel with religion, nor with any particular religion; we are, however, provided with a method of analysis which enables us to understand how religion works or fails to work, and to separate the living from the dead.

THE RÔLE OF THE PHILOSOPHER

T. V. SMITH

THERE is no philosophy — only philosophers and their philosophies. Before philosophers were philosophers they were men; some remain men throughout; and all become men again, if but at last to die. Men seek to adjust themselves to other men and to the world; they seek a method in the otherwise madness that is life; and philosophies arise to memorialize this human attempt at orientation. If there be anything common to the varying philosophies of diverse men, it is this attempt on the part of all to come to terms with the whole reach of their environment. But science, when conceived as both understanding and power, may also be described as an attempt at adjustment. And religion certainly has been so described. Nevertheless science goes the long way at it — so long a way indeed as to leave complete individual adjustment a mere ideal. Religion, on the contrary, goes at it the short way — so easy a short-cut indeed as renders it more suspect the more intelligence advances. No scientist even attempts to adjust himself through his rigorous methodology to the whole of the world. No, he takes his environment piecemeal, and is content to profess ignorance of things-in-general if only he can boast full knowledge of something in particular. There are not merely scientists and their sciences; but also there is — in a sense not true of philosophy — science itself. But no individual scientist embodies the whole of it. He forgets himself through specialization into the immortality that is science. At least for purposes of knowledge he does, though not for purposes of action. He goes on acting; and there is little action inside the laboratory and perhaps none outside it that does not transcend scientific knowledge, little indeed that does not outrun knowledge altogether. Science is a tiny but shining oasis of order amid vast expenses of disarray. Beyond science there is common sense with only animal faith to guide. This animal faith manifests itself now as shrewdness, now as skill, now as taste, and on rare occasions as art. So one does not have to be completely dumb merely because he does not know everything. At the boundary of knowledge a kind of wisdom begins that is of great utility.

I

The philosopher is etymologically, be it remembered, a "lover of wisdom." Both the terms throw light upon his rôle. As a lover, he must accept his emotional nature as among his assets. The scientist may disallow emotion in his quest for precision and he may discount temperament as "personal equation," but not so the philosopher. He is by fate a lover — a lover of an object that love does not defeat, of wisdom.

> Our knowledge is a torch of smoky pine
> That lights the pathway but one step ahead
> Across a void of mystery and dread.

> *   *   *   *   *   *

> It is not wisdom to be only wise,
> And on the inward vision close the eyes,
> But it is wisdom to believe the heart.

The scientist is a philosopher in his off moments, if he uses the intelligence he has, to make an art of his extra-scientific relations of citizen, of friend, of parent. The common man is a philosopher so far as he has a philosophy of life. Perhaps no person altogether lacks a philosophy of life; perhaps no person has an altogether satisfactory one. To know and to remember that all men share thus in varying degrees in the honors of philosophy will render more sane our further discussion of the rôle of the philosopher in a class sense.

As commonly conceived the philosopher is a hybrid between a common man and a scientist: not merely professing wisdom, but having more knowledge than the common man and yet not enough to make him a scientist. The knowledge he does have he treats not as an end in itself nor yet primarily as a means of getting more knowledge, but rather as a clue to conduct. He is preoccupied with a way of life rather than with a technique of understanding. This does not mean that he must be always devoted to practice in any narrow sense; he may indeed live under the light of distant stars, as witness the legend of Thales. But his quest for the meaning of things relates at last to his own adjustment to the world at large.

It will be noted that I speak of the philosopher, not of the historian of philosophy. Historians are many: notable philosophers are few. Any man that can become an historian at all can become an historian of philosophy. It may take a little different flair and a little more tolerance and patience and a little greater thinness of blood, but it is within the reach of any diligent student. But to know the history of philosophers does not make one a philosopher, save in the general sense already admitted for all men. In so far as it begets the conceit, it indeed perhaps militates against the actuality; and since it seems to do this very thing, it is not unlikely that other studies than the history of philosophy conduce more readily to make one a philosopher. An historian is most likely to make philosophy from philosophies by isolating ideas and stringing them on some developmental thread. It was not the mere having of ideas that made philosophers philosophers; it was the having of such ideas at a given time and place as adjusted life to that time and place. Without this latter one can be neither wise nor a lover of wisdom, though he may be an historian of philosophy. An historian sees another historian when he looks at a philosopher, since it is precisely what cannot be reduced to knowledge that makes a philosopher; and consequently what is called philosophy is not infrequently the set of ideas one man has about the ideas another man had about those still another man had. Philosophy degenerates, as a not too outworn textbook defines it, into " the derivation of rational knowledge from concepts as such."

History of philosophy and philosophizing are easily confused, moreover, because a knowledge of the history of the philosophies of dead men usually happens, for reasons largely adventitious, to be tied up with a function of all real philosophers — the function of teaching. The genuine philosopher will certainly be a teacher; for having found a way of life, he will not be able to keep it to himself. Effective ways of life are too rare indeed and far too much in demand for a man to squander such wisdom upon himself alone. Philosophy is not what a man does with his solitariness. If the philosopher does not teach in one way he will in another. As the modern world is organized, he may well become a professional teacher of youth, taking money for his work. Modesty, if nothing else does, will forbid his merely teaching wisdom. So he must affect at least to teach something else in order to do by indirection what he cannot do directly — insinuate into his students a way of life.

Caught in this predicament and finding through the refined distribution of academic labor all other fields pre-empted by technicians, what is more natural than that he, too, should turn specialist and teach as his subject-matter the history of philosophy. That is, he takes the literature that other technicians have found no use for and expounds it as his specialty. If, however, he realizes that what those other men thought were not just thoughts, but thoughts about things and institutions and persons, he will either become an ardent " new historian " and realize himself in a reconstruction of the total context of which their ideas and doctrines were functions; or he will use this historical knowledge for the ulterior purpose of setting himself and his students fruitfully in their own time and place. Either way, an honest assumption of his rôle as a teacher demands that he master the material at which he makes his living, as other specialists master their material.

But if, taking the latter cue, he become a philosopher, his major rôle is other than either the mastery or the presentation of his historical material. He will teach students as well as the history of philosophy. The latter will enable him to make a living, but it will never build a life either for him or for his students. I might without seeming unduly to labor the matter dwell somewhat more upon the potentiality of teaching for effecting this metamorphosis of the historian into the philosopher. We shall in the discussion see the subject-matter get subordinated to the subjects, the teacher get transformed into an educator, and the student pass from immobile chrysalis to winged freedom beating with the wise teacher the philosophic empyrean for enlarged vistas. The philosopher will stand forth in the sequel as interpreter of value, as mediator between otherwise isolated realms of appreciation, as emancipator from outworn institutions, and, finally, as creator of his own personality and through friendliness as grower of souls as well.

II

I have said that the philosopher will be a teacher. Now the teacher in the course of his job at once extraverts himself and writes his values large in the habits and sentiments and ideas of his hearers, while he discusses as a ruse whatever he discusses. This out-writing of himself he may do unconsciously and unintentionally, as in the natural sciences, by desensitizing the student to slipshod methods and sensitizing him to rigorous methods of thinking and of research. Or he may do it consciously, as the philosopher; for have not philosophers always had as their dearest

goal the meaning and value of things and the subsequent dissemination
of these meanings and values in the human community? Zeno built himself a school; Epicurus repaired to a garden; Plato, and after him Aristotle,
exploited the academy for the sake of community, and through the maximum sharing of insight in the small community, they hoped, especially
Plato hoped, to achieve at least some promissory minimum distribution
of the same insight in the largest community conceivable in his world of
caste. But we need not call the roll of philosophers to make out this case.
Philosophers who have been willing to hide their light under a bushel
have possessed also that other differentia of non-existence — hand palms
with heavy mustache. Even the Spinozas who have declined the vantage
of an established chair have done so in order to achieve the freedom of a
larger sounding-board in some other way. There is an astute modesty
that hides its blushes by retiring to the privacy of innumerable posterity.

However high the philosopher may mount for his vision and however
esoteric he may conceive the moment of illumination, he counts himself
poor and his mission incomplete until he has shared the fruits of his toil
or fortune with the denizens of some earthly cave. This will-to-disseminate with which all philosophy is so instinct might have long ago indicated
to the philosopher that the value he really sought under the guise of metaphysical objectivity was the largest possible human community to share
with him his emotions and his hopes. At any rate whatever meaning may
remain for the reality-gesture when socialization is complete, the clearest
implication of this philosophic will-to-disseminate itself is universal
community.

The very medium in which the philosopher becomes expert and which
he exploits in teaching throws some light upon his rôle. Words are his
implements; they are his sword as well as his pen; they are " all his science
and his only art."

> From these create he can
> Forms more real than living man,
> Nurslings of immortality.

The conditioning principle that any part of experience may become
through proper association a substitute for any other part constitutes every
verbal incarnation a permanent possibility of value; in the beginning, as
religious insight has clairvoyantly discerned, was the Word, and it was the

highest religious value; it was God. There is indeed more than good humor in a definition recently suggested for philosophy: "the attempt to go from the known to the unknown by means of words." The common meaning of symbols, which language primarily represents, would not be possible, however, without a substructure of shared non-verbal experience. The life in which each philosopher participated before he became a philosopher and into which he dips intermittently to rest his wings is the world of common activities, of daily routine. If one wishes to see the relation of language in which philosophy primarily deals and more fundamental shared experiences, let him read Bronislaw Malinowski's account of the relation of the language of a primitive tribe in the Trobriand Islands to the communal activities of that tribe. (Ogden and Richards, *The Meaning of Meaning,* Supplement I.) Malinowski seems to me completely to make out his case, that language arises as a form of shared experience to further another type of experience that would cease to be common and effective but for the function of the vocal gesture in its on-going. Acquiring its meaning from conditioning in shared work or play, language has as its continuing function the further sharing of work and play.

The scientist uses words only when he cannot manipulate anything else, and then for the sake of furthering particular experimentation. The theologian mistakes words for things and by hypostatization raises them to powers and then through personification to gods good enough to use their power for human ends. The artist exploits words for what they are in themselves. All of these have other materials also than words save, perhaps, the theologian; and he certainly thinks he has. But the philosopher eschews if not by choice then by necessity all other means of experimentation and achievement save that of words. He becomes — no invidiousness is intended — a purveyor of words. But words, as we have seen, are coins of exchange whose cash value lies buried not exclusively in any scientific sector and certainly not in any transcendental elysium, but buried yonder in the vault of common human activities which constitute their meaning. Every gesture, therefore, of the philosopher has as its real result — if it have any result beyond the waste of breath — either the intensification of shared experience by stirring up the environmental and habitual complex of which it is the part or the extensification of basic experience by the initial sharing of some symbolic experience.

There are important implications of the philosopher's choice of tools.

He cannot elect but to participate in the whole process from which language arises and to the furtherance of which it contributes. It is at once his fate and his vocation. He may make of the necessity the glory of his vocation if he attend well to two conditions: (1) simplicity of phrase, (2) friendliness of manner.

If language is to commemorate by way of appreciation or to extend by way of creation the realm of shared experience, then the philosopher must use a common language. It is a sure mark of apostasy through pride when a philosopher begins to glory in a technical terminology; he wants to be like the experts around him and to associate with technicians. This tendency shows a predilection for the meaning of values rather than an appreciation of the values themselves. It is because of the compartmentization of life through science as well as through social classes that the philosopher as mediator is imperatively needed in the modern world. He has no methods of his own for getting at new facts; the scientist humbles any pride he may have here by performing the function far better. But the scientist becomes so highly specialized that what he discovers is unintelligible to all but a few of his fellows in science. Likewise social cliques get nuances each of its own esoteric realm and corner each some type of value experience; but others are excluded from the values by prestige symbols or by the deterring fences of private property. And yet value experiences — so the philosopher's vocation commits him to hold — must not be shut up in a corner; value should not be allowed to go to waste. If the philosopher is himself a man of broad sympathies, of large inflamed sensitized areas, and is modest enough to use the language of common sense, he may be able to help diverse groups understand and eventually to share their otherwise exclusive experiences. He may become in part an interpreter of the technicians to each other; but he must become the mediator between the technicians and the people. Dissolving scientific novelties and artistic extravagancies into a way of life for himself, he can project their significance onto the plane of conduct for others. The *sine qua non* of this rôle, however, is the use of the language of common sense as his medium.

Its use implies a persisting lack of pride and an equally persisting conviction that no experience is inexorably private in its nature. The technicalities of science have a meaning, often a great or even terrible meaning, for all men. This meaning becomes a value, positive or negative, to common men when understood; but it must be explained in terms that common men know, with as much regard to the connotative as to the denotative side of the language of common sense. The philosopher must not be ashamed to be a poet when only poetry suffices. Primarily the philosopher must hold himself to be what all men are and no man to be other than what he is; and since he equates all men with himself *seriatim,* he equates all men with each other through himself. He will talk the language of common men because all experiences of value are potentially sharable and the only way to make them actually so is to talk up to the level of his faith. Using thus a universal medium, the philosopher can become even in an age of science, necessarily becomes in an age of science, as well as in a caste-ridden society, the intermediary of man to man. In so far as he makes understandable to all what is otherwise intelligible to the few, he is achieving the objectification of whatever specific values the shared experiences has; and, what is more, he is objectifying in an enlarging society as such the highest possible value, the felt value of sharing itself — the appropriation of the values of others, regardless of content, awakens new values in one himself.

In the performance of this function, the philosopher's manner is of high import. The aristocratic mien, possible elsewhere, is suicidal in this rôle. As a certain basic element of friendliness is involved in all sharing of value experiences, so the philosopher as the plenipotentiary of value must be himself a friendly man. Only the friendly at heart shall find grace. His words must retain some of their original warmth after they have been polished as pointers. All value suffers at the hands of frigidity. What can so unavoidably be seen in the classroom relations of the philosopher as teacher of youth can without large danger of error be imputed to him as he functions on a larger scale through all the reach of his influence, however extensive that may be. The tone of his reports upon life will outweigh the content of them in the supreme function to which he is devoted. He will not achieve greatness in his special vocation if he act out the philosophy attributed recently by an athlete to a contemporary coach: "In his presence," said the athlete, "no man ever does his best." The philosopher cannot further his high cause by keeping men at arms-length; and unless he learns deeply to respect that life of experienced value that lies under the connotative side of language, his skill in marshalling the denotative aspects of meaning will leave him still greatly circumscribed in influence — an impotent pseudo-scientist rather than a "divine philosopher."

But for the social clairvoyance that led Aristotle to humanize his "proportional justice" with the virtue of friendship, his ethics would be no more than a hard class rationalization. With this it becomes a singularly humane treatment, a vision of potentiality outrunning Greek actuality. A man finds himself in his friend, who is his second self. "As then everyone desires his own existence, so or similarly he desires the existence of his friend. . . . We require therefore the consciousness of our friend's existence, and this we shall get by living with him and associating with him in conversation and thought." [1] As one comes to know and love himself through seeing himself in a friend, so the intrinsic good of friendship, when further objectified, furnishes a goal in terms of which to conceive an ideal community where all would not only have but also be friends; and this social good set up as a human objective gives energizing motivation for its own progressive actualization.

Though Aristotle explicitly emphasized friendship, it remained for Plato to demonstrate how language could be used to make all things available for sharing. Plato was at once scientist and poet. He used all the available science not for its own sake, but for the sake of human improvement; he used the devices of the artist to make accessible the content of science; he differed from the theologian as every philosopher should differ, in knowing when he was out-talking his information [2] and in evaluating the gods in terms of his own most mature value experience. Every philosopher who rises to the highest level of his vocation will become a cross between the scientist and the poet, resolving the idiosyncrasies and dissolving the privacies of each in terms of the language of the common man, being neither poet nor scientist but what is common to them and so common to all men, and finally speaking to men as the incarnation of human friendliness. Such a person with such a procedure could objectify the values that he senses up to the optimum limit of universalization. A mere word committed to the ear or entrusted to paper remains at the lowest a permanent possibility of felt experience; but phrases and propositions rising from so rare an organic matrix as this type of personality would

---

[1] *Nichomachen Ethics*, IX, x.

[2] One of his finest myths he appraises as "a tolerably credible and possibly true though partly erring myth." (*Phaedrus,* 265.)

constitute must remain to the end of time a magic call to enriched community. Plato measured highest of any philosopher who lived before democracy had broken the crust of class prejudice. Combine George Santayana, the poet-philosopher, and John Dewey, the scientist-philosopher, both speaking from a democratic scene, and there would emerge from this fusion of fires a personality whose style would even through symbolic means extend the boundaries of value experience beyond the far reaches of Plato himself.

III

It perhaps appears that I am unduly discounting the knowledge element in the philosopher's equipment. Is the philosopher as teacher to mediate value without creating knowledge? The more knowledge the philosopher has, the better, of course — knowledge of the history of philosophy, knowledge of the history of everything, knowledge particularly of science. But knowledge unassimilated is merely an ornament. To assimilate knowledge for purposes of living, if not also for purposes of getting more knowledge, means for it to become taste, clairvoyance. The unconscious use of means for the achievement of ends that burn in consciousness is the highest wisdom. The philosopher, be it remembered, is devoted to wisdom, not to knowledge. He succeeds in his vocation as he discovers a way of life, and he prospers as he disseminates it. And what are his efficacies to this end? Logic? Yes; he must clearly know the nature, the function, the utility, the limitation of ideas. Ethics? Yes; he must surely know the natural history of wants, the life-cycle of desires, the abiding elements of satisfaction that constitute value, the place and potency of sublimation. Aesthetics? Yes; he must know kinaesthetically the feel of beauty as well as experimentally the educative function that art serves in society. Metaphysics? Yes and no.

Metaphysics is sometimes conceived as knowledge of a larger or better reality, or both, than can be known scientifically. The scientist's extremity becomes the metaphysician's opportunity. At the boundary of research the metaphysician appears to confound the timid, agnostic, silent scientist by telling what's what — or is it after all telling what's *not?* Well, I must admit that this type of metaphysician confounds me as much as he does the scientist. I for one do not doubt that the several sciences through their own plodding trials and errors will give us all the knowledge that we shall ever have about the nature of reality. They will not tell us every-thing; but when they close their mouths in discreet silence, no trustworthy philosopher will attempt to bark forth final truth. No; they will not tell us all that we want to know about the world. But what have wants to do with it? They cannot, as the tender-minded in every age have be-lieved, guarantee their own satisfaction. If they could, the beggars would all be riding cushions instead of rods. No; metaphysics as cognitive short-cuts to reality is not for the sane philosopher, however much the apologist may exploit it. To call reality the emotive force back of such words as Whole, Infinity, Absolute, Eternal is to be superstitious, not philosophic. The wise man will know that words have their pathology as well as their etiology.

But must not the universe be friendly? Yes; I suppose it must, if out-talking one's information is good warrant. It is sorry business for a grown man, this metaphysical conjuring of our wants into the substructure of the universe. Metaphysics has never been a discovery of something back of physics, but the unacknowledged invention of a balm for the wounds of physics. That there are wounds, all of us know from experi-ence; and we know that we dare not be indifferent to their cure. But deception is no cure even though it be self-deception; and the best con-solation that is available for a mature mind is to take without repining what cannot be helped, and to help without delay what is open to remedy. Whether the universe as such is friendly or not, we know from common-sense experience that we can make it more friendly than it is by the simple expedient of making more friends. The wounds of physics can be greatly lessened by scientific research wisely placed and can be progressively healed by human kindness and co-operation. Whatever the universe as such may prove to be, " real defeat," as Professor Max Otto says in con-cluding his fine *Things and Ideals,* " will overtake man only when men themselves forgetting that they are comrades in doom and agents of each other's woe or weal go down the years estranged from the one friend they have — each other." Physics and chemistry and other basic sciences furnish after all the only content for metaphysics as a theory of reality. The metaphysician if he so will can make one part of his task the accept-ance of what they find and the other part the developing of the resources for betterment offered by nature through human ingenuity and co-operation.

In this rôle he will understand and interpret and further whatever potency tradition has for social solidarity. He will evaluate institutions with reference to their influence upon growth as well as upon order. The metaphysics of the past has in its determined attempt to discover a better reality than appeared upon the surface been too ready to apologize for institutional dominance under cover of holding that the real reason why anything comes to be what it is, as Socrates said, " is that it is better for it to be that way than any other." Upon this view whatever at any given time is, must be accepted by natural piety as rational and be perpetuated as such.

IV

When the modern philosopher becomes aware of what the sociologists have long described as " institutional lag," of the great truth long ago described by Thomas Jefferson in his remark that " all experience hath shown that mankind is more disposed to suffer while evils are sufferable than to right themselves by abolishing the forms to which they are accustomed," he is likely to see that as custodian of value he must count as part of his rôle that of emancipator. The baneful influence of outworn institutions upon the life of value appears not merely in the sense that to extend value is sometimes to thin it, but also in the form that to institutionalize often means to freeze what ought to be freed. Bone is a necessity for body, but ossification marks the cessation of growth; and arteriosclerosis conducts the hot blood of life through cramping narrowness to the grave. To hazard a formula: *Permanence of value varies proportionately, but intensity of value inversely, with its institutionalization.* To habituate impulse deadens satisfaction, and individual habitation is, of course, the counterpart of institutionalization.

The philosopher who prizes growth need not turn iconoclast regarding institutions, but he will not be blinded by the *status quo*. He will see that institutionalization of values even by those who most insist upon it is not regarded by them so much as maximizing the life of satisfaction as it is minimizing danger to their own satisfaction. Euphemistically, it is a means of order and security — order for the majority, security for the minority in its independent and often illicit quest for maximum satisfaction. If there be doubt, note, for example, in England today the rigor of law for the populace and the laxity of practice among favored classes

regarding monogamy. Note the same thing in America regarding prohibition. It is arguable that more freedom for all would augment value
as it is surely believed in practice to augment it for the favored few. There
are many goods that might be enjoyed save for the sole reason that we
will not let each other enjoy them. We forbid in fear what in wisdom
we should encourage. Society allows itself too wide a margin of safety
at the expense of its individual members. It is the way of institutionalization. We do not yet know what are the fruitful limits of tolerance in
human relations, and we are not making very rapid strides towards finding
out.

When the philosopher sees that institutions tend to take care of themselves, because habit and tradition have a momentum from the past and
a present meat to eat that simple men know not of, he is likely to appraise
highly his rôle as emancipator of individuals from institutional dominance
and preach tolerance for variation as among the greatest of human goods.
Not palliatives for unrest, but creation of finer human hungers, becomes
his guiding star. In a tolerant society where to the uttermost limits imposed by demonstrable and immediate harm (as Mr. Justice Holmes cautiously puts it) individuality were encouraged, there would be the greatest
possibility of moral inventiveness. Each citizen would from a logic of the
inner life itself seek to share every experience he found self-justifying
with as many others as could be brought to it. Certainly sharing increases
in extent and in import as it is divorced from compulsion. But more than
the sharing of individual experiences in detail would be the permanent
fact of community itself. It is no little triumph for the human spirit in
its mundane provincialism to achieve an ability to let other people live
their lives while one lives his own. There are few realizations that carry
deeper joy than that one is a part of a community of the tolerant — primarily because such a realization even more than rigorous law and forcibly
maintained order, carries the guarantee that the experience of each has
after all the best chance of being shared by all. A great added advantage
remains; and that is that sharing under such conditions guarantees, as
rigid institutions cannot, that what does not have intrinsic appeal will not
persist to be shared in the market place of spiritual goods.

What the philosopher can do, then, to make respectable in its own
right every tinge of joy, is a duty laid upon him by the potentiality of his
rôle. As the discipline of sociology takes institution-culture for its field and

the newer science and art of social service exploits the public side of the individual, a defence of the private side of the individual marks a challenging part of the philosopher's contemporary opportunity. To make institutions flexible — easily formed, easily disbanded — is to make of them a maximized value. Through his emphasis upon tolerance as the social bond and growth as the prime institutional objective, institutions are promoted from a plane of physical constraint to a level of spiritual insight. When freshly experienced good becomes the basis of one's own value theory, and joyous unconstrained sharing of it by others the social bond, institutions lose their debit to intensity and retain whatever credit for permanency they at any time possess.

I have now spoken of what I regard the major tasks of the philosopher: he is an articulator of the way of life which constitutes his wisdom; he is a mediator between isolated groups each with some value of its own worthy of being shared; he is a conservator of whatever value he discovers in tradition; and he is an emancipator from the inertia and tyranny of outworn institutions. There remains a word regarding his rôle as creator.

V

If the way of life which one's total philosophy constitutes and recommends is really an achievement rather than a borrowed thing, it betokens a creative process out of which emerges the philosopher's own personality as the thing created. Philosophy, like charity in the proverb, begins at home. To achieve a single personality out of a medley of relatively conflicting desires through a process of integration, rounded out by sublimation, and confirmed by enlarged satisfaction — this is to top merit with dividends. To lead the criticized life has been claimed as a special philosophic duty and prerogative since Socrates. Whether any given philosopher achieve through criticism a harmonious personality is more modest for him to admit than to assert; but it is enough here to remark that he sets himself this task by his very profession and that in so far as he effect it, he is a creator of no mean object, i.e., of a soul. This is to achieve a firm and fruitful personality. An impulse balked by absence of environmental means of satisfaction remains purely private as a ghostly stirring in the subconscious or leads a lonely existence as an impotent reverie in the realm of would-be robust ideas. At best it becomes a sort of idea of an idea instead of an idea of concrete means of satisfaction. To see life steadily and to see it whole implies that one has become himself a whole and has steadied himself by participation in a larger whole than he himself is. " Become a whole by joining one " — this, then, is to correct Goethe's famous maxim by a paraphrase. No community short of mankind answers for aspiration, and no norm of criticism is needed other than the universal sharability of a questioned value.

Contrary to Shaw's witticism that those who can, do; those who cannot, teach, one is not likely indeed to teach what the philosopher stands for — wisdom, a way of life — unless he has first inculcated it in himself, for his personality with its assets and deficiencies will speak more effectively than his words, unless they speak to the same intent. If he as educator of youth or of fellow-citizens hopes to procreate robust personalities, he must first have achieved one himself. To have laughed and loved; to have suffered and grieved; to have laid hold on goods with modest pride, and to have met failure without repining; to have developed understanding without cynicism, and a sense of humor without satire — this is out of the raw material of heredity and environment, of stress and strain, of brute and man to have created a philosopher. The first thing that the philosopher creates, then, is his own personality; and the initial contribution he can make to mankind is himself — a product of whom he may not with impunity be proud, of whom he dare not be ashamed. Without such a self the modern philosopher degenerates into just a professor; with it, cosmic weather favoring, he may become at once artist-scientist, teacher-friend.

A METHODOLOGY OF THOUGHT

John Storck

I

THE point of view of the following paper is methodological. In it we shall not be told what really is, nor shall we learn whether the things we study are good or true or beautiful. A methodologist is not even entitled, officially, to use the optative mood. His verb is not *ought* but *can*. His primary concern, in other words, is with possibility. " One can regard these things in this manner " — a person who speaks thus is for a moment, at least, talking methodologically. As we shall see, however, not all things are possible. In fact, when we understand it better the methodologist's *can* will begin to approximate the character of a *must*. In terms of the data he is considering no other possibility is possible, though it may be true that no inescapable necessity is laid upon anyone to consider precisely these things. The vicissitudes of human affairs make it more than likely that no one else ever will.

The particular subject-matter of the paper is human thinking considered in its systematic aspects. Thought is given systematic form, among other places, in science, in art, in the activities of practical life, in religious exercises, and in the speculations of philosophers. Such organizations of thought, though they are capable to some extent of independent development, can also often be exhibited as interdependent, or as severally dependent upon a hierarchically superior system of thought. In addition, systems of thought are on occasion subjected to alteration. It seems desirable, if possible, to offer a logical rendering of these facts about systems of thought, without appealing too hastily to psychology, metaphysics, or ethics.

The aim of the paper, then, is to develop a position in terms of which other positions can be exhibited without doing violence to their otherness. This position is to have no metaphysical status. The various systems will remain different from each other and from the system here to be developed, but by being brought into this setting their extra-systemic meaning and utility will have been given a logical rendering. The effort, in other words, is to provide a logical bridge between different systems of thought that will place them in communication without necessary destruction of sovereignty.

A methodologist is not entitled to judge the materials he organizes. He must take them exactly as they are, and insure them a perfectly adequate logical setting. These materials may not serve his purposes, and therefore may not themselves exhibit methodologies, but he must take it for granted that they serve their own. He must " save the phenomena." He must even save the theories about the phenomena. In this respect he is more empirical than the empiricist, for his empiricism includes the empirical fact of rationalism itself. He is not bound to demonstrate the truth or falsity of these theories, but he is obliged to insure them a logical setting. He must also develop his position so that the occurrence of mistakes in judgment and fallacies in reasoning is logically possible, since they obviously occur.

The methodological position can be illustrated by indicating how psychiatrists are beginning to treat their patients. Here is a woman suffering from hysteria. Her right hand is anaesthetic. She does not wince or pull it away when it is pricked with a pin. In a variety of situations she treats it as foreign to herself. And yet the psychiatrist can find no obvious physical basis for her condition. He does find, however, that the anaesthetic area stops quite suddenly at an arbitrary line on the patient's wrist — a line corresponding more accurately to the terminus of the colloquial notion of " hand " than to any recognizable anatomical or physiological unit. No competent psychiatrist treating such a patient would begin his cure by telling her that she is acting wrongly, either morally or in the sense that she is anaesthetic in an area that anatomy and physiology do not countenance. Instead he would take it for granted that the behavior he has witnessed is the very best possible under the circumstances. The anaesthesia, however peculiar, has a setting which makes it reasonable, indeed logically necessary. That setting may, of course, be narrow and perverse from the point of view of some other conceivable setting, but in its own terms it is logically justifiable. It is the psychiatrist's function to discover this setting, and then to exhibit it to his patient in such a manner that a " normal " functioning of the woman's hand is logically possible. He does not refute the logic that leads to the anaesthesia; he assimilates it to another logic that does not include the anaesthesia. This must be done, not merely to his own satisfaction (he will, of course, require that), but in terms agreeable to his patient — that is to say, in a second setting which she herself accepts, just as she accepted the first setting whose overt manifestation was the anaesthesia.[1] When this has been accomplished, the woman is cured. The grounds of her peculiar behavior have been removed, and though she still has no indisputable reason for being just the person she is, she *can* be that person. Indeed, she *must* be, though previously she could only be a divided self.

The patient need not know why she is acting as she does. She need not even know what she is doing, nor that such-and-such principles are being invoked to cure her. But the treatment must be functionally relevant just the same; it must be a treatment of *her* case. In a similar fashion, the treatment must be functionally relevant to the psychiatrist; it must be *his* treatment of the case. He need know no more about himself, nor what he is doing, than his patient need know about herself.

It follows from what has been said that methodologies are implicit in their subject-matters. No psychiatrist could ever cure a patient who was completely recalcitrant — one, as the term has it, who was entirely lacking in orientation. He would possess no means of contact with the disordered mind. It is the total situation of the discordant and competing ways of life in the patient that on the one hand generates the peculiar problem and on the other provides the means of its solution. Similarly, it is the total situation in the psychiatrist that on the one hand leads him to understand the patient exactly as he does, and on the other leads him to believe that certain procedures will result in a cure. The situation, in other words, is a functional one. Were anything in the situation different, other things there would also be different.[2] The fact that methodologies are always *of* something and *for* something (e.g., of " hysterical patient " and for " restoration of this patient to normality ") is basic. The *of*, the *for*, and the *how* reciprocally determine each other.

---

[1] More strictly, no doubt, the logical basis of the anaesthesia is to be found in the juxtaposition of the two settings. (Actually, also, many more than two logical settings were probably involved.) In the case cited, the woman, for reasons that need not be mentioned, has been a shoplifter. Her thefts made her unhappy. She was led to disown them, and therefore the hand that had committed them. Hence the anaesthesia.

[2] What it means to be " in the situation " will, I hope, become clear during the course of the paper. That in a way is its theme.

If this paper succeeds in making its point, it too will be found to possess the formally tautologous character so intrinsic to systems of thought. The approach outlined will be in agreement with the materials of which cognizance is taken and with the results that are reached, the agreement itself being of a kind appropriate to just this enterprise. This does not involve a claim to absence of predilection. The formally novel elements in a system of thought when it is viewed from the standpoint of another system may be regarded alternatively as its insights or as its prejudices.

It may be added that this paper does not discuss the advisability of one's becoming a methodologist. Reasons historical, psychological, and logical, might be given for the methodological attitude, but they would not be pertinent to the task in hand. Since no position generates itself, the conditions of its generation are always a legitimate subject for discussion; but the topic of this essay is the methodology of human thinking and not the rationale of methodology.

II

Modern philosophy has been greatly influenced by the concepts, procedures, and ideals of mathematics. This is true whether one considers the continental rationalists or the English empiricists. In this section I shall discuss only a single phase of this influence — that indicated by the effort to demonstrate truths in the mathematical order. The mathematical order is one in which propositions are proved by showing that they follow with logical necessity from certain basic assumptions. Two remarks are necessary. In the first place, mathematical thinking has itself undergone a considerable development in modern times. It is today held, for example, that the assumptions basic to mathematical systems are not axioms or self-evident truths, but simply postulates. Mathematical systems are now exhibited by developing the formal implications of certain undefined terms and certain primitive propositions. The elements of such a system are neither true nor false. In fact they are supposed to be perfectly meaningless when taken singly. Their significance lies entirely in the fact that when taken together they are capable of yielding the theorems or propositions that complete the system. The formal procedures summarized above by the term " yielding " are themselves members of the postulate set basic to the system.

In the second place, the notion of mathematical order is to be distinguished from what might be called the mathematical method. The latter is employed whenever mathematical entities (numbers, measures, etc.) are used as principles of interpretation. The initial significance of most mathematical entities is not derived from the fact that they can be obtained deductively from one or another postulate set. As the terms are here being used much of modern science is mathematical in method, although the results of scientific research are seldom exhibited in the mathematical order. It has only been within recent years, as for example in Whitehead and Russell's *Principia Mathematica,* that mathematicians have attempted to exhibit the whole of mathematics itself in the mathematical order. In this endeavor they have found it all but necessary to develop a special symbolism to condense and clarify their procedures.[3]

Philosophies that take their start from clear and distinct ideas thereby announce their allegiance to the mathematical order. So, too, do philosophies that begin with simple psychical elements and the principles of association. However different these schools of thought may be in other respects, they are alike in this, that they aim to start from certain simples from which, by severe processes, other more complicated materials are to be derived. It is worthy of note, however, that neither of these traditions ever succeeded in providing a measurably integrated presentation of their data in the strict mathematical order. Perhaps the most notable attempts were those of Spinoza and David Hartley. Spinoza finds it difficult to account for the concrete individual and for " inadequate ideas " in terms of his principles, while Hartley and the other associationists struggled in vain to reduce association by similarity to mere contiguity in space or in time.

The critical movement in philosophy initiated by Kant can be regarded as a reaction against the attempt to render philosophic data in terms of elements in accordance with the ideals of mathematical order. The claim was raised that there is a synthetic element in the data which must be taken account of. The absolutistic and pragmatic offshoots of the critical philosophy in somewhat different ways also emphasize the same point. Yet, although it is perhaps not too much to say that *The Critique of Pure Reason* opened the door into a new world, the philosophies at whose births

[3] C. I. Lewis, *A Survey of Symbolic Logic* (Berkeley, Univ. of Cal. Press, 1918) is an admirable guide to this field.

it has assisted in one respect have managed to retain a somewhat old-fashioned air. In each of them hypostatization occurs, whether it be of the thing-in-itself and the categories, the absolute, or " experience." The doctrine of elements has all but disappeared, but the brute fact of revelation at some point or other remains. Something in each instance is not only uninterpreted, but fundamentally uninterpretable. It just simply is, and those who do not see it are blind.[4] And these hypostatized items are really mathematical primitives, for from the attributes assigned to them everything else in the system follows.

If one were to retreat beyond the confines of modern philosophy into the realm of Greek thought, one would find that the chief principle of organization there is not mathematical, but dialectical. Truth is sought in the opposition and conflict of opinions rather than in deductive elaboration. In Plato opinions are dramatized with such skill that he is often credited with the views he puts into the mouths of his characters — which is as though Polonius' advice to Laertes were credited to Shakespeare. Aristotle is in the habit of wending his way through such a cloud of witnesses (most of them very obliquely referred to and summarized) that we are often left in no little doubt as to the particular position he is himself expounding. So strong, however, is the modern predilection for the mathematical order that even an acute and original work like Mr. Mortimer J. Adler's *Dialectic* is conceived of largely in a deductive setting. This is the more curious in that Mr. Adler considers dialectic to be the realm of " statements about statements."

III

I shall now point out that the mathematical or deductive exhibition of a system must of necessity contain elements that have not been given a logical rendering. This fact in no wise affects the status of such a system as a series of implications; indeed, it follows from the nature of a deductive system that it must always contain materials that have not been given a strictly logical reading. The presence of these arbitrary elements, how-

---

[4] This might be called the mystical strain in western philosophy. Its perpetuation in the body of western thought is no doubt due to Near Eastern (Christian) influences. Its presence, however, can be demonstrated even in Greek thinking. It would seem as though modern thinkers have aimed to know " the world " in precisely the same manner that mystics influenced by the Near Eastern tradition have sought to know " God."

ever, makes the mathematical order unsuitable for a methodology designed to exhibit the organization of thought.[5] A methodology must tell us how to get the materials we need, and how to use them. The materials of a mathematical system are its primitives. From the point of view of this paper these primitives are unsatisfactory in a double sense: (1) No method is given for getting precisely them and nothing else; (2) If they are really what they are asserted to be, the theorems cannot have the meanings usually assigned to them. These matters are so important that it seems best at this point to let contemporary logicians speak for themselves. I shall confine myself largely to the writings of Mr. Adler the dialectician and M. Couturat and Professor Lewis the mathematical logicians, but the difficulties to which I shall point are by no means peculiar to their systems. As a matter of fact, these individuals seem to be more acutely aware of the difficulties than most of their coworkers.

(1) Mathematically ordered logics can offer no logical account of the manner in which their primitives are obtained; in fact, a whole realm of human activity is placed outside the pale of logic. The two passages quoted below are in substantial agreement, although they make somewhat different points. Mr. Adler says: [6]

Synthesis . . . is a process of finding the system capable of demonstrating the proposition, the doctrine and the theorems which the given isolated proposition presupposes, and by which it is implied. But this act of finding, this act of synthesis, is not a logical act in the strict sense, for it is only after the system of propositions of which the original proposition is a member has been found that relationships of implication can be exhibited or actualized. Following implications and employing presuppositions are in this important respect utterly dissimilar. The act of synthesis requires the exercise of intellectual imagination, an act of insight rather than an act of logical analysis. The difference between analysis and synthesis is the familiar difference between detecting the postulates of a system, and deducing the theorems of a system from the postulates; there is no rule for the former process; the latter is guided by the rules of implication and demonstration.

From this quotations we see that synthesis — Mr. Adler's name for the act of finding a postulate set — is placed outside the boundaries of logic. Postulate sets must be found if we are to have mathematically ordered

[5] Mathematically ordered systems may, of course, be useful for other methodological purposes than that here being considered.

[6] Mortimer J. Adler, *Dialectic,* New York, Harvourt, Brace, 1927, p. 161.

logics; but these logics do not state the logical operations necessary to obtain them. Indeed, it is stated that these operations fall outside of logic. Upon the same basis it is not difficult to see that following implications ("analysis") demands insight — not all of us do it so easily or so well — and therefore also should have no place in logic. Do we not find in contemporary views of the relation between postulates and the theorems they imply a lively ghost of the old notion of cause? It used to be said that one can reason from causes to their effects, but not *vice versa;* today it is said that postulates imply ("generate") their theorems, but are not implied by them. This, of course, is a consequence of a linear view of the logical situation.

M. Couturat points to another difficulty; for mathematically ordered logics any one of a number of postulate sets is often equally satisfactory. He says: [7]

For any given deductive theory there is not *any one* system of fundamental notions nor *any one* system of fundamental propositions; there are generally several equally possible, i.e., from which it is equally possible to deduce correctly all the theorems. The two systems, of course, depend on one another, and if we change the fundamental notions, or even one of them, we shall be obliged to change the axioms, for these are relative to the notions. Hence the choice of this double system is not arbitrary but to a certain extent free and optional; from the logical point of view it is a matter of indifference, and if one system appears preferable to another it is either on account of reasons of convenience and facility or for quasi-aesthetic reasons of order.

The dualism involved in this position is incurable within the limits of the effort to display data in the mathematical order. The applicability of logic to a certain field of data is definitely abandoned. The discovery of postulate sets, and the choice between competing sets equally satisfactory from the deductive point of view, is held to be governed by extra-logical considerations. And logic is in the uncomfortable position of standing in an indeterminable relation to these nonlogical factors in the thinking situation.

(2) If the primitives of a mathematical system are what they are asserted to be, the theorems they imply have no meaning, since they are the verbal echoes of the postulates and the postulates themselves are devoid

[7] Louis Couturat, The principles of logic; in *Encyclopaedia of the Philosophical Sciences*, Vol. I, *Logic*, London, Macmillian, 1913, p. 186.

of meaning. This fact is somewhat obscured because the professions of deductive logicians differ widely from their actual practices. Deductive systems are supposed to be based on undefined terms and undemonstrated propositions, and on nothing else; but as these primitives are presented they are always embedded in symbolic settings the meanings of which are taken for granted, although these meanings are themselves external to the systems in question. No one has gone further than Professor C. I. Lewis in the effort to develop a " mathematics without meaning " — a mathematics " dealing, not with certain denoted things — numbers, tri-angles, etc. — nor with certain symbolized ' concepts ' or ' meanings,' but solely with recognizable marks, and dealing with them in such wise that it is wholly independent of any question as to what the marks represent." [8] Yet Professor Lewis is at pains to point out that the principles according to which these " strings of marks " are to be manipulated are themselves extra-logical. These principles are given, not in meaningless conventional signs, but in literary form. No one has as yet succeeded in presenting the primitives of a mathematical system without the help of (non-mathe-matical) literary devices. These primitives cannot be so rendered that they will of themselves be declarative; their logical status depends upon their standing in certain relationships, literary or otherwise, not provided for by the principles of mathematical ordering.[9]

If the point I am making is not entirely obvious, it is probably because we are not yet accustomed to thinking in terms of an indefinite number of equally satisfactory logical procedures. A group of expressions com-posed merely of meaningless primitives, such as $(p < q)$, $(q < r)$, $(p < q)$ $(q > r) < (p < r)$, have by themselves no logical force. They secure logical force only when they are embedded in one or more of an indefi-nitely large number of meaning-matrices. Not even, for example, if p, q, and r are " propositions " and if $<$ means " implies," does the last expres-sion mean "*If p implies q, and q implies r, then p implies r.*" The *if, and,*

---

[8] Lewis, p. 355. See the whole section entitled " A heterodox view of the nature of mathematics and of logistic," pp. 354–362.

[9] It is important to note that the meaning these symbols must have external to the deductive order is logical meaning. Whether they must also possess psychological meaning, or meaning of still some other variety, or whether, indeed, there is any such thing as psycho-logical meaning, or whether there is any other kind of meaning, are questions not pertinent to this paper. Nor am I discussing whether a set of marks could ever be experienced in such a manner as to be completely devoid of logical significance. I am here considering only the *logical* prerequisites of mathematical reasoning.

and *then* form part of the expression only in terms of a certain fund of meanings not appearing in the statements themselves. And, of course, the fact that *p, q,* and *r* are here to be " propositions " and that < here is to mean " implies " does not define the logical existence of these terms, unless these words themselves figure in more precise logical settings than the terms to which they have been attached. Mathematical logicians when confronted with this difficulty are likely to reply that the terms they use may be taken to mean anything at all, provided the meanings assigned to them are consistent with the relations exhibited. From such a statement, however, we see at once that the relations exhibited are themselves supposed to be unambiguous, and that the notion of " consistency " itself is also supposed to be, not a logical primitive but a term capable of only a single meaning. In making these assumptions, therefore, mathematical logicians violate their own canons of the nature of a mathematical system. In addition they ignore the empirical existence of a multiplicity of logical systems resting on different definitions of consistency.

It is possible to view the undefined terms and undemonstrated propositions of contemporary logic as lingering remnants of Descartes' clear and distinct ideas, and to interpret the difficulties here being considered as due to an important shift that makes the transition from mediaeval to modern philosophy. Descartes' clear and distinct ideas are intuitions, not (modern) concepts or definitions. That is to say, they exist objectively in the mind and subjectively in nature, and not *vice versa.* They exist objectively in the mind in the same unequivocal fashion, e.g., that the word " cow " exists in the sentence, *the cow jumped over the moon.* Whatever interpretation we offer for this sentence, it must be such that *cow* exists objectively in the sentence. Clear and distinct ideas also exist in nature as subject-matter, i.e., as possible materials for intellectual consideration. They do not exist subjectively in the mind, as more or less esoteric aspects of its being; and they do not exist objectively in nature, as things that knowledge hopes to reach. They are not the hypothesized termini of knowledge but its materials.

The primitives of contemporary mathematically ordered logics are hardly even subjective in the modern sense. They are almost entirely literary, things dependent on print and books. It seems very doubtful whether anyone ever actually thinks them, whether in the Cartesian " objective " or in the modern " subjective " sense. At best the logician probably thinks something else which, by an extra-logical process of interpretation, bears a more or less remote resemblance to the absolutely content-less logical primitives. Thus mathematically ordered systems are not only developed, but they are also interpreted in an external setting. This situation is partially revealed in the following quotation from Mr. Bertrand Russell.[10]

It frequently happens that we have a deductive mathematical system, starting from hypotheses concerning undefined objects, and that we have reason to believe that there are objects fulfilling these hypotheses, although, initially, we are unable to point out any such objects with certainty. Usually, in such cases, although many different sets of objects are abstractly available as fulfilling the hypotheses, there is one such set which is much more important than the others.

The reasons we have for believing that objects fulfill the conditions established by the postulate set lie outside the range of deductive logic. Two additional remarks are pertinent. The above statement assumes that we are already in possession of postulate sets; but it does not tell us how we are to obtain them. In the second place, the " importance " of one or another set of objects held to be capable of fulfilling the postulate conditions is a matter of no importance to mathematical logic.

At the various points that have been mentioned, then, mathematically ordered systems of thought exhibit their lack of autonomy. Nor is this all. The great emphasis laid upon proof in these systems is also extra-logical. In the strict sense logics never prove; they exhibit compatibility. In this sense they are precisely like works of art. In a satisfactory art object materials, techniques, and purposes are focused to form a functional unit. The completed work seems to justify everything that went into its making. At whatever point it be approached psychical energies are intensified and given materials to discharge themselves upon. As a consequence strong emotions are aroused and sublimated — that is to say, they secure a distanced expression in a locus furnished by the art object, rather than a more personal expression in terms of conditions pertinent only to the appreciator. This, no doubt, is the artistic catharsis.[11] In

[10] Bertrand Russell, The Analysis of Matter, New York, Harcourt, Brace, 1927, pp. 4–5.

[11] I have written at some length on this topic in Chapter 16 of a previous work entitled Man and Civilization, New York, Harcourt, Brace, 1927. The concept of psychical distance is expounded in an article by Edward Bullough in the Brit. Journ. of Psych., Vol. V (1912), pp. 87–118.

such a situation the prevailing feeling is one of beauty, and there is little or no question of proof. Precisely the same analysis applies to systems of thought. When they are understood, we begin to see that their parts hang together and tend to exhibit a totality. It is possible to go from one place to another in the system in just the same sense that one can move about in a work of art. There is mutual dependence rather than the type of linear dependence implied in proof.

The overemphasis on proof in mathematically ordered systems is, I think, a concession to psychology and pedagogy. It is a testimony to the strength of the very human demand for certainty, and an evidence of our very modest powers of learning. On the one hand, faith must be fed and doubt exorcised, and on the other, the complexities of life situations must be accommodated to the needs of education.

In brief, then, modern logics developed in accordance with the ideal of mathematical order necessarily contain within themselves a diversity of materials that have not been given a logical rendering. The premises of such systems are logically arbitrary in a double sense — we are not told how this particular set was obtained, nor are we told why it was preferred to other equally satisfactory sets; the meanings assigned to the theorems are logically arbitrary; and the emphasis placed upon proof is a logical irrelevance. In particular, hypothesis (i.e., postulation) figures in contemporary logical systems in an undisciplined fashion. There is urgent need of a method for postulation, as is shown by the inanity of existing criteria of a good hypothesis. It is usually stated that hypotheses must be simple, must explain all the facts, must lead to new knowledge, must be capable of verification, etc. These criteria will not help us to find hypotheses, and they are all but completely useless in helping us to test the hypotheses we somehow obtain. They fit very inadequately scientific hypotheses whose functioning power is great. What is logical simplicity? What types of explanation shall we admit — theological, superstitious, practical, for example? Who knows what a fact is, apart from a theory to give it a setting — or what a theory is, apart from the facts it " explains " ? What kinds of new knowledge are we willing to accept? Was a hypothesis ever framed that did not tell us something? What is verification, in and of itself? These are but a few of the questions that might be raised to show the precarious position of hypothesis in contemporary logical thinking.

Nor are the criteria of a good postulate set as they are stated by mathematical logicians more illuminating. They are usually named, as for example by Professor Young,[12] as consistency, independence, and categoricalness. But these tests take one outside of mathematical logic. A postulate set is consistent if there exists a concrete interpretation that satisfies it; postulate k is independent if we can find " one concrete representation for which all the assumptions, except No. k, are satisfied and for which No. k is not true "; a postulate set is categorical if there exists but one concrete interpretation that satisfies it. Of these criteria only the first is named as absolutely essential, and, like the others, it takes us outside of the logic. It is clear, then, that postulation has not been rendered logically responsible.

If this were a historical paper it would now be appropriate to show at some length that Francis Bacon was keenly aware of the logical shortcomings of hypothesis, and that one of the chief aims of his philosophical thinking was the development of a method for the restraint and direction of man's postulatory energies. This is his statement of the case in the " Prooemium " to *The Great Instauration:* [13]

The primary notions of things which the mind readily and passively imbibes, stores up and accumulates (and it is from them that all the rest flow) are false, confused, and overhastily abstracted from the facts; nor are the secondary and subsequent notions less arbitrary and inconstant; whence it follows that the entire fabric of human reason which we employ in the inquisition of nature is badly put together and built up, and like some magnificent structure without any foundation. For while men are occupied in admiring and applauding the false powers of the mind, they pass by and throw away those true powers which, if it be supplied with the proper aids and can itself be content to wait upon nature instead of vainly affecting to overrule her, are within its reach. There was but one course left, therefore, — to try the whole thing anew upon a better plan, and to commence a total reconstruction of sciences, arts, and all human knowledge, raised upon the proper foundations. . . . Certainly the two ways of contemplation are much alike in this — that the one, arduous and difficult in the beginning, leads out at last into the open country; while the other, seeming at first sight easy and free from obstruction, leads to pathless and precipitous places.

[12] J. W. Young, *Lectures on the Fundamental Concepts of Algebra and Geometry,* New York, Macmillan, 1911, pp. 43–57. Cf. Couturat, pp. 187–188.

[13] Quoted from J. M. Robertson's edition of *The Philosophical Works of Francis Bacon,* London, Routledge, 1905, p. 241.

A little later (p. 246) he states that his aim is to establish "a true and lawful marriage between the empirical and the rational faculty, the unkind and ill-starred divorce and separation of which has thrown into confusion all the affairs of the human family." In *Valerius terminus* he says that forms are to be discovered through "the freeing of a direction" — i.e., through the purification and control of the processes by which hypotheses are engendered and put to use. Bacon's thought has been grievously misunderstood for at least two reasons: (1) No effort has been made to see it in the setting in which it arose. The most important affiliations of his doctrine of forms, for example, are with the Aristotelian doctrine of formal causes, rather than with the modern doctrine of scientific law. (2) He is looked upon as a thinker who failed to understand the basic features of modern science. On the contrary, he was vividly aware of the place of both mathematics and experiment in science, and of the logical shortcomings of these enterprises. His experimental cautions are now commonplaces; and he was keen enough to foresee the difficulties that contemporary mathematical logicians are now being forced to face. The serious study of his writings in the terms which they themselves suggest, rather than with reference to the manner in which they succeed or fail to accord with the development of modern science, should prove extremely fruitful for the clarification of contemporary logical problems.

IV

It is now in order to exhibit in another than the deductive manner what I mean by a system of thought. I shall begin by discussing the meaning to be assigned to the term "fact." This term as I shall use it is intended to possess its familiar colloquial denotation. It is not in any sense to be taken as a logical primitive. After it has served its purpose in the discussion that follows, it will be replaced by other terms of great descriptive power. Nor will these other terms be primitives; they will be more like mathematical functions.

That I must begin my exposition at a certain place is to me a literary matter. It is a feature of literary exposition that words follow one another in linear order. The things I am talking about, however, are to be regarded as logically co-present. The order of my remarks, in other words, is not so important as what I am saying. It is worth noting that I am not here declaring myself with respect to the presence, absence, or irrelevance of time to logical systems. The logical co-presence of which I speak can sometimes be exhibited — as, for example, in painting or in the moment of insight — without regard to the flow of time. In literature and in music perhaps it cannot. The general status of time in logic is identical with the general status of any other item. It figures in logic " if, when, and as issued."

My main point will be that the simplest possible logical locus of a " fact " relates it to at least two systems of thought. A " fact " at best stands in a double logical setting. It is an item appearing in one system and taken over for use in another system. For an item to be a " fact," it must be both established and relevant. These are both systemic require-ments, but they point in different directions, the one backward to a system which gives the fact weight, the other forward to a system which puts it to use. Any item under appropriate conditions can take on this status, since everything can be questioned with respect to its logical foundations, and anything can be argued from.

I am not saying merely that the facts we find depend upon the theories we have. The dependence exists, though it is no doubt mutual. I am indicating the mediatory position of " facts " in logical systems. The whence, the whither, and the what reciprocally define each other. In the mathematical sense of the term, they are functions of each other. An absolutely isolated " fact " would be completely elusive. It would not even be meaningless, since " lack of meaning " itself presupposes an ex-tremely complicated systemic setting to give it whatever logical values it may possess. The following passage, describing how military operations are sometimes interpreted in the interests of nationalism, will illustrate the point: [14]

If facts are hurriedly issued, fresh from the mint of battle, they cannot be expected to supply an account which is either well-balanced or exhaustive. On the other hand, it is equally certain that, when once the fight has been fairly lost or won, it is the tendency of all ranks to combine and recast the story of their achievement into a shape which shall satisfy the susceptibilities of national and regimental vainglory. It is then already too late for the pains-taking historian to set to work. He may record the orders given and the

[14] Ian Hamilton, *A Staff Officer's Scrap-book during the Russo-Japanese War* (5th impr., London, 1907, I, v. Quoted from F. J. Teggart, *Prolegomena to History, Univ. of Cal. Publ. in Hist.*, Vol. IV (1916–17), p. 187.

movements which ensued, and he may build up thereon any ingenious theories which occur to him; but to the hopes and fears which dictated those orders, and to the spirit and method in which those movements were executed, he has forever lost the clue. On the actual day of battle naked truths may be picked up for the asking; by the following morning they have already begun to get into their uniforms.

Of course, the " naked truths " referred to in the quotation would themselves be clothed systemically, though this clothing might not be a nationalistic " uniform." We are none of us privileged after the manner of the somewhat paradoxical Aristotelian in Butler's *Hudibras* who " had first matter seen undress'd, before one rag of form was on."

The whence, the whither, and the what spoken of above are all to be conceived logically. The whence in this setting is not necessarily the genetic origin; it is the system from which the " fact " is taken. The whither is not necessarily the finalistic purpose; it is the system in which the " fact " is used. And the what is not necessarily the metaphysically true or real; whatness consists in fulfilling a certain logical function at the meeting point of two or more systems. An item is found by getting something to point to it; we know about it by considering what it points to; and it is appreciated or understood by its being experienced in this mediatory position, as being both pointed at and pointing.

Systems of thought tend towards formal circularity. In this respect they can be compared to the layout of a geographical region. A completely exhibited system would present the aspect of a field or universe of completely related constituents. The formal specifications of the system would be such that one might move from any point in the system to any other point. We might have to pass through intermediate positions to get from some places to certain others, but the lines of passage would not necessarily be unidirectional, nor would we have to start at any particular place in the system in order to be able to move about in it at all. This fact about systems is hidden when the deductive order or presentation is looked upon as a logical norm. It is worth noting, therefore, that some mathematical logicians, as, for example, Couturat, are aware of the alterations and distortions that are introduced whenever systems are rendered in the mathematical order: [15]

[15] Couturat, pp. 186–7. The dualism that Couturat takes for granted has already been noted above.

The deductive order, according to which this proposition is an axiom and that a theorem, is something subjective which depends on our methods and our procedure, on our preference and our convenience, and which seems almost an illustration of the infirmity of the human mind. One is tempted to believe that a more powerful mind would see intuitively the simultaneous truth of the entire theory, without distinguishing axioms and theorems, principles and consequences, merely by recognizing the reciprocal interlacement of all the propositions. It seems as though the objective and whole truth had the form of a vicious circle, or of a complex net which has no end and in which everything mutually implies everything else. It is our discursive reason which, imposing on partial truths a linear and successive concatenation, breaks the circle or the net and imposes upon them, more or less arbitrarily, a beginning or a point of departure.

The same point is put a little more briefly, and without some of the assumptions unnecessarily introduced by Couturat, in Weiss's definition of a logic as " a set of formal tautologies, capable of systematization through the use of no other symbolic principles than those which it itself asserts." [16]

As things go, however, the development of systems is always more or less incomplete. Not all of the " facts " that might have been used are actually employed in any given case, nor are the " facts " that actually figure in the system pressed to yield an absolute maximum of fruitage. " Facts " that are logically necessary for the development of a system are often unknown or even unavailable. The door is probably always left open for further logical activity, even within the confines of a single logical system.

In addition systems necessarily contain elements of novelty as respects each other. The logical demands laid upon an item when it is taken over to be used in the construction of a system are seldom if ever the exact logical conditions that led to its appearing as a product in the course of the development of another system. It is present in the new country as a stranger trying to make himself feel at home. Its allegiance is, as it were, divided; and it is this conflict of loyalties that provides the element of novelty in systems of thought. In even the simplest possible situation a " fact " is logically obligated in many different directions. For it to maintain its status it must not deny or be denied by anything in any of the systems in which it figures, and it must both assert and be asserted by

[16] See the summary of a paper entitled " Alternative Systems of Logic " in the *Journ. of Philos.*, Vol. XXVI (1929), p. 129.

everything in these systems. Standing in this mediatory position, the life of a " fact " is not an easy one. It is subject to strong systemic stresses in even the simplest situations. It has no non-systemic norm to correspond to; and it is expected to be coherent with a number of different systemic settings. In the light of their intersystemic position, " facts " might well be defined as " loci of systemic stresses."

In the preceding discussion a " fact " was described as an " item appearing in one system and taken over for use in another system." But the analysis has made it clear that items do not remain unchanged when thus transplanted, since systems of thought are novel as respects each other. In what sense, then, can an item in one system of thought be regarded as similar to an item in another system? The various items of a single system are, of course, logically similar. This is involved in the tendency of systems towards tautology. But were a system to become completely tautologous it would thereby become irrelevant to all other systems. It would lack orientation and be incurably itself. It is in the " fact " situation that systems take logical cognizance of each other, and so it is there that we must look for intersystemic similarity. The conditions of similarity can be stated logically in terms of formulae of translation.[17] Let xRy be a relationship set up by a given system, and let T be a formula of translation.[18] When T is applied as operator to x we get z; and when it is applied to y we get w. Then z and w are similar to x and y respectively; and the relation Q between z and w (if there be such — and there will be if these terms belong to a system) is analogous to the relation R.

Formulae of translation are generally provided by systems whose change rates are low with respect to the systems they are used to translate. Translation systems can, of course, be arbitrarily developed, but those most frequently employed are expressive of the major social institutions of a period, in terms of which nearly all the activities of the group are interpreted. Among the most stable of these systems are those provided by language. Words usually long outlast their meanings. In fact, the mere statement of a position to some extent stiffens and formalizes it. " The

---

[17] Cf. Bertrand Russell, *Introduction to Mathematical Philosophy*, 2nd ed., London, Allen and Unwin, 1920, pp. 53–54.

[18] T will itself be systematically exhibitable; but our explanation is concerned, not with the system of which it forms a part, but with the system it generates when applied to xRy. The reason for its being taken as operator is that it has the power to generate this other system.

letter killeth, but the spirit giveth life." This is the reason why innovations are seldom as revolutionary as at first sight they appear to be. Until they can make a language of their own, they must clothe themselves in the old terms and make more or less vain efforts to force these terms to the new uses.

An illustration will sum up the points that have been made. In the body of historical tradition shared by ourselves and the Arabs, there stands at a certain place (variously named by the two traditions) a series of events that we shall call " the threatened invasion of western Europe by the Arabs in the early eighth century." These events culminated in the retreat of the Arabs back into Spain after the Battle of Tours in 732 A.D. In most standard European histories this repulse of the Mohammedan forces is regarded as a fortunate escape for Europe. But here is how the same series of events is understood by an Arab historian: [19]

Standing on the Pyrenees, the dauntless Viceroy conceived the project of conquering the whole of Europe. . . . The cautious and hesitating policy of the Damascene Court lost the glorious opportunity, with the consequence that Europe remained enveloped in intellectual darkness for the next eight centuries.

The logical situation here may be stated as follows. The data of the historical tradition, itself a highly organized logical system, are taken as " facts " in two very different systemic settings, provided respectively by the western European Christian and the Mohammedan culture systems. These systems act as translators of the historical data, so that in the one setting the run of events figures all but tautologously as a God-send, while in the other it figures all but tautologously as a misfortune. The two interpretations are each of them similar to the events of the historical tradition because they are derived from it by processes of translation. They are novel as respects each other because they figure in different logical settings. The situation is complicated somewhat further by the fact that the Mohammedan historian very clearly has assimilated certain elements of the western European tradition as it prevailed when he was writing. For instance, he regards the whole period up to about 1500 as a period of intellectual darkness; and he speaks of " Europe " as remaining in this intellectual darkness when more properly he might have spoken

[19] Ameer Ali, *A Short History of the Saracens,* London, 1899, p. 111; quoted from F. J. Teggart, *Theory of History,* Yale Univ. Press, 1927, p. 40.

of "western Europe." If the period preceding the Renaissance was a period of intellectual darkness, it lasted much beyond 1500 for eastern and northern Europe. Finally, he assumes in the Viceroy his own knowledge of the map of Europe, since it is asserted that he formed the plan of conquering that continent upon his having won his way to the crest of the Pyrenees.

V

It is now time to provide a set of terms to fit the analyses that have been offered. The logical situation, then, is one in which instruments act upon materials in such a way as to yield products. The materials, the instruments, and the products are functions, in the sense that they reciprocally depend on each other. The relation of materials, instruments, and products, in other words, is formally tautologous. The products are of two types, finished goods and surds. The surds are logically generated by the system, but are not logically renderable by it. They are the occasion for new logical activity, which, if successful, renders them as products, while leaving yet other items (perhaps the items previously rendered) in the status of surds. Thus surds represent the incompleteness of logical systems, but they represent that incompleteness not metaphysically but logically. They are logically generated, and they are the occasion of new logical analyses. It is their presence that provides the intrusive element of novelty in logical systems.

INDIVIDUALISM AND AMERICAN LIFE

JAMES H. TUFTS

I

IT is more or less commonly assumed that the outstanding and even the essential characteristic of American life is Individualism. Since the Great War with its extraordinary experiments in collective and unified control of our productive system the pendulum has swung towards individualistic policies. "Less government in business, more business in government" has been a popular slogan. The War showed what could be done, even though several millions of the most vigorous men were withdrawn from our productive forces, when the great aim was to produce rather than to make a profit, but the War also opened vistas of more magnificent possibilities in business enterprise. And undoubtedly war sets a pace too stiff to be easily maintained in time of peace.

Moreover, after a temporary pause, general prosperity seemed to prevail and attain unexampled heights — except, of course, among the farmers. The climax of success seems to have been reached when millions have been added to bank accounts by shrewd speculation without the necessity of any productive industry. Prosperity has apparently set its seal upon the policy of non-interference with the individual, particularly upon the unchecked expansion of the profit motive.

The courts have to some degree appeared to sympathize with this return to individualism: After reaching a maximum of control in the Oregon case limiting the working day for women, and in the Oklahoma case upholding the state in requiring banks to guarantee mutually their deposits, the Federal Supreme Court refused its sanction to a law restricting child labor in the District of Columbia, to the Kansas Industrial Court Act, and recently to a statute of Tennessee declaring the trade in petroleum to be affected with a public interest.

Legislative bodies have shown a similar trend. Few state legislatures have approved the proposed Child Labor amendment; the railroads have been returned to private management; a resentment against any social control which might threaten a check to prosperity has been frequently in evidence. The eighteenth amendment may seem to be an exception, but the opposition to its enforcement voiced by many who cannot be suspected of merely selfish interest is at least in part indicative of impatience with any restriction by government upon the freedom of the individual, no matter what the consequences for social welfare.

Recently individualism has received more distinguished sponsorship than that of academic authority. Mr. Hoover, when Secretary of Commerce, gave the sanction of his great name and prestige to which he called American Individualism. As a candidate for the presidency he re-asserted his faith, and his election may seem to imply the acceptance of this doctrine by a large majority of the American people. It is, however, important in the interest of clear thinking to discover just what qualification of individualism is covered by the adjective " American." It may be that the magic of the phrase owes more to the association of the term " American " — standing as it does for a sum of patriotic, religious, and moral institutions, for the adventurous spirit of the pioneer, and the restless creative genius of the inventor, and indeed for a large share in those ties of kin, of place, of tradition, of familiar environment without which life is meager and for ordinary folk scarcely conceivable — than to any very intelligent conviction as to the merits of individualism. Moreover, Mr. Hoover's exposition of the content of individualism seems to include two distinct meanings. On the one hand, self-interest as motive and free competition as social process for selection are approved; on the other hand, the great propelling force of progress is found in " right ideals " by whose growth " through education the selfish impulses become less and less dominant," and of the " impulses which carry us forward none is so potent for progress as the yearning for individual self-expression, the desire for the creation of something." Of these two meanings the first is obviously the historic meaning of individualism. The second is in part an ideal of social as *versus* selfish nature, and in part the creative spirit — scientific, inventive, or artistic, the " instinct for workmanship," which is ordinarily included under " individuality," but has no necessary relation either to self-interest or to the opposite. We get additional light upon the importance of the adjective " American " when we see that Mr. Hoover contrasts the social system of his choice with " old world individualism " (autocracy), with a system of fixed hereditary classes, and with bureaucracy. He refuses to identify individualism with capitalism although economists tell us that the United States is the most capitalistic country in the world. His dislike of anything savoring of socialism is a logical consequence of his attachment to individualism in the first or historic sense of the term.

The ambiguities thus involved in Mr. Hoover's conception of the actual and the ideal social system and its motivation suggest the two divisions of this paper.

(*a*) How far and in what respects is the American social system properly termed individualism?

(*b*) Is the greatest need at present to protect and strengthen the individualistic motive of self-interest or on the other hand to encourage the constructive, scientific interest, and the agencies of social solidarity?

(1) In its economic phase it may be freely admitted that American life is individualistic to a great though by no means exclusive extent. The essential character of individualism, so far as its motivation is concerned, is to center regard in those interests which are exclusive as contrasted with those that are shareable or social. Material goods as objects of desire or considered as property, are fundamentally exclusive. Acquisitiveness is undoubtedly an active factor in American business life. True, as Justice Holmes points out, the man of great wealth cannot consume more than a fraction of what he owns but the title is his; and to a great extent the power to decide whether goods shall be consumed and how. Economic power is at present largely autocratic. Its taxing power, exercised through price and wage, is seemingly less coercive, but really more omnipresent than that of government.[1] And in so far as it is gained and administered under the profit motive economic power is individualistic. It may or may not be so exercised as to benefit consumers and workmen. But this is as such irrelevant. As Professor Mitchell puts it: " It is no fault of the individual business leaders that they take profits as their own guide. On the contrary they are compelled to do so, for the men who mix too much philanthropy with business soon cease to be leaders." The theory has been that ultimate power rests with the consumer, and that the competition of the market selects as leaders the ablest and those who best supply wants. In some cases this is largely true, but supply of wants need

---

[1] The price of coal since the war is a good example. Every user who pays the doubled price has found the pressure as actual as if administered by the sheriff.

not enter into the motives of the " leader." He need only consider profits, and these will sometimes be greatest by making what men need and sometimes by judicious sabotage with a corresponding scarcity price. In the frenzied stock speculation of the past year which a high financial authority has characterized as " incomparably the most gigantic gamble of history," the speculator is obviously guided by the profit motive. No question of contributing to social welfare, or of rendering any equivalent for value received need enter into the process. The motive of something for nothing is thoroughly individualistic, for it aims at adding to the possessions of the individual without requiring any expenditure of possessions or labor.

But while profit serves as a vigorous incentive to business and as a necessary condition if business is to remain solvent, it is far from being the sole actual incentive. Three other motives are active: first, the desire to make a fair return in some form — labor, ideas, useful material things, money — for what is gained or received; second, the adventurous spirit of the inventor and enterpriser, the instinct of workmanship; and third, the sporting interest of rivalry which in the opinion of William James is the principal incentive for getting the hard and disagreeable work of the world done. Of these three, the first — the desire to deal justly — is distinctly social; the second — the scientific or inventive, craftsmanship spirit — is an objective, " disinterested " motive to achievement, and as such is neither social nor individualistic; the third is mixed, for in so far as it is a desire to win it is individualistic, in so far as it is a desire to win by fair means against an equal opponent it presupposes either a voluntary contest in which both parties share in the agreeable stimulation of the match as in sports and games, or a respect for a fellow being which makes the victor reluctant to press a brave rival too far. In other words it is what Veblen is fond of calling the attitude of Live and Let-live. We wish to examine these three non-individualistic motives briefly.

As regards the desire to deal justly, to give a fair return, it is doubtless possible to give this a turn by which just dealing is practised as a means to greater self-interest. " Honesty is the best policy " is a maxim which reflects such a view. Accounts by economists of the principle of exchange of commodities and services are likely to run in this form: If you want something which another man has, you must either get it by force as under militarism and slavery, or by his consent, as in voluntary exchange.

And to gain his consent you must offer what he considers a satisfactory equivalent. It cannot be questioned that this is the theory of much of the bargaining or higgling of the market. It could be stretched to justify unconscionable exploitation of native tribes provided their " consent " was secured to the exchange of furs or lands or gold for glass beads or whiskey. And in modern business it may be said to have found an enlarged sphere in the strategy of " overcoming sales-resistance " where the salesman aims, not so much at winning consent, as at the more fundamental task of creating desire. But it is needlessly damnatory of human nature, and in particular of American business and industry, to assume that this theory exhausts the meaning of dealing justly. What the law recognizes under the terms " reasonable " or " equitable," what was included under " honorable," and later became the ethical standard of many bankers, merchants, and manufacturers, not merely excludes fraud, but forbids taking advantage of the ignorance of the other party; it implies a fair equivalent — fair in the estimation of a reasonable, disinterested third party; it implies under " honorable dealing " the equality which holds in a group of mutual confidence and good will rather than the cautious suspicion of the primitive trader who must be ever alert and on the defensive.

Industry is in its essence more naturally governed by the theory of a fair equivalent than is business. The craftsman makes something. His labor and skill are real and the product is a visible, tangible thing, whereas in business honesty and fairness are less easily tested and departures into the different scheme of speculative values are less subject to any criterion except that of the market. The " double standard " which the working man resents is that whereas he is expected to give a full equivalent for his wage, the man of business is esteemed shrewd in proportion as he makes large profits with a minimum expenditure of time and effort.

The adventurous, inventive scientific motive which has had a large place in American life is not individualistic except in that sense of the word in which it signifies the disposition to resent dictation and to seek a free field. It has no preference for that meaning of individualism which is identified with reliance upon self-interest. In fact a spirit of adventure, except on the part of chief executives, is likely to find the great business corporation as formidable as a bureaucracy. And the really great inventors, scientists, and creative minds are notoriously neglectful of self-interest.

The greatest scientist I have known has said that he has prosecuted his investigations " for fun," and an inventor-manufacturer of my acquaintance, when arranging for the gift to education of a large part of his fortune, remarked: " It was fun to make it, but I don't want the bother of it." The scientist wants a comfortable livelihood; the inventor wants means to develop his ideas and place his products before the public, but this is a different matter from making self-interest the chief motive.

Resentment of dictation is undoubtedly a strong force in American life. It had a large place in the restless frontier. It survives in the farmer. It is strong in many captains of industry who resist all government interference except that of a protective tariff. But the sweeping change in American life by which, instead of a nation of self-sufficient, independent farmers, each his own master, we have become a people in which at least two-thirds work for other men or corporations and are therefore in Aristotle's classifications of those who are directed by others, has scarcely favored this aspect of individualism. Indeed those familiar with the labor movement know that it is far from being solely a matter of wages and hours. The laborer of independent spirit resents the military discipline of the factory in which all orders issue from management, and no initiative or participation in determining conditions of work on the part of the employee is welcomed. Against this trend of " individualistically " conducted industry union has appeared to be the only defence. In union organization, standardizing labor conditions, setting a more democratically chosen control over against employer control, though often requiring a sacrifice of individual advantage in the common interest, is found at least a measure of what Mr. Sidney Hillman has called " citizenship in industry." The tendency on the part of some to emphasize the free field for the selection of leaders is liable to pass over the case of the rank and file.

As regards the final aspect of business mentioned above, viz., that of rivalry, motives are mixed. There is a well-known difference between cut-throat competition and fair competition. In the first the motive of individual self-interest is unchecked by any scruples. If scruples arise as to the ethics of ruining the competitor or taking his job, they are met by the comforting doctrine of survival of the fittest, nature's method of selecting leaders. In fair competition the motive of self-interest is held in restraint, subject to a regard for the competitor as a fellow human being and to rules of fair play which have come to formulation in the first instance usually as the decent or becoming behavior towards members of the same group and then have become broadened to such ethical principles as the golden rule, and to such legal doctrines as those relating to " unfair competition." It was not under the influence of self-interest that these conceptions gained recognition; it was through the legal or judicial premise of the public good, or the moral principle of Live and Let-live, or the sporting principle of fair play among fellows — all social as distinguished from self-interest and individualism.

I conclude this brief survey of motives in business and industry with the summary: Business and industry are carried on from mixed motives of self-interest, of regard for fellow men and for the common weal, and of interest (neither self-interest nor social necessarily) in solving problems by constructive work, and in achievements.

(2) In its political and legal phases also American life combines individualistic with social and even with socialist doctrines. If our Declaration of Independence declares natural rights to be prior to governments our Constitution emphasizes not only common defence but justice and the general welfare. When we were a nation of farmers individualism was a natural policy of government, but the shift first to slavery as a great commercial system and later to a system of business and industry collective and corporate has compelled a shift in governmental policy. The individual as a person has made way for the impersonal corporation of limited liability and unlimited term of life. Men increasingly live in cities stratified into social groups by the rent they are able to pay. The advance of science has made possible not only governmental control of railroads, banks, and other public utilities, but positive aid in promoting agricultural welfare, in conserving natural resources, in the zoning of cities, in providing parks and playgrounds. Most revolutionary of all, and registering a well-nigh complete abandonment of earlier individualistic views of property was the addition of the Income Tax Amendment to the Federal Constitution which embodies at least one fundamental principle of socialist doctrine, " From each according to his ability." All labor legislation has been in restraint of individualism, and the courts, at least, have upheld the Eighteenth Amendment even though this exercise of police power has been resisted by individualists to the verge of nullification and anarchism. The Fourteenth Amendment has not enacted for the United States Herbert Spencer's *Social Statics*. It is at least probable that as business and industry

become more and more nation-wide and gigantic in corporate power and resources the American people will dare, not merely to control this power in the interest of the common weal, but themselves as a collective unit to do what cannot be safely entrusted to individual or corporate interest motived by profit.

(3) The religious consciousness of American life has shown a similar trend from a more individual to a more social point of view. Not that the earlier period was wholly concerned with saving individual souls. The Massachusetts colony was notably regarded by its members as a " Holy Commonwealth." The kingdom of God, the *civitas dei,* the hope of the ages, was here at last to be established. The state was ruled by the clergy as a soviet. Later the presence of increasing numbers in the community who were motivated by secular interest, added to the influence of religious individualists and of religious societies other than those which had sought to establish the commonwealth, brought about a change. The kingdom of God was again transferred to the other world. The elect, the converted, were here to prepare for heaven. The task of the clergy was to call to repentance. This was the typical conception during the eighteenth century and the early part of the nineteenth. But when slavery became a national problem the churches were forced to take account of a social institution. From that time the churches have never been without a social question. The temperance cause, the labor movement, municipal government, civic duties, social justice, the campaign against child labor — all these in turn have enlisted the sympathies and active philanthropic interest of the churches. The Friends, who were by tradition the most individualistic of all religious groups, were in the Great War foremost in succoring the unfortunate victims. Missionary policies have reflected the changed attitude and have been directed increasingly toward education, and improvement of social conditions. Despite contemptuous epithets from the " hard-boiled," the churches continue to make their voices felt for humane conditions of labor, for world peace, and for the supremacy of social welfare over individualistic attitudes in the use of alcoholic beverages. The churches represent a very real and vital expression of the American spirit. And what they stand for is not individualism.

(4) The same is true in even higher degree in the activities and point of view of what has come to be called " social work." Perhaps the distinctive characteristic of this work is that it combines in a high degree

the spirit of humane brotherhood which has been the inheritance of Christianity with scientific method of enquiry and experiment. Finding its beginnings in problems of voluntary charity on the one hand and of public provision for delinquents, defectives, sick, and insane on the other, the scope of enquiry and outlook has widened to embrace city planning, recreation, race adjustments, immigration, juvenile courts, and indeed the whole field of social relations.[2] Numbers professionally engaged in social work may be relatively few, but the influence of these leaders has been wide. The response of the public in its care of the sick and insane, of the blind and defective, in its provision for parks and playgrounds, in its factory and child labor legislation, and legislation for protection of women in industry, in the establishment of great foundations dedicated to the tasks of preventing disease and otherwise improving social conditions, has been as characteristic of American life as the great development of business and industry.

(5) But neither the spirit of the churches nor that of social work is so peculiarly American as the general interest in education. Amid the extreme inequalities in wealth, in social status, in power and opportunity, produced by our economic individualism here is at least an approach to that equality which is asserted by Mill to be the only school for true morality. If we have largely escaped the grim bitterness of soul, the sense of injustice in a land of plenty, and the hopeless sodden misery which are equally fatal to a good life and to a healthy society this is chiefly due to our system of public education. It seems probable that such an institution is the only means of making workable an economic system which produces extremes of inequality and a political system based on equal suffrage. For our educational system is not merely an agency for the selection of " leaders " through free competition. It is also an agency for giving the common man and woman and child a share in those goods of the mind which are our social inheritance. Those goods — a knowledge of the written word, of the world of nature and of man, of high thought, deep feeling, and noble deeds — are at least not wholly reserved for the few.

Equal opportunity, which Mr. Hoover esteems so highly as tempering the hardness of pure individualism, has had in our educational system much larger scope than in other fields of American institutions — even

---

[2] R. A. Woods, *The Settlement Horizon;* Jane Addams, *Twenty Years at Hull House;* J. H. Tufts, *Education and Training for Social Work.*

though it is painfully true that as the child moves on beyond the age of compulsory attendance he finds obstacles in the ignorance or poverty of his parents which too often close the door.

This great educational system, from the elementary grades to the advanced research of the universities is in its conception, its financial support, its personnel, its motivation, social. It is even socialistic rather than individualistic. As carried on by government it violates the canons of Mill and Spencer. It aims to include all children on an equal basis, and relies for support upon all members of the community. In its provision for different classes it exemplifies the maxim " To each according to his needs." It bases its claim upon the welfare of the community and the aim to give every child a fair chance. Teachers and scientists give their services with very little profit motive. As members of a profession they feel that they perform a function in the social process, and find their chief reward in the consciousness of making some contribution to the welfare and progress of society. In the case of the more originative minds in the profession the scientific and constructive motive plays an important rôle.

" The aim to give every child a fair chance " is, it may be said, only another aspect of individualism, and particularly of American individualism. For this means giving every individual his opportunity, equipping him to hold his own, encouraging him to develop his individualty. This, however, is not individualism in the sense of motivation by self-interest. There is a chasm here between each-for-himself and each-for-all, as impassible as the similar chasm in Bentham's Utilitarianism. Individualism of a liberal sort would not put a competitor out of the race, by fouling, or fraud, or violence, but it has never regarded it as a duty, to pay for the competitor's training, or to provide him with the best running shoes.

This brief discussion of American life and institutions may then be summarized in the statement: American business, industry, and government are mixed in their conceptions and motivation; they are in part individualistic as recognizing self-interest and private property, and in part non-individualistic as recognizing fairness, constructive interest, and the public good; American religious life, social work, and education are decidedly social in purpose and appeal. It is then inappropriate to choose individualism as an adequate term to characterize American life and institutions.

II

Is it desirable, even for the best interests of business, to stress at this time the appeal to self-interest?

The basis of shrinking from socialism — aside from the inappropriateness of a class war to American traditions — is perhaps due chiefly to two causes: (1) the desire by enterprising men of affairs that the fields for capitalistic exploitation of natural resources, of scientific discovery, of inventive genius, and of the concentration of great populations should remain open for private management, private profits, and private property rather than become the property of the commonwealth; (2) unwillingness to allow both economic power and political power to be concentrated in one authority and under one administration. Probably both these motives will continue to operate. The first has been given a longer lease by an increasing disposition on the part of some at least of the great organizations to distribute more widely the surplus profits either by higher wages or by reduced prices or by both. The prodigal wastes of natural resources, and of our distributing and selling systems, can be in part covered up, in part shifted to government or charity account, in part charged to economic reasons, or to interference by government with the economic free hand ("less government in business"). The force of this last plea in avoidance is strengthened by the circumstance that economic power exerted through price is impersonal and therefore seems less coercive than the personal political power exerted by legislatures, sheriffs, and courts, although for the great mass of the working people the economic control over wages and prices touches daily life at a dozen points where the legal and political power touches it at one. Taxation administered through process of rent or food is accepted as if proceeding from laws of an impersonal nature. Hence it seems not worth while to waste words upon warning the American people against state socialism.

But is there no evil in the economic motive of profit and self-interest? Mr. Hoover considers that there is danger, but also considers that this is met by public regulation and by the ideal of equal opportunity, which in American society qualifies individualism. I wish to suggest that even on economic grounds the profit motive in its extreme form of " something for nothing " is suicidal, and that the most needed line of emphasis at present is the scientific and constructive spirit on the one hand, the principle of fairness and an active interest in the common good on the other.

Lest any economic suggestion from an academic source should be regarded as " destructive criticism of minds too weak or too partisan to harbor constructive ideas " the " criticism " of individualism may be taken from one who can scarcely be accused of a " passion for ignorance of its constructive ideals." Mr. Roger Babson writes [3]

Prosperity cannot last forever in a country where the speculators are making most of the money while the producers of the necessities of life are barely making both ends meet. . . .

The weakest factor in the situation today is the growing belief that it is easier to make money in the stock market than at one's legitimate job.

Yet it is hard to see why, on the principles of individualism, each individual should not do what will yield him most profit. Of course, if one asks whether general and sound prosperity can be secured by gambling that is something else. That doubtless depends on producing and distributing useful goods. Efficiency in such production and distribution depends largely on scientific advance and on the human factor, especially the good will of labor. If these are fundamental why not aim at them directly? It is not a case of substituting " altruism " for self-interest. It is rather (1) recognizing and restoring to a normal place the scientific, constructive, or craft interest which is likely to be submerged in the race for profits, and (2) enlarging the range of vision to include not only the individual customers, capitalists, or laborers with whom one bargains or competes, but also society, and the community as a whole, in which there are functions to be performed, duties to be met, and larger ends to be achieved than the competitive process is likely to reckon with. American progress, it is commonly reputed, is due in largest degree to the substitution of machinery for manual labor, but inventors greater and lesser have been notoriously neglectful of pecuniary considerations in comparison with their absorption in working out the solution of a problem. To one who considers the extent to which a high sense of professional honor and public service has replaced the acquisitive motive in the field of government it does not seem incredible that a similar conception of business as a profession and economic power as a trust because " affected by a public interest " may become increasingly common. Mr. Owen D. Young believes that the shift in re-

[3] In *Collier's Weekly*, January 5, 1929.

sponsibility from stockholders to a management which regards itself a trustee to the institution, embracing the interests not only of owners, but of workmen and the public as well, is a forward move towards what is right in business.

If we turn from business to the larger ends of civilization, and ask what at the present time we need especially to guard and strengthen in the realm of motives, I should place first the promotion of good will between groups, classes, races, and nations. Individualism and the competitive spirit are scarcely adapted to secure this end. The Great War is still too near for us to forget that one factor in the complex situation of mutual fear, competition in armaments, and reaching out for markets and natural resources, was the individualistic motive of self-interest whether in its individual or in its national manifestation.

Even for family life, which perhaps ranks second only to international peace and good will, the path to good dwellings, to sanitation, hygiene, and protection against the risks of modern industrial society is likely to lie more and more through concerted action in which the state in its administrative functions does for individuals what they cannot well do for themselves. One instance may not prove a general proposition, but one instance made an indelible impression upon the mind of the writer. Traveling across England my eye was caught by a charming little village, with neat stone dwellings of attractive design. Enquiry brought the information that it was a mining village recently rebuilt by the government. I involuntarily compared it with the hideous, dreary, and forlorn mining dwellings which one sees from a train en route from New York to Chicago. In the one it was easy to imagine children growing up with love for home and community. In the other the only agreeable associations would seemingly attach to the public school.

Has not the time come when we may consider on their individual merits in each case methods for solution of the complex problems of a machine age, organized in huge and impersonal corporations, without presuming to settle the matter in advance by epithets of individualism and socialism?

LOOKING TO PHILOSOPHY

Matilde Castro Tufts

I

In an address before the Sixth International Congress of Philosophy, Professor Dewey pointed out that philosophy is a phenomenon of culture, and that the presence or absence of a native-born philosophy is a " severe test of the depth of unconscious tradition and rooted institution among any people, and of the productive force of their culture." For the conversion of this culture into consciousness is a further movement of civilization itself. The United States of America has not yet achieved a culture " which eventuates in an imaginative formulation of itself." Further, " a deliberate striving for an American philosophy as such would be only another evidence of the same emptiness or impotency."

Professor Dewey's brief paper packed with constructive suggestion seems to contain an implication of the possibility of an American philosophy in spite of the absence of tradition and weathered institution. Is it not conceivable that America may find another basis, another *vis a tergo* to impel it to definition of its own characteristics? Lacking the leisure to reflect, as indeed the fulfilled culture upon which to direct contemplation, it cannot come as an overflow, a welling-up into conscious " wonder " at a mellow heritage, but may perhaps be born of the complexity of its civilization. Writers in every field of the social sciences make constant reference to this as the most complex civilization the world has known, and seem agreed that America is facing first, the full force of grave problems which are the by-products of that complexity, with which European civilizations, also, must reckon in the near future.

Complexity has always been a challenge to philosophy; philosophers are wont to claim that their task is to " see life steadily and see it whole " and to " make man at home in the universe." For this reason philosophy has perhaps never been more significantly " indicated " than in America at present. Not that this is a sick or decadent world; notoriously it is a young world, virile in its recuperative powers, unremitting in its expenditure of energy, faced forward towards constantly new endeavors and successes. Never a world so filled with the contagiousness of being alive, yet so difficult to live in. It may be a simple life for the type of person who swims along with the stream of passing events, mingling with people and things on the level of surface contacts — the kind of person dubbed " a typical extrovert." That he is not an entirely mythical personage, witness the psychology of behaviorism, which gives so admirable an account of him in terms of all-sufficient muscular adjustments, reflexes, habits. But for the majority of those who do not, in Stevenson's phrase, " swallow the universe like a pill," there is a disturbing sense of complexity. Increasingly there is being voiced a call for philosophy to " come out of the cloisters " of metaphysical preoccupation with *Oneness,* and lend a hand in resolving the perplexing many-ness of everyday affairs into manageable portions.

The widespread consciousness of complexity is a signal that the first step toward a reflective attitude is being taken. A sense of confusion is one stage at least beyond the level of taking everything for granted. Confusion does not occur in the wholly impoverished mind; it is an index of some resource; it comes from the realization of various possibilities, uncertainty as to what to do next. It is a sort of preliminary inventory or taking stock of the predicament. Such appears to be the *status quo* of America regarding its complex life. Philosophy has therefore the advantage of a pupil already partially astir with the sense of a problem, and the time seems favorable for pupil and teacher to seek the truth together.

But philosophy finds itself in a dilemma. To be a useable philosophy it must attempt to record a civilization as it is, put into intellectual form the pattern which is in the weaving, base its interpretation and fashion its guidance upon that. However, there is the danger that such a statement will be looked upon as a mere justification of the civilization which it reports, a " rationalization," and therefore an influence towards perpetuation of traits which are already too much in the ascendancy. Note the trend of criticism toward the philosophy of James. When he blew the clarion blast of giving men a malleable universe to work with, an assurance of the part man himself plays in building the truths he lives by; when he emphasized the need of rigorously testing the value of truths by the worthwhileness of the returns they yield; when he stressed man's never-relaxing responsibility in taking a hand in directing the course of the universe, one might have supposed that here man had been proffered a job big enough to test all the larger human qualities — character, social insight, high ideals of effective endeavor. But the drift of the discontent was evidently, that here was a philosophy truckling to popular taste, rubbing in the go-getter, commercial ideals, or lack of them, of our society, with its already too worldly standards of expediency and immediate success. What was needed, instead, was a philosophy to offset this, and to encourage the spiritual and cultural interests so obviously lacking in our generation. Had James been reporting the philosophy of an idealistic, spiritually-minded people, the verdict would probably have been that he was encouraging an arrested infantilism, or something of the sort.

It appears that any interpretation of a civilization on its present level of development is unsatisfactory, and not chiefly because an attempt to put the enterprise of living into an intellectual formulation distorts by selection, and throws out of focus, the facts it finds, but because it reads them in terms of the present and shuts them within the limits of the meaning they have already achieved. The effect of this is to make a civilization seem ignoble, lacking in one form or another, the essentials of worth and dignity. Philosophy, like education, may be said to have a threefold function; that of taking cognizance of tendencies as they manifest themselves, of eliminating those which have outgrown their function, and of cultivating those which have implications for future growth. A philosophy which has a clear vision of a present civilization because it can discern the meaning of its possibilities for the future, can fulfill with reference to it the true function of philosophy: interpretation, on the basis of this, prophecy, hence guidance. It should thus satisfy the demand for a philosophy which shall be true to the realities of life, yet shall formulate a program of the something over and above the limitation and deficiencies which it finds at any cross-section reading.

II

In the foregoing discussion the term " complexity " has been used without indicating any of its specific aspects. It is not in place here to review the large social, economic, and industrial problems with which specialists in those fields are concerned — complexities which are presumably the sequence of the whirlwind changes in labor-saving machinery and all the other devices by which modern science has multiplied man's needs as well as his satisfactions. Rather the purpose here is to suggest briefly some familiar instances of the sense of complexity induced in individuals by this world, " which is so full of a number of things." Moreover, the choice of illustrations is not from problems which reflect the need for guidance in serious moral and spiritual issues, but rather those which lend themselves to brief and simple description, which yet present conditions under which, in general, the sense of confusion arises.

A few of the counter tendencies which make for the sense of conflict may be noted. This is an age of experiment and not of authority. Only that is accepted which stands the test of experimentation and critical investigation. On the other hand only a small fragment of investigation can be carried on by any one person. To know by trying out — to be expert — in one field means to be subject to authority of experts in all other fields. Nor is there longer the one-time comfort that judgment developed in one field guarantees good judgment, wisdom, in another. That is, the older belief that a mental power could be formally trained by some subject-matter destined to discipline the mind, and prepare it to render sound judgments on any occasion thereafter, is no longer available — the promise of this unity is denied us. Balancing the method of careful research is the necessity of taking much on faith, nay, of even the most facile credulity. Hence that institution of modern life, the great Sophist, Salesmanship, ready to persuade as to " wares of the soul " as well as " wares of the body." Nor is this provincialism the fate merely of the average, intelligent citizen, but of the learned as well. A case in point is that of an eminent young sociologist informing a group of students that modern sociology is built upon two psychological doctrines; the behaviorism of the Watsonian school and the psycho-analysis of the Freudian! Not a stir of curiosity from the group, or any evidence on the part of the lecturer that sociology had accomplished a feat of " reconciliation of opposites " which most psychologists would consider somewhat miraculous. And so the learned biologist who " solves " his problem of freedom and determination by recourse to a metaphysics which would be an invitation to lively controversy among metaphysicians.

From another point of view the complexity appears in the form of the loosening up of the grip of the universe on man. Neither good nor evil is felt to be a metaphysical fixture of the universe, but a condition coming to be more and more under man's control. Further, current psychology has released him from the mooring of fixed instincts, so long held to be the inescapable inner drives which forced him to determined modes of behavior; has given him not one chance, but many, of refashioning his habits into new capacities; has freed him from the thrall of heredity which makes him a slave to a pre-established pattern. Even the psychology which shuts him up to a definitely limited mental endowment gives him the opportunity of making good through the cultivation of habits which will make possible the best investment of his hereditary capital. And the psychology which finds him grown to adult estate with all sorts of physical, mental, and spiritual handicaps offers him the grace of complete rehabilitation and a fresh start. With all this enfranchised energy, with the pervasive belief that men can make of themselves and the world what they will is the complementary difficulty. The possibility of wide choice means hesitation; procrastination in a world so specialized as this means failure. Free choice, but made quickly, and followed without swerving thereafter, is the price of " success."

This is essentially the dilemma of youth. Our educational theory is to give youth every chance to find itself, to offer an opportunity to sample the various possibilities of careers open to it. We give every aid, to be sure, such as the analysis of capacities, the invitation to explore interesting fields and to experiment freely, yet throughout is the anxious undercurrent, " Choose quickly lest you will never be one of the competent ones of the world." We speak much of the prolongation of infancy as the mark of a higher civilization, a longer period of plasticity, yet in effect we are lessening that by the pressure of early professionalism and specialization. The technique of expertship grows more and more exacting, and the requisite time longer, so that one must fix one's end early in youth. The long period of preparation to live which our modern régime requires of youth is in marked contrast to our exalting of youth for its own sake; we fear nothing so much as the tragic hand of time. Hence the tendency, so much bewailed, of youth to take its youth by using it, of making short cuts through the long lane of getting-ready-to-live, of searching for some alchemy by which to achieve results without the intervening drudgery. Hence the hold on the popular imagination of spectacular successes through risks, of thrilling achievements as if accomplished through the magic of courageous endeavor alone, desperate taking of chances — in short, the cult of luck. " The only alternative to luck is art," says Professor Dewey, but art means slow trekking over the long, long, interval between means and ends.

Anthropologists and psychologists who have studied the mind of primitive man are now fairly in agreement that primitive mind does not differ so much from that of civilized man as was formerly supposed. It is rather that the environment of man is today more complex, and therefore calls out capacities which are not developed in simpler societies. If complexity of environment makes for intelligence this should be a supremely intelligent age, provided that the stimulation is to something more than agile manipulation, swift adjustment to novelties, and uncurious acceptance of whatever comes to pass. Nothing could be more unfortunate than that there should be a preponderance of the purely " objectively- " minded, who make no attempt to re-evaluate the ends which are proffered them as worthy of possession and attainment. The multiplicity of ends " on sale " in our world today, may not be ends which are ultimately desirable. At any rate there is bound to be some reconstitution of ends or patterns which our civilization sets for itself, and the throwing overboard much useless ballast. Somehow we shall have to develop a method of enlarging our grasp of meanings, or of simplifying through reduction the multiplicity of ends. There must be a deepening of reflective power, that is, of the ability to establish working relationships between the diverse aspects of experience.

We look to the philosopher to aid in raising the sensory-motor level of our living to a reflective plane which will relegate the cohort of things to a marginal background, at least, and free us for constructive thinking along the front. In other words, we look to the philosopher to help man to come into his greatest human heritage, capacity for taking thought. Obviously it were idle to look to a philosophy which follows its promise of a unified view of the universe by luring the pilgrim into the Slough of Despond of the how-is-knowledge-possible problem, and then into the bottomless pit of perceptual analysis. From the technical, dialectical controversies of much present-day philosophy there can be little hope of guidance through the maze of living. As one youth, in stage whisper, exhorted a learned dialectician: " Come on. Let's go! let's get a look under the Big Tent."

III

It is part of the picture that there should be at the present time a number of trends of philosophy all vigorously alive. To say that they are fundamentally in agreement is to deny their own insistence that they are different, and in nothing so different as in the rôle they ascribe to thought. All are, however, agreed upon what is a particularly opprobrious criticism and what is an especially " honorific " epithet. No philosophy cherishes the charge of subjectivism; all covet the merit of telling the story of reality. And since thought has usually been accused of breathing out the contagion of subjectivity into the world, beware of it. Let us isolate the germ of reality and get a sort of germ-plasm capable of transmitting its own realness to its offspring, pure and emergent, without the contamination of characteristics acquired by thought. Thus in effect the realist who contends that reality is what it is regardless of our thought about it, and that our thinking effects no change in it. But where is the simple, simon-pure sample given in awareness (with which the critical realist, for example, has started) by the time he has evoked through an amazingly intricate thought-gymnastic, his trinitarian theory to keep thought out of it. Like the poor little beaver at sight of the Great Boojum, it has " suddenly and silently vanished away." It is interesting to note that although thought is denied a part in the up-building of a real object, thought can apparently analyse its reality into nothingness. Like Descartes' soul, seated in the pineal gland, it can get in its little " push " — at least in one direction.

As for the naïve realist, if any such there be, and his one hundred per cent. objectively real world, it is strange support that he finds in the doctrine of behaviorism for denying the constructive rôle of thought. It is not the purpose here to point out what seems an unfortunate circumstance (both for behaviorism and for philosophy), namely, the attempt to make a philosophical position of a psychological doctrine, but rather to suggest that the realist omits the positive contribution of behaviorism. Far from lending aid and comfort it should prove embarrassing to him in his stand as to the all-thereness, the given-ness of realities. For behaviorism in foregoing consciousness (or thought viewed as adjustment through consciousness) has nevertheless been careful, on the one hand, to abandon the belief in a fixed invariable instinct, or fixed immediate response, to a given stimulus, and has insisted that every response is a learned reaction, one acquired through a process of various steps. On the other hand, the stimulus (the realist's " object ") is anything but the fixed and given thing it seems. For the behaviorist, by his machinery of shifting associations, " conditioning reflexes," may make an " objective " stimulus stand

for anything he pleases. Thus there is no end of the sliding and shifting
and making of stimuli into "directly given" objects. Certainly there is
nothing of the "reals" of the realist here. The behaviorist, moreover,
has at least some arrangement by which he can keep the world moving,
and behavior, whether it is called thought-less or no, certainly plays a very
large part in what the world comes to be. The realist could not have
chosen to build his house upon more shifting sands than the changing
world of the behaviorist.

The intent of this discussion is not primarily critical reference to realism, but an emphasis on the need of a philosophy which instead of attempting to withdraw thought from circulation, will stress it as the dominant
force in the forward movement of civilization. As a concession to its
philosophical critics it must first and foremost take away the subjectivity
complex which has grown about it. However one choses to account for
thought — and the account of it as an "emergent quality" seems recently
to bring the most philosophic peace of mind — it has *come* upon the scene,
has put in *an appearance*. If it is really a novel, an emergent quality, why
not make it such in good sooth, by giving it the benefit of a variant heredity which will enable it in turn to produce something novel? To make
man wait upon "reality" to do all the emerging when he is heir to the
emergent quality, par excellence, would mean to be a spendthrift philosophy at best. But considerations of consistency aside, what might not be
accomplished by a great drive in philosophy to emphasize the positive
rather than the metaphysically negative aspects of thought!

The great need is for a useable philosophy. This does not mean a
philosophy stripped of "profundities" or popular-ized. It is doubtful if
philosophy can be made popular in this sense. Ideas about philosophy
may be simplified by selection of outstanding aspects and be presented in
interesting narrative form; there is doubtless a legitimate place for this.
But as Professor Dewey has pointed out with reference to many textbooks
written for young students by specialists, they simplify by omitting the
thought-provoking processes by which the content of the subject becomes
intelligible. Much in the same way popularized philosophy is often not
philosophy at all, or is even more abstract than the philosophy of which
it renders an account. There is a difference between ideas about philosophy and "philosophical ideas." Philosophical ideas "find their simplification in their power to clarify and unify, in their capacity to get us

under way with our problem. Briefly, it is possibly fair to claim for instrumentalism that it has yielded more genuinely " philosophical ideas " than any of the other extant philosophies.

Without developing the implications of such ideas, especially fertile as they are in the fields of education, conduct, and social problems, a brief memorandum of a few of them will be offered. Although they are in a sense corollaries of the main thesis of instrumentalism as to the constructive and reconstructive function of thought, the emphasis here is in the main on their testimony to the " objectivity of thought for this philosophical position."

First comes to mind the insistence that the method of thought is the same for reflective judgment as for practical affairs. This affords one source of encouragement in the search for a method of unifying the diversities of experience. This identification, however, does not reduce the significance of the intellectual aspect of life to a mere " doing," as superficial critics of its educational import have sometimes maintained, or critics of its alliance with pragmatism have urged. On the contrary, it has made even of practical adjustments a reasoned affair. It offers no comfortable intellectual holiday, no waiting for a special period of childhood, for instance, adolescence, to burgeon into reasoning power, but its challenge is to cultivate the way of thinking throughout the waking hours of life. It is preëminently a philosophy which makes focal the responsibility for taking thought. " There is no rest for the thinker save in the process of thinking."

Thought is objective in another sense. There is no direct communication of mind with mind; no contagion or convoy of meaning except through the medium not merely of a " social," but, indeed, ultimately, of a physical environment in which there has been a shared or common experience. Except as an idea points to such a common medium, revives imaginatively that shared experience, its meaning is not intelligible. That is, an idea establishes communication by way of an environment which is objectively real.

The importance of language in gaining knowledge is doubtless the chief cause of the common notion that knowledge may be passed directly from one to another. It almost seems as if all we have to do is to convey a sound into his ear.[1]

---

[1] *Democracy and Education*, p. 17.

And the only way that any person can modify the mind of another is by using physical conditions, crude or artificial, so as to evoke some answering activity from him.[2]

In a more technical, metaphysical context this same point is brought out under the term " denotation."

The value of experience as method in philosophy is that it compels us to note that *denotation* comes first and last, so that to settle any discussion, to still any doubt, to answer any question, we must go to some thing pointed to, denoted, and find an answer in that thing.[3]

Another aspect of the objective nature of thought is its connection with habit. The ideo-motor theory of thought is tenable only with reservations. Between the appearance of the idea and its issuance into action is the history of its connection with appropriate habits, former responses, and occupations with an environment. An idea can become " motor " only to the degree that such habits are available for use in reshaping to new action. To use a simple illustration, an idea that is " told " over and over again, such as " Be neat " or " Be industrious," has no roots in habit; as simple exhortation it cannot be conveyed as an idea with propulsive power. It lacks the conditioning " practice habits " which can convert it into an idea, an ideal, with objective consequence. An idea is the conscious formulation of habit, and the reconstructing of habit depends in turn upon the expression of it in idea form. But it is " not thought as idealism defines thought which exercises the reconstructive function — only action, interaction, can change or remake an object — this is because intelligence is incarnate in overt action, using things as means to affect other things." [4] Thus since habits are the carriers of our adjustment to environment, and environment is only as extended as our habits of response to it, thought is objectively conditioned, both in its origin and operation.

In still another sense thought is objective. Its products are incorporated in the environment; they are there in the form of weighted stimuli. " The savage deals largely with crude stimuli; we have *weighted* stimuli." Thought leaves permanent monuments, or is incarnate in them, or remains as coefficients of them. Institutions, constructions of stone and mortar, conserve the drama of human thinking just as a book holds be-

[2] *Ibid.,* p. 40.   [3] *Experience and Nature,* p. 10.   [4] *Ibid.,* p. 158.

tween its covers stored memories of our intimate acquaintance with it. The products of thought are everywhere, outward and visible signs of our social heritage; the life of culture is there to reawaken for every human reader who comes to learn the technique of deciphering the hieroglyphics. So much for the evidence of thought's " increment " to reality. So much for the evidence of thought's objective existence if we look for it not as a noun, but as an adjective. " Thought, reason, intelligence, whatever we choose to use is existentially an adjective (or better an adverb), not a noun." [5]

Thought viewed thus objectively as process and product is not an inner, private, mysterious gift which makes inspired or lucky transmutations, or the possession of a few of the mentally superior, but may be extended as an operative force as far as education is made available. But education in its widest, most virile sense means the opportunity, first, and foremost, of fuller sharing, in experiences. Only in so far as that participation is widened will intelligence itself overcome its partiality and specialization. " Intelligence is partial and specialized, because communication and participation are limited, sectarian, provincial, confined to class, party, professional group."

Participation is the central category of instrumentalism. It leads to new vision in the " applied " philosophy of education, to fresh interpretation of social problems, and to suggestive restatement of deadlocks in controversial metaphysics. It is in essence the putting back into working relationship of two seemingly irreconcilable elements, by finding a basis for such co-operation in their common origin. But the synthesis thus effected is not a schematic unity, a Hegelian dialectic of opposites. It is a solution of a concrete kind, for it sets itself the problem of locating the level at which these incompatibles, now set up as abstract elements, were in active association. This is the task of thought made so familiar now through instrumentalism's " analysis of an act of thought." The study of origins, does not however, determine for instrumentalism present " validity " but because of liberated alliances, helps to keep values moving in the direction of wider fulfilments.

Because instrumentalism builds its philosophy upon participation, it above other philosophies, should be of service in our present-day confusion of tongues. Conditioning intelligence upon communication, and com-

[5] *Experience and Nature*, p. 158.

munication upon participation, it conceives the office of philosophy as that of opening the thoroughfares between insulated centers. Its rôle is that of messenger, interpreter, and guide, "making reciprocally intelligible, voices speaking provincial tongues."

The emphasis placed upon the objectivity of thought has been for the purpose of establishing the claim, that the interpretation which instrumentalism gives of its chief instrument, thought, makes it an essentially useable philosophy. It is only in passing that reference can be made to the capacity of thought for outreaching its grasp. Because thought can shake off the shackles of the concrete in its inflexible wholeness and can experiment in terms of ideas, instead of with physical objects and material conditions, it can find new directions and fashion new forms. The method of intelligence is the method of discovery and creation. It is possible that, encouraged to exercise its genius freely, intelligence will dare to find for us some new way through our blocked paths, some new route which will foreshorten the distance between means and ends, some transatlantic flight over the arid wastes of futile controversy; some new philosophy which will bring a larger human grasp, hence a more manageable world. Until then — instrumentalism.

SOME IMPLICATIONS OF LOCKE'S PROCEDURE

Frederick J. E. Woodbridge

Locke states his purpose in writing the *Essay* with evident care and de-liberation: " This, therefore, being my purpose, to enquire into the original, certainty, and extent of human knowledge, together with the grounds and degrees of belief, opinion, and assent, I shall not at present meddle with the physical consideration of the mind, or trouble myself to examine wherein its essence consists, or by what motions of our spirits or altera-tions of our bodies we come to have any sensation by our organs, or any ideas in our understandings; and whether those ideas do in their forma-tion, any or all of them, depend on matter or not. These are speculations which, however curious and entertaining, I shall decline, as lying out of my way in the design I am now upon. It shall suffice to my present pur-pose, to consider the discerning faculties of a man, as they are employed about the objects which they have to do with." [1] The reader of today — and, possibly, the reader of Locke's day — may conclude, on finishing the book, that the *Essay,* as a whole, is a more intelligible document in the matter of belief, opinion, and assent, than it is in the matter of the original, certainty, and extent of human knowledge. Locke is primarily a moralist and not a logician. He gives abundant evidence of a greater interest and a greater competence in practical than in theoretical considerations. The moral effect of the *Essay* is to encourage the reader to believe that our knowledge is suited to our place and station, that " the candle that is set up in us shines bright enough for all our purposes," and that " our business here is not to know all things, but those which concern our conduct." [2] The knowledge which is so suited, comprises those conclusions which we reach by exploring the evident and obvious situations in which we find ourselves when we think and act; and the candle which is bright enough is simply our natural ability to observe what we are doing when we do it. It is vain and profitless to wish for other instruments than those we have or to speculate about situations which are not those in which we daily live

---

[1] Bk. I, ch. I, sec. 2.   [2] Bk. I, ch. I, sec. 6–7.

and labor. And it seems quite clear that Locke would have his readers stop bothering about the nature of things in so far as that nature was irrelevant to human living, and proceed rather to use their talents in the service of society. He wrote to stop what he thought was a bad habit and to encourage what he thought was a good one. His practical sanity is pronounced. It robs the theoretical difficulties and contradictions in the *Essay* of controlling importance in interpreting the book as a human document. As such a document time has not seriously impaired its effect. There is still profit in reading it.

The *Essay* is, however, an enquiry into the original, certainty, and extent of human knowledge. It has escaped neither the criticism nor the effect of such an enquiry. And, as such, it has not escaped the repeated charge of unintelligibility. On the theoretical side, Locke seems to find himself caught in a net from which he cannot extricate himself. He gets involved in contradictions. When he finally raises [3] the question of the " reality of knowledge," he can answer only by an appeal to faith. The problem of knowledge ultimately raised by the *Essay* is not solved, but left unsolvable. It has, consequently, provoked many subsequent essays dealing with the same problem, sometimes critically, sometimes constructively. The *Essay* may be read and judged in terms of them. It has, however, an independent interest in terms of its own procedure. The implications of this procedure may be explored without raising the question of the value or soundness of the *Essay* as a theory of knowledge. One may take his clue from the third book of the *Essay*. There Locke urges that terms should be understood in terms of their use and context and not independent of them. The definitions which are made of terms should find their explication in the distinctions which they introduce into the subject-matter with which a given enquiry is concerned. They are relevant to that subject-matter and meaningless apart from it. When this principle is applied to the *Essay,* its difficulties may not disappear, but they become, I think, clarified. Indeed, their character may be changed. Instead of appearing as difficulties or inconsistencies in Locke's argument, they may appear ultimately to enforce distinctions which are necessary if the argument is to be intelligible.

A limited attempt of this kind is here proposed. Locke's hypothesis about the mind as originally empty and devoid of ideas will be examined

[3] Bk. IV, ch. IV.

in the hope of clarifying the mutual implications between it and such terms as "experience" and "idea." This hypothesis required another about the world of bodies in consequence of which "experience" and "ideas" became matters of the world of bodies before they became matters of the world of mind. Locke does not seem to have seen this clearly although he seems to stick rather stubbornly to its implications. The obviousness — obvious to him at least — of his controlling convictions was such that their evident clearness seemed to clarify what was otherwise obscure. It was so clear to him that we get all our ideas from experience and that, consequently, we are at liberty to suppose that our minds were originally without them, that the light of this conviction was still shining when "ideas" had ceased to be ideas and "experience" had ceased to be experience. In other words, Locke's procedure involved a radical shift in context of radical significance for his terminology. Terms which are supposed to have a logical or trial and error significance lost it and acquired a significance of a different character. The shift was obscured because the light in which it was made was so bright. "Real knowledge" became well-nigh impossible, because the situations in which it was "impossible" were situations to which knowledge in the sense defined was irrelevant.

"Let us then suppose the mind to be, as we say, white paper, void of all characters, without any ideas." [4] What is the reader to suppose in response to this invitation? A mind without any ideas is scarcely an intelligible conception without a context, and the context from which it derives its meaning must, obviously, be more fundamental than the conception itself. Locke states: "We know certainly, by experience, that we sometimes think, and thence draw this infallible consequence, that there is something in us that has a power to think." [5] But the consequence is neither necessary nor infallible. It may express a rooted conviction of Locke's, but it is not so rooted that he cannot later subject it to criticism. He tells the reader quite plainly [6] that, apart from revelation, there is not more contradiction in supposing that matter thinks than there is in supposing that there is annexed to matter something which has the power to think. So far as the procedure of the *Essay* is concerned, Locke is well enough aware that the supposition of a "mind without any ideas" means no more than the supposition — which with him is an obvious truth — that men do not think always, that their thinking is an occasional incident

---

[4] Bk. II, ch. I, sec. 2.   [5] Bk. II, ch. I, sec. 10.
[6] Bk. IV, ch. III, sec. 6.

in their history, that all the ideas they have are acquired; consequently we are at liberty to suppose that they are at times and originally without ideas. The hypothesis about the " mind " turns out to be an hypothesis about man. " Mind " is not necessary to the procedure. It is a concession to revelation and to the human belief in a soul. Locke can say even that " all the great ends of morality and religion are well enough secured, without philosophical proofs of the soul's immateriality." [7] It is man, not mind, we are to suppose to be without any ideas, and this supposition requires an antecedent conception of man so situated that the transition from not having ideas to having them may be considered.

How is this transition affected? How does a man without ideas come to be a man with them? Locke answers, by experience. But what is " experience "? The term had and has a meaning which is rarely troublesome. To observe, to try out, and to reflect on what one observes or tries out, is to have experience. It is clear enough that such experience we are constantly having and that it is a great source of ideas. But we are to conceive a situation in which " experience " occurs and produces them. How is Locke's procedure affected by this demand? It requires another hypothesis. We are to suppose — and the supposition embodies another of Locke's rooted convictions — a world of bodies including the human body from which, as such, thinking and ideas are absent. In this world bodies are related to one another solely in terms of mutual contacts. It is hardly too crude to say that they do nothing but collide. Space is filled with bodies which move about in it, meet and part, and agitate one another in consequence of their motions. Among these bodies are the bodies of men. They are equipped with what we call sense organs, but these organs are also bodies subject to contacts with other bodies. There is, however, a peculiar consequence arising from the contact of other bodies with the sense organs of the human body. This contact issues in ideas. To have it so issue becomes thus fundamentally what it is to have " experience." This term has consequently acquired a meaning which is initially irrelevant to the operations of a man when he thinks. Its meaning is relevant initially to the operations of bodies generally and to the operations of the human body in relation to other bodies specifically. We may say that " experience " has become fundamentally physical, if by " physical " we mean a matter of bodily contact. It is something which happens, not

[7] *Loc. cit.*

between a mind and bodies, but between bodies, and although the consequence is peculiar when the human body is involved, the consequence is none the less a consequence of the contact of bodies. When this consequence has happened, a man may think about it or reflect upon it and so have an experience of a different kind, but the consequence must have happened first. There must be physical experience before there is reflective or thinking experience.[8]

It is this second hypothesis about the world of bodies and the shifting of the meaning of " experience " consequent upon it, that give to Locke's first hypothesis about the mind, whatever intelligibility it has. To suppose a mind without any ideas is not to suppose an empty mind waiting somewhere to be filled. It is rather to suppose a world of bodies in which something has not yet happened, a world of bodies in which " experience " has not yet occurred. But given " experience " in that world, the consequence of it is given. There are ideas and a man may then reflect upon them. The second hypothesis and not the first is the controlling one in the procedure and gives to " experience " and " mind " their fundamental and initial meaning. " Experience " becomes, initially, bodily contact and " mind " becomes, initially, the locus of the consequence of this contact when the human body with its sense organs is involved. Thus meaning is given to the supposition that the locus is absent when the circumstances of it are absent. It is as easy and as intelligible to suppose a mind without ideas as to suppose a man asleep or in a faint. Apart from the procedure and its implications, the supposition of a mind without any ideas is meaningless.

---

[8] That what I have here called " physical experience " without a mind, is a possibility clearly admitted by Locke is evident from Bk. IV, ch. III, sec. 6, to which I have already referred. " What certainty of knowledge can any one have, that some perceptions, such as, e.g., pleasure and pain, should not be in some bodies themselves, after a certain manner modified and moved, as well as that they should be in an immaterial substance, upon the motions of the parts of body? Body, as far as we can conceive, being able only to strike and affect body; and motion, according to the utmost reach of our ideas, being able to produce nothing but motion; so that where we allow it to produce pleasure or pain, or the idea of a color or sound, we are fain to quit our reason, go beyond our ideas, and attribute it wholly to the good pleasure of our Maker. For since we must allow he has annexed effects to motion, which we can no way conceive motion able to produce, what reason have we to conclude that he could not order them as well to be produced in a subject we cannot conceive capable of them, as well as in a subject we cannot conceive the motion of matter can any way operate upon? " This is clear evidence not only that " experience " is initially physical without involving mind, but also that " ideas " may also be equally physical in the first instance.

That Locke prefers the term " mind " or " understanding " to the term " man " is probably due to his personal conviction that there is " something in us that has a power to think." He had a bias for the soul. Yet mind as the locus of ideas was, in a very real sense, a consequence of his procedure and its implications. " Experience " as physical generates a product, ideas, which does not fit well into the world of bodies. The consequence of that contact of the human body with other bodies which is " experience," is not comparable with the consequences of the contacts of bodies generally. It is not, strictly, a bodily event in the world of bodies. As an event it cannot be dated and located in that world as other events are dated and located. If it has time and place at all, its time and place are the time and place of the body responsible for it. It happens as a consequence of the operations of bodies, but it does not happen in their world as Locke conceives their world to be constituted. The locus of ideas is, consequently, an extra-bodily locus. It becomes the " mind " or " human understanding." Ideas are thus a product of the world of bodies without being parts or elements of that world. Their existence is not relevant to that world at all. It is relevant only to what is done with them when they exist. After " experience " has produced them, a man may experience them in a new way. He may observe them, try them out, and reflect on them. He will then get new ideas and be on the way to knowledge.

Under the influence of Locke's hypothesis, " experience " becomes, thus, in its primary sense, a technical term to be understood, not according to common usage, but strictly in terms of the procedure in which it is employed. It denotes something which happens between bodies and not something which happens between them and a mind. It is essentially a physical operation. Something similar happens to " idea." As already noted, " experience " issues in " ideas," and " ideas," although their locus may be called " mind," may, for all we know, be attached to bodies or exist in them without involving mind in an immaterial sense.[9] The term " idea " is troublesome. Locke himself feels the importance of calling the reader's attention to it early in the *Essay:* " Thus much I thought necessary to say concerning the occasion of this enquiry into human understanding. But, before I proceed on to what I have thought on this subject, I must here in the entrance beg pardon of my reader for the frequent use of the word

[9] See footnote 8. Locke is quite clear on the point that an immaterial thinking substance does not explain why " ideas " exist as a consequence of " experience."

' idea,' which he will find in the following treatise. It being that term which, I think, serves best to stand for whatsoever is the object of the understanding when a man thinks, I have used it to express whatever is meant by phantasm, notion, species, or whatever it is which the mind can be employed about in thinking; and I could not avoid frequently using it." [10] Later, he gives illustrations: " Every man being conscious to himself that he thinks, and that which his mind is applied about whilst thinking, being the ideas that are there, it is past doubt that men have in their minds several ideas, such as are those expressed by the words whiteness, hardness, sweetness, thinking, motion, man, elephant, army, drunkenness, and others." [11] A number of questions readily suggest themselves: are we to conclude that there is no difference between an object of thought and an idea of that object; no difference between an elephant and the idea of an elephant, or between drunkenness and the idea of drunkenness; no difference between " whatever is the object of the understanding when a man thinks " and " what a man thinks about that object " ? Locke clearly recognizes such a distinction when " experience " is reflective experience, but he withholds the distinction when " experience " is not reflective. He falls easily into the clutches of dialectic. Restricting " idea " to " what a man thinks about," how is it possible to think about anything which is not an idea, and how can we think of anything — " substance," for example — of which we have no idea? If a man thinks of the world of bodies, is not that world an idea and do not ideas then exist whether a man thinks or no? If we emphasize " when a man thinks," does the world of bodies exist only when he thinks of it, and what is he thinking of when that world is not an idea? Strictly construed, it would seem that, apart from reflective experience, " idea " has no logical or cognitive meaning whatever and is only an alternative word for " object of thought." Locke does not escape the clutches of the dialectic. It bothers him, however, only when circumstances or his convictions about " real " knowledge force him to face it; only when he is forced to recognize that the term " idea " has, obviously, a logical and cognitive significance. His procedure is little troubled by it. Here " ideas " are initially nothing but the objects of thought. They are the products of bodily " experience," and, when produced, they are not what a man thinks, but what he thinks about or the occasions of his thinking. He would not think at all, unless they were first produced, but his

[10] Bk. I, ch. I, sec. 8.   [11] Bk. II, ch. I, sec. 1.

thinking has nothing to do with their production. Like the world of bodies and " experience," " ideas " belong to a situation or state of things which must be supposed, before there is any genuine operation of the human understanding.

Although Locke puts the definition of idea at the beginning of his inquiry, it is evident from the whole *Essay* that the definition is a consequence of his hypotheses and procedure. These control the definition, it does not control them. The effect is, as I have said, to rob the term " idea " initially of all logical significance. " Ideas " are, in the first instance, not logical entities at all. The only discoverable reason for calling them ideas is to link them with man's thinking. But his thinking is irrelevant to their production. They are produced by bodily operations and by nothing else — except, of course, when we have ideas of reflection. " As the bodies that surround us do diversely affect our organs, the mind is forced to receive the impressions, and cannot avoid the perception of those ideas that are annexed to them." [12] Consequently " ideas," like " experience," might, in the first instance, be called physical were it not that their locus in the physical world is so difficult to imagine. When they exist, it may be necessary that they be perceived and reflected on, but their own nature is quite irrelevant to these operations. It may be that these operations give them something of a logical status, but such a status they do not have in their own right any more than the operations of bodies with the effects they produce have such a status. For all we know, " ideas " might exist simply as events attached in some desultory way to the world of bodies.

This use of the term " idea " without logical significance is apt to trouble the reader as it troubled Locke himself. Ideas are usually associated with the operations of thought and not with the operations of bodies. They are, normally, not the objects of knowledge, but products arising from reflection on such objects. One does not ordinarily think of an elephant or drunkenness as ideas. But the procedure of the *Essay* warns both Locke and the reader not to think in the ordinary fashion. And it must be said that Locke, for the most part, heeds the warning, and, at times, checks himself when he is in danger of forgetting it. The most notable example of this is, perhaps, the chapter " Of Solidity." [13] Solidity is the first " idea " to which Locke pays specific attention. It is, obviously, an important " idea " in view of his hypothesis of a world of bodies. He has

[12] Bk. II, ch. I, sec. 25.　　　　　　　[13] Bk. II, ch. IV.

much to say about solidity as a result of his reflections upon it. He calls it that which " hinders the approach of two bodies when they are moved one towards another." He distinguishes it from space and hardness in order to make clear what it is. He declares that impulse, resistance, and protrusion depend on it. In short, he elaborates his thought about it — one might say, his idea of it. But then, as if a little distrustful of what he had done, he says at the end: " If any one ask me what this solidity is, I send him to his senses to inform him." Clearly the *idea of* solidity is not solidity, the " idea." What one gets by going to the senses is not what one gets by reading Locke's elaboration. Solidity, the " idea," is clarified by the *idea of* solidity. " Ideas " which are the products of bodily " experience " must be elaborated in discourse — or reflective experience — before they are significant in human understanding.

It is an obvious consequence of the procedure that Locke should regard knowledge as a matter of reflective experience. It is a contemplation of " ideas." He defines it as " the perception of the connexion and agreement, or disagreement and repugnancy of any of our ideas." [14] It is a lame definition which did not carry Locke very far or very sturdily. It could be bettered. The *Essay* as a whole is sufficient proof of this, for it is a shrewd, homely, honest, and sympathetic reflection on the objects of the understanding when a man thinks. But, as I have already suggested, Locke found himself caught in a net from which he did not extricate himself. He was haunted by the suspicion that knowledge ought to be something fundamentally different from the conclusion he had reached about it. It ought to be " real." And to be " real," there ought to be some sort of a knowledge relation between " ideas " which are the products of bodily experience and the world of bodies itself. This relation his hypotheses and procedure could not deliver. His honesty leads him to face the matter squarely in the fourth chapter of the fourth book. His handling of the difficulty is about the weakest part of the whole *Essay,* so weak that many have taken it to be the *reductio ad absurdum* of his general position. He is led to make of such " real " knowledge as we may hope to attain in this world a pretty poor instrument for our present happiness — " something very short and scanty " — but, possibly, a foretaste of what intellectual creatures are capable of in a better state. He flies to belief, opinion, and assent, to judgment and probability. These are " suitable, I presume, to

[14] Bk. IV, ch. I, sec. 2.

that state of mediocrity and probationership he [God] has been pleased to place us in here; wherein, to check our over-confidence and presumption, we might, by every day's experience, be made sensible of our short-sightedness and liableness to error; the sense whereof might be a constant admonition to us, to spend the days of this our pilgrimage with industry and care, in the search and following of that way which might lead us to a state of greater perfection: it being highly rational to think, even were revelation silent in the case, that, as men employ those talents God has given them here, they shall accordingly receive their rewards at the close of the day, when their sun shall set, and night shall put an end to their labours." [15]

Such an outcome was probably due more to Locke's temper and the temper of the group of men in whose labors he was interested than to the requirements of his procedure. For him a new stage had been set for philosophical performance. Man appeared essentially as the explorer of nature in the interests of his life here. For this he was adequately equipped. Revelation was not denied, but it had to do with life hereafter and could not alter the necessity or the wisdom of properly comprehending what life here is. Whatever God had proposed for men hereafter, he had put them on earth to live and to live by finding out what kind of a world it was which he had given them. There was no need to speculate about him or to use him as an explanation of what men could find out by the use of their own wits. The candle set up within us shone bright enough for all our purposes here. God had made the world discoverable and it was part of man's business to discover it. Now men had discovered, or thought they had discovered, that the world in which their bodies were placed was a different world from the one which they perceived. Between them as perceivers and the world which owned their bodies appeared intervals of something quite different from the bodily world. During these intervals and in terms of what they contained, men worked out their discoveries. The status of these intervals was troublesome. They were fleeting while the world of bodies was permanent. They were a riot of qualities while the world of bodies was serene in its quantitative relations. They were full of mistakes, while the bodily world was not. All this seemed very evident. It was also perplexing. Its perplexity, however, could be discounted and even neglected in practice. After all, it seemed

13987

[15] Bk. IV, ch. XIV, sec. 2.

to be no barrier to making useful and workable discoveries. One did not have to get rid of the perplexity in order to work profitably. Why, then, should the perplexity be allowed to interfere with what men had perforce to do and could do if they tried? Locke's *Essay* is a bible of this attitude.

But Locke, like many of his contemporaries and successors, could not escape the conviction that unless these intervals were adequately disposed of, human knowledge was radically impaired. Real knowledge would be knowledge untroubled by the perplexity which these intervals occasioned. As long, however, as these intervals remained, or were not adequately disposed of, real knowledge was impossible or, at best, something very short and scanty. We must be content with probability. When contented with it, we find it sufficient for our guidance during this earthly pilgrimage.

Now it is interesting to observe that Locke did dispose of these intervals in a certain way. His honesty in sticking relentlessly to his procedure and in holding fast to his convictions, led to conclusions about these intervals which are difficult to set aside. If we are not fussy about terms, if we are not committed to some unalterable meaning to be attached to " experience," " ideas," or " knowledge," but are willing to find their meaning in the context in which they are used and in the procedure which employs them, then Locke has said something about ideas and experience and knowledge which wears the look of finality. He has said, for example, that ideas which are not the products of reflection create no logical problem. In the face of many a theory of knowledge, that is an important thing to say. He has said also that ideas which are the products of reflection are not and do not give us the subject-matter on which we reflect. And he has said that reflection on subject-matter and not some antecedently or subsequently discovered relation between subject-matter and something else, is the sole source of stable convictions. In sum, he has said that a theory of knowledge which is a theory of bodily experience and not a theory of reflective experience is not worth the paper it is written on. All this he has said in terms of, and in spite of, his hypotheses. One has not to be convinced of them in order to be convinced.

There is, perhaps, no portion of the *Essay* which brings all this out more clearly than the chapter " Of Solidity " to which I have already referred. Solidity is first of all a bodily experience. It is subject-matter. If we ask what it *is?* It tells us: it is its own information. But as such it is nothing more. If we ask *what* it is or what we mean by solidity, we try to define it and explore the implications and distinctions which the definition involves. Only by doing the latter do we ever reach any convictions about solidity, and these convictions are not something of which the senses inform us, nor something more solid than solidity itself. The distinction between what solidity is as subject-matter and what it is as elaborated in discourse looks like a distinction more fundamental than any other and one not likely to give way to a demand for its justification. Clearly Locke damaged every attempt to turn logic into physics or to turn the implications of subject-matter into a subject-matter more fundamental. The irony of the situation is that he seems so little aware of what he had done.

Kant made little improvement over Locke. With an imposing terminology, with the advantage of the intervening discussion, with an acuter mind, and with a more profound acquaintance with philosophy generally, the German ingeniously reversed the Englishman's position, but left the latter's hypotheses looking like a skeleton in a closet. He could say with confidence that reflective experience, that is, developing in thought what we perceive, is the only kind of experience that we can intelligibly be said to have, and that, consequently, a critique of reflective experience was the thing urgently needed before one bothered much about anything else. But he was haunted by Locke's hypotheses. He could believe that there was merit in saying that there were things-in-themselves and that an experience of them, which we cannot possibly have, would be, none the less, a more solid kind of experience than we can ever hope to attain. One may wonder whether current philosophies of experience have successfully laid that ghost.

La Bibliothèque
Université d'Ottawa

The Library
University of Ottawa

Échéance

For failure

OCT